p 2 purpose of study
p.4 purpose of the study
p.52 Zwickau Prophets
53 Melanch's identity crisis.

Phil 118

DA79 28

£26

Breen - see bibliography p.64 Anabaptists

p.61 - curriculum
p.69 - 1527 and its importance
p.70-71 - lex naturae (p.95)
p.78 - Zwingli on civil disobedience
p.98 - w/o faith we cannot fully understand the human soul
p.99 Kristeller
p.100 the task of natural phil
101 - anatomy 103 - know & th
118ish - 120 - Vesalius
p.124 - Luther + Mel. see p w/ their own age + II Pe
p.127 - astronomy
p.139 - arithmetic prepares for knowing G
140 - phil. teaches know. of G
p. 142
p.159 - goal of nat. phil. = obed. of civil magistr.
165-6 - nat. phil. = know. of the law

Jon SERAK

REC: November 5 2010

suggested to me by Ole Peter Grell during a meal at Wittenberg conference in Oct 31 2010.

This book proposes that Philip Melanchthon was responsible for transforming traditional university natural philosophy into a specifically Lutheran one. Motivated by the desire to check civil disobedience and promote Lutheran orthodoxy, he created a natural philosophy based on Aristotle, Galen and Plato, incorporating contemporary findings of Copernicus and Vesalius. The fields of astrology, anatomy, botany and mathematics all constituted a natural philosophy in which Melanchthon wished to demonstrate God's Providential design in the physical world. Rather than dichotomizing or synthesizing the two distinct areas of 'science' and 'religion', Kusukawa advocates the need to look at 'natural philosophy' as a discipline quite different from either 'modern science' or 'religion': a contextual assessment of the implication of the Lutheran Reformation on university education, particularly on natural philosophy.

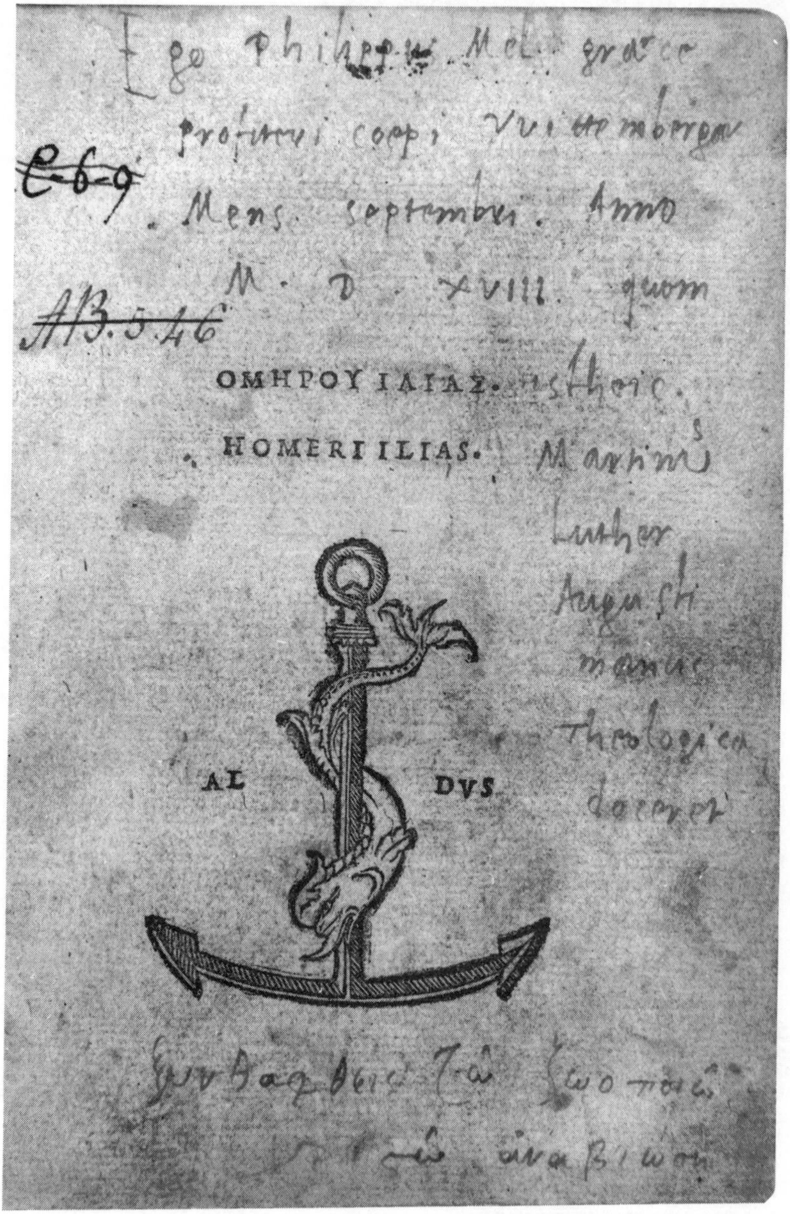

Title-page of Melanchthon's copy of the *Iliad*

IDEAS IN CONTEXT

THE TRANSFORMATION OF NATURAL PHILOSOPHY

IDEAS IN CONTEXT

The books in this series will discuss the emergence of intellectual traditions and of related new disciplines. The procedures, aims and vocabularies that were generated will be set in the context of the alternatives available within the contemporary frameworks of ideas and institutions. Through detailed studies of the evolution of such traditions, and their modification by different audiences, it is hoped that a new picture will form of the development of ideas in their concrete contexts. By this means, artificial distinctions between the history of philosophy, of the various sciences, of society and politics, and of literature may be seen to dissolve.

The series is published with the support of the Exxon Foundation.

A list of books in the series will be found at the end of the volume.

THE TRANSFORMATION OF NATURAL PHILOSOPHY

The case of Philip Melanchthon

SACHIKO KUSUKAWA

Christ's College, Cambridge

CAMBRIDGE
UNIVERSITY PRESS

Published by the Press Syndicate of the University of Cambridge
The Pitt Building, Trumpington Street, Cambridge CB2 1RP
40 West 20th Street, New York, NY 10011–4211, USA
10 Stamford Road, Oakleigh, Melbourne 3166, Australia

First published 1995

Printed in Great Britain at the University Press, Cambridge

A catalogue record for this book is available from the British Library

Library of Congress cataloguing in publication data

Kusukawa, Sachiko.
The transformation of natural philosophy: the case of Philip Melanchthon / Sachiko Kusukawa.
p. cm. – (Ideas in context)
Includes bibliographical references.
ISBN 0 521 47347 0
1. Melanchthon, Philip, 1497–1560. 2. Reformation.
3. Religion and science – History – sixteenth century.
4. Education, higher – Europe – History – sixteenth century.
I. Title. II. Series.
BR339.K87 1995
230'.41'092–dc20 94–18291 CIP

ISBN 0 521 47347 0 hardback

CE

For Hiroko and Toru Kusukawa

Contents

Illustrations

Notes on the text

For English translations of the Bible, I have used the 'Authorized Version' (1611).

For most primary and secondary sources, references are given by the name of the author and year of publication, followed by Roman numeral(s) indicating volume number(s) and Arabic number(s) specifying page or column number(s). Full titles are given in the Bibliography.

When quoting from printed primary sources, conventional and unconventional abbreviations have been expanded without indication. When quoting from manuscript sources, expansions of conventional and unconventional abbreviations have been indicated by italics. Within quotations and translations, square brackets [ ] denote my interpolations.

Unless otherwise stated in notes, all translations are mine. The following abbreviations have been used for frequently cited sources.

SIGLA

CR	*Corpus reformatorum Philippi Melanthonis opera quae supersunt omnia*, ed. C. B. Bretschneider and H. E. Bindseil, 28 vols. (Halle, 1834–52; Brunswick, 1853–60); *Huldrich Zwinglis Sämtliche Werke*, ed. E. Egli *et al.*, 6–3, *Corpus Reformatorum*, vol. 93–3 (Zürich, 1983).
Hartfelder	*Philipp Melanchthon als Praeceptor Germaniae*, by K. Hartfelder, Monumenta Germaniae Paedagogica 7 (Berlin, 1889).
Lohr	*Latin Aristotle Commentaries* II. *Renaissance Authors*, ed. C. H. Lohr (Florence, 1988).
LW	*Luther's Works* (English translation), ed. J. Pelikan and H. T. Lehman, 55 vols. (St Louis, 1955–76).

MBW	*Melanchthons Briefwechsel: kritische und kommentierte Gesamtausgabe, im Auftrag der Heidelberger Akademie der Wissenschaften*, ed. H. Scheible (Stuttgart, 1977–).[1]
StA	*Melanchthons Werke in Auswahl: Studienausgabe*, ed. R. Stupperich, 5 vols. (Gütersloh, 1963).
Urkundenbuch	*Urkundenbuch der Universität Wittenberg*, Teil I. *1502–1611*, ed. W. Friedensburg (Magdeburg, 1926).
VD	*Verzeichnis der im Deutschen Sprachbereich erschienenen Drucke des XVI. Jahrhunderts* (Stuttgart, 1983–).
WA	*Dr Martin Luthers Werke, kritische Gesamtausgabe*, 63 vols. (Weimar, 1883–1987).
WBr	*Dr Martin Luthers Briefwechsel*, 17 vols. (Weimar, 1930–83).

1 With its detailed critical apparatus, cross-reference, commentary and exhaustive index incorporating biblical references, this modern edition promises to meet the long and acutely felt need for a modern critical edition of Melanchthon's texts. For parts of Melanchthon's correspondence, I have used the dating and the Latin text of this modern edition and consulted the German summary for my translations. At the time of going to press, vols. I–VI, XXII were available to me.

Acknowledgements

First and foremost I wish to thank Dr A. R. Cunningham for his guidance and encouragement. He was the most critical and most sympathetic reader of the numerous drafts of my thesis and the revised manuscript for this book. In person and in print, he has been an inspiring historian: much of what I had to say was easier to find, since he had already shown the way. I am also grateful to Professor Nick Jardine for his unwavering support. I learnt from him the riches and fascinations of renaissance thought. I am further indebted to Dr Elisabeth S. Leedham-Green not only for teaching me palaeography and how to find rare books, but also for her encouragement. Professor Eckhard Kessler and Ms Constance Blackwell offered me a precious opportunity in Wolfenbüttel to realize that I was not writing in a vacuum. I have also received valuable advice and encouragement from Professor Peter Barker, Dr Lawrence Brockliss, Professor Mordechai Feingold, Professor Luce Giard, Professor Donald R. Kelley, Dr Heinrich Kuhn, Dr Steven Pumfrey, Dr Helga Robinson-Hammerstein, Dr Simon Schaffer, Professor Nancy Siraisi, and the anonymous readers for the Press. I alone am responsible for the errors and shortcomings that remain in this book.

The foundational works of Charles Lohr, the late Charles B. Schmitt and Paul O. Kristeller have naturally been indispensable to my work. The cheerful and efficient help provided over the years by Sue Wray, Nancy Sempers and Rebecca Bertoloni-Meli at the Whipple Library, Cambridge, expedited my research. The staff of the Rare Books Room and Main Reading Room of the University Library of Cambridge have, as ever, been helpful, understanding and accommodating.

I thank the Master and Fellows of Christ's College, Cambridge, for offering me a chance to pursue my interests further, as well as providing me with a congenial and stimulating environment for research. I am especially indebted to Professor Quentin Skinner for encouraging me to have my thesis published. During my time in Cambridge I benefited much from the encouragement of friends. In particular, I thank Drs Christine F. Salazar and Frances Willmoth not only for sharing with me their expertise, but also for providing salutary advice and support. At times when confidence was lagging Ros Hunt offered reassurance and Ms Marina Frasca-Spada enthusiasm. Dr Keith M. Ball has brought precious moments of laughter and peace into my life. I thank them all.

If the past is a foreign country and history a journey through that country, I have tried to travel in order to understand 'what those ways of life, those churches, those vineyards, meant to the natives' (C. S. Lewis, *The Discarded Image*, Cambridge, 1964, p. x). For I have been an optimistic traveller, believing that there is scope for understanding between different countries, be they separated in time, or in space. To my parents, whose encouragement and support made my journey to a foreign country possible, I owe my greatest debt.

Introduction

Of the countless ways in which historians may try to understand what sixteenth-century people made of the natural world, I offer in this book an account of what Philip Melanchthon, colleague and ally of Martin Luther, meant by natural philosophy. By the beginning of the sixteenth century, natural philosophy was a well-established subject in universities, a subject in which the nature of the natural world was discussed. In this study, I have looked at Melanchthon's idea of this natural philosophy in a way which is different from traditional accounts found in the histories of science, of renaissance philosophy or of universities. A different approach has meant a different picture. On my reading, natural philosophy emerges as undergoing a significant transformation at the hands of Melanchthon. In the following pages, I have tried to chart this transformation which, to my knowledge, has never been fully appreciated.

Today Melanchthon is best remembered for his attempts to explain Luther's theology of 'justification by faith alone' in his *Loci communes* and for his influential educational reforms which earned him the title of the *Praeceptor Germaniae*. Amongst the innumerable products of his prodigious writing and editing activity, there were two textbooks on natural philosophy, the *Commentarius de anima* and the *Initia doctrinae physicae*. These and their revised editions were read widely across Northern Europe throughout the sixteenth century.

Historical assessments of the significance of Melanchthon's natural philosophy have, however, remained oddly fragmented. For instance, historians have congratulated Melanchthon on the swift incorporation into his textbooks of some of the new findings of Copernicus and of Vesalius; on his enthusiastic promotion of mathematics; and on his success in educating a series of students of astronomy and botany.[1] Yet this 'progressiveness' of Melanchthon has remained largely irreconcilable with his apparent dependence on Aristotelian teleology and Galenic anatomy, and his unabashed enthusiasm for astrology.[2] It is a problem, I believe, that has arisen for historians of science who have tried to understand the sixteenth century in terms of the 'Scientific Revolution' – a movement which broke away from the Aristotelian qualitative explanation of natural phenomena to pursue the mathematical, quantitative explanation of natural change, and culminated in the triumph of experiment and observation over the occult, the superstitious and the religious.[3] In other words, they have tried to tease out of the past some elements of 'modern science', the end-product of this 'Revolution', thus dissociating those elements from the 'non-modern', superstition and religion.[4] Because it is a search for what modern historians themselves regard as respectable science or modernity, their history has been and forever will be about a past trapped in a strange mixture of 'modernity' and 'non-modernity'.

In this study, I propose a different way of understanding Melanchthon's natural philosophy. My aim has been to understand what natural philosophy meant *to Melanchthon*.[5] Why was it that Melanchthon thought it important and necessary to write about natural philosophy and how did he do it? For an answer I have looked at his own words in his correspondence, textbooks, theological tracts, disputations and poems, as well as at a number of pictures connected with him. As I hope will become apparent, Melanchthon's natural philosophy, which was built on classical as well as contemporary material, closely reflects issues of faith which were immediate and important to him.

To historians of renaissance thought, it may seem less than

[1] For Melanchthon's partial adaptation of Copernicus, see Westman (1975); for his use of Vesalius, see Nutton (1993); for his promotion of mathematics and astronomy, see Westman (1980b); and for his students of botany, see Dannenfeldt (1972).

[2] For Melanchthon's 'Aristotelianism', see Petersen (1921), 38–108; for a study of his Galenic sources, see Rump (1896); and for traditional treatments of his astrology, see Warburg (1919) and Thorndike (1923–58), v, 378–405, but see now also Bellucci (1988) and Caroti (1982).

[3] Representative works of this approach in the history of science are Koyré (1961), Dijksterhuis (1961) and Hall (1983).

[4] For a recent re-examination of the historiography of the 'Scientific Revolution', see now the essays in *Reappraisals of the Scientific Revolution*.

[5] For philosophical reasons for adopting this kind of historical approach in intellectual history, see Skinner (1969), and Baxandall (1985) for history of art. Cf. also a review of the current state of the history of ideas in Kelley (1990).

surprising that a parallel can be found between a man's faith and his classical scholarship in an age when the fruits of humanist scholarship were ripe and when faith had become a hotly contested issue. Is that not just what we might expect of a 'Christian humanist'?[6] Yet, according to its most influential modern proponent, the term 'humanism' (be it Christian or not) cannot be identified with any particular ideological, theological or philosophical position.[7] That is, the term cannot account for the particular way in which individuals in the sixteenth century quoted from classical authors: a 'Christian humanist' did not, for instance, need to write about natural philosophy using Aristotle or Galen in the way that Melanchthon did. Nor was it imperative for a 'Christian humanist' to write about natural philosophy at all.

Yet Melanchthon did write about natural philosophy in a way which was different from his predecessors, and he did so by building on writings of classical authors such as Plato, Aristotle, Galen, Ptolemy and Cicero. Individual studies have gauged the extent to which Melanchthon was indebted to Aristotle, Galen and Plato.[8] It is nevertheless insufficient to explain what Melanchthon was doing by simply characterizing him an Aristotelian or a synthesizer of Platonic and Aristotelian philosophies. Melanchthon's use of Plato is quite different from that of a Ficino and there seem to be as many forms of Aristotelianism as there were people who wrote about Aristotle.[9] Instead, taking natural philosophy as a whole, I have asked why Melanchthon chose to follow Aristotle, Galen or Plato on certain points, and modify or ignore them on others. My concern was thus to understand why Melanchthon chose to write natural philosophy in the particular way that he did, and why he needed natural philosophy at all. It is, I believe, by paying attention to the immediate context in which Melanchthon wrote his words that we can understand the significance of natural philosophy for

6 Christian humanists are defined as those 'who applied their classical scholarship to biblical and patristic studies and who adopted and defended in their writings some tenets of Christian religion or theology', in Kristeller (1988a), 133.

7 Kristeller (1988a), 113f. For a study of the religiosity of several Italian humanists, see Trinkaus (1970).

8 For an estimation of the extent of Melanchthon's debt to Aristotle, see Petersen (1921), 48–108; Melanchthon's Platonism receives ample examination in Maurer (1967–9), I, and Belluci (1988); and for Melanchthon's use of Galen, see Rump (1896).

9 For a recent assessment of Ficino's Platonism, see the essays in *Marsilio Ficino e il ritorno di Platone* and *Ficino and Renaissance Neoplatonism*; for the various forms of Aristotelianism, see Schmitt (1983).

Melanchthon and the uniqueness of his use of authors. As a result, we may arrive at an understanding of what was in fact a much stronger bond between Melanchthon's scholarship and his faith – Melanchthon in fact used classical as well as contemporary authors in such a way as to render his natural philosophy *Lutheran*. That is, Melanchthon transformed traditional natural philosophy into a natural philosophy new and different from its predecessors *because* he believed in a faith which was also new and different.

I shall be arguing in this study that Melanchthon's natural philosophy was a *Lutheran* one to the extent that his use of authors and his aim in writing natural philosophy textbooks can be accounted for through his Lutheran conviction: Melanchthon saw in natural philosophy a potent response to issues which he believed to be seriously jeopardizing Luther's cause; he reinterpreted classical and contemporary authors along Lutheran principles; and he made natural philosophy an integral part of a pedagogy which was aimed at establishing and consolidating Luther's message. This understanding of natural philosophy enables us to see for the first time how disparate fields of study such as human anatomy, astrology, mathematics, geography and botany all formed a unity at Wittenberg in achieving a single goal: the knowledge of the Providence of God in this world. It is precisely for this same reason – to know the Providence of God – and not because he wanted to be 'progressive', that Melanchthon also adopted the findings of Vesalius and of Copernicus in the particular way that he did.

Modern scholars are ambiguous in their assessment of the authenticity of Melanchthon's 'Lutheran' faith. Some have underlined the importance of Melanchthon's humanistic skills for Luther's reading of the Bible, while others, including his contemporaries, have questioned the Lutheran orthodoxy of his stance on the Eucharist and other doctrinal matters.[10] Yet, the morphology of Lutheranism itself owes as much to Melanchthon as it does to Luther. At times, as Erasmus would say, Melanchthon was 'more Lutheran than Luther himself'.[11] Whatever their differences, we should therefore remem-

[10] For studies on the relationship between the two, see Lohse (1983), Pauck (1984), 41–65, Green (1980) and Hildebrandt (1946). An erstwhile student, Mathias Flacius Illyricus, attacked Melanchthon and his followers for pusillanimously compromising the original teachings of Luther. For Flacius, see Olson (1981) and for the dissension within the Lutheran camp, see Stupperich (1966), 133–45.

[11] '... est [Melanchthon] ipse, pene ut ita dixerim, ipso Luthero lutheranior'. Erasmus to John Lasky, 5 March 1534, Erasmus (1956–68), x, 363, no. 2911. My interpolation.

ber the large overlap of interests and concerns of Luther and of Melanchthon, most significant of which was the pursuit of Reform in order to establish the teaching of justification by faith alone. They pursued this Reform through their respective vocations: Luther the dynamic and charismatic preacher who heard the Word of God; Melanchthon the irenic scholar and teacher who wanted to see the Providence of God in nature. It is Melanchthon pursuing this vocation whom we see creating a new kind of natural philosophy.

This work is about Melanchthon as well as natural philosophy. Because Melanchthon lived a life in which faith mattered, this book is as much about religion as it is about natural philosophy. I wish to stress, however, that I do not want to depict this natural philosophy as something between 'science and religion'. Modern interpretations of the historical relationship between 'religion and science' vary tremendously: some claim that religion (Puritanism in particular) actively promoted and developed 'modern science' and others argue that religion was a hindrance to the formation of 'modern science'. There are also those who take an 'indifferent' stance that religion had no decisive impact on the development of 'modern science' either way.[12] It was not my aim to take any side in this debate. We have recently been shown, in fact, how and why this particular theme of 'science and religion' is riddled with problems: not only do the variety and complexity of each historical case defy any attempt to reach a simple generalization about the relationship of 'science and religion', but also historical exposition on this theme has been confused by the partisan interests of modern historians and further complicated by the inherent artificiality of the pairing of the concepts 'science' and 'religion', whose definitions seem equally confused.[13] The problem of historical interpretation of 'science and religion', it thus seems, is essentially a problem created by historians who have tried to find elements of 'science and religion' in something that may have had a different identity altogether.

What I have attempted in this study is to understand natural philosophy as a whole, as something with a distinct identity of its

[12] For representative works on the positive contribution of religion to 'science', see Merton (1970), Mason (1962) and Hooykaas (1972); the conflict thesis was most famously presented in Draper (1875) and White (1955); and for a stance between these two positions, see Deason (1985). For a recent re-examination of the Merton thesis, see the collection of essays in vol. 3–1 (Spring 1989) of *Science in Context*. For a critical and comprehensive survey of the secondary literature on 'science and religion', see now Brooke (1991), 348–403.

[13] Brooke (1991), esp. 1–116.

own. It was inherent in the discipline of natural philosophy that it was to be about nature understood as a Creation of the Christian God; that its arguments could elucidate points about God and the Christian Church; and that it was part of learned knowledge produced in universities, often in the service of orthodoxy or the status quo.[14] Melanchthon was by no means the first or the last to espouse this view of natural philosophy. The significance of Melanchthon's endeavours, as I hope to show, was that he transformed a traditional natural philosophy into a peculiarly Lutheran one.

In this study I have focused rather sharply on Melanchthon's natural philosophy. My immediate aim was to offer a picture of Melanchthon's natural philosophy which seemed less fragmented or blurred. The picture, I nonetheless hope, will further illustrate the importance for historians in general to take stock of the identity of natural philosophy,[15] and to ask, therefore, a different kind of question about the natural philosophy of the past.

[14] For universities as religious authorities, see Lytle (1981).

[15] The necessity to understand natural philosophy as something *sui generis* was first argued in Cunningham (1988) and (1991).

CHAPTER I

The way of the Schoolmen

> Just as for the people of God there was an exile in Babylon while Jerusalem was their homeland, so ignorance is the exile of the inner man though *sapientia* is his homeland ... The route from this exile to the homeland is *scientia*, for *scientia* deals with earthly matters, while *sapientia* is concerned with divine matters. One should pass along this route not by steps of the body, but by desires of the heart. Indeed this route leads to the homeland through the ten directing arts and through the books cleaving to the way and serving it like so many towns and villages along a route.
>
> *On the exile of the soul and on its homeland, or, On the arts,*[1]
> Honorius of Autun (*c.* 1156)

The University of Wittenberg was founded in 1502. By then, men in the universities had been learning, teaching, disputing upon and writing about natural philosophy for at least three hundred years. Natural philosophy was firmly embedded in the arts curriculum and had become an integral part of medieval learning. Its standard texts were Aristotle's *libri naturales*, such as the *Physica*, the *De caelo*, the *De generatione et corruptione*, the *De anima*, the *Meteora* and the *Parva naturalia*. These were tackled following a set of logical procedures and recognized authorities. Together with logic and metaphysics, natural philosophy formed the core of learning undertaken in medieval universities. The University of Wittenberg began by inheriting the kind of learning characteristic of late fifteenth-century German universities. It is this learning, including natural philosophy, that

1 'Sicut Populo Dei exsilium erat in Babylonia, Jerusalem vero patria, sic interioris hominis exsilium est ignorantia, patria autem sapientia ... De hoc exsilio ad patriam via est scientia, scientia enim in rebus physicis: sapientia vero consideratur in divinis. Per hanc viam gradiendum est non passibus corporis, sed affectibus cordis. Haec quippe via ducit ad patriam tendentes per decem artes, et libros sibi adhaerentes, et quasi per totidem civitates et villas sibi servientes.' *De animae exsilio et patria alias de artibus*, Honorius of Autun (1854), 1243.

Luther violently objected to, in person at Wittenberg and more generally in print. I shall therefore begin with a summary of how the medieval Schoolmen dealt with natural philosophy.

Medieval university learning had a unitary character in that, despite certain recognizable disciplinary boundaries, areas of study were closely related to each other. Amongst Northern European universities where faculties of theology dominated, the arts curriculum was mainly orientated towards theology.[2] The seven liberal arts were considered propaedeutic or instrumental to the study of theology.[3] Logic was the fundamental procedure of intellectual discourse, and the *quaestio* method was originally developed as a technique to resolve seeming contradictions and inconsistencies when reading the Bible.[4] 'Nature' in natural philosophy was frequently identified with God's Creation and moral philosophy dealt with the happiness of a Christian man.[5] Metaphysics dealt with the mode of being in its highest abstracted form and had the status of 'divine science' in which some aspects of the Divine Being were considered.[6] Thus, as a whole, studies in the arts faculty could contribute in one way or another towards knowledge of the Christian God.

Medieval natural philosophy was orientated towards theology in a variety of ways. For instance the thirteenth-century Dominican interest in a natural philosophy based on Aristotelian causation and the Franciscan interest in the nature of light and *perspectiva*, it has been shown, can best be understood as a Christian enterprise whose origins can be traced to the personal experiences and senses of mission of the founders of these orders, St Dominic and St Francis respectively.[7] Although the process by which Aristotle's *libri naturales*

2 For the difficulty, in fact, of separating theology and philosophy in this period, see Vignaux (1959), 9–16 and Marenbon (1987), 83–90.

3 This is understood as a continuation of the role of liberal arts as propaedeutic to scriptural wisdom in cathedral schools in McInery (1983).

4 Marenbon (1987), 13f. and 35–49, 80–2 for the importance of logic in theology. Cf., however, the case of Henry of Langenstein who rejected the universality of Aristotelian logic as applicable to theological tenets such as the Trinity, in the wake of his failure to convert the Jews in Vienna, Shank (1988).

5 See for instance Albertus Magnus' treatment of Aristotle's *Physica* as pertaining to Christian Creation in Lang (1992), 125–60. For Christian happiness in medieval moral philosophy, see Wieland (1982b).

6 For various ways in which the subject matter and theological orientation of metaphysics were defined in the Middle Ages, see Wippel (1982).

7 I am grateful to Dr Andrew Cunningham and Dr Roger French for allowing me to read an earlier draft of their forthcoming book, *Before Science: The Friars' Natural Philosophy*.

were established as canonical texts of natural philosophy needs further investigation, especially in the light of the condemnation of 1277, natural philosophy continued to be taught and learnt in arts faculties.[8] In the fourteenth century, topics which closely reflected contemporary theological concerns were developed and expounded upon in natural philosophy. For instance, William of Occam's analysis of the concept of quantity was developed in order to overcome (in Occam's eyes) the inadequate explanations of Christ's quantity in the Eucharist by Aquinas and Scotus, and studies of measuring motion closely reflected contemporary theological attempts to 'measure' the relationship between God and His Creation.[9]

Natural philosophical arguments were also frequently and extensively used in theological discussions, such as on the power of God in the Sentences commentaries, on Creation in the Hexaemeron commentaries, and on transubstantiation in Eucharist treatises.[10] Although as philosophy, or human rational knowledge, natural philosophy was never sufficient for a theologian to deal with divine matters, it was a powerful means by which some parts of Christian doctrine could be elucidated, developed and maintained. It was an integral part of learning for university men who increasingly saw themselves as 'professors of orthodoxy' and saw the universities as a universal authority on a par with that of the Pope and of the Emperor.[11]

Natural philosophy was taught in universities in the form of lectures, exercises and disputations, though the extent to which these academical exercises were required for degrees varied.[12] By the end of the fourteenth century, it generally seems to have been the

8 Marenbon (1987), 67. For the limited impact of the condemnation of 1277 on arts teaching, see Hissette (1977), 316–18; for a synthetic account of modern scholarship on the Parisian condemnations, see Wippel (1977); for the introduction of Aristotle to the West see Steenberghen (1955) and Weisheipl (1964).

9 For Occam, see Sylla (1975), 361–72 and now Tachau (1988) for the relationship between his optical theory and theory of knowledge. For studies of measurement, see Murdoch (1975), 289–97.

10 For Hexaemeron literature, see for instance Steneck (1976) for Henry of Langenstein, and Southern (1986), esp. 205–19, for Robert Grosseteste. For an overview of the doctrine of transubstantiation, see McCue (1968).

11 For the 'authority' of professors and universities, see Lytle (1981); for the medieval triadic division of authorities, see G. H. Williams (1962b), 166–83. For clerical control over issues in natural philosophy in the later Middle Ages, see Lohr (1988b).

12 For the variety of degree requirements at different universities, see Rashdall (1936) and Thorndike (1975).

case that students wishing to obtain arts degrees were required (amongst other things) at least to have heard lectures on most, if not all, of Aristotle's *libri naturales*. Students usually first heard lectures on logic, followed soon after by lectures on natural philosophy and finally on Aristotle's *Metaphysica*.[13]

Logic was the starting point and building block of scholastic learning in universities. It provided the means by which most subjects were discussed in commentaries or in disputations. It is, in fact, the logically rigorous procedure of exposition which has been regarded as one of the distinctive features of medieval learning.[14] Mastery of logic was therefore essential before proceeding to philosophy.

Natural philosophy was thus expounded in a rigorously logical way. For instance, commentaries on natural philosophy frequently followed the *quaestio* form.[15] A section of a commentary began with a disjunctive question about the meaning of Aristotle's text. It was followed by a list of arguments found in Aristotle or other commentators which seemed to support the view opposed to the favoured answer. These (opposing) arguments were then refuted or resolved one after another into the favoured view by way of syllogistic reasoning, utilizing logical distinctions and definitions from Aristotle or other commentators. By way of logical reasoning, the question was eventually resolved into the favoured view. This kind of logical reasoning, which reconciles various authorities and the teaching of the Church, is representative of the procedure of the 'scholastic method'.[16] Thus, whilst some historians have called medieval natural philosophy a 'handmaiden' to theology,[17] others have called it a natural philosophy 'without nature', because of its rigorously analytical character.[18]

The centrality of logic and the unitary character of university

[13] For the order of learning at Paris, see Rashdall (1936), I, 439–54; for Oxford, see Fletcher (1984), 376–86 and for Cambridge, see Leader (1988), 89–107, 155–69. For the relatively late establishment of metaphysics in the arts faculty, see Gabriel (1963).

[14] Ueberweg (1926–8), II, 152–7.

[15] A concise introduction to the *quaestio* technique can be found in Marenbon (1987), 25–34, whom I follow here.

[16] A standard definition of the 'scholastic method' is that it is 'essentially a rational investigation of every relevant problem in liberal arts, philosophy, theology, medicine and law, examined from opposing points of view, in order to reach an intelligent, scientific solution that would be consistent with accepted authorities, known facts, human reason, and Christian faith', *New Catholic Encyclopedia*, XII, 1145.

[17] Cf. an examination of the extent of interdependence between natural philosophy and theology in Sylla (1975).

[18] The characterization is from Murdoch (1982).

learning was much in evidence when different ways of teaching (the *viae*) in the arts faculty were introduced for the first time in the fifteenth century. In 1425, the Saxon princes ordered the University of Cologne to provide for a new way of teaching by the *moderni* in order to counter the spread of the Prague heresy.[19] This heresy which promoted communion in both kinds and severely criticized the conduct of the clergy was led by John Huss (*c.* 1372–1415) and others who espoused the realist views of John Wyclif (*c.* 1330–84).[20] In the fifteenth century the *moderni* stood for those who took a nominalist stance about universals, claiming that there was nothing in reality that corresponded to abstract concepts. On the other hand, the *reales* (often equated with the *antiqui*, in opposition to the *moderni*) denoted men who believed that universals had in one way or another a foundation in reality.[21] The Cologne masters were then predominantly realist, following the teaching of Thomas Aquinas. Faced with a threat to their own established way, they remarked: 'The connection of the [faculty] of arts with the faculty of theology is so inseparable that to prohibit the use of this teaching [of Thomas] in arts amounts to much the same thing in theology, and to allow [his teaching] in theology [is to do so] in the arts.'[22]

Because of its theological orientation, the manner of teaching in the arts faculty was pertinent to the problem of heresy. Moreover, because logic was central to the whole scholastic teaching, it was in terms of a different logical stance (concerning universals) that an alternative way of (theological) education was expressed. In order to check the spread of the Prague heresy, the *via moderna*, which meant in this case the teachings of Marsilius of Inghen and Jean Buridan, was thus introduced at Cologne, in addition to the pre-existing *via antiqua*, which meant the teachings of Albertus Magnus and of Thomas Aquinas.[23] This meant that the arts curriculum, including natural philosophy, was to be taught thereafter in two different ways.

19 For a brief summary of this case of Cologne, see Ritter (1922), 39–44. For a full transcription of the response of the masters, see Ehrle (1925), 36–65.

20 For an account of this heresy, see Kaminsky (1967) and for Huss' realist views and his attitude towards Wyclif, see Spinka (1968), 36–65.

21 The meaning of the terms *antiqui/moderni* were fixed in the fifteenth century, Gilbert (1974), 85. For fourteenth-century antecedents of this distinction, see Courtenay (1984).

22 '...(dicimus) quod Artium cum Facultate Theologiae tam indissolubilis est connexio, quod per idem valere est, prohibere hujus doctrinae usum in Artibus et in Theologia, et permittere in Theologia et in Artibus'. Ehrle (1925), 284, my brackets.

23 Ritter (1922), 39.

After Cologne, all German universities came to offer two different ways of teaching in the arts faculty during the course of the fifteenth century. Their reasons for introducing a new way in addition to the pre-existing one ranged from Dominican influences to rivalries between neighbouring universities.[24] Consequently there was little consensus as to which Schoolmen should be followed under either *via*. Under the *via antiqua* some people followed Albertus Magnus, Thomas Aquinas or Duns Scotus, while under the *via moderna* others followed William of Occam, Marsilius of Inghen, Jean Buridan or Duns Scotus again![25]

The co-existence of the *viae* did not necessarily lead to conflict (the so-called *Wegestreit*), and even when it did, the nature of the conflict had more to do with individual ambitions, factional power struggles and puerile rivalry than with serious ideological conflict.[26] In several instances, the *viae* seem to have existed peacefully alongside each other, and there was some flexibility in changing from one to the other. As competition grew between the two *viae*, a formal division was introduced in the arts faculty.[27] At Tübingen the institutionalization of the *viae* extended into the theology faculty, where it was stipulated that each *via* was to be represented by two theology lecturers.[28] Although the two *viae* in the arts curriculum spread mainly amongst German universities, Padua also introduced the *via Thomae* and the *via Scoti*, in connection with the teaching of the Dominican and Franciscan convents there. These *viae* applied to the teaching of metaphysics and theology, but there were also efforts by both Dominicans and Franciscans to align the contents of natural philosophy with the kind of metaphysics taught in their respective *via*.[29]

By the end of the fifteenth century it thus became common,

[24] In German universities other than Cologne, it was usually the old way (*via antiqua*) which made its way into predominantly nominalist universities. For a comprehensive survey of the establishment of the two *viae* in German universities, see Gabriel (1974).

[25] At the University of Freiburg, Thomas Aquinas was followed for the *via antiquorum* and Duns Scotus for the *via modernorum*, Kaufmann (1888–96), II, 361. For possible *moderni* authorities, see Oberman (1987b), 24f.

[26] Overfield (1984), 49–60.

[27] See the suggestion at Ingolstadt in 1472 to have separate deans, matriculas, chests and halls, Gabriel (1974), 476.

[28] *Urkunden zur Geschichte der Universität Tübingen*, 264f. For the inherent tension between the *viae* at Tübingen, see Oberman (1981), 30–44.

[29] Poppi (1983). Cf. the Scotist, Filippo Fabri's work on natural philosophy at post-tridentine Padua in Schmitt (1984).

especially in German universities, to offer two different ways of arts instruction as part of a system of knowledge with different theological emphases. For natural philosophy, it meant that it too could be taught in different ways, with different theological orientations.

In form and in content, the University of Wittenberg inherited many of the characteristics of its predecessors. In 1502 Frederick the Wise (1463–1525), the Elector of Saxony, founded a university at Wittenberg.[30] As most Northern European universities did, it followed the 'Parisian archetype' of a university of masters.[31] Imperial and Papal charters were procured as necessary conditions of founding a *studium generale* whose masters could claim their *ius ubique docendi*. Although the anomaly of officially opening the university before receiving a Papal charter has been noted,[32] there is no indication in the sources that Frederick the Wise deliberately intended to start a university which was different in structure or in kind from its predecessors. Ecclesiastical approval was sought and procured the following year and, albeit minor, an ecclesiastical officer was appointed to the chancellorship.[33] Frederick the Wise's principal aim, it seems, was to found a full university in his own territory, with all the rights and privileges of a traditional university, just like its archetype Paris, or its neighbouring rival, Leipzig.[34]

In the format of its teaching, Wittenberg was 'a direct daughter of Tübingen'.[35] This was due to Johann Staupitz (1470–1524), an Augustinian who was entrusted with the organization of the university. Staupitz himself had graduated from Tübingen and had been the prior of the Augustinians there.[36] From Tübingen, he brought several men from the university as well as some Augustinians, who

[30] See Frederick the Wise's letter of invitation to the opening of the university, *Urkundenbuch*, 3f. For background of the foundation of the university, see Grossmann (1975), 24–46.

[31] For the seminal classification of the two 'archetypes' of medieval universities of Bologna and of Paris, see Rashdall (1936), I, 17. For German universities following the Parisian model, see *ibid.*, II, 210–88.

[32] Clark sees this as an indication of the growing importance (relative to Papal privilege) of imperial privilege in founding universities, which culminated in the foundation (deliberately without acknowledgement of Papal authority) of the University of Marburg (1527). Clark (1986), 220f., 227f.

[33] The *praeceptor* of the Antonines at Lichtenberg was appointed as chancellor. Friedensburg (1917), 29. For the financial implication of ecclesiastical approval, see Grossmann (1975), 41.

[34] *Urkundenbuch*, 2f. The University of Leipzig was in the territory of the rival Albertine line of the house of Wettin.

[35] Bauch (1897), 299.

[36] Steinmetz (1968), 4–6; Grossmann (1975), 44–6.

took up key posts at Wittenberg.[37] The statutes of the arts faculty at Wittenberg, dating from 1504, were copied also from Tübingen.[38]

The Wittenberg arts statutes stipulated that students wishing to obtain a bachelor's degree should hear lectures on logic: Porphyry's *Isagoge* and *Predicamenta*, Aristotle's *Priora analytica*, *Posteriora analytica*, *Sophistici elenchi* and *Topica*. Furthermore, attendance at exercises on Aristotle's *Physica* and the *Parva logicalia* and participation in disputations were required. For a master's degree, the lectures on Aristotle's *Physica*, *De caelo et mundo*, *De generatione et corruptione*, *De anima*, *Metaphysica*, *Ethica* and *Parva naturalia* had to be heard in addition to exercises on the *Ethica* and the *Parva naturalia* and participations in disputations.[39] Thus, whilst mastery of logic was essential for a bachelor's degree, for a master's degree knowledge of the whole of Aristotle's philosophy was imperative. Natural philosophy was part of the requisite knowledge for a master's degree at Wittenberg.

At Tübingen lectures were given according to two *bursae* ('chests') of two different ways.[40] All the clauses pertaining to the *viae* in the Tübingen statutes were copied out into the Wittenberg arts statutes.[41] We have, however, little direct evidence for assuming that teaching according to different interpretations of 'universals' was implemented from the very beginning at Wittenberg.

What is known, however, is that at least one way came into existence in 1503. In autumn that year, the dean of the arts faculty, Sigismund Epp, who was one of the Augustinians who came from Tübingen with Staupitz, asked Frederick the Wise to have textbooks in the *via Scoti* printed.[42] This request resulted in the establishment of a university printer, Wolfgang Stöckel,[43] and three textbooks were

37 For a list of Augustinians and/or Tübingen graduates at Wittenberg, see Grossmann (1975), 44f.

38 The 1504 statutes are the earliest extant statutes. For the text of the Wittenberg statutes, see Muther (1874). The only alterations occurred in the pecuniary and penalty clauses, Bauch (1897), 301. Borrowing of statutes was fairly common; the Tübingen statutes of 1477 were themselves copied from Basle and those of Basle in turn from Erfurt, *ibid.*, 300.

39 Muther (1874), 184–7.

40 They were called the *Bursa realium* and the *Bursa modernorum*, *Urkunden zur Geschichte der Universität Tübingen*, 402–5.

41 See the collation of the clauses touching the division of the *viae* between Tübingen and Wittenberg, Ehrle (1925), 224f., 230 note 1. The *viae* also appear in the statutes of the Wittenberg theology faculty of 1508, which are the earliest extant ones for the theology faculty, see *Urkundenbuch*, 34.

42 *Urkundenbuch*, 6, Grossmann (1975), 91f.

43 Grossmann (1975), 91f. For a list of publications by the early Wittenberg printers, see Grossmann (1971).

duly printed by him in the autumn of 1504. These textbooks were commentaries of Petrus Tartaretus (*fl.* 1480–90), a Scotist at the Sorbonne.[44] One textbook dealt with Peter of Spain's textbook on logic, the *Summulae logicae*, another with Porphyry and Aristotle's *Organon*, and the third with all of Aristotle's *libri naturales* and the *Metaphysica*.[45] All profess to be commentaries following John Duns Scotus (*c.* 1265–1308).

Tartaretus' commentary on natural philosophy follows the *quaestio* form.[46] He begins his commentary on the *Physica* with the question, 'whether there is a "*scientia*" of natural things, having [as] its prime and adequate subject, "body", considered insofar as it is natural (*sub ratione naturalitatis*)'.[47] Then arguments from Aristotle which seem to support a negative answer (which is the opposite of the favoured view) follow: it seems that there cannot be a *scientia* of natural things because, according to the *Posteriora analytica*, *scientia* deals only with necessary things which cannot be otherwise, but natural things are contingent, corruptible and can be otherwise than they are, because they are composed of matter and form. In addition, *scientia*, according to the *Posteriora analytica* again, can deal only with universals and not singulars, but natural beings are singular. Moreover, the subject matter of *scientia* should adequately contain characteristics deducible from that subject within that *scientia*. 'Natural body' cannot be the essential subject of mobility, the prime demonstrable characteristic of natural philosophy, because there are mobile things which are not natural, such as angels and the soul.[48]

Then arguments refuting these opposing views are introduced. The argument is conducted in three steps: first, definitions and distinctions which are necessary to tackle the question are intro-

44 Rector at Paris in 1490. For his logical standpoint and popularity, see Prantl (1855–70), IV, 204–10.

45 The titles were: *Expositio magistri Tatareti supra summulas Petri hispani cum allegationibus passuum Scoti doctoris subtilissimi*, *Expositio magistri Petri Tatareti super textu logices Aristotelis cum allegationibus passuum Scoti doctoris subtilissimi*, and *Clarissima singularisque totius philosophie nec non metaphysice Aristotelis magistri Petri Tatareti exposicio ac passuum Scoti allegatio*, Grossmann (1971), 25f.

46 I have not been able to consult the original commentaries of Tartaretus printed in Wittenberg. My following argument is based on the *Commentarii Petri Tartareti in libros philosophie naturalis et metaphysice Aristotelis* (Paris: F. Regnault, 1514).

47 'Quaeritur primo utrum de rebus naturalibus sit scientia: habens pro subjecto primo et adequato corpus sub ratione naturalitatis?' *Commentarii Petri Tartareti in libros philosophie naturalis* . . ., fo. iir.

48 *Commentarii Petri Tartareti in libros philosophie naturalis* . . ., fo. iir.

duced (*notabilia*); then further possible objections are countered (*dubia*); and finally the question is resolved by way of logical reasoning into the favoured view.[49]

In the *notabilia*, a sharper definition of *scientia* is introduced in order to distinguish it from other kinds of knowledge such as faith or opinion. Following Scotus, there are four conditions of *scientia* to note: it should be certain and evident knowledge; it should be about necessary objects; this knowledge should arise from principles; syllogistic reasoning should be applied to these principles which are better known in nature.[50] Tartaretus further explains that natural things are defined as a composite of matter and form. This definition is contrasted with definitions of other extra-mental entities, such as God (who have forms separated from matter) and mathematical numbers and figures (which are abstracted from material things but do not include matter in their definitions). This indicates how a composite of form and matter is a definition exclusive to natural things. This definition, Tartaretus notes, is not determined by the difference of individuals but, rather, is a *generic* definition. Tartaretus then introduces distinctions and definitions of terms such as 'subject' and 'being' either from Scotus or Aristotle.[51]

Then, the opinions of other authorities are listed. Albertus Magnus, Avicenna and Aegidius Romanus have posited 'natural body' (*corpus mobile*) as the subject matter of the whole of natural philosophy. By a 'whole' natural philosophy, they mean an aggregate of all conclusions demonstrated in all of Aristotle's *libri naturales*. Aquinas, Jean Buridan and others have defined the subject matter of this whole natural philosophy as 'mobile being' (*ens mobile*). Tartaretus agrees with neither because an aggregate of such conclusions are beings (gathered together) *per accidens*. Recent Scotists also come under attack. They have posited 'natural body' (*corpus naturale*) as the subject of the whole of natural philosophy, claiming that 'mobility' is the attribute convertible with body, namely that everything mobile is a body and every body is mobile. For Tartaretus, this does not fit the teaching of faith, because faith, for instance, is mobile but

[49] 'In hac questione et in ceteris sequentibus erunt tres articuli. In quorum primo erunt notabilia. In secundo erunt dubia. Et in tertio respondebitur ad questionem: ponendo conclusionem rationalem et cum hoc solventur rationes ante oppositum.' *Commentarii Petri Tartareti in libros philosophie naturalis* ..., fo. iir.

[50] For the original formulation by Scotus, see *Lexicon scholasticum philosophico-theologicum*, 612f.

[51] *Commentarii Petri Tartareti in libros philosophie naturalis* ..., fo. iir.

has no body, and angels and rational souls are mobile but are separated from bodies.[52]

Having dismissed the opinion of other Schoolmen, Tartaretus introduces Scotus' definition of the subject matter of natural philosophy. For Scotus, it is 'finite being taken in its common concept considered insofar as it is natural ... because mobility is interchangeable with finite natural being'.[53] This, Tartaretus says, is different from Aristotle's definition. According to Tartaretus, Aristotle had defined the subject matter of natural philosophy as natural body (*corpus naturale*) because the terms '*mobile*' and '*natural*' were interchangeable to him. That everything mobile is a body (*corpus*) is against the teaching of the Catholic Church, since faith and angels are mobile but do not have body. Hence 'mobility' is an accident that should be separated from the subject.[54] Scotus' definition of the subject of natural philosophy above gets round this problem by Aristotle's original definition.

In the *dubia*, further possible questions are raised such as whether the prime and adequate subject of a *scientia* contains all necessary truths of the subject, or whether consideration of all things pertains to natural philosophy. These are tackled, again via Aristotle and Scotus, and it is concluded, for instance, that natural philosophy considers at best all things as species, but it does not treat 'being', 'thing' or 'whatness' (*quidditas*), which can only be dealt with in metaphysics.[55]

Tartaretus' examination of what the subject matter ought to be reveals that he is not simply trying to recover what Aristotle meant, but, more importantly, is trying to reach a definition of the subject matter which is also theologically correct. Therefore, the *quaestio* is resolved in the following way: 'There is a *scientia* about natural things ... and body considered insofar as it is natural is the prime subject of natural philosophy treated by Aristotle; but not of philosophy dealt with completely, but finite being is [the latter's] subject.'[56] As we may recall, the latter definition of a 'complete' natural philosophy is Scotus'.

52 *Commentarii Petri Tartareti in libros philosophie naturalis* ..., fo. iivf.

53 '... ens finitum acceptum in suo conceptu communi sub ratione naturalitatis est subjectum adequatum philosophie naturalis complete tradite: quia mobilitas convertitur cum ente finito naturali'. *Commentarii Petri Tartareti in libros philosophie naturalis* ..., fo. iir.

54 *Commentarii Petri Tartareti in libros philosophie naturalis* ..., fo. iiv. 55 *Ibid.*

56 'Conclusio responsalis. de rebus naturalibus est scientia ... Et corpus sub ratione naturalitatis est subjectum primum philosophie naturalis tradite ab Aristotele non tamen philoso-

Essentially the same format is followed throughout Tartaretus' commentary on Aristotle's *libri naturales*.[57] The *quaestiones* relating to Aristotle's texts are resolved using distinctions and definitions mainly from Scotus and drawing conclusions from those definitions using syllogistic reasoning. Great care is taken to point out and refute theologically unacceptable views. Tartaretus' commentary is thus an exposition of Scotist natural philosophy as a study of finite beings, rather than a straightforward textual exposition on Aristotle.

In Tartaretus' commentary, a distinction is frequently drawn between natural philosophy and metaphysics. In it, following Scotus, metaphysics is defined as a study of infinite being, whilst natural philosophy is a study of finite beings. The nature of a Scotist natural philosophy is, in fact, best understood in conjunction with a Scotist metaphysics.

Scotus sought to establish as a legitimate form of knowledge of God a metaphysics which did not depend on a physical knowledge of God. He rejected the then current Thomist idea of natural knowledge of God which took as its starting point sensory knowledge and claimed that, by way of analogy and negation of knowledge gained through the senses, man could gain knowledge about God.[58] Against Aquinas' position, Scotus claimed that a notion of God gained through such physical knowledge was only physical knowledge of God and, as it were, of a God 'gripped' in nature. Through such a physical knowledge, Scotus argued, one could not know of a God who had brought into existence the very being of this Creation. Instead Scotus created a metaphysics whose object was the most abstract and indeterminate notion of being which applied indifferently to everything that is, namely the 'univocal' notion of being *qua* being. The most perfect knowledge man can form of God is that of 'infinite being' and it is the metaphysician's task to prove that there is an 'infinite being'.[59]

Scotus' metaphysics of God which transcended natural philosophy did not imply, however, that natural philosophy became redundant or theologically useless. The stark distinction between

phie complete tradite: sed ens finitum.' *Commentarii Petri Tartareti in libros philosophie naturalis* . . ., fo. iiiv.

57 The *libri naturales* are treated in the following order: the *Physica*, the *De caelo et mundo*, the *De generatione et corruptione*, the *Meteora*, the *De anima*, the *De sensu et sensato*, the *De memoria*, the *De somno et vigilia* and the *De longitudine et brevitate vitae*.

58 For Scotus' metaphysics, I have paraphrased Gilson (1957), 97–110.

59 Gilson (1954), 455–61.

the subject matters of natural philosophy and metaphysics had significant bearing on a central issue of Scotist theology. Scotus was concerned with freeing God from the Thomist subordination of the Divine Will to the Divine Intellect.[60] For Scotus, the only necessary object of God's Will is God's essence. There is no reason why God would necessarily will the existence of finite essences: 'God creates if he wills to do so, and only because he so wills.'[61]

Thus the radically different natures of the infinite being and finite beings are necessarily prescribed by Scotus' theology of the Divine Will. Consequently it becomes important that a clear distinction is made between the two areas of philosophy, natural philosophy and metaphysics, which deal with two radically different kinds of beings. By pointing out the contingent relationship between the infinite being and finite beings, a Scotist theologian can stress the significance of the Divine Will in Creation. In this sense, Scotist natural philosophy ought to be considered together with Scotist metaphysics, and the two as a whole form an important basis for Scotist theology.

Epp's choice of Scotist texts was most probably related to his experience as an Augustinian under Staupitz. At Tübingen, all Augustinian friars under Staupitz's priorate attended the lectures of the Scotist, Paulus Scriptoris (d. 1505).[62] Staupitz himself had been impressed by Scriptoris' lectures on Scotus' commentary on the Sentences.[63] At Tübingen, Staupitz partook in what is now termed an 'Augustine renaissance', a revival not only of Augustine as an authority but also of his pastoral theology and Christology.[64] For the kind of Augustinian theology Staupitz espoused, Scotus' doctrine of Divine Will was in fact crucial.

Staupitz's theology based hope in the work of Christ rather than in the works of men, and this conviction was based on a Scotist understanding of God's covenantal relationship to His Creation.[65] Scotus had placed stress on the distinction between the *potentia Dei absoluta* (the absolute omnipotence of God) and *potentia Dei ordinata* (God's omnipotence within the limits of the laws which He has himself established).[66] By understanding that this Creation was

60 Bettoni (1961), 153–9. 61 Gilson (1954), 461.
62 Oberman (1981), 103 note 173.
63 Steinmetz (1968), 4. 64 Oberman (1981), 75–91 and Wetzel (1991).
65 For Staupitz's thought, I have followed Steinmetz (1968), esp. 51–5.
66 Korolec (1982), 639f.

created from the *potentia Dei ordinata*, the principles governing justification were also ordained by God from His *potentia ordinata* and thus had no other grounding than in the Divine Will which brought them into being. Thus good works lost their inherently meritorious grounding. On the basis of this Scotist view of God's (covenantal) relationship to His creation, Stauptiz believed that the elect will be justified not because they deserve it, but because God has willed Himself to be faithful to His decree of election.[67] We have already seen how Scotist natural philosophy and metaphysics could serve Scotist theology of Divine Will, especially with respect to God and His Creation. Scotist natural philosophy, taken together with Scotist metaphysics, may well have been conducive to those who professed the kind of theology that Stauptiz believed in.[68] We may safely surmise that Epp's choice of texts was agreeable, if not necessary, from Staupitz's point of view.

Epp himself could not have taught with these textbooks of Tartaretus at Wittenberg since he returned to Tübingen in 1504 to take up a rectorship there. His successor Ludwig Henning, a Franciscan, adopted other texts by another Scotist, Antonius Sirecti, in order to invigorate logic training.[69] This, however, seems to have been a temporary measure since we know from records of accounts that the textbooks of Tartaretus were in use until May 1519.[70] Owing to Staupitz, the Augustinians at Wittenberg may well have attended these lectures.[71] We thus find natural philosophy first taught at Wittenberg in a Scotist way, using the commentaries of Tartaretus, in support of the kind of Scotist-Augustinian theology Stauptiz favoured.

By 1507 another way of teaching had come into existence at Wittenberg. The *Rotulus doctorum Vittemberge profitentium*[72] was published in that year by Christopher Scheurl (1481–1542) as part of a campaign to attract students.[73] It listed the names of the lecturers and the content of lectures offered by them, an Italian convention adopted by Scheurl who had just arrived from

67 For an estimation of Staupitz's influence on Luther's theology, see Steinmetz (1980).
68 For the close connection between Duns Scotus' thought and the Augustinian school from an early stage, see Gilson (1954), 454–71.
69 Bauch (1897), 306. 70 Bauch (1897), 307f.
71 The Augustinian convent at Wittenberg was founded at the same time as the university.
72 Reprinted in *Urkundenbuch*, 14–17.
73 For the background of this reorganization, see Grossmann (1975), 55f.; for student numbers at Wittenberg, see *Album academiae Vitebergensis*, III, 803f.

Bologna.[74] According to this *Rotulus* two kinds of lectures on natural philosophy were offered in 1507, one on Aristotle's *Physica* and the *De anima*, the other on the *De caelo et mundo*, the *De generatione et corruptione*, the *Meteora* and the *Parva naturalia*.[75] Furthermore, these lectures were each offered in two different ways, one in a Scotist way (*via Scoti*), the other in a Thomist way (*via Thomae*). Besides natural philosophy, lectures on logic were similarly offered in these two ways, whilst the *Ethica* and the *Metaphysica* were assigned only one lecturer each.[76] We lack further evidence to ascertain what kind of texts were used for these Thomist lectures on natural philosophy in 1507.

We have, however, a later example of a Thomist textbook on natural philosophy by Martin Polich von Mellerstadt (*c.* 1450–1513), professor of theology and physician to the Elector.[77] He was most probably responsible for initiating the Thomist way. In 1511, he published his commentary on logic, in which he offered a Thomistic exposition of the *Organon* following Gilbert de la Porée.[78] This was followed by Polich's commentary on natural philosophy, *Exquisita cursus physici collectanea*, which appeared posthumously in 1514.[79] Both commentaries were based on his lectures from his Leipzig days.[80]

Like Tartaretus' commentary, the *Exquisita cursus physici collectanea* is set out in a *quaestio* form which is strictly followed throughout the exposition of the *Physica*, the *De caelo et mundo*, the *De generatione et corruptione* and the *De anima*. In Polich's case the supreme authority is Thomas Aquinas, whose definitions and distinctions are utilized. Polich asks whether the subject matter of natural philosophy is 'mobile being' (*ens mobile*) or something else.[81] Again, arguments which seem to deny that the subject matter is 'mobile being' are

74 Grossmann (1975), 60–4. 75 *Urkundenbuch*, 15f.

76 Andreas Bodenstein von Carlstadt was assigned to lecture the *Metaphysica*. For his Thomism at this stage, see Bauch (1897), 319–22 and Sider (1974), 6–15. For the hitherto unexplained irrelevance of Aristotle's *Ethica* to the *viae* in general, see Wieland (1982a), 670.

77 For Polich, see *Lohr*, 346f., Grossmann (1975), 42–4, and French (1989), 139–41.

78 Prantl (1855–70), IV, 273. Polich's logical commentary was entitled *Cursus logici commentariorum nostra collectanea*, Bauch (1897), 325.

79 According to Otto Beckmann's preface to Polich's *Exquisita cursus physici collectanea*, Polich had compiled his notes on the *Metaphysica* with a view to publication but died prematurely. Bauch (1897), 327.

80 Polich, *Exquisita cursus physici collectanea* (Leipzig: M. Lother, 1514), fo. iir.

81 'Utrum ens mobile vel aliquod aliud sit subjectum naturalis philosophie arguitur', *Exquisita cursus physici collectanea*, A1r.

introduced: it seems that the subject matter ought to be 'motion' because its properties such as unity, contrariety and divisibility are dealt with in the last four books of the *Physica*; the subject matter cannot be investigated unless it is in metaphysics; and the subject matter in fact ought to be 'mobile body' (*corpus mobile*).[82] Against these views, following Aquinas and Aristotle, Polich argues that natural philosophy is a complete and perfect cognition of something common to all natural being; that the attributes to be considered ought to be essential attributes of natural beings; that these attributes are matter and form; that 'natural being' contains the species of motion and mutability; and that metaphysics considers only being as being.[83] Then, Polich concludes that the subject matter of natural philosophy is indeed 'mobile being'.[84]

Thomist natural philosophy also had a significant bearing on Thomist metaphysics. Aquinas believed that natural reason could obtain certain knowledge about God and His attributes.[85] Since all human knowledge originates in sense perception, human knowledge of God takes its starting point in the senses. Knowledge concerning the attributes of God can be gained from such knowledge arising from the senses by way of analogy and negation. What we know about the sensible world through natural philosophy thus can and should provide a basis on which the existence of God can be demonstrated. For instance, from our senses we know that there is motion. Whatever is moved is moved by something else. If that by which a thing is moved is itself moved, it is moved in turn by something else, which in turn is moved, and so on. This cannot proceed to infinity and therefore there must be an unmoved prime mover, which is God.[86] Because movement means change from potency to act, for a metaphysician God as an unmoved mover implies that He is pure act, and thus His mode of being is an 'act-of-being' (*ipsum esse*). Utilizing Aristotelian concepts and reasoning in natural philosophy, Aquinas produces rational proofs about the Christian God.[87] Such rational proofs about God are necessary for Aquinas because the existence of God, which is neces-

[82] *Exquisita cursus physici collectanea*, A1r. [83] *Exquisita cursus physici collectanea*, A1r–A3r

[84] 'Convenientissime potest poni ens mobile subjectum naturalis philosophie.' *Exquisita cursus physici collectanea*, A3r.

[85] Here I follow Gilson's account of Thomas Aquinas' philosophy in Gilson (1957).

[86] This is one of the five famous proofs for the existence of God, see Gilson (1957), 59–83.

[87] For Aquinas' commentary on Aristotle, see Chenu (1964), 203–32 and for his Christian transformation of Aristotle's philosophy, see further Pegis (1946).

sary knowledge for salvation, is not immediately evident (because self-evidence presupposes adequate knowledge of divine essence, which is impossible for a finite mind). Thus, a Thomist natural philosophy, together with metaphysics, provides a basis from which a Thomist theologian could prove the existence of and other attributes of God.

Why Polich chose to follow Aquinas is not altogether clear. We lack other independent sources for his theological ideas.[88] It was perhaps due to a multitude of reasons. Polich wrote in the preface to the *Exquisita cursus physici collectanea* that, as an appreciation of the Elector's favour to him, he had decided to render his final service to the Elector's university by aiding the learning of the students.[89] It may well have been Polich's way of asserting his presence and power in a university which had been dominated by Staupitz's influence.[90] There is no indication that Polich himself taught any of these subjects at Wittenberg, although he clearly intended his commentaries for student use. The initial cost of the printing of Polich's commentary was met by either the university or the Elector, perhaps as a tribute to a recently deceased senior member of the university.[91] It soon seems to have been adopted as a textbook in the university and was in use until May 1518.[92]

In 1508 yet another way was introduced. Jodocus Trutfetter (d. 1519), a renowned 'modern' according to Scheurl,[93] came to Wittenberg at the end of 1506 at the invitation of Frederick the Wise. His name appears in the *Rotulus* of 1507 as professor of theology.[94] Scheurl drew up a whole new body of statutes, including the arts statutes, as part of the reorganization of the university in 1508.[95] Perhaps in order to accommodate the increased number of the ways of teaching, the natural philosophy lecture was now reduced to just one kind: to read in the course of one year the *Physica*, the *De anima* and, after these, the *Parva naturalia*. This lecture was required to be heard for the master's degree. The natural philosophy lecture, together with the logic lectures, was now to be taught in

88 Polich conducted a bitter dispute with Konrad Wimpina on the relationship between theology and poetry, but I have been unable to consult the original documents. See Grossmann (1975), 43f.

89 *Exquisita cursus physici collectanea*, A iiv and Friedensburg (1917), 47 note 2.

90 Bauch (1897), 299.

91 Bauch (1897), 327, cf. Friedensburg (1917), 47.

92 Bauch (1897), 308.

93 Obermann (1981), 140 note 45.

94 *Urkundenbuch*, 15.

95 For background on this revision, see Grossmann (1975), 56.

three different ways – the *via Scoti*, the *via Thomae* and the *via Gregorii*.[96] This third way was the way of Gregory of Rimini (d. 1358), an Augustinian philosopher and theologian influenced by Occam, whom Trutfetter regarded highly as an exponent of the *via moderna*.[97]

Much attention has been drawn to this extra way, not least for its being unusually a 'third' way, but especially because of modern-day interest in the nominalist influence on Luther.[98] This third way, however, seems to have died out prematurely at Wittenberg. Apparently upset by the hostility of the existing professors, of Polich in particular, Trutfetter went back to Erfurt in 1510.[99] We have no information about the kinds of texts that could have been used for the teaching of natural philosophy in the third way.[100] In fact, we have no record to confirm that the actual teaching of natural philosophy in the third way took place at all, whilst the teaching of the two other ways (the *via Scoti* and the *via Thomae*) in natural philosophy can be confirmed until 1516/17.[101]

During the early years at Wittenberg, then, natural philosophy was to be taught in different (logical) ways following the Schoolmen. That there had to be a plurality of ways, it seems, was partly due to convention (other universities did so) and partly due to personal conviction (it was necessary for the kind of theology one believed in). What is important is the very similar nature of these ways of natural philosophy: the texts were exclusively Aristotle's books on nature; these were taught with commentaries by Schoolmen who were in turn following in the footsteps of earlier Schoolmen; authors were confident in the power of logic and the authority of Aristotle and of the Schoolmen; together with metaphysics, natural philosophy formed a system of thought which was consistent

96 '[I]ndifferentur [sic] profitentur via [sic] Thome, Scoti, Gregorii, estate quinta, hieme sexta legatur major logica per illas tres vias; estate septima, hieme octava libri physicorum et de anima, quibus finitis parva naturalia, similiter per tres vias, hora duodecima minor logica, id est Petrus Hispanus, similiter per tres vias, secunda libri ethicorum et post illos metaphysica, item in mathematica, tercia grammatica; septima hieme, octava estate et prima et quarta humane littere.' *Urkundenbuch*, 56.

97 Obermann (1987a), 447.

98 For studies on late medieval nominalism and Luther, see the collection of essays in *Gregor von Rimini* and Oberman (1981). Luther was assigned to teach moral philosophy in the *via Gregorii* in 1509. See his letter to Brann, 17 March 1509, *WBr*, 1, 17.

99 For this conflict, see Bauch (1897), 316.

100 Cf. Trutfetter, *Quam Judocus Eysennaiensis philosophus et theologus tocius philosophie naturalis summam nuper elucubravit* ... (Erfurt: M. Maler, 1517).

101 Bauch (1897), 307f.

with and necessary for theology. In short, natural philosophy at early Wittenberg shared the essence of its predecessors' learning.

In contrast to this learning of the medieval Schoolmen at early Wittenberg, the existence of humanist elements at Wittenberg, even before the foundation of the university, has been carefully traced.[102] If, however, following Kristeller, we take 'humanism' to mean 'the general tendency of the age to attach the greatest importance to classical studies and to consider classical antiquity as the common standard and model by which to guide all cultural activities',[103] we see no drastic change to the teaching of logic, natural philosophy or metaphysics. The *humaniora* subjects such as grammar, rhetoric, history and poetry, were not necessary for taking degrees.[104] Although Polich spoke highly of humanist skills, he hardly practised them in his commentary on natural philosophy.[105] His commentary followed the traditional *quaestio* method and understood natural philosophy in a Thomist way. Chilian Reuther adopted a new translation of the *De anima* by Johannes Argyropulos (*c.* 1415–87), but it accompanied Aquinas' commentary on the *De anima*.[106] An improved translation of a text of Aristotle in order to interpret Aristotle in a Thomist way can hardly count as an attempt to guide the study of natural philosophy towards the standard of classical antiquity. 'Humanism' may indeed have come into existence in Wittenberg owing to individual interests and initiatives, but it hardly had an impact on the nature of traditional university subjects like natural philosophy.[107]

Similarly, the introduction of mathematics lectures had little effect on the nature or the way natural philosophy was taught. In 1514, hearing lectures on mathematics became a requirement for both the bachelor and master of arts degrees.[108] Not much is known how the first mathematics lecturer, Bonifazius Erasmi, taught these lectures, though his successor, Johannes Volmar, seems to have

102 Grossmann (1975) and Schwiebert (1958).
103 Kristeller (1961), 95. Cf. the somewhat ambiguous definition, in Grossmann (1975), 7.
104 See *Urkundenbuch* 54f. Moral philosophy, of course, had been taught in the form of lectures on Aristotle's *Ethica*. Cf. Kristeller (1988b) for humanist ethics.
105 See the estimation in Bauch (1897), 325f.
106 Overfield (1984), 214. I have not been able to consult the original. Reuther was a Thomist, Grossmann (1975), 65, 73f. For Argyropulos' partial debt to the medieval translation by William of Moerbeke, see Cranz (1976), 361.
107 Cf. the case of secondary schools in Grafton and Jardine (1986).
108 Instead of being treated as an appendix to metaphysics, mathematics was introduced from 1514 as preparatory to Aristotle. See Friedensburg (1917), 106f., *Urkundenbuch*, 73f.

taught medical astrology.[109] There is no indication, however, that these mathematics lectures affected the nature or content of natural philosophy in any substantial way.

At the beginning of the sixteenth century Wittenberg had thus essentially followed in the footsteps of the Schoolmen. The goal of natural philosophy was directed neither to 'nature itself' nor to 'the recovery of Aristotelian natural science', but to something else, namely, knowledge about God and His Creation – just as there was a Jerusalem, not an Athens, at the end of the *viae* of the Schoolmen. These Schoolmen were confident that 'Jerusalem' could be reached through human rational knowledge. They believed that human rational knowledge could and should deal with some aspects of God.[110] As we shall see in the next chapter, it is this very learning, including natural philosophy, that Luther soon challenged and rejected, because of his new faith.

[109] Erasmi is known to be the author of an astronomical table printed in 1515 with Cranach's woodcut, Koepplin and Frank (1974), I, 231. Volmar succeeded Erasmi in 1518/19, Friedensburg (1917), 134. Volmar's notes on medical astrology are now in the Thüringer Universitäts- und Landes-Bibliothek, Jena: 'Tabulae resolutae et quarta pars summae astrologiae', MS El. f. 77; and 'Altera pars astrologiae', MS El. Phil. 9. 3. For further details of these manuscripts, see J. C. Mylius, *Memorabilia bibliothecae academicae Jenensis*, (Jena, 1746), 348, 405f.

[110] Lohr (1988b), 91f.

CHAPTER 2

Law and Gospel: the reforms of Luther and Melanchthon

Beware lest any man spoil you through philosophy and vain deceit, after the tradition of men, after the rudiments of the world, and not after Christ.

Colossians 2. 8

In October 1517 Martin Luther (1483–1546), an Augustinian teaching theology at Wittenberg, composed ninety-five theses attacking the validity of the indulgence system, and much more. It was an attack resulting from his new understanding of justification – that man is justified by faith in the crucified Christ alone. Luther called for the rectification of the failings of the Church and the establishment of the true message of the Gospel. This call for reform culminated in the complex and wide-ranging movement which we now call the Reformation. It was a movement in which the traditional teachings of the Papacy were first criticized, then challenged and finally rejected, while a new Lutheran theology and Church, with a distinct identity of its own, emerged. It was also a movement with significant intellectual implications.

In this chapter I rehearse some of the most well-known events of the Reformation amidst which significant changes took place in the arts faculty at Wittenberg. The philosophy teaching inherited from the medieval Schoolmen was rejected at Wittenberg by Luther on grounds of his new faith, and Philip Melanchthon (1497–1560) in turn found a new meaning and value for philosophy in defence of Luther's cause. My discussion of natural philosophy in this chapter may seem to be submerged under discussions about a greater change, but it is indeed only as part of the larger movement of the Reformation that we may understand the attitudes of Luther and Melanchthon towards the teaching of natural philosophy.

1 Salvation by good works.
The Dying by Lucas Cranach the Elder (1513/18)

LUTHER'S REFORM – ESTABLISHING THE MESSAGE OF THE GOSPEL

When Luther reached a new understanding that man is justified by faith alone, he began to reread the Bible and reorientate all theological arguments to focus on the importance of the crucified Christ.[1] Luther saw the whole Scripture as a 'Gospel' which taught that God had promised to send, and did send, His Son to be crucified so that all men will be saved.[2] In order to understand the message of the Gospel fully, however, man also had to understand the meaning of 'Law', that fallen man had no ability whatsoever to merit salvation on his own.

> The Law is the Word in which God teaches and tells us what we are to do and not to do, as in the Ten Commandments. Now wherever human nature is alone, without the grace of God, the Law cannot be kept, because since Adam's fall in Paradise man is corrupt and has nothing but a wicked desire to sin ... The other Word of God is not Law or commandment, nor does it require anything of us; but after the first Word, that of the Law, has done this work and distressful misery and poverty have been produced in the heart, God comes and offers His lovely, living Word, and promises, pledges, and obligates Himself to give grace and help, that we may get out of this misery and that all sins not only be forgiven but also blotted out ... See, this divine promise of His grace and of the forgiveness of sin is properly called Gospel.[3]

This message of Luther's was fundamentally different from the traditional teaching of salvation, as two paintings by Lucas Cranach the Elder illustrate in stark contrast. One painting was commissioned from Cranach around 1518 by Henricus Schmitburg, a law professor at Leipzig[4] (Fig. 1). It is based on the *ars moriendi* motif in which the struggle takes place between the good and the evil over the soul of the dying man.[5] At the bottom half of the panel, a man is

1 For introduction to Luther's theology, see Althaus (1970) and Ebeling (1970).

2 For Luther's definition of the Gospel as different from the four gospels, see Althaus (1970), 74 note 7.

3 As translated in Christensen (1979), 126. Though this statement dates from 1522, the Law and Gospel doctrine becomes most prominent from around 1530. For the central role of the Law and Gospel doctrine in Luther's theology, see further McDonough (1963).

4 For an earlier dating of this panel (i.e. 1508), see Vogel (1907). For this panel as embodying the ideology of the papacy, see *Kunst der Reformationszeit*, 42f.

5 Friedländer and Rosenberg (1978), 89. For the *ars moriendi* motif, see Rudolf (1957) and more recently Chartier (1987), 32–70.

2 A Lutheran salvation.
Verdämnis und Erlösung, Lucas Cranach the Elder (1529)

dying in his bed, presumably receiving extreme unction from a priest, while on the far left of the bed a lawyer is taking down the last will of the dying man. At the right of the bed stands a physician inspecting a urine sample, and at the foot of the bed, most probably the son and the wife of the man are looking into an empty chest. All indicate the last moment of a man's life in this earthly world. Above this worldly scene the spiritual and eternal world is depicted. The naked figure above the dying man represents the soul of the man. The devils at the right of the man's soul offer the trappings of various stages of human life, and the angel on the opposite side offers forgiveness by indicating good works (*bona opera*) in its hands.[6] The Holy Trinity, adored by the Virgin Mary, St John the Baptist and other saints and angels, presides over this struggle for the man's soul. At the top of the panel, the family of the commissioner are depicted praying to the Virgin Mary who symbolizes the Church, thereby demonstrating their piety.[7] The panel thus depicts the salvation of man through good works and the commission of the panel becomes a 'good work' in itself.[8]

Cranach's picture of Luther's way of salvation was quite different. Luther rejected the efficacy of good works in justification, the necessity of the medium of the priesthood for salvation and the validity of extreme unction as a sacrament.[9] As Christensen has convincingly shown, although categorically opposing the idea of art as good work, Luther nevertheless regarded visual images as useful for didactic purposes.[10] It is in this didactic context that Cranach frequently painted Luther's way of salvation in a very different manner.[11] The panel is divided in the centre downwards by a tree, the right side of which is living and the left side dead (Fig. 2).[12] To the left of the tree are a group of Old Testament prophets, and

6 For medieval views of the moral trappings of various stages of human life, see Goodich (1989). The angel is saying 'Etsi peccavi, tamen Deus Meus nunquam negavit', my transcription from the original.

7 *Kunst der Refomationszeit*, 43.

8 For the Catholic practice of commissioning art as good works, see Christensen (1979), 13–23.

9 Strictly speaking, there are only two sacraments in Luther's theology, namely baptism and the Eucharist. For Luther's reasons for rejecting the traditional seven sacraments, see further Althaus (1970), 345–8.

10 See Christensen (1979), 42–65. For the place of images in the Lutheran Church, see also Stirm (1977), 69–129.

11 On the motif of 'Law and Gospel' in art, see Christensen (1979), 124–30, and the use of that motif in Johannes Hoffer, *Icones Catecheseos* (Wittenberg: J. Crato, 1558).

12 Here I paraphrase the detailed description given in Ehresmann (1966/7), 35.

Moses points to the Tables of the Law. To their right, death and the devil drive a naked man towards the fire of hell. In the left middle ground Adam and Eve stand before the tree. To the right of the tree there is a naked man praying, to whom St John the Baptist points out the crucified Christ. A stream of blood pours out from the crucified Christ towards the naked man and the Holy Spirit as a dove glides along it. In front of the crucifixion the ascending Christ blesses with His right hand. Thus the left of the panel represents (original) sin, death, the devil and hell, which are pointed out by the Law. The right of the panel represents salvation, eternal life and triumph through the crucified Christ alone. The panel thus concisely depicts salvation through Law to Gospel.

In Luther's eyes the traditional teaching of the Church failed to teach the message of the Gospel that faith in the crucified Christ alone sufficed for salvation. Luther began to criticize and attack everything that stood in the way of establishing this message of the Gospel. Before long, he showed his dissatisfaction with the arts curriculum at Wittenberg which, as I have sketched out in the previous chapter, had inherited a traditional medieval learning orientated towards theology. Luther objected to this theology and consequently to the whole system of learning which supported it.

In February 1517 Luther voiced his objection to Aristotle:

> We are to believe everything, always obediently to listen and not even once ... wrangle or mutter against Aristotle and the *Sentences* ... I wish nothing more fervently than to disclose to many the true face of that actor who has fooled the Church so tremendously with the Greek mask, and to show them all his ignominy, had I only time! I am working on short notes on the First Book of *Physics* with which I am determined to enact the story of Aristaeus against this, my Proteus.[13]

Luther thus objected to the unquestioned authority of Aristotle and claimed that the latter had deceived the Church. We do not know, however, the specific nature of Luther's criticism of Aristotle's *Physica*, since his notes on it have not come down to us.[14]

In the 'Disputation against Scholastic Theology' held the following September, Luther elaborated on how Aristotle was a deceiver

[13] Letter to Johannes Lang, 8 February 1517, translated by G. G. Krodel in *LW*, XLVIII, 37f. In classical myth, Aristaeus captured the sea-god and magician Proteus, in spite of the latter changing his shape, see Virgil, *Georgics*, IV, 387. For other names by which Luther called Aristotle, see Rokita (1970) and Nitzsch (1883).

[14] *LW*, XLVIII, 37 note 9.

of the Church.[15] In this disputation Luther rejected the righteousness of good works and the freedom of the will in salvation, tenets traditionally propounded by medieval theologians such as Duns Scotus, Gabriel Biel, William of Occam and Pierre d'Ailly. Luther also denied that syllogism was a valid form of inquiry in theology. He further declared that Aristotle's *Ethica* was the 'worst enemy of grace' because it taught that man became righteous by doing righteous deeds.[16] Luther identified the main error of scholastic theology in their conviction that theological truths were attainable by human reasoning. For Luther, Aristotle embodied this error.[17] Luther's attack on Aristotle in the 'Disputation against the Scholastic Theology' was thus an attack on the whole basis on which scholastic theology rested. Here Luther did not make specific attacks on Aristotelian natural philosophy, but it would not have stood much chance, given Luther's blanket rejection of Aristotle such as the following:

43) It is an error to say that no man can become a theologian without Aristotle. This in opposition to common opinion.
44) Indeed, no one can become a theologian unless he becomes one without Aristotle.
45) To state that a theologian who is not a logician is a monstrous heretic – this is a monstrous and heretical statement. This in opposition to common opinion.
...
50) Briefly, the whole Aristotle is to theology as darkness is to light. This in opposition to the scholastics.[18]

In Luther's own theology, in contrast, the Bible was the sole authority in divine matters. It enjoyed the highest authority as the only record of God's Word. It is only through the Scriptures that man could learn that the promise of God was fulfilled in the historical Jesus of Nazareth who died on the Cross for us all.[19] It was only on the basis of the Scriptures that Luther was prepared to argue theological matters. The supreme authority of the Bible in Luther's theology thus meant that a good knowledge of Greek, Hebrew and

15 'Disputation against Scholastic Theology' (1517), *LW*, XXXI, 9–16.
16 *LW*, XXXI, 12. See also his *Lectures on Romans*, *LW*, XXV, 152.
17 For the function of the critique of Aristotle within Luther's critique of scholastic theology, see further Eckermann (1978).
18 Translated by H. J. Grimm in *LW*, XXXI, 12.
19 For the necessity of the 'Spirit' when reading the Scripture, see Luther's letter to Spalatin, 18 January 1518, *LW*, XLVIII, 53f.

Latin was required of a Lutheran theologian in order to read the Bible accurately.[20]

When the major figures of the university were won over to Luther's new theology a revision of the curriculum was felt imperative. Luther spearheaded this move.[21] As a result, several lectures were added to the arts syllabus in 1518: professors of Greek and of Hebrew were to be newly appointed and two masters (forming a *pädagogium*) were to oversee the language instruction of younger students.[22] Texts of Quintilian and Priscian were to be taught. In addition, probably owing to the arrival of a staunch humanist Aesticampianus (Thomas Rhagius, d. 1521), a lecture on Pliny the Elder was also to be established.[23] Lastly, lectures using the 'new translations' (*secundum novam translationem*) of the *Logica*, the *Physica* and the *Metaphysica* of Aristotle were to be taught and the *De animalibus* was to be read as well.[24] These lectures did not replace lectures on Aristotle according to the different *viae*, and in this sense the curricular reform did not go as far as Luther would have had it,[25] but the first crucial step towards facilitating Luther's theology had been made.

Compared to the previous syllabuses at Wittenberg, these new additions exhibit a marked change of emphasis in being primarily concerned with reading in the original language and in reading classical authors, thus breaking away from the traditional way of teaching by Latin translations and commentaries. Although on the surface this new syllabus suggests that Wittenberg had kept abreast of the fashionable trends of humanistic instruction in other universities,[26] their purposes differed radically. The introduction of

20 The classical languages are not necessary for ordinary Christians, but imperative for those who interpret the Scriptures, see 'To the Councilmen of All Cities in Germany that They Establish and Maintain Christian Schools' (1524), *LW*, XLV, 363.

21 Brecht (1981–7), I, 264–74. Spalatin, the Elector's secretary, was instrumental in carrying out this reform, see Höss (1989), 106–9.

22 *Urkundenbuch*, 85f.

23 *Urkundenbuch*, 86 note 1. Aesticampianus left Leipzig owing to a conflict there. He had already attempted to read Pliny at Leipzig without success. For his dispute at Leipzig see Overfield (1976), 415f. For Aesticampianus' arrival at Wittenberg see Friedensburg (1924).

24 *Urkundenbuch*, 85f.

25 Salaries were still paid out to those teaching Aristotle in the middle of 1520, see *Urkundenbuch*, 100. Cf. Luther's optimism in his letter to Johannes Lang, 21 March 1518, *WBr*, I, 155.

26 For instance, new translations of Aristotle were adopted in Leipzig, Erfurt, Vienna and Heidelberg by 1518, Overfield (1976), 413–17.

humanist studies at other German universities was due to a complex of reasons such as individual ambitions, personal preferments and factional interests. If the introduction of humanist studies had any definite goal beyond such interests at all, it seems to have been to improve some features within the traditional framework of the university.[27] At Wittenberg, however, the changes were introduced with the clear intention of accommodating a new kind of theology. The humanists' attitude towards and skills of approaching texts had indeed played a crucial role in Luther's reading of the Bible and his understanding of justification.[28] What I wish to stress here, however, is that it is precisely because Luther's reading and interpretation of the Bible had to be facilitated and accommodated that humanist subjects and readings came to have a significant place in the arts syllabus at Wittenberg.

Meanwhile counter-attacks on Luther's 'Ninety-Five Theses' intensified, and a war of pamphlets broke out between Luther and the Dominicans such as Tetzel, Konrad Koch (Wimpina) and Johannes Eck, a theologian at Ingolstadt.[29] Through Dominican agitation, the Pope directed the General of the Augustinian Order, Gabrielle della Volta, to restrain Luther. As it became clearer that the issue was not simply a matter of the validity of the indulgence system but that Luther's claims challenged the teaching and authority of the Church, Cardinal Cajetan, a champion of Thomist theology and the General of the Dominican Order, began to see the serious need of silencing Luther. Luther, however, refused to retract his statements.

Amidst these attacks, Luther stepped up his attack on Aristotle. For a disputation held at Heidelberg in April 1518,[30] Luther had prepared twenty-eight theses defending his views on grace, justification and free will, while in twelve other philosophical theses he attacked the validity of Aristotle's philosophy. Besides demonstrating the errors of traditional theology, Luther said he had intended in this disputation to show that the scholastic theologians had misread Aristotle, and that even the original Aristotle was useless:

27 For the limited usefulness of the humanism/scholasticism dichotomy for pre-Reformation Germany, see Overfield (1984). A concise survey of current scholarship on humanism in Germany is found in Brann (1988).

28 For Luther's debt to humanism, see Junghans (1984).

29 Mackinnon (1925–30), II, 18–31.

30 For background of this disputation, see also Brecht (1981–7), I, 225–8.

if we should hold to his [Aristotle's] meaning as strongly as possible (as I proposed here), nevertheless one gains no aid whatsoever from it, either for theology and sacred letters or even for natural philosophy (*ad ipsam naturalem philosophiam*). For what could be gained with respect to the understanding of material things if you could quibble and trifle with matter, form, motion, measure, and time – words taken over and copied from Aristotle?[31]

In the disputation, Luther pointed out that Aristotle had erred in asserting the infinity of the world and the mortality of the soul, and in seeking understanding of nature through meaningless jargon.[32] Luther thus considered Aristotelian natural philosophy useless even for its own subject area, the understanding of material things. Here, Luther's objection to Aristotle was very strong: no matter how it is read, Aristotle's philosophy is useless.

Compared to his earlier 'Disputation Against Scholastic Theology', here in the 'Heidelberg Disputation' Luther's critique of Aristotle has gone a step further. It is not only in the area of theology but also in its own right that Aristotelian philosophy is useless. This in turn implies a stronger critique of traditional theology in that any theology which draws on such Aristotelian philosophy must be invalid. Luther's attack on Aristotelian natural philosophy in the 'Heidelberg Disputation' may thus be seen as furnishing him with a stronger argument against traditional theology. This harsher critique of Aristotle may well have been induced by the intensifying Thomist attacks.[33] As Luther said, 'Thomas wrote a great deal of heresy, and is responsible for the reign of Aristotle, the destroyer of godly doctrine.'[34]

A few months after returning from Heidelberg, in August 1518, Luther heard an inaugural lecture by Philip Melanchthon, who had arrived in Wittenberg in order to take up the lectureship in Greek newly established earlier that year on Luther's suggestion. As a great-nephew of Johannes Reuchlin (1454/5–1522), Melanchthon himself had shown great linguistic and literary talent from a very young age.[35] As most ambitious young men with literary gifts of the

[31] 'A Statement Concerning the Heidelberg Disputation, Made Apparently soon after its Conclusion', translated by H. J. Grimm, *LW*, XXXI, 70; *WA*, IX, 170.

[32] Theses 29, 31–4, 40, in 'The Heidelberg Disputation', *LW*, XXXI, 41f.

[33] For the intensifying Thomist attacks from 1518, and Luther's redirection of criticism against Thomism, see Grane (1970), esp. 245.

[34] 'Against Latomus' (1521), translated by G. Lindbeck in *LW*, XXXII, 258.

[35] For Melanchthon's humanist background, see the most exhaustive study in Maurer (1967–9), I, 23–83.

time did, Melanchthon revered the literary elegance and style of Erasmus and actively sought the latter's recognition.[36] Through contacts with various humanists at Pforzheim, Heidelberg and Tübingen, Melanchthon had also come to cherish linguistic clarity as a key to sound and certain knowledge.[37] Melanchthon had already earned a reputation as a teacher of classical literature at Tübingen[38] and he now arrived in Wittenberg to take up the Greek lectureship. By training, reputation and vocation, therefore, we may see a 'humanist' in the figure of Melanchthon.[39] This is not to say, however, that he was entirely indifferent to theological issues. In fact, he strongly believed that linguistic clarity was necessary to understand theological truths.[40] Yet, it is clear that the inaugural lecture heard by Luther was delivered by a man whose expertise lay primarily in the area of classical literature and languages.

Melanchthon's inaugural lecture entitled *De corrigendis adolescentiae studiis* was duly ambitious and couched in elaborate Latin,[41] calling for the 'rebirth of the Muses'. Melanchthon reviewed the history of learning since the fall of the Roman Empire in order to illustrate how the decline of learning and of Christianity went hand in hand with the neglected state of Greek studies.[42] As for the contemporary situation, Melanchthon pointed out for instance how the Schoolmen such as Tartaretus, Bricot, Versor and the like had polluted true dialectics with their convoluted logic.[43] Melanchthon claimed that a proper course of study should begin with grammar, dialectics, rhetoric and history, and then proceed to philosophy, by which Melanchthon meant the 'knowledge of nature' (*scientiam naturae*) and 'grounds and examples of conduct' (*morum rationes et exempla*).[44] Greek learning in particular was impor-

[36] See for instance Melanchthon's preface to the 1516 edition of Terence, *MBW* no.7, T-i, 451. For the details of exchange between Melanchthon and Erasmus, see the survey in *Contemporaries of Erasmus*, II, 426–9; and Maurer (1967–9), I, 17–214.

[37] For the centrality of rhetoric in the early thought of Melanchthon, see Schneider (1990), 65–95; 205–62.

[38] Melanchthon also acted as corrector to the Anshelm Press, see Maurer (1967–9), I, 30f.

[39] For a definition of the term 'humanist' see Campana (1946), 66 and Kristeller (1961), 9.

[40] For Melanchthon's early theological concerns as deriving from humanist and nominalist traditions of South Germany, see Schneider (1990).

[41] *StA*, III, 29–42. The elaborate style is perhaps due to Melanchthon's awareness that other professors at Wittenberg preferred a more established figure for the post. Manschreck (1958), 21.

[42] Melanchthon (1988), 47.

[43] Melanchthon (1988), 50f.

[44] 'Complector ergo Philosophiae nomine scientiam naturae morum rationes et exempla.' *StA*, III, 39.

tant in recovering the pure philosophy of the ancients.[45] In short, Melanchthon claimed that elimination of barbaric teaching and restoration of pure learning were only possible through Greek studies, which he had come to teach. Melanchthon ended his lecture by summing up his message:

We have in hand Homer, and we have Paul's letter to Titus. Here you can see how much a sense of appropriate language contributes to understanding the mysteries of sacred things: and also what difference there is between learned and unlearned interpreters of Greek ... Take up sound studies, and bear in mind what the poet said: Well begun is half done. Dare to know, cultivate the Romans, embrace the Greeks without whom the Romans cannot be properly studied.[46]

It was a typical humanist lecture stressing the need to purge the ancient authors of barbaric commentaries through sound linguistic and classical studies. Melanchthon thus stressed the importance of his profession of teaching Greek and classical literature. It should be noted that at this point he made no criticism of ancient philosophy *per se*, but was even intent on improving the texts of Aristotle.[47]

Luther was impressed with this inaugural lecture and he quickly found in Melanchthon a loyal friend and an able collaborator, besides an excellent teacher of Greek.[48] Melanchthon too was quickly drawn to Luther's theology and it was not long before he began to pursue a degree in theology.[49] For his degree of the *baccalaureus biblicus*, Melanchthon defended twenty-four theses on justification by faith alone, which delighted Luther.[50] At the instigation of Luther, Melanchthon also began lecturing on Paul's Letter to the Romans, which developed into the first organized exposition of Lutheran theology, the *Loci communes*, first published in 1521.[51]

Soon after Melanchthon's inaugural lecture, Luther (among

[45] Melanchthon (1988), 56. [46] Translated by R. A. Keen in Melanchthon (1988), 56.

[47] See Melanchthon (1988), 49, 54. For Melanchthon's project to prepare a new translation of Aristotle with Franz Stadian, see Schneider (1990), 29f. and also Oberman (1981), 29f.

[48] See Melanchthon's assistance with Luther's interpretation of the Bible, Green (1980) and Pauck (1984), 41–53. Cf. also Luther's *Lectures on Galatians* (1519), in *LW*, XXVII, 377.

[49] For Melanchthon's nominalist background as a common denominator of the theology between Melanchthon and Luther, see Maurer (1967–9), I, 37, which is further elaborated in Schneider (1990).

[50] For the theses, see *StA*, I, 23–5. Cf. Maurer's conjecture that only the first twelve theses were composed by Luther, Maurer (1967–9), II, 102–4.

[51] For lecture notes of Melanchthon's early lecture on Paul, see Bizer (1966). For the background of this 1521 edition of the *Loci communes* see the introduction by W. Pauck in Melanchthon (1969), 3–17.

other things) began his campaign to eliminate Aristotelian philosophy from the arts syllabus. In September 1518, he asked for the removal of the *Ethica* from degree requirements.[52] Three months later, Luther and the rector of the university wrote to the Elector's secretary, Georg Spalatin:[53]

it seems to be good not only to eliminate the course of Thomistic *Physics* (which is now being dropped by Master Gunckel, who is taking over the [rector's] reading course), but also to eliminate the course on Thomistic logic, which is now taught by Master Premsel from Torgau. Instead the same master is to lecture on Ovid's *Metamorphoses*, since he is well qualified to teach classical literature. For we consider the course on Scotistic philosophy and logic, together with the reading course in *Physica* and logic, to be enough until such time as the chair of the Scotist Sect – that equally useless and unfruitful occupation of gifted men – is also abolished. In this way the subtle hair-splitting finally may perish altogether, and genuine philosophy, theology and all the arts may be drawn from their sources (*in fontibus suis hauriantur*).[54]

Luther was recommending what he had been hoping for earlier on in the revision of spring 1518 and what he could not quite achieve then, namely the abolition of the lectures on Aristotelian philosophy taught according to the *via Thomae* and *via Scoti*.[55] It is noteworthy that Luther recommends a gradual abolition of these lectures, starting with the Thomist ones. It may have been due to the fact that Luther realized that the Elector was not going to effect changes all at once.[56] The Thomist lectures were recommended to be abandoned first, probably because Aquinas was the supreme authority of Luther's opponents, especially the Dominicans, while Scotus had the merit of having opposed the authority of Thomas,[57] as well as of being connected with the teaching of the Augustinian order.

No decision seems to have followed. Two months later, apparently frustrated, Luther broached the topic once more. The abolition of the *Physica* lectures was mentioned again, but this time for the sake of increasing Melanchthon's salary, and Luther's hostility

52 For Luther's campaign against Aristotle, see also Brecht (1981–7), I, 264–71.
53 For a biography of Spalatin, see Höss (1989), esp. 117–23 for his role in the educational reforms as Elector's secretary with financial concerns.
54 Luther to Spalatin, 9 December 1518, translated by G. G. Krodel in *LW*, XLVIII, 95f., *WBr*, I, 262, my interpolation.
55 See above p. 34. 56 Höss (1989), 118.
57 See Luther to Staupitz, 31 March 1518, *WBr*, I, 160.

to the Thomist lectures is toned down.[58] This time Luther reinforced his request by appealing directly to the Elector with other major professors of the university.[59] This time Spalatin indicated that Melanchthon should take on the lectureship on the *Physica*.[60] This was a reasonable suggestion on Spalatin's part, were Melanchthon to receive the salary assigned to that lectureship. Luther's outburst against Spalatin's suggestion, however, conveys in no uncertain terms what he thought of the teaching of Aristotle's *Physica*:

Aristotle's *Physics* is a completely useless subject for every age. The whole book is a debate about nothing ... I know this book inside out since I have already explained it privately twice to my fellow friars without using the [usual] commentaries. As a result, I think that the [*Physics* lectures] should be continued only until they can be abolished – and this had better be soon, since an oration of Beroald would be more useful by far. In [Aristotle's *Physics*] there is no real knowledge of the world of nature. His works on Metaphysics and the soul are of the same quality. It is, therefore, unworthy of [Melanchthon's] intellect to wallow in that mire of folly.[61]

On the same day, 13 March 1519, most probably urged on by Luther, Melanchthon himself wrote to Spalatin, expressing his own objection to the *Physica* lecture:

On what you write about the *Physica*, it seems to me thus: if Aristotle has to be read I would reap a more fruitful harvest in dialectics ... But the commentaries on Aristotelian natural philosophy are so chilling that nothing could be read with greater discomfort. It would be better to have taught something by Galen on nature or by Hippocrates.[62]

Melanchthon had already expressed his distaste for medieval commentaries on Aristotle in his inaugural lecture. Here he seems to have gone a step further. In his preference for medical authors to be taught in the *Physica* lectures, we may detect his reluctance to teach even the original Aristotle, to which he had not objected earlier

[58] Luther to Spalatin, 7 February 1519, *LW*, XLVIII, 106f. For this change of tone by Luther as a manœuvre to make his proposal sound more acceptable to Spalatin, Friedensburg (1917), 128.

[59] Letter to the Elector on 23 February 1519, with Carlstadt, Burchard, Bernhardi and Amsdorff. *Urkundenbuch*, 89; Höss (1989), 119.

[60] This letter by Spalatin is now lost to us, but its content can be inferred from Luther's letter of 13 March 1519, *LW*, XLVIII, 111f.

[61] Letter to Spalatin, 13 March 1519, translated by G. G. Krodel in *LW*, XLVIII, 111–15.

[62] 'De Physicis quod scribis, mihi sic videtur: Si sit legendus Aristoteles, plus frugis fecero in dialecticis, ... Sed Physicorum Aristotelicorum adeo frigida sunt ὑπομνήματα, ut nihil possit incommodius legi; praestiterit interim aliquid Galeni de natura, sive Hippocratis tradidisse.' Melanchthon to Spalatin, 13 March 1519, *MBW* no.46, T-i, 110.

on.[63] We may well assume Luther's influence behind this negative attitude towards Aristotle's natural philosophy.

We do not know Spalatin's reaction to these requests. Apparently the discussion about curricular reform and Luther's campaign against Aristotelian philosophy was interrupted by a more pressing issue, a debate at Leipzig with one of Luther's staunchest opponents, Johannes Eck.[64] It seems, however, that Melanchthon was spared from teaching Aristotle's *Physica* and managed to elicit some temporary salary increase by teaching Pliny the Elder after Aesticampianus' death, though Luther was irritated by the fact that Melanchthon was not concentrating on theology.[65] Despite the interruption, Luther's campaign bore some fruit: Johann Dölsch of Feldkirch (d. 1523), then probably teaching the *De anima*, petitioned the Elector to discharge him from teaching Scotist lectures on the grounds of his new faith. The discharge was granted and Spalatin was given the responsibility to see to the future of the Scotist lectures.[66] The case of Dölsch and perhaps of Melanchthon indicates the effect of Luther's campaign against Aristotle's natural philosophy at Wittenberg.

On 25 January 1520, Melanchthon publicly pronounced the limits of the whole classical philosophy with respect to the evangelical theology. In his *Declamatiuncula in divi Pauli doctrinam*, Melanchthon argued how Paul succinctly taught the message of justification by faith alone.[67] Pagan philosophy, however, could not teach the message of the Gospel.

> Many men adore philosophy because it puts man before his own eyes, and the ancients regarded the fruit and end of philosophy thus: to know oneself. But how much more felicitously has Paul surpassed this, in whom it is to discern, as in a mirror, whatever was placed in the inner recesses of man! Nowhere could you contemplate more completely about the grounds of imperfections and nowhere more precisely about the power and founts of virtue.[68]

[63] See p. 38 above. [64] For the details of the Debate, see Brecht (1981–7), I, 285–332.

[65] Luther to Spalatin, 13 June 1520, *LW*, XLVIII, 165f.

[66] Letter of Frederick the Wise to Spalatin, 29 September 1519, *Urkundenbuch*, 90f. and the resolution, *ibid.*, 108. Dölsch was teaching natural philosophy in the *via Scoti* in 1516 and, at the time of his plea to the Elector, he was probably teaching the books of the *De anima*, *ibid.*, 77, 100. For Melanchthon's testimony on Dölsch's faith, see *MBW* no. 186, T-i, 399–405.

[67] *StA*, I, 26–43; for an analysis, see Schneider (1990), 163–87.

[68] 'Philosophiam plerique deamant, quod hominem sibi ipsi ante oculos ponat, et veteres aliquot fructum et κολοφῶνα Philosophiae censerunt, sese novisse. At quanto felicius hoc Paulus praestitit, in quo ceu in speculo est cernere, quidquid est in intimo hominis secessu

The self-knowledge taught by pagan philosophy did not teach that man does not have the power to justify himself or that faith in Christ alone was necessary for salvation.[69] In short, classical philosophy was ineffectual for salvation. Melanchthon thus firmly delineated the limits of pagan philosophy with respect to the message of the Gospel.

After the Leipzig Debate, which only confirmed Luther's difference with traditional Catholic theology, a papal bull (*Exsurge, Domine*) was issued by Pope Leo X on 15 June 1520, condemning Luther as a heretic and threatening excommunication if he did not recant. In response, Luther published three tracts, *An Address to the Christian Nobility of Germany*, *The Babylonian Captivity of the Church* and *The Freedom of a Christian Man*, in which he defended his position, denounced the errors of the Papacy and called for the rectification of those errors. It was in the *Address to the Christian Nobility of Germany* that Luther set forth for the first time in print a clear programme of university reform: the arts faculty should retain Aristotle's *Logica*, *Rhetorica* and *Poetica* because they were useful for learning the skill of speaking and preaching. History, mathematics and the three languages were also approved of as useful subjects.[70] However, all the philosophical books of Aristotle – the *Physica*, the *Metaphysica*, the *De anima* and the *Ethica* – had to be abandoned.

> ... my advice would be that Aristotle's *Physics*, *Metaphysics*, *Concerning the Soul*, and *Ethica*, which hitherto have been thought to be his best books should be completely discarded along with all the rest of his books that boast about nature, although nothing can be learned from them either about nature or the spirit ... I dare say that any potter has more knowledge of nature than is written in these books. It grieves me to the quick that this damned, conceited, rascally heathen has deluded and made fools of so many of the best Christians with his misleading writings. God has sent him as a plague upon us on account of our sins.[71]

The abolition of lectures on Aristotelian philosophy was what Luther in person had been campaigning for in his own university. Now, in print, Luther called for all universities to follow suit.

Melanchthon defended and elaborated on this position of

positum. Nusquam absolutius vitiorum rationes, nusquam exactius virtutis vim atque fontes contempleris.' *StA*, I, 41.

69 Cf. Rice (1958) for the humanist idea of 'wisdom' as ethical self-knowledge.

70 *LW*, XLIV, 201f.

71 'Address to the Christian Nobility of Germany' (1520), translated by C. M. Jacobs and revised by J. Atkinson in *LW*, XLIV, 200f.

Luther's in his *Adversus Rhadinum pro Luthero oratio* (February 1521).[72] This was written in reply to an attack on Luther by Thomas Rhadinus, a professor at the University of Paris.[73] Against Rhadinus' accusation that Luther had rejected all kinds of philosophy because he knew so little about it, Melanchthon asserted that Luther approved of the knowledge of gems, plants and living beings written by Pliny the Elder, Dioscorides, Theophrastus and others, including Aristotle, as they were necessary for sacred studies.[74] In short, Melanchthon wrote, Luther approved of the knowledge of the nature of things (*de rerum natura*) which was written by medics.[75]

Melanchthon then endorsed at great length Luther's rejection of the rest of Aristotelian philosophy. Luther condemned, Melanchthon confirmed, whatever was written by Aristotle on physical things, metaphysical matters and ethical topics.[76] In the *Physica*, nothing is taught other than verbal monstrosities such as 'matter', 'form', 'privation' and 'infinity', which only furnish prating men with stuff to chatter about and enervate young minds with competitions and over-exactness.[77] Furthermore there are several points in the *Physica* itself which contradict the Scriptures, such as the eternity of the world, the eternity of celestial motions and the mortality of the human soul. Such teachings weaken the critical minds of the students by the time they reach the theology faculty.[78] Aristotle's *Metaphysica* and the *Ethica* are no better. Basing themselves on Aristotle's discussion about God, the unity of the intellect, the will, and the like in the *Metaphysica*, theologians have aimed to dominate theology for themselves. Thence rose factions of Thomists,

72 *StA*, I, 56–140.

73 *Thomae Rhadini Todischi Placentini in Lutherum Oratio*, published in October 1520, *VD*, R84.

74 'Non damnat Lutherus eam philosophiae partem, quae mathemata, quae gemmarum, plantarum et animantium naturas descripsit. Nam horum cognitionem fatetur ad sacra necessariam esse, soletque in loco uti, quoties res postulat, probat, inquam, pinguem illam rerum descriptionem, cuius auctores habemus apud latinos Plinium, apud Graecos Athenaeum, addo, si vis, Aristotelem, Theophrastum, Dioscoriden, ut poetas interim taceam.' *StA*, I, 72.

75 'Breviter collaudat Lutherus, quae de rerum natura fere sunt a medicis conscripta.' *Ibid.*

76 'Damnat autem, si ignoras, eam philosophiae partem, quae de rerum principiis, ventorum ac pluviarum causis prodigiosas nugas comminiscitur, adeoque quidquid id est, quod Aristoteles vocat physica ἀκροάματα καὶ μετὰ τὰ φυσικά, damnat, quidquid de moribus a philosophis proditum est... Atque hic mihi nolim veterum calculos suffragari, quorum alii legibus, alii conscriptis orationibus, alii poematis philosophiam damnarunt, homines ingeniosi, quantum intelligo, videbant enim, hoc sapiendi genus inutile rebus publicis esse, videbant, anxia et curiosa disceptatione mascula iuventutis ingenia enervari, videbant perpetuis digladiationibus verum obscurari magis, quam explicari.' *StA*, I, 72f.

77 *StA*, I, 74. 78 *Ibid.*

Scotists and Occamists.[79] Melanchthon argues that it is outrageous that the human mind should assume knowledge of the divine majesty, since fallen man does not have the ability to comprehend God by his own reason. The Stoics, the followers of Democritus, Epicurus, the Cyrenaics and Aristotle are all atheists (ἄθεοι) because they try to seek by human reason what cannot be known to man.[80] By further assuming man's ability to live virtuously without the Holy Spirit, Aristotle's *Ethica* fundamentally opposes all three Christian teachings of law, sin and grace.[81] In short, Aristotle and the theologians who used Aristotle, have confused and exhausted students with chicanery, obstructing the message of the Gospel. By invoking Paul's caveat 'Beware lest any man spoil you through philosophy...' (Colossians 2. 8), Melanchthon attacked Rhadinus' dependence on Aristotle which left no room for the teaching of Christ.[82]

As Melanchthon thus explained and confirmed, Luther was indeed hostile to Aristotelian philosophy because it contradicted or obstructed the message of the Gospel. In effect Luther was criticizing the very foundation of medieval learning, that human reason could and should contribute towards the knowledge of God. The natural philosophy traditionally taught at universities and at early Wittenberg was thus also attacked, as part of that medieval learning.

A year later, in early 1522, Luther repeated his opposition against Aristotelian natural philosophy in perfect unison with Melanchthon. In a sermon prepared as homiletical material for preachers on the topic of the festival of Epiphany (Matthew 2. 1–12), Luther explained how Epiphany, Christ's appearance to the three gentile Magi, illustrated ironically the spiritual degeneration of the people of God.[83] In explaining the kind of knowledge the three Magi possessed, Luther further illustrated the degenerate state of con-

79 *StA*, I, 75.

80 'Palam enim ἄθεοι sunt Stoici et qui Democritum secuti sunt, Epicurei, item Cyrenaici, ἄθεος est et vester ille, Hirce, Aristoteles, quo duce, o Titanicam audaciam, coelum oppugnatis.' *StA*, I, 76.

81 *StA*, I, 79–85.

82 'Annon tandem videmus, cur tam sollicite caveri praecipiat hominum doctrinas Paulus, tam gravis Apostolus, certe praevidens animo miseranda nostrorum temporum fata, cum ait: "Videte, ne quis vos depraedetur per philosophiam et inanem deceptionem." Scilicet ad vos ista, Hirce, non pertinent, qui Aristotelem, qui hominum somnia docetis? atque ita pertinaciter tuemini, ut ne locum quidem Christo in Scholis vestris esse velitis.' *StA*, I, 78f.

83 *LW*, LII, 159–286, *WA*, XI-I, 555–728. This was written during Luther's confinement at the Wartburg. For an analysis of the homiletic character of Luther's sermons in comparison to medieval and modern ones, see Kiessling (1971), 60–7.

temporary university teaching: the Magi were experienced in the knowledge of nature (*natürlich Kunst*) previously called 'magic' but now called 'physiology', the 'knowledge which discovers the powers and processes of nature'.[84] The Magi, however, could only imitate true knowledge of nature (*natürlich Kunst*) because they did not have the Spirit of God.[85] Luther claimed that there was a good and most natural kind of knowledge granted by the Spirit of God, for instance to Solomon (1 Kings 3. 16–27) and to Jacob (Genesis 30. 37–9). It is also the source of all medical knowledge.[86] Contemporary universities, however, far from teaching this true knowledge of nature, do not even profess what the pagan Magi had known. Luther thus attacks the Aristotelian natural philosophy taught in the universities as vain.[87] Quoting Colossians 2. 8 and 1 Timothy 6. 20–1, Luther wrote:

> the apostle truly condemns what the universities teach because he demands that everything not from Christ must be avoided. So every man must confess that Aristotle, the highest master of all universities, not only fails to teach anything concerning Christ, but also that what he teaches is idle nonsense ... [The apostle] ... calls the natural philosophy of Aristotle un-Christian, idle words without substance; in fact, it is opposed to Christ; he says, it is 'falsely called knowledge' ... There is no greater reputation than that which is derived from the knowledge of Aristotle in the universities. Yet that reputation is false, for that knowledge is nothing; it is simply opposed to Christ and has arisen to destroy him.
>
> Therefore, dear man, give up this natural philosophy (*Darumb, lieber Mensch, laß naturlich Kunst faren*) ...[88]

St Paul's caveat in Colossians 2. 8 – 'Beware lest any man spoil you through philosophy and vain deceit, after the tradition of men, after the rudiments of the world, and not after Christ' – was frequently invoked by both Luther and Melanchthon when criticizing Aristotle.[89] In fact this caveat aptly characterizes the attitudes both of Luther and of Melanchthon towards the traditional university teaching of Aristotelian philosophy. It had to be abandoned because it supported the wrong kind of theology and hindered the teaching of the true message of the Gospel.

Luther enacted St Paul's admonition with great vigour. It was

84 *LW*, LII, 162, *WA*, XI–1, 562. 85 *LW*, LII, 160, *WA*, XI–1, 560.
86 *LW*, LII, 161.
87 *LW*, LII, 165. 88 Translated by S. P. Hebart, *LW*, LII, 166f., *WA*, XI–1, 569.
89 See for instance Luther, 'Lectures on Romans' (1515–16), *LW*, XXV, 362 and Melanchthon, 'Preface to Aristophanes' *Clouds*' (1521) *MBW* no. 89, *CR*, I, 205.

Luther's own contention that one could not be too severe with 'wolves', the enemies of the true faith.[90] Some people were shocked at Luther's severe criticisms, to the extent that some humanists thought he had become an obscurantist.[91] A broadsheet woodcut by Hans Holbein the Younger (1497/8–1543), dating from 1522, depicts Luther through the eyes of such people (Fig. 3).[92] Although in a monk's garb and with a monk's tonsure, Luther as a German Hercules is here depicted as quite a savage and gruesome figure. The figure of the Pope is dangling from Luther's 'hooked nose',[93] a literal visualization of a Latin hyperbolic metaphor of contempt, 'to hang on one's nose an object of contempt' (*suspendere naso*).[94] Next to the figure of the Pope we can see the skin of a lion worn over the monk's habit, a reference to the skin of the Nemean Lion which Hercules had overpowered,[95] and perhaps also a reference to Pope Leo X. Luther as Hercules is about to slay with his club Hoogstraten, the famous Dominican inquisitor. At his feet are several figures already slain. We can read the name-tags of Occam, Aquinas, Scotus, Holcot, Lyra, Peter Lombard (labelled '*sentencius*') and the largest and the clearest of all, in the foreground, Aristotle. All of them had been severely criticized by Luther in print. If, following Lucian, Hercules was meant to be a figure excelling in eloquence,[96] the whole woodcut becomes a sharp satire of Luther's use

90 'A Sincere Admonition by Martin Luther to All Christians to Guard Against Insurrection and Rebellion' (1522), *LW*, XLV, 73. On the visual representation of the good shepherd parable, see Scribner (1981), 50–8, and illustrations 19, 20, 39–42. Luther called Aristotle's *Ethica* 'a wolf', Schwiebert (1950), 299.

91 See note 11 to *LW*, IL, 34.

92 The woodcut appeared from the Froben press in autumn 1522, Weber (1989), 156. I am grateful to Dr B. Weber for drawing my attention to his article. For an interpretation of this woodcut I mainly follow Saxl (1957).

93 The text at the bottom of the woodcut reads,

'Nonne vides, naso ut triplicem suspenderit unco
Geryonem, et lasset pendula crista caput?'

94 'Non
... naso suspendis adunco
ignotos, ut me libertino patre natum.' Horace, *Satires*, I, vi, 1, 5f.

For the Horatian saying, see also Erasmus, *Adagia*, I, viii, 22 in Erasmus (1974–), XXXII, 136.

95 Cf. Lucian, *Heracles*, 1.

96 '...we consider that the real Heracles was a wise man who achieved everything by eloquence and applied persuasion as his principal force.' Lucian, *Heracles*, 6. In the renaissance reception of Lucian's portrait of the (Gallic) Hercules, Hercules is primarily seen as god of inspired eloquence, Hallowell (1962), 243, cf. MacDonald (1976). For Lucian's influence on Erasmus, see Robinson (1979), 165–97. See also Sparn (1984) for an

3 Luther as Hercules Germanicus.
Hercules Germanicus, Hans Holbein the Younger (1522)

of savage language which railed at the Papacy, the scholastic theologians and Aristotle. The text attached to the bottom of the woodcut calls for reform within the (Roman) Church itself, without Luther.[97] Rather than being a piece of pro-Lutheran propaganda, the message of the woodcut is more in the spirit of Erasmus with whom the woodcut was associated at that time.[98]

It was indeed with the vigour of a Hercules that Luther put into practice St Paul's caveat. Luther set out to eliminate everything that supported and perpetuated traditional theology and anything that was an obstacle to accommodating his true message of the Gospel. In terms of university teaching, this meant that the major part of the arts curriculum which taught Aristotelian logic and philosophy had to be abandoned, because it ultimately served the traditional (and in Luther's eyes the wrong kind of) theology.[99] It is within this comprehensive onslaught on the traditional teaching of Aristotelian philosophy that natural philosophy was rejected by Luther and to some extent abandoned in practice at Wittenberg. Although neither Luther nor Melanchthon denied the validity of a knowledge about nature altogether, especially that of a medical kind, their attitude towards the teaching of natural philosophy and Aristotle was thoroughly negative. As aptly captured by the Holbein cartoon, Luther and Melanchthon were intent on abolishing the natural philosophy traditionally taught in the universities, the natural philosophy that did not teach Christ.

It is one thing to oppose and reject a traditional form of education and its content and quite another to provide an alternative education equally systematic and effective but compatible with the reformed theology. As we have seen, in the early years of the movement for reform spearheaded by Luther, Luther's emphasis, which was endorsed by Melanchthon, was always on the former. In the wake of the ensuing radical movements within the evangelical camp, the course of the movement for Luther's reform was redirec-

examination of the role of classical mythology in early modern theology, especially 76–81 for Luther.

97 Saxl (1957), 282.

98 Saxl (1957), 282f. Erasmus frequently expressed his disapproval of Luther's harsh language, e.g. his letter to Melanchthon in June 1520, Erasmus (1974–), VII, 313. Melanchthon disapproved of the depiction of Luther in the woodcut: 'Et quid dissimilius veri, quam quod fingunt de Hercule Germanico, de filiis Herculis apud nos, et multa hoc genus?' Melanchthon to Andreas Althamer, c. 1527, *CR*, I, 928.

99 For the necessity to understand Luther's attack on Aristotle in the context of his theology, see Ebeling (1970) 89f., 230f. and Eckermann (1978).

ted to what is now called the 'Magisterial Reformation'.[100] This period was to mark Melanchthon's redirection of his career from a theologian back to a Greek teacher. It was this Melanchthon who took to heart the necessity for a more positive programme of arts and philosophy education, after his experience in what turned out to be only the beginning of a series of tumultuous events.

MELANCHTHON'S REFORM – LAW AND PHILOSOPHY

In April 1521 an Imperial Diet was held at Worms to which Luther was summoned to submit his case. The Emperor Charles V dismissed Luther's case and an edict was issued outlawing Luther.[101] On the way back from Worms Luther disappeared, which, as was later known, was a precautionary measure by Frederick the Wise who feared for Luther's life. Luther was confined to the Wartburg, while at Wittenberg the leadership of the movement for reform was passed on to Melanchthon.

When discussions for curricular reform resumed at Wittenberg after the Diet of Worms, Melanchthon led the negotiations. We can read from his correspondence with Spalatin that Melanchthon was trying to realize a curricular reform along the lines proposed by Luther in his *Address to the German Nobility*.[102] Amidst this discussion we find Melanchthon consistently objecting to refilling the lectureship on the *Physica* which had been vacated by a Jodocus Mörlin.[103] Melanchthon had earlier suggested replacing the lectures on the *Physica* with the teaching of mathematics and argued that other studies should be restored first.[104] The curricular reform was finalized in June that year when an Electoral visitation took place.[105] The result was that Melanchthon's requests were largely fulfilled, but for one exception – the lectureship on the *Physica*. To our surprise, we find that Heinrich Stackmann (d. 1532), then a licentiate of medicine, was appointed to teach the *Physica* lecture.[106]

100 For the effect of this reorientation on education, see Strauss (1978).

101 For the background, see Brecht (1981–7), I, 413–53.

102 See *Urkundenbuch*, 111–18; Höss (1989), 203–5.

103 Mörlin was assigned to the pedagogue post in March 1518. In May 1520 he was paid five gulden for teaching the *Metaphysica*, *Urkundenbuch*, 86, 100.

104 See Letter to Spalatin, 21 March 1521, *MBW* no. 130, T-i, 130, and 14 June 1521, *MBW* no. 146, T-i, 298.

105 Result in *Urkundenbuch*, 118f.

106 'Stacmannus ... profiteatur lectionem physicam modo et ratione de qua Philippus noster Melanchthon cum eo egerit'; *Urkundenbuch*, 118. Stackmann became professor of medicine

Spalatin seems to have insisted on its continuation.[107] However, its teaching, it was stipulated, was to be done in the way Melanchthon had 'negotiated' with Stackmann.[108] Melanchthon was soon to express his satisfaction with Stackmann's lectures in which students were learning 'purely physical matters'.[109] The content of the *Physica* lecture thus seems to have been transformed, as Melanchthon further testified:

it seems to me that Stackmann should by all means be retained here, such an erudite man, especially in a medical school thus flourishing. Since even those who were once content to learn in the physical lectures those verbal monstrosities from Tartaretus and who knows what others, for the sake of obtaining the Master's degree, those men now hear the medics for the sake of learning about nature (*cognoscendae naturae*), and not for the sake of any title.[110]

Stackmann pleased Melanchthon because he was teaching an agreeable version of 'the study of knowing nature' (*studium cognoscendae naturae*), instead of an Aristotelian natural philosophy based on the commentaries of Tartaretus. Melanchthon further endorsed this new study about nature as a liberal art.[111]

Melanchthon's remark above and Stackmann's position as licentiate of medicine strongly suggest that some medical authors were read for this new study of nature. Stackmann, with Melanchthon, seems to have commended the study of Hippocrates,[112] but we have no positive evidence for Stackmann having actually taught Hippo-

at the end of 1524, and then ordinary professor of practical medicine in 1531. On Stackmann, see Friedensburg (1917), 132f., 139.

107 Spalatin was against abolishing the *Physica* lecture, as he wrote (during a discussion of salary redistribution in 1521) 'Also ver[b]lib die lectio physica noch ungestift, der man in kein weg mangeln kan.' *Urkundenbuch*, 117. My interpolation.

108 See note 106 above.

109 'Dicitur ille [Stackmann] et utiliter et frequenti auditorio profiteri, id quod nescis quantae mihi voluptati sit, discere iuventutem pure res physicas." Melanchthon to Spalatin, July 1521, *MBW* no. 153, T-i, 316.

110 '...modis omnibus retinendus hic mihi videtur Stagmannus, vir tam eruditus, praesertim medica schola sic florente. Nam et ii, qui antea contenti erant, φυσικὰς ἀκροάσεις, illa verborum portenta, ex Tartareto et nescio quibus aliis magisterii adipiscendi causa, discere, nunc cognoscendae naturae, non tituli alicuius gratia medicos audiunt...' Melanchthon to Spalatin, 5 November 1522, *MBW* no. 241, T-i, 501 (dated April 1522 in *CR*, I, 569).

111 '...nam et naturae cognoscendae studium liberale esse iudico; et ex Tartaretis illis quid omnino peteres non ineptum?', *ibid.*, For a classical precedent for including knowledge about nature in the liberal arts, see Cicero, *De oratore* II, 127.

112 See Petrus Burckhard, *Parva Hippocratīs tabula* (Wittenberg: J. Grunenberg, 1519), *VD*, H3801. I have not seen the original.

crates for the lectures which used to teach Aristotle's *Physica* following Tartaretus. It has also been suggested that Pliny's *Historia naturalis* replaced Aristotelian natural philosophy at Wittenberg around this time.[113] The *Historia naturalis* was read primarily for medical knowledge during this period,[114] and Melanchthon had also expressed his wish to have Pliny read for such knowledge.[115] Furthermore, we may recall that both Luther and Melanchthon approved of knowledge of nature which had a medical use.[116] The arts faculty at Wittenberg also had stipulated that Pliny the Elder be taught.[117] Yet, we have no concrete evidence that Pliny's *Historia naturalis* became the text for Stackman's *Physica* lecture.[118] Due to the paucity of available information, it is perhaps best to leave the matter here, with a tentative statement that, as a compromise between Spalatin and Melanchthon, the *Physica* lecture continued to be taught, but its content was transformed into a positive 'knowledge of nature' which had a medical use.

Towards the end of 1521, tumultuous events, now called the 'Wittenberg Movement',[119] occurred in Wittenberg. This was to test Melanchthon's calibre as a leader of reform in place of Luther. A period of unrest resulted from the determined efforts of Andreas Bodenstein von Carlstadt and of Gabriel Zwilling to realize the reforms that Luther had been calling for. Carlstadt impatiently called for the abolition of the Mass and the administration of communion in both kinds and further urged people to abandon university education.[120] Zwilling, an Augustinian, called for the abandonment of begging and the abolition of private masses. Excited by such preachings by Carlstadt and by Zwilling, townsmen and students, some armed, took part in riots and iconoclasm. The university was left in a desolate state: student numbers had plummeted and virtually no one was attending the arts course.[121] The remaining students seemed to be rioting.

113 Dannenfeldt (1972), 227, and repeated in Nauert (1979), 80.

114 On the reading of Pliny as a medical authority, see French (1986). See also Erasmus' praise of Pliny as a medical authority in his 'Encomium medicinae' (1519) in Erasmus (1974–), XXIX, 35–50.

115 See letter to Spalatin, 14 June 1521, *MBW* no. 146, T-i, 298f.

116 See above pp. 43–5.

117 Pliny the Elder was stipulated to be taught by a pedagogue in 1521, *Urkundenbuch*, 118.

118 For the adoption of the *Historia naturalis* as a textbook later on, see below pp. 136f.

119 For details of this movement, see Müller (1911). For this movement as a 'social' movement, see Scribner (1987), 145–74.

120 For Carlstadt's role in the Movement, see Sider (1974), 152–77.

121 Schwiebert (1950), 603–6; Friedensburg (1917), 158.

The arrival of three men from Zwickau claiming to be prophets further fuelled the already excited situation. The three men, Nicolas Storch, Thomas Dreschel and Marcus Stübner, all claimed to be prophets who held direct colloquies with God.[122] They questioned the validity of infant baptism and prophesied that existing governments would be overthrown. The Zwickau Prophets made a great impression on Melanchthon. Luther had claimed that it was not enough simply to read the Bible to gain faith. One had to pray for the Holy Spirit to arrive.[123] The Zwickau Prophets claimed to possess this Spirit. Melanchthon did not know how to judge these Prophets, and he begged the Elector to recall Luther so that he might judge them:

Your Highness is not ignorant of how many varied and dangerous disagreements concerning the Word of God have been excited in your Highness' town of Zwickau. Some of the rebels – I know not what they were calling for – were thrown into chains. Three of the authors of these disturbances have swiftly flown hither, two illiterate weavers [Storch and Dreschel], and the third literate [Stübner]. I have heard them. What they claim about themselves is amazing: they claim that they have been sent by the clear voice of God to teach; that they have private conversation with God; that they foresee the future; and that in short, they are prophets and apostles. But I cannot explain easily how I am affected by them. I am certainly led by great reasons not to ignore them. For it is apparent from many arguments that there are certain spirits in them, but no one can easily judge these spirits besides Martin.[124]

Both the Elector and Luther himself thought it unnecessary to return. Disturbance at Wittenberg continued, and Melanchthon

[122] For details of the Zwickau Prophets, see Karant-Nunn (1987), 106–9.

[123] See for instance, Luther to Spalatin, 18 January 1518, *LW*, XLVIII, 53f.

[124] 'Non ignorat celsitudo vestra, quam multae, variae et periculosae dissensiones de verbo dei in urbe celsitudinis vestrae Zuiccavia excitatae sint. Sunt et illheic in vincula coniecti qui nescio quae novarunt. Ex horum motuum auctoribus huc advolarunt tres viri, duo lanifices, literarum rudes, literatus tertius est. Audivi eos; mira sunt quae de se praedicant: missos se clara voce dei ad docendum esse sibi cum deo familiaria colloquia, videre futura, breviter, viros esse propheticos et apostolicos. Quibus ego quomodo commovear, non facile dixerim. Magnis rationibus adducor certe, ut contemni eos nolim. Nam esse in eis spiritus quosdam multis argumentis adparet, sed de quibus iudicare praeter Martinum nemo facile possit." Melanchthon to the Elector, 27 December 1521, *MBW* no. 192, T-i, 416f. My interpolation. A letter with a similar content was sent to Spalatin on the same day, see *MBW* no. 193, T-i, 417f. For Spalatin's role in the deliberation on whether Luther ought to return or not, Höss (1989), 217–20, see also Luther's letter of 12 March 1522, *WBr* II, 467–70.

exclaimed, 'I cannot hold back the water!'[125] The town council asked for Luther's return and Luther returned on 1 March 1522.[126] He immediately began preaching that force was unnecessary to bring about the Word of God and that if a thing did not violate the Word of God, it might be tolerated. The situation was resolved. Luther judged the Zwickau Prophets as bogus and they quickly left for Thuringia. Zwilling confessed his errors. Carlstadt was banned from preaching and was later banished from Saxon lands.[127] Peace was restored in Wittenberg.

It is generally agreed that Melanchthon underwent what we would now call an 'identity crisis' as a leader of reform during the Wittenberg Movement.[128] Melanchthon's inability to judge the spirits of the Zwickau Prophets pinpoints the problem. Luther in contrast had no problem in testing their spirits, as he explained to Melanchthon:

> In order to explore their individual spirit, too, you should inquire whether they have experienced spiritual distress and the divine birth, death and hell. If you should hear that all [their experiences] are pleasant, quiet, devout (as they say), and spiritual, then don't approve of them ... The sign of the Son of Man is then missing, which is the only touchstone of Christians and a certain differentiator between the spirits ... Therefore examine [the Zwickau Prophets] and do not even listen if they speak of the glorified Jesus, unless you have first heard of the crucified Jesus.[129]

We may recall Luther's struggle with the meaning of justification that led to his famous discovery. It was precisely through such a spiritual struggle that the Holy Spirit came to man.[130] For Luther, whose theology was the fruit of precisely such a struggle, there was no problem in judging the spirit. In contrast, Melanchthon had come to distrust human reason through the influence of Luther, but he had not reached an understanding of Luther's theology through a

125 'Ich kahn aber das wasser nicht halden; were von nodten, das man zu solchen Sachen, so der seelen heyl betreffen, ernstilicher thette.' Melanchthon to Hugolt von Einsiedelius, 5 February 1522, *MBW* no. 209, T-i, 444.

126 For Luther's intention to return in order to resume leadership, see Viner (1972), 51–63.

127 For events after Luther's return, see Viner (1972), 73–7. Carlstadt led a peasant's life for a while and then wandered around Germany until he became a self-appointed preacher in Orlamünde, Sider (1974), 174–97.

128 Manschreck (1958), 79f.; Maurer (1967–9), II, 152–229.

129 Luther to Melanchthon, 13 January 1522, translated by G. G. Krodel in *LW*, XLVIII, 366f.

130 For Luther's autobiographical account of this famous struggle, see his preface to his complete Latin writings (1545), *LW*, 34, 336f., and Brecht (1977) for an analysis of the process of the famous 'discovery'.

similar spiritual struggle. As one biographer of Melanchthon put it, 'reason he did not trust; revelation he did not have'.[131] Melanchthon was not a theologian in the sense that Luther was. This, Melanchthon, and perhaps Luther too,[132] came to realize after the Wittenberg Movement. On Luther's return, therefore, Melanchthon wished to withdraw from theology:

I hear that Martin wants someone else to be asked to give the Greek teaching, which I do not wish to be done. I would rather leave out theology which I had begun to lecture on for the *Baccalaureus* [*Biblicus*], as is customary. For so far, my work was only a substitute for either when Martin was absent, or more profitably engaged. I also see the need of many earnest teachers of the classics [*humanarum literarum*], which are no less neglected in this age than in that sophistic age.[133]

Melanchthon chose to concentrate on teaching Greek, and what such Greek studies stood for, namely classical literature.

Significantly, Melanchthon was to write, some time later in his life, the following words on the title-page of his own copy of Homer's *Iliad* (Frontispiece):

I, Philip Melanchthon, began to teach in the Greek language at Wittenberg in September 1518 when at this very place Martin Luther, the Augustinian, was teaching theology.[134]

Judging from the handwriting and the use of the past tense, it seems that the inscription was written later than the annotations in the text which resemble Melanchthon's earlier small, thin and neat handwriting. The copy itself may well have been the text from which he gave his first lectures at Wittenberg in 1518. We may recall that Melanchthon also taught Paul's letter to Titus then.[135] Of the two texts with which he began his lectures at Wittenberg, Melanchthon chose the copy which represented (Greek) classical studies, and

131 Manschreck (1958), 79. 132 Edwards (1975), 29–31.

133 'Doctorem Martinum audio velle, ut Graeca praelectio alteri demandetur; quod nolim ego. Nam theologica, quae praelegere ceperam propter baccalaureatum, ut mos est, omittere malim. Hactenus enim mea opera vicaria tantum fuit, vel absente vel foelicius occupato Martino. Et humanarum literarum et multis et adsiduis doctoribus opus esse video quae non minus hoc seculo quam sophistico illo negligentur.' Melanchthon to Spalatin, July 1522, *MBW* no. 237, T-i, 492.

134 'Ego Philippus Mel. graece/ profiteri coepi VVitembergae/ Mens. Septembri. Anno/ M.D.XVIII. quom/ istheic/ Martinus/ Luther*us*/ Augusti/ nianus/ Theologica/ doceret.' Inscribed on the title-page of the Greek text of Homer's *Iliad* (Venice: A. Manutius, 1504) now in Cambridge University Library (classmark Adv.d.13.4). For the significance of the Greek inscription at the bottom, see p. 197 below.

135 See p. 38 above.

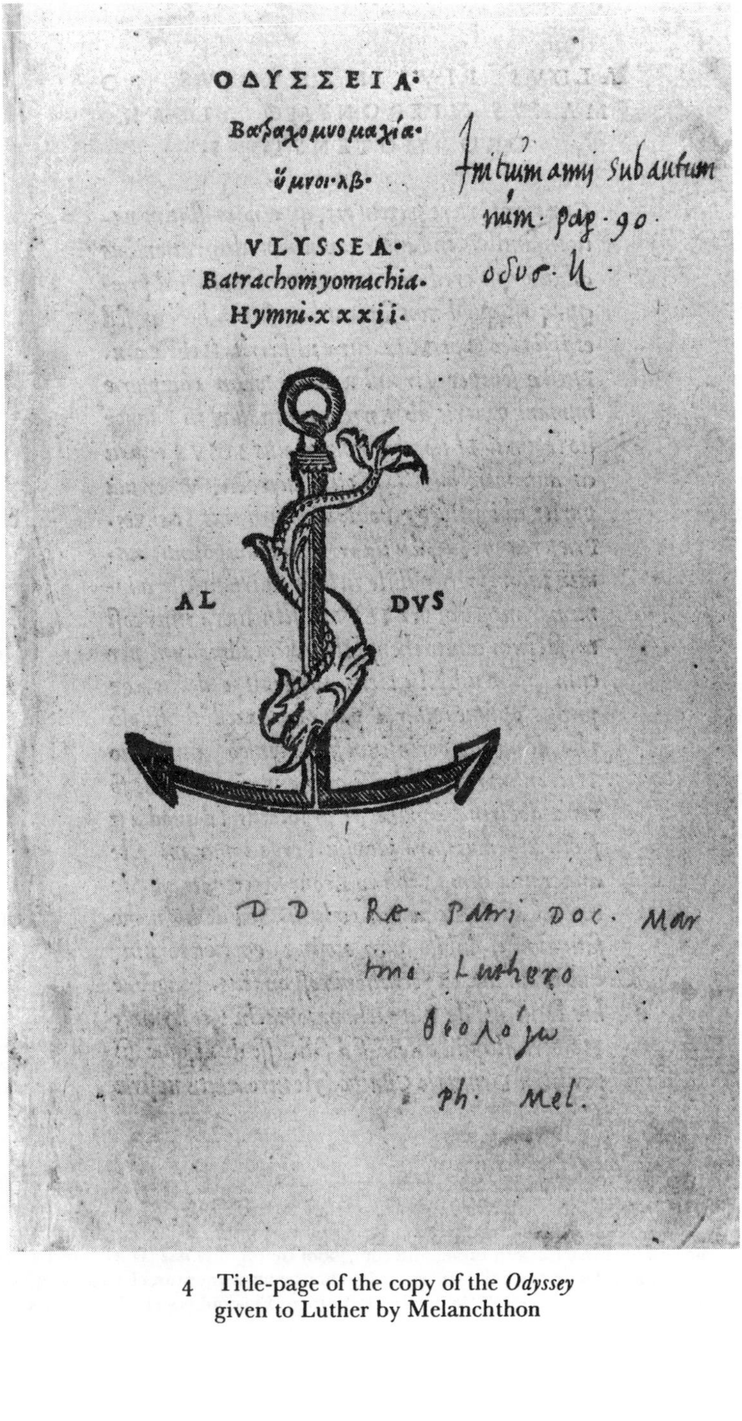

4 Title-page of the copy of the *Odyssey* given to Luther by Melanchthon

inscribed in it what he later saw himself as doing, in contrast to Luther. Melanchthon always knew that Luther was the theologian, as many of his addresses, including an inscription on Homer's *Odyssey* which he gave to Luther, indicate (Fig. 4).[136] Melanchthon's inscription in the *Iliad* may thus be read as what Melanchthon saw (or did not see) himself as: the teacher of Greek and classical studies (and not theology). He chose Homer rather than St Paul.

That Melanchthon chose Homer rather than St Paul did not imply, however, that he became a humanist in the vein of Erasmus. Although Melanchthon showed a lifelong respect for Erasmus' promotion of classical studies, especially for their moral content, he clearly saw that the two of them differed in their theology.[137] Thus, in a pamphlet in which Melanchthon set forth a plan of learning based on the humanities, he remarked:

> In theological matters, we require most importantly two [things]. One, by which we are consoled against death and the judgement of God and also lift our mind against all snares of the Devil, against the power of the gates of Hell. And this is a true, evangelicial and Christian proclamation unknown to the world or to any human reason. This Luther teaches. And this is the justice of the heart which afterwards produces good works. He who follows this in reading the Scriptures easily understands many mysteries of the Scriptures. The other is good manners or politeness. This indeed Erasmus teaches but so did the gentile philosophers ... Those who follow this one teach charity but not faith.[138]

The difference between Luther and Erasmus became unmistakably clear, especially after their bitter dispute over the Freedom of the

[136] The inscription reads: 'D[ono]. D[edit]. Re. Patri Doc. Mar/tino Luthero/ θεολόγῳ/ Ph. Mel.' For this copy of Homer, see Volz (1954), cf. Smith (1911). Melanchthon often called Luther 'the theologian', the first instance of which seems to be 4 April 1525 in a letter to Camerarius, *MBW* no. 387 (*CR*, I, 734, dated 12 April). For a list of allegorical names Melanchthon used, see *CR*, x, 317–24.

[137] For Melanchthon's reservation about Erasmus' interpretation of the Eucharist, see *CR*, I, 840–8. The difference between Melanchthon and Erasmus is pointed out in Maurer (1967–9), I, 171–6, 182–5, 206–8, and Scheible (1984). Cf. Boyle (1981) for Erasmus' Christocentric theology which *necessitates* his promotion of classical studies.

[138] 'In rebus theologicis duo potissimum requirimus. Alterum, quo nos consolemur adversus mortem, et iudicium dei, quoque animum erigamus adversus omnes insidias satanae, adersum vim portarum infernarum. Ea demum vera, evangelica, et christiana praedicatio est, ignota mundo, et omni rationi humanae. Hanc profitetur Lutherus. Et haec iusticia cordis est, quae postea bona opera parit. Hanc qui in scripturis legendis sequitur, facile intelliget multa mysteria scripturae. Alterum, boni mores, civilitas. Haec fere Erasmus docet; sed et gentiles philosophi docuere ... Qui hoc genus sequuntur, charitatem quidem docent, sed fidem non docent.' 'De Erasmo et Luthero Elogion' (1522), *CR*, xx, 700f.

Will in the mid-1520s.[139] Erasmus' judgement on Melanchthon was entirely reciprocal to that of Melanchthon. Whilst acknowledging Melanchthon as the only humanist in Wittenberg, Erasmus thought that his talent was wasted on theological issues.[140] When Melanchthon reconfirmed his vocation as a Greek teacher after the Wittenberg Movement, it was to be not in the footsteps of Erasmus but in an entirely different and new way – in support of Luther's cause. As Erasmus eventually remarked, Melanchthon became 'more Lutheran' than Luther himself.[141]

Luther too could see the importance of the study of Greek and classical literature.[142] It was, however, from the point of view of theology that he saw it:

> I myself am convinced that without the knowledge of the [Humanistic] studies, pure theology can by no means exist, as has been the case until now: when the [Humanistic] studies were miserably ruined and prostrate [theology] declined and lay neglected. I realize there has never been a great revelation of God's Word unless God has first prepared the way by the rise and the flourishing of languages and learning, as though these were forerunners, a sort of [John] the Baptist. Certainly I do not intend that young people should give up poetry and rhetoric. I certainly wish there would be a tremendous number of poets and orators, since I realize that through these studies, as through nothing else, people are wonderfully equipped for grasping the sacred truths, as well as for handling them skilfully and successfully.[143]

For Luther classical studies were preparatory and necessary (St John the Baptist) for something more important, namely theology (Christ himself). The message of Christ, however, was what Luther was most preoccupied with. Therefore he was very keen for Melanchthon to teach theology rather than wasting his talent on other basic subjects.[144] Quite literally, Luther was a theologian by vocation.[145]

139 For this controversy, see Boyle (1983) and Brecht (1981–7), II, 21–34. For Melanchthon's part in this dispute, see Maurer (1958).

140 See *Ciceronianus*, Erasmus (1974–), XXVIII, 427 and his letters, Erasmus (1974–), V, 29; VII, 313; VIII, 210.

141 Erasmus to John Lasky, 5 March 1534, Erasmus (1956–68), X, 363, no. 2911. For the text, see p. 41 note 11 above.

142 See for instance his use of humanist rhetoric in the 'Dictata super psalterium', Junghans (1984), 240–73.

143 Luther to Eobanus Hessus, 29 March 1523, translated by G. G. Krodel in *LW*, IL, 34.

144 See Luther's letter to Frederick the Wise, 23 March 1524, *LW*, IL, 75f.

145 See for instance his famous remark: 'I would not exchange my doctor's degree for all the world's gold. For I would surely in the long run lose courage and fall into despair if, as

Many historians have written about the differences between Luther and Melanchthon, in particular about the calibre and judgements of the latter as a Lutheran theologian.[146] Here I only wish to contrast what Luther and Melanchthon saw themselves as doing: Luther was a theologian, Melanchthon a Greek teacher. I do not wish to imply that either of them pursued his interests to the exclusion of the other's. Melanchthon was persuaded to teach theology after all, when he had time to,[147] and he also took part in numerous theological controversies and wrote numerous theological treatises. Similarly Luther actively sought to establish sound and good education, to an extent that his persistence sometimes annoyed the Elector.[148] Nevertheless, their reactions and approaches to the same problems differed, and that is because, I believe, they pursued different vocations. Luther responded to the claims of the authors of the Wittenberg Movement in his theological writings.[149] Melanchthon on the other hand responded to the problems stemming from the Wittenberg Movement in the field of arts education where he felt most comfortable.

In 1523 Melanchthon explained in a speech how he wanted to reinvigorate the arts faculty which had been left desolate. In this speech, *Necessarias esse ad omne studiorum genus artes dicendi sive encomium eloquentiae*,[150] Melanchthon rigorously defended rhetoric as a basis of all branches of knowledge. Melanchthon wrote that speech is essential for mankind.[151] Eloquence, however, is more than an arbitrary heaping of words.[152] Against Pico della Mirandola, who had argued that eloquence is simply about rhetorical flair and thus of no use,[153]

these infiltrators, I had undertaken these great and serious matters without call or commission. But God and the whole world bears me testimony that I entered into this work publicly and by virtue of my office as teacher and preacher, and have carried it on hitherto by the grace and help of God.' 'Against Infiltrating and Clandestine Preachers' (1532), translated by C. Bergendoff in *LW*, XL, 387f.

146 For a concise review of Melanchthon scholarship in this respect, see Stupperich (1966), 151–9.

147 Keen (1988), 7.

148 See for instance, *To the Councilmen of All Cities in Germany that They Establish and Maintain Christian Schools*, *LW*, XLV, 363. For Luther's request for school visitations, see his letter to Spalatin, 16 April 1525, *LW*, XLV, 102–5; and for the Elector's annoyance, see *LW*, IL, 131f. The difference of emphasis in educational reforms between Luther and Melanchthon is pointed out in Benrath (1970), 69.

149 'Against the Heavenly Prophets in the Matter of Images and Sacraments' (1525), *LW*, XL, 73–223.

150 Reprinted in *StA*, III, 43–62. 151 *StA*, III, 45. 152 *StA*, III, 47.

153 This refers to Pico's defence of philosophy over and against rhetoric. In 1485 Ermolao Barbaro wrote a famous letter in reply, defending rhetoric, Breen (1952a). The two letters

Melanchthon argued that just as a painter cannot paint or draw without any order (*ratio*), so eloquence cannot do without rhetoric.[154] With an allusion perhaps to Horace (*Ars poetica*, 361–5), Melanchthon said that with rhetoric, thoughts of the mind should be represented just as things are depicted with colours. To be eloquent, Melanchthon defined, is to be able to place the sentiment of your own mind clearly and fittingly under the eyes of others and to express aptly everything the subject matter requires – this is to speak elegantly indeed.[155]

Not only is eloquence an accurate representation of the sentiment of one's mind, but it also sharpens the judgement of the mind through imitation (*imitatio*) and practice (*exercitium*). Poets such as Homer and Virgil and historians such as Thucydides and Xenophon should be read as examples so that students may learn the power of words, the structure of orations and figures of speech.[156] Melanchthon then goes on to say how neglect of this eloquence has been the source of confusion and of errors by theologians. Although Melanchthon is careful to point out that the human mind cannot penetrate into divine truth on its own, he does claim that rhetoric is nevertheless necessary for preaching the true faith and passing it down to posterity.[157] This oration has been noted by scholars for its rigorous defence of rhetoric[158] and indeed in this sense we should note the typically humanistic ideal of learning Melanchthon is projecting. We should also take note that by claiming the basic necessity of rhetoric for all branches of knowledge, what Melanchthon is in effect doing is stressing the importance of arts studies in relation to the higher faculties. It is a strong defence of the necessity of studying in the arts faculty against those who inopportunely rush to what they believe are more important disciplines.

were printed together in Melanchthon's *Elementorum rhetorices libri duo* (1547). For Melanchthon's rhetoric, see Mouchel (1992).

154 'An vero recte corpus imitabitur pictor, si nulla ratione penicillum regat, si temere feratur manus, nec ducantur arte lineae? Ad eum modum nec animi tui sententiam aliis ob oculos posueris, ni propriis et illustribus verbis apta vocum compositione, iusto sententiarum ordine utare.' *StA*, III, 47.

155 'Adeo non quovis orationis genere lectori satisfeceris, sed cura studioque paranda facultas est, qua animi tui sententiam perspicue aliorum oculis subiicere possis, omniaque commode quae res poscit, eloqui, id est enim eleganter dicere.' *StA*, III, 47f.

156 *StA*, III, 47–53.

157 *StA*, III, 48f., 59. Cf. Erasmus' much stronger belief in oratorical power, see Boyle (1977).

158 Most notably in Breen (1952b), though Breen's definition of rhetoric and philosophy is rather idiosyncratic and does not take into account later developments of Melanchthon's philosophy.

Some are 'snatched away by the hope for profit to learn law and medicine, and reach for theology before building up strength in the study of the art of speaking',[159] – an allusion, perhaps, to the sorry state of arts education during the Wittenberg Movement.

This ideal of arts studies founded upon rhetoric was put into effect by Melanchthon towards the end of 1523 when, as rector, he implemented a set of regulations concerning the studies and behaviour of students.[160] Concerning student behaviour, explicit injunctions were introduced against students rioting in town, pillaging gardens, defaming others in print, and wearing arms,[161] obviously a reaction against the student riots during the Wittenberg Movement. As for the studies, tighter control over the young students by the rector was introduced to ensure their instruction: beginning students had to submit their names to the rector, who would assign them a pedagogue, who in turn would prescribe each student an order of studies and supervise their literary and linguistic studies. Students who neglected these studies were to be fined. Rhetorical exercise was introduced in the form of declamations: twice a month, declamations were to be held, one by a grammar or rhetoric teacher, another by a student whose declamation had been authorized and checked by the rhetoric teacher.[162] In addition, disputations were to be held twice a month by the *Physica* teacher or by the mathematics teacher, or by whoever was deemed fit to do so. They were to dispute on the knowledge of nature and of mathematics (*naturae mathematumque cognitio*) because such knowledge was 'very necessary for human affairs (*rebus humanis*)'.[163] Again, it is not clear from these regulations what exactly was taught by the *Physica* lecturer as 'knowledge of nature' (*cognitio naturae*). The stress on the utility for human affairs, however, indicates that it may well have been the kind of liberal art with a medical use which was introduced in 1521.[164]

If the regulations of 1523 were limited in scope in that they dealt

159 'Nunc vestrum est cum elegantiore litteratura in gratiam redire eamque cupide amplecti. Video plerosque intempestive properare ad graviores, ut vocant, disciplinas, quosdam ad Iura discenda, ad Medicinam spes quaestus rapit alii ad Theologiam contendunt, priusquam robur aliquod fecerint in studio artium dicendi.' *StA*, III, 61.

160 *Urkundenbuch*, 128–30.

161 *Urkundenbuch*, 129.

162 *Urkundenbuch*, 128f.

163 '[E]t quia naturae mathematumque cognitio perquam necessaria est rebus humanis, volumus ut itidem singulis mensibus disputent vel physici ac mathematici professores vel alii, quos ei rei idoneos esse professores judicaverint.' *Urkundenbuch*, 129.

164 See pp. 49–51 above.

only with young beginners at university, the resolutions passed by the arts faculty at the beginning of 1526 clarified the scope of the whole arts syllabus.[165] A student was to begin with Latin grammar, dialectic, and the elements of rhetoric and of mathematics. Terence, Cicero's letters, Virgil, Erasmus' *Copia verborum* and Proclus' *Sphaera* were to be learnt during this course. No student was to proceed to more advanced subjects without the permission of his instructors.[166] When a student had mastered these subjects thoroughly and was allowed to proceed to the more advanced lectures, he was granted the title of a *Baccalaureus*. The students were then to master the *scientia* of judging correctly and certainly about the whole of nature and conducts (*scientiam de tota natura et moribus recte et certi judicandi*), in addition to the art of explaining complex and weighty matters perspicuously.[167] The mathematics and the *Physica* lectures taught the 'knowledge of nature' (*scientia naturae*).[168] Works of various orators and poets were to be taught privately and publicly for learning proper conduct.[169] Knowledge of the Greek language was necessary because many things concerning both the knowledge about nature and conducts were to be tackled from the Greek authors.[170] Students who mastered these subjects were granted the title of Master.[171]

In the resolutions, further explanation was given as to the importance of these subjects in relation to the higher faculties. The languages, rhetoric and dialectic were all necessary for tackling theological matters.[172] The knowledge of nature, in contrast, was very important for those who pursued medicine: those who wished to pursue medicine would be at a loss in their disputations without '*physiologia*' and mathematics.[173] This '*physiologia*' seems to indicate the content of the *Physica* lectures in which Stackmann had earlier begun to teach medical knowledge. Once more, however, we are left without being told exactly what was to be taught in these lectures.

165 *Urkundenbuch*, 146f. 166 *Urkundenbuch*, 146.

167 'Ab his initiis gradus fit ad superiora. porro qui volet utiliter discere, danda opera est, ut totam ἐγκυκλοπαιδείαν cognoscat, ut et scientiam de tota natura ac moribus recte et certo judicandi et facultatem quandam dilucide explicandi, et illustrandi res abstrusas et de gravioribus causis clare dicendi sibi comparet.' *Urkundenbuch*, 146.

168 'Ad naturae scientiam conducent mathematicae et physicae praelectiones.' *Ibid.*

169 *Ibid.*

170 'Et quia pleraque de natura et moribus a Graecis autoribus petenda sunt, debet ad haec accedere etiam studium ejus linguae.' *Urkundenbuch*, 147.

171 *Ibid.* 172 *Ibid.*

173 '[Q]ui vero se ad medicinam contulerit, nisi eo hoc adferet instrumentum φυσιολογίαν et mathemata, haerebit ubique tanquam in luto in eius artis disputationibus.' *Ibid.*

Reinvigorating the teaching in the arts faculty meant finding a positive meaning for the arts studies. In a typically humanist fashion, Melanchthon based his programme of arts education on classics. It was, however, only after Melanchthon had encountered more disturbing events that he saw in a decisive way the necessity of re-introducing classical philosophy teaching in a new way in the universities.

Unrest was spreading over Germany. Thomas Müntzer, an erstwhile sympathizer of Luther now in Allestedt, was passionately calling for the establishment of the living and eternal Word of God spoken to the Elect (as opposed to the 'dead' letter of Scriptures).[174] For Müntzer the Elect were the common people, who by God's will had to destroy the Godless in order to bring about the impending apocalyptic transformation of the world. Even the princes, should they prove Godless, needed to have their swords taken away.[175] The newly transformed community of Elects was to hold goods commonly.[176] After leaving Allestedt, Müntzer wandered around Germany, finally ending up in Mühlhausen. Meanwhile, peasants who had been frustrated and dissatisfied with their condition took up arms in several places.[177] Melanchthon wondered whether one of the Zwickau Prophets, Storch, was behind such riots.[178] The peasants in Upper Swabia published their manifesto in the 'Twelve Articles' and claimed (among other things) their Christian right to disobey and to revolt.[179] Convinced by the peasants' uprising nearby that the final apocalyptic battle against the Godless had begun, Müntzer joined the peasants. Luther violently objected to the rebellious spirits of both the peasants and Müntzer. He harshly rejected Müntzer's cause in the *A Shocking History and God's Judgement on Thomas Müntzer*.[180] In his tract *Against the Murdering, Thieving*

174 For an analysis of the gradual development of Müntzer's radical apocalyptic theology, see Scott (1989) and Friesen (1990) who stresses the independence of Müntzer's theology.

175 See his 'Sermon to the Princes', *The Radical Reformation*, 11–32. For analysis of Müntzer's conviction in destroying the Godless to maintain the purity of Church, Friesen (1990), 168–268.

176 Stayer (1991), 107–22. For the invocation of community of goods as a medieval topos of popular grievance, Scott (1989), 87.

177 For a close analysis of the historiography of the Peasants' War, see Scott (1979).

178 See letter to Joachim Camerarius, 16 April 1525, *MBW* no. 391 (dated 17 April in *CR*, I, 739f.).

179 For the text of the 'Twelve Articles', see *The Radical Reformation*, 231–8; for recent studies on the Peasants' War, see further *The German Peasant War of 1525*.

180 *WA*, XVIII, 367–74.

Hordes of Peasants, Luther called for the rulers to counter such disturbances with force.[181] Melanchthon too objected to the peasants' resort to violence in his *Confutation of the Articles of the Peasants*.[182] In May 1525 the Peasants' War came to an end. The peasants and Müntzer were quickly and ruthlessly put down. This did not mean, however, that the root of civil disobedience had been extirpated, as both Luther and Melanchthon were soon to realize.

In the summer of 1527 a visitation of the Ernestine territory of Saxony was conducted by representatives of the faculty of Wittenberg in order to survey the extent of the chaos created by Müntzer and the extent to which reformed doctrines were being taught and preached. Melanchthon went to Thuringia and he was appalled at what he found there.[183] The pastors were instructing the people poorly, they preached on the remission of sins but hardly on penitence, and several knew nothing beyond the Decalogue, the Creed and the *Pater Noster*.[184] In Kahla and Orlamünde Melanchthon found some 'Carlstadters', unbaptized children and the practice of adult baptism.[185] Melanchthon saw the disturbances at Kahla as caused by Carlstadt.[186]

Melanchthon took his findings at Thuringia very seriously. By October 1527 he began to write against those disruptive people and called them 'Anabaptists' for the first time.[187] The work was completed in a few months and was published as the *Adversus anabaptistas Philippi Melanthonis iudicium*.[188] A German translation was available within the same year. The 1528 edition of the *Loci communes* also incorporated a new section on infant baptism.[189] In the *Adversus anabaptistas*, Melanchthon defended the efficacy of infant baptism on traditional and scriptural grounds. By declaring that baptism was

181 See *LW*, XLVI, 45–55. 182 *Confutatio articulorum rusticanorum*, *CR*, XX, 641–62.

183 For Melanchthon's experience in the Thuringian visitation of 1527, I follow Oyer (1964), especially 140–78.

184 Oyer (1964), 143.

185 See letter of Melanchthon *et al.* to Elector John, 13 August 1527, *MBW* no. 574, Melanchthon (1910–26), I, 369.

186 Melanchthon to Joachim Camerarius, before 9 August 1527, *MBW* no. 571 (*CR*, I, 881, dated 11/12 August).

187 See Melanchthon's letter to Hieronymus Baumgartner, 23 October 1527, *MBW* no. 609 (*CR*, I, 900).

188 No copies of the Latin edition of the *Adversus anabaptistas Philippi Melanthonis iudicium* of 1528 survive, Oyer (1964), 144 note 2. The Latin edition from 1541 is reprinted in *CR*, I, 955–73. An English translation by C. L. Hill (probably based on the 1528 German edition) is available in Melanchthon (1962), 102–22.

189 Oyer (1964), 147.

valid only when the heart began to have faith in the forgiveness of sins, the Anabaptists erred in imposing an arbitrary human interpretation on an act which carried the Spirit of the Divine. The other issue besides infant baptism that Melanchthon turned his attention to in this treatise was the community of goods. Melanchthon saw this latter claim as most disruptive to society, as he assoicated it with the claims of the peasants in the Peasants' War.[190]

A great deal of modern scholarship has been devoted to distinguishing different kinds of Anabaptism and to demonstrating that the Anabaptists did not necessarily advocate civil unrest.[191] In Melanchthon's eyes, however, Anabaptism and civil unrest were inseparable, as was the case with other magisterial reformers.[192] In the case of Melanchthon, this was because his idea of Anabaptism was shaped by his experiences in Thuringia.[193] In the visitation to Thuringia, Melanchthon encountered the practice of adult baptism and denial of infant baptism alongside civil unrest. Denial of infant baptism and disruption of society are what the Zwickau Prophets had also called for in Wittenberg. Furthermore, there was a close parallel in the nature of the claims made by the Anabaptists and the Zwickau prophets: in his *Adversus anabaptistas* Melanchthon called the Anabaptists 'fanatic spirits' or 'Schwärmer', as the German edition translated the term,[194] and condemned their interpretation of baptism as arbitrary. The Zwickau Prophets had similarly claimed possession of the Holy Spirit and contradicted each other with differing interpretations.[195]

For Melanchthon there was not only a parallel between the authors of the Wittenberg Movement and the Anabaptists in Thuringia, but also a geographical and causal connection. Thuringia was where Thomas Müntzer began to preach his 'revolutionary theology' and where he joined the Peasants' War. It is also where the Zwickau Prophets originated from and where at least

[190] For details of Melanchthon's argument, see Oyer (1964), 144–54. See also Stayer (1991) for the Anabaptist claim for community of goods as drawing from the social protests of the Peasants' War. Cf. Clasen (1972).

[191] For the difficulty of reducing the origin of Anabaptism to a single cause or person, see Stayer, Packull and Deppermann (1975). For a review of the historiography of Anabaptism, see Coggins (1986).

[192] See also the case of Johannes Brenz in Brecht (1966), 260–6, 302–8. For how these views of Melanchthon and Luther have in fact led to modern historiographic confusion, see also Bender (1980).

[193] This point is argued convincingly in Oyer (1964), 239–42.

[194] Oyer (1964), 148.

[195] See Luther's letter to Spalatin, 4 September 1522, *WBr*, II, 597.

Storch returned to and preached sedition after leaving Wittenberg.[196] Melanchthon suspected further the influence of Carlstadt on the disturbances at Kahla and Orlamünde. This meant that the disturbances encountered in Thuringia by Melanchthon alongside the practice of adult baptism and denial of infant baptism could be traced back to Müntzer, the Zwickau Prophets and Carlstadt.[197] Melanchthon thus saw in what he found in Thuringia the latest manifestation of what was begun in the Wittenberg Movement. Hence by 1530 Melanchthon came to believe that any Anabaptist would oppose civil government in one way or another.[198]

Melanchthon's experience in Thuringia not only resulted in a strong refutation directed specifically against the claims of those whom he regarded as the Anabaptists, but also effected a fundamental shift of emphasis in his thought. In August 1527 a short disputation on Colossians 2.8. by Melanchthon was printed.[199] This passage had been the favourite scriptural source for both Luther and Melanchthon when attacking scholastic philosophy. In the disputation, Melanchthon indeed repeats his earlier criticism of philosophy: it wrongly teaches that civil justice suffices in the eyes of God (*coram Dei*), and it also wrongly assumes that reason, without the Holy Spirit, can oppose evil on its own.[200] In sum, to affirm as certain what reason or philosophy cannot discern, namely theological truths, is inane.[201]

The force, however, of St Paul's caveat is now positively, and

196 For a summary of Müntzer's activities at Zwickau, see Karant-Nunn (1987), 96–106. For an analysis of Müntzer's (limited) debt to the Zwickau Prophets, see Scott (1989), 21–8 and Friesen (1990), 73–99.

197 Clasen (1972), 34, 171. Though Müntzer questioned the efficacy of infant baptism, he preserved the rite, Scott (1989), 53. For the Swiss appropriation of Carlstadt's view on baptism, see Pater (1984), 117–67. For a general overview of the radical wing of the Reformation, see G. H. Williams (1962a).

198 Melanchthon's specific identification of the origin of Anabaptism with the Zwickau Prophets and Carlstadt owing to his personal experiences is also noted in Oyer (1964), 247.

199 'Philipi Melanchthonis in locum ad Colossenses, videte ne quis vos decipiat per philosophiam inanem dissertatio' (August 1527), *CR*, xii, 691–6.

200 *CR*, xii, 692–4.

201 'Non est enim philosophia, cum de divina voluntate ex ratione iudicamus, sed sunt inania somnia, sicut Epicurus negavit, Deo res nostras curae esse, item Platonici disputaverunt, Deum gignere cogitationem quandam; et Aristoteles disputat, mundum esse aeternum, nec aliquando coepisse. Et admiscuerunt doctrinae christianae philosophiam, qui docuerunt, quod nostris meritis iustificemur, Et quidam scripsit, fundamenta doctrinae christianae philosophiam Platonicam esse. Sic pro certis adfirmare, quae ratio aut philosophia non potest adfirmare, immo quae prorsus sunt extra iudicium rationis aut philosophiae posita, ea est inanis deceptio . . .' *CR*, xii 695.

quite definitely, qualified: 'Paul did not say "philosophy is bad", but he said "See to it that no one makes prey of you by philosophy", just as if he should say "Beware lest wine should deceive you" [Romans 14. 21].'[202]

St Paul did not mean that all philosophy was inherently bad. It is only the abuse of philosophy in Christian matters, Melanchthon argues, that St Paul is objecting to. Melanchthon thus spells out at length what St Paul meant:

When Paul said 'Beware lest any man spoil you through philosophy', it should not be understood thus: that that philosophy which teaches us to speak well and teaches the natures of remedies and of bodies, is empty: for Paul permits us to use that very judgement of reason like clothing or provision. He does not forbid us to count or measure bodies, he does not forbid us to build, to paint, to heal illnesses of our bodies or to exercise our judgement. Rather, because you hear that these gifts of God were implanted in nature, you should all the more respect this philosophy which God gave for the sake of the procurement of necessities of life . . .[203]

The seeming contradiction of opposing scholastic philosophy on the one hand and praising a useful philosophy on the other under the same scriptural passage is resolved by a clear distinction between the Gospel and philosophy.

The Gospel is the teaching of spiritual life and of justification in the eyes of God; but philosophy is the teaching of the corporeal life (*doctrina vitae corporalis*), just as you see that medicine serves health, the turning points of storms serve navigators, civil conduct serve the common peace of all men. The use of philosophy in this way is very necessary and approved of by God; as Paul says in many places, that creatures of God may use it with thanksgiving [1 Timothy 4. 4].[204]

202 'Ita Paulus non ait, philosophiam esse malam, sed sic ait: videte ne quis vos decipiat per philosophiam, ut si dicat: vide, ne te decipiat vinum.' *CR*, XII 695

203 'Cum igitur Paulus ait, Cavete ne quis vos decipiat per philosophiam, non est sic accipiendum, quod illa philosophia, quae docet loqui, ac remediorum naturas, aut corporum, sit vana: permittit enim uti nobis isto iudicio rationis sicut vestitu et victu, non vetat numerari aut metiri corpora, non vetat aedificare, non vetat pingere, non vetat mederi morbis corporum, non vetat iudicia exercere, immo quia audis haec dona Dei esse insita naturae, multo magis debes hanc philosophiam venerari, quam Deus dedit ad vitae praesidia paranda . . .' *CR*, XII, 692.

204 'Sed Evangelium est doctrina vitae spiritualis et iustificationis coram Deo, Philosophia vero est doctrina vitae corporalis, sicut vides medicinam valetudini servire, navigantibus discrimina temptestatum, mores civiles communi hominum tranquillitati. Est autem huiusmodi usus necessarius et a Deo probatus, sicut multis locis docet Paulus, utendum esse creaturis Dei cum gratiarum actione.' *CR*, XII, 695.

Philosophy was thus re-defined positively as the teaching about the corporeal (as opposed to the spiritual) life. By drawing a clear distinction between philosophy and the Gospel, Melanchthon thus gave a new meaning to philosophy which was at once positive and compatible with his earlier criticisms.

The ethical implication of this positive philosophy was most significant. In the disputation it was in particular the philosophy that taught civil conduct to 'serve the common peace of all' that Melanchthon elucidated in detail. On the basis of Romans 2.15, Melanchthon claimed that all men are endowed by God with the ability to judge with reason about natural and moral matters. That nobody should be hurt and that magistrates should be obeyed are just such divine laws written in the hearts of all men.[205] This law, given to all men by God, is for Melanchthon the strongest possible justification for civil obedience since it implies that even those who do not have true faith are subject to civil justice.[206] In the light of his experience with the Anabaptists in Thuringia, this message becomes particulary poignant. This disputation may well have been the disputation with which he claimed to have brought some 'Carlstadters' back to their senses.[207]

In the summer of 1527, Colossians 2. 8 took on a positive meaning for philosophy. A *Scholia* on the whole of Colossians containing a more lengthy re-interpretation of the same passage was printed in Latin and in German in 1527.[208] By 1530 Melanchthon recommended his *Scholia* on Colossians as an essential supplement to his *Loci communes*.[209] Melanchthon's confidence in the positive value of

205 'Est [Philosophia] enim ipsum iudicium rationis, quod in rebus naturalibus et civilibus moribus Deus dedit humanae naturae, verum et certum, quia dicit Paulus Rom. 2.: Gentes habent legem Dei scriptam in cordibus, id est, habent iudicium, quo iudicare possunt, neminem laedendum esse, gratiam pro benefactis habendam esse, magistratibus obsequendum esse, et similia.' *CR*, XII, 692.

206 'Neque vero tollit christiana doctrina civiles mores, sed eos exigit, et philosophiam seu rationem praecipientem de civilibus moribus approbat, sicut et civiles magistratus approbat, et testatur, se authorem esse civilium ordinationum, Roman. decimo tertio: omnia, quae ordinata sunt, a Deo ordinata sunt. Et ab his qui non habent spiritum sanctum, tamen exigit, ut frenentur civili iusticia. Ut dicit Paulus: lex est iniustis posita. Item: lex est paedagogus.' *CR*, XII, 694.

207 Melanchthon *et al.* to Elector John, 13 August 1527, *MBW* no. 574, Melanchthon (1910–26), I, 369f.

208 *Hartfelder*, 586. For an English translation of the *Scholia*, see Melanchthon (1989).

209 'Iuberem et meos communes locos legere, sed multa sunt in illis adhuc rudiora, quae decrevi mutare. Facile tamen intelligi potest, quid mihi ibi displiceat ex meis Colossensibus, ubi locos aliquot mitigavi.' 'Discendae theologiae ratio' (1530), *CR*, II, 457. The

5 *The Close of the Silver Age*, Lucas Cranach the Elder

philosophy never wavered after 1527. It was in fact to mark the beginning of Melanchthon's active and lifelong occupation of writing and rewriting of philosophy textbooks. Melanchthon began this with the teaching of moral philosophy and the publication of a revised edition of his dialectics manual.

In late August 1527, Melanchthon announced his intention to teach Aristotle's *Ethica Nicomachea*.[210] It is not known which book he then commented upon, if at all, but in 1532, he definitely began teaching the fifth book of the *Ethica*, as he announced:

> The poet depicted Astraea, exiled from towns and states [*Aratus Phaenomena*, lines 115–28], to have conversed with men of the least corrupt kind in the countryside. Nowadays one philosophizes almost only in schools. Therefore it is befitting for us to cherish and attend to her willingly. Therefore I shall explain the fifth book of the *Ethica*, so that the students may hear Justice addressing them in that book ... For these arguments are useful for civil behaviour as well as for preparing the mind to the teaching of law and many theological matters. This book should thus be retained and inculcated in the young.[211]

The exiled Astraea, the goddess of justice, represents the Silver Age when strife and impiety abounded.[212] The times were troubled enough in the late 1520s and the early 1530s to draw a parallel with this Silver Age, as Cranach increasingly came to depict, perhaps on the advice of Melanchthon (Fig. 5).[213] In such an age of discord, Melanchthon saw all the more the need to teach moral philosophy and civil justice. The book he began to teach for this purpose was the fifth book of the *Ethica* which deals with the ideal of civil justice and with human excellence as consisting in abiding by civil law. That the fifth book was the text which Melanchthon taught most fre-

decisive impact of the spiritualists on Melanchthon's theology is also pointed out in Engelland (1961), 62. See also Herrlinger (1879) and F. Hübner (1936).

210 See letter to Justus Jonas, 28 August 1527, *MBW* no. 580, *CR*, I, 888.

211 'Astraeam pulsam ex civitatibus et imperiis finxit poëta aliquamdiu in rure concionatam esse generi hominum adhuc minus corrupto. Nunc quidem propemodum tantum in scholis philosophatur. Ideo decet nos eam colere et libenter audire. Enarrabo igitur quintum Ethicorum, ut in eo libello concionantem iustitiam studiosi audiant ... Nam hae disputationes cum moribus prosunt, tum vero praeparant ingenia ad iuris doctrinam et plerasque Theologorum materias. Quare hic libellus retinendus est et inculcandus adolescentibus.' 'To the Students' (1532), *CR*, II, 579f.

212 For the classical origins of the idea of Golden/Silver Age, see Baldry (1952); for the renaissance reception of the myth of the Golden Age in general, see Levin (1969); for Astraea as a figure of justice for imperial monarchies in the sixteenth century, see Yates (1975).

213 Friedländer and Rosenberg (1978), 31.

quently from the *Ethica* signifies his specific interest in the issue of civil obedience.[214] The *Ethica* had been condemned by Luther for its false teaching on justification, but now Melanchthon found the necessity to use it, not for a theology of justification or of good works, but for teaching a moral philosophy of civil obedience.

In a manuscript entitled *Epitome ethices* dating from 1532, Melanchthon explained the nature of moral philosophy:

Philosophy is neither gospel nor any part of it, but it is a part of divine law. For it is the law of nature itself divinely written in men's minds, which is truly the law of God concerning those virtues which reason understands and which are necessary for civil life. For philosophy, properly speaking, is nothing other tha[n] the explanation of the law of nature. But I call philosophy not all of men's opinions but the sure perceptions and those which can be demonstrated.[215]

Moral philosophy is not Gospel but part of Divine Law, because it demonstrates precepts of civil life from the 'law of nature' (*lex naturae*), which is divinely bestowed on all human minds. In the Roman jurist tradition, the '*lex naturae*', often identified with the law divinely bestowed on all humans according to Romans 2. 15, served as the basis for, or was identified with, the '*ius gentium*', the law of the peoples.[216] Possibly through Reuchlin, Melanchthon adopted the idea of innate ideas which underlies the Roman jurist tradition.[217] Melanchthon elsewhere defined the 'law of nature' as 'a common judgement to which all men give the same consent'.[218] This law was not specific to Christians, and thus furnished the basis of the political philosophy of both Luther and Melanchthon.[219] Luther had argued

214 Melanchthon taught the *Ethica* in the years 1527, 1529, 1532, 1533, 1537, 1543, 1544, 1545 and 1546. Except for 1545 (Book One), all were on the fifth book. *Hartfelder*, 555–65.

215 *Epitome Ethices* (1532), translated by R. A. Keen in Melanchthon (1988), 204. My correction.

216 See Thomas (1976), 63–5 for the place of '*lex naturae*' in Roman Law. For a survey of definitions of the '*lex naturae*' in the works of medieval canonists and civilians, see Crowe (1977), 72–110. For the significance of Roman Law for the Reformers, see Strauss (1986), esp. 199–234. For the theological significance of the '*lex naturae*', see Arntz (1965). Cf. the nominalist origin of the idea of 'law of nature' as explanatory law of the workings of nature specifically, in Milton (1981).

217 Kisch (1967), 45–9, who sees Melanchthon's turn to Roman Law as prompted by the unrests of 1525.

218 'Loci communes' (1521) translated by L. J. Satre and revised by W. Pauck in Melanchthon (1969), 50.

219 For the centrality of '*lex naturae*' in Luther's political philosophy, see McNeill (1941) and for a detailed analysis of Melanchthon's interpretation of the '*lex naturae*', see Bauer (1951).

against the rioting peasants of 1525 that by taking up arms against civil authority they had defied the law of nature (not to mention Christian Law) which even the heathens recognize.[220] Melanchthon thus proved in his moral philosophy that activities which disturbed the peace of society had to be punished and that civil authorities had to be obeyed. In fact, for Melanchthon, ethics *was* political.[221] It was concerned to prove the precepts of civil life both public and private, to all human beings, irrespective of their faith. This is precisely why Melanchthon could legitimately use pagan philosophy.[222]

After the turbulence of the 1520s, just as Luther and Melanchthon turned to the 'godly' princes who governed the masses (because both Luther and Melanchthon regarded the majority of the masses as un-Christian) to lead the reform of the Church, so the 'law of nature' became central to a moral and political philosophy which proved the necessity for all people (irrespective of their faith) to obey civil authorities.

An intense interest in classical moral philosophy is often regarded as a hallmark of a sixteenth-century humanist, but it should be understood that Melanchthon's development of moral philosophy with specific interests in certain books of Aristotle's *Ethica* is a response to a specific issue of his times. Furthermore, Melanchthon's moral philosophy, as part of the Divine Law, always had to be understood in contrast with and alongside the Gospel. In 1532, the same year as we have the first concrete evidence that he taught the fifth book of the *Ethica*, Melanchthon wrote a poem about that book. In it he praised God the Creator who had fashioned absolutely everything with design. He had placed in man the law of nature about civil virtue which the *Ethica* teaches usefully. Christ, however, is necessary in order that the Word of God may live in man.[223]

220 See his 'Admonition to Peace: A Reply to the Twelve Articles of the Peasants in Swabia' (1525), *LW*, XLVI, 25, 27.

221 'Aristoteles hoc loco admonet hanc ipsam ethicen vere esse eam politicam seu practicam, quae principaliter privatos mores et publica officia regit.' *Enarratio libri I Ethicorum Aristotelis* (1546) *CR*, XVI, 285. Melanchthon's identification of ethics and politics is noted also in Wieland (1982a), 671.

222 Cf. Kraye (1988), 324.

223 'Non casu volucres atomi sine mente ruentes,
Hanc mundi formam progenuere novam.
Formatrix sed mens sapiens, bona, libera, casta
Omnia miranda condidit arte, Deus.
Utque homines essent divinae mentis imago,
Attribuit radios lucis habere suae,
Notitias, quales diurno in pectore lucent,

Dedicated though Melanchthon was to teaching civil obedience in moral philosophy, he was always at pains to point out that controlling external actions did not merit salvation.

Melanchthon also regarded demonstration as crucial for distinguishing true philosophy from mere opinions. As I argue elsewhere, the increasing emphasis on methodical skills and Aristotelian demonstration in Melanchthon's dialectical textbooks from 1528 onwards reflects his concern to teach the proper procedures of philosophy with which absolute certainty can be guaranteed for conclusions drawn.[224] Possibly following Cicero, Melanchthon gave three criteria for certain statements: innate knowledge (*principium*), experience and syllogistic conclusions.[225] In the *De dialectica libri quatuor* (1528), the following example is given as certain moral demonstration:

Actions which disturb the society of mankind are to be prohibited.
Thefts, freebooting and the like disturb the society of mankind.
Therefore thefts, freebooting and the like should be prohibited.

The major premise is a principle (*principium*). The minor premise has the evidence of experience and both are therefore most certain. And what the lawyers call the law of nature, or strictly speaking law of the peoples (*ius naturae aut gentium proprie*) is nothing unless it is knowledge of certain principles of behaviour and civil life.[226]

Addidit et legi congrua corda suae,
Eheu dissidium sed nostro crimine venit,
Utuntur flammis iam mala corda vagis.
Notitiae mansere tamen, legesque severae,
Recte factorum regula ut esse queant,
...
Ex his notitiis divinis haec quoque fluxit
Doctrina, est ista quae recitata libro.
In quo virtutum prodest simulachra videre,
Qualia mens hominis pingere docta potest.
Sed Sol iustitiae radios in pectora spargens,
Christus et adsimilans nos sibi luce sua.
Virtutem accendit meliorem, nescia mortis,
Quae vivit flatu non moriente Dei.
His igitur scriptis doctrinam adiungito Christi,
Ut vivens in te sit λόγος ipse Dei.' In *Ethica*, *CR*, x, 537f.

224 Kusukawa, '*Vinculum concordiae*', forthcoming. Cf. L. Jardine (1988) for humanist dialectics in general.

225 Engelland (1965), XXVIIIf.

226 'Facinora quae perturbant societatem generis humani, sunt prohibenda
Furta, Latrocinia, et similia perturbant societatem generis humani.
Ergo furta, Latrocinia, et similia sunt prohibenda.

Melanchthon thus proves with absolute certainty a precept of civil law which prohibits actions of disturbance. This, no doubt, reflects what Melanchthon regarded as a most pressing issue in the wake of his experiences in 1527 in Thuringia, namely the establishment of civil obedience.

Melanchthon further stressed the necessity to master methodical procedure in his dialectics. The methodical procedure was essentially rhetorical in that it was primarily concerned with finding the proper *locus* of argument by using questioning procedures found in Aristotle's *Topica* and *Posteriora analytica*.[227] For Melanchthon, the main aim of dialectics had been to teach the skills of epideictic oratory, or the *genus demonstrativa*.[228] Aristotle had classified oratory according to the attitude of the listener: the deliberative kind of speech urges the listener to make decisions about future events; the forensic kind defends or accuses somebody as in legal cases in order to urge the listener (often judges) to make a decision on past acts; the epideictic kind praises or censures somebody, and presents a case to listeners as if they were spectators.[229] Melanchthon's aim was not, however, to produce orations of 'praise or blame', but to *teach* succinctly.[230] Perhaps following Wimpfeling, Melanchthon saw the style of epideictic oration as particularly fit for inculcating moral lessons because it moved the audience to virtuous living, as if watching a drama.[231] It is this epideictic style that was powerfully put into service by Melanchthon for his subsequent promotion of studies.

Melanchthon's insistence on teaching 'method' in order to achieve certainty in his dialectical manuals earned him the title of the '*artifex methodi*',[232] and the series of his lectures and publications on moral

Maior est principium. Minor testem habet experientiam, utraque igitur certissima est, Et quod Iurisconsulti vocant Ius naturae aut gentium proprie nihil est, nisi principiorum quorundam de moribus de civili vita, noticia.'

De dialectica libri quatuor (Wittenberg: J. Klug, 1531), L6r–v.

227 For an examination of Melanchthon's concept of '*loci communes*', see further Joachimsen (1926) and Breen (1947).

228 To make the *genus demonstrativa* as the formal link between dialectic and rhetoric is regarded as original with Melanchthon, Schneider (1990), 71.

229 Aristotle, *Rhetorica*, I. 3, 9.

230 Cf. Cicero, who rather pejoratively speaks of epideictic oration as 'display' fit for the sophists at gymnasiums, see Cicero, *Orator*, XIII, 37–42. For a survey of classical theories on epideictic oratory, Burgess (1902) is still useful. For the revival of epideictic oratory in renaissance Papal courts as a style particularly apposite to praise the Papacy and its theology, see J. W. O'Malley (1979).

231 Schneider (1990), 37.

232 Gilbert (1960), 125.

philosophy in turn earned him the name of the 'Ethician of the Reformation.'[233] The two titles complement each other. His teaching was a product of his determination to counter unrest and civil disobedience. In early 1521, Melanchthon had stressed the limits of classical philosophy with respect to the Gospel – that it was not effective for salvation. Then, it was important to establish the true message of the Gospel. From 1527 on, Melanchthon began to stress the positive role of classical philosophy for divine Law. Turbulent events of the 1520s had brought out the pressing need to counter civil disobedience.

When Melanchthon knew he was no Luther, he returned to teaching Greek and the classics. When Melanchthon encountered the Anabaptists in Thuringia, he turned to classical philosophy. It was dialectics and moral philosophy that Melanchthon first developed in response to the civil disobedience of the Anabaptists. Melanchthon's moral philosophy acquired the status of Divine Law through the 'law of nature' and demonstration, and as Divine Law, it was always to be contrasted with and placed alongside the Gospel. The difference of vocation between Luther and Melanchthon may be understood as a difference of choice between Law and Gospel. In their university reforms, Luther, the theologian, sought to establish the Gospel, Melanchthon, the Greek teacher, the Law: Luther attacked and endeavoured to eliminate traditional philosophy, including natural philosophy, because it obstructed the true message of the Gospel; Melanchthon restored the teaching of classical moral philosophy as part of the Divine Law. And, as I shall argue in the next two chapters, within this same concern to establish knowledge of 'Law', Melanchthon began to develop a new kind of natural philosophy, using classical as well as contemporary philosophy.

233 Keen (1988), 23.

CHAPTER 3

The soul

Wherefore the law was our schoolmaster to bring us unto Christ, that we might be justified by faith.

Galatians 3. 24

From the late 1520s, another dimension developed in the task of defending Luther's cause. The doctrinal rift with the Zwinglians and the continuing threat of civil disobedience showed up the necessity to clarify and delineate Luther's cause ever more sharply. As Melanchthon grappled with these problems, he continued his educational reforms at Wittenberg. He also began working on natural philosophy from the early 1530s. In this chapter I shall discuss Melanchthon's first natural philosophy textbook, the *Commentarius de anima*, which closely reflected the issues of his time.

DEFENDING LUTHER'S CAUSE

In the autumn of 1529 a conference was held at Marburg to resolve doctrinal differences among the Evangelicals concerning the Lord's Supper. This conference was called by Philip of Hesse whose ambition was to form a political alliance among the Evangelical Swiss, the southern German cities and upper Germany, and thus challenge the house of Habsburg. Doctrinal differences between Zwingli and Luther had to be resolved in order to clear the way for such an Evangelical political alliance.[1] Zwingli and Oecolampadius attended from Zurich; Jacob Sturm, Caspar Hedio, Martin Bucer from Strasburg; Luther, Melanchthon and Justus Jonas from Wittenberg; and several others such as Myconius, Cruciger and Osiander convened at Marburg.[2] The conference took place but no agreement was reached on the interpretation of the Lord's Supper.

[1] Potter (1976), 378–84. [2] Potter (1976), 323.

Luther adhered to the real presence of the body and blood of Christ while Zwingli advocated a 'commemorative' interpretation of the Eucharist.

Perhaps owing to his own experience of suffering and surviving pestilence in 1519, Zwingli had a strong sense of God's overwhelming power over all creatures, including the physical body.[3] Every single action of man was due to God's doing and thus foreknown to Him. The Holy Spirit effects faith but it does not depend on the external Word to do so. This is because the saving grace of God is already predestined for the elect. In order to establish the true sovereignty and Providence of God, Zwingli rejected the Catholic interpretation of sacraments in which man's own works could merit grace. John 6.63: 'It is the spirit that gives life, the flesh is of no avail' became the key text for Zwingli's understanding of the Lord's Supper. For Zwingli, 'flesh' denoted Christ's physical body, and it was in Christ *as God* and not as man that the saving faith existed and thus the bodily presence of Christ cannot of itself produce faith. Following Erasmus, Zwingli thus drew a sharp distinction between the soul and body.[4] By the time of the Marburg Colloquy, Zwingli had already reached the conclusion that 'This is my body' meant 'This signifies my body.' The Eucharist signified that Christ had died and His body was given for us. The Lord's Supper, Zwingli thus argued, was an act of thanksgiving for the death of Christ.

For Luther, in contrast, the divinity and humanity of Christ were inseparable. Forgiveness of sin could only be understood through the understanding that the promises of the Old Testament were really fulfilled in the historical Jesus of Nazareth, when the Word was made 'flesh', as the New Testament bears witness. It was precisely in Christ who died on the cross *as man* that Luther saw the divinity of God.[5] This Christ as the incarnate Word of God was central to Luther's theology, and the meaning of sacrament was redefined accordingly. For Luther, a sacrament meant a sign of the promise of the forgiveness of sin.[6] The words 'This is my body' were necessary in the Lord's Supper precisely in order to effect the sign of

[3] For Zwingli's theology, I have followed the excellent study by Stephens (1986).

[4] For Zwingli as an Erasmian-humanist, see Gestrich (1967), 25–7 and Bosshard (1978), 13–15.

[5] 'That These Words of Christ, "This is My Body," etc., Still Stand Firm Against the Fanatics' (1527), *LW*, XXXVII, 72.

[6] Althaus (1970), 345–52.

the promise of the forgiveness of sins.[7] As forgiveness of sin can only be gained through trust in Christ as the incarnate Word of God, Christ is necessarily and really present in the Eucharist. Thus Luther's own words bring into stark contrast his difference with Zwingli's interpretation of the Lord's Supper:

> Our fanatics, however, are full of fraud and humbug. They think nothing spiritual can be present where there is anything material and physical, and assert that the flesh is of no avail. Actually the opposite is true. The Spirit cannot be with us except in material and physical things such as the Word, water, and Christ's body and in his saints on earth.[8]

For Luther, it was in the physical things, things which Zwingli would discount precisely on grounds of their 'creatureliness', that spirituality existed.

The controversy was not simply over the interpretation of the Lord's Supper but it was also about what God, the Holy Spirit and Christ meant and how they were related to each other. Whilst Zwingli would stress God's absolute sovereignty over this world, Luther would stress the divinity as revealed through physical things. By the time of the Marburg Colloquy, both Zwingli and Luther had each developed their own theology. The Colloquy was in fact a confrontation of different understandings of matter and spirituality, arising from different sets of beliefs, and in this sense Luther and Zwingli were arguing 'at cross purposes'.[9] The Marburg Colloquy, therefore, ended without achieving what it was called for.

Although several questions still need to be answered about Melanchthon's precise interpretation of the Lord's Supper,[10] he seems to have tried, in one way or another, to adhere to the real presence of Christ until the very end of his life.[11] On the issue of the Eucharist, however, Melanchthon preferred to refrain from taking a

7 'Against the Heavenly Prophets in the Matter of Images and Sacraments' (1525), *LW*, XL, 212f. and *WA*, XX, 478.

8 *LW*, XXXVII, 95.

9 See the perceptive summary in Stephens (1986), 178f. For an interpretation of the difference between Luther and Zwingli according to their debt to the *via moderna* and the *via antiqua* respectively, see Oberman (1987b). Their difference extends also to outward forms of worship: see the issue of iconoclasm in Eire (1986), 65–88.

10 For the historical questions posed from a non-confessional point of view, see Fraenkel (1961b).

11 See Melanchthon (1988), 132. For an attempt to systematize Melanchthon's view of the real presence of Christ, see Quere (1977). Cf. Neuser (1968).

polemical stance like Luther because he believed that disagreement was the worst enemy of truth.[12]

For Melanchthon, there was another issue which had to be tackled head on, refuted and treated with the utmost severity. Four months after the Marburg Colloquy, Melanchthon wrote to Myconius on the necessity of the death penalty for the Anabaptists, recounting his own experience:

At the beginning, when I first came to know Storch and his faction, from whom the whole lot of the Anabaptists arose, I was stupidly lenient. Others too thought that heretics should not be put down by the sword. And then Prince Frederick [the Wise] became extremely angry with Storch and unless he had been protected by us, he would have received the [death] penalty as an insane and excessively malicious man. I am in no little way sorry for my leniency. What troubles and which heresies did he not arouse after that? So you should understand that just as in the story a whole race of armed men were born from the teeth of the dragon, so from one Storch all those factions of Anabaptists and Zwinglians arose. Therefore you should understand that the magistrates ought to exercise the utmost severity in checking spirits of this kind. You see how despised the authority of the magistrates is, how secure the evil ones are, because they see that there is so much leniency or rather complaisance in government.[13]

For Melanchthon there is not much difference between the Anabaptists and the Zwinglians since both camps advocate civil disobedience.[14] What is noteworthy is Melanchthon's strong sense of guilt concerning the disturbances caused by them all. By identifying Storch, the leader of the Zwickau Prophets, as the sole cause of all the current disorder created by the Anabaptists and by the Zwinglians, Melanchthon takes his own lenient attitude in the Wittenberg Movement as having been directly responsible for the troubles

[12] See Melanchthon's letter to Oecolampadius, 8 April 1529, as translated by R. A. Keen in Melanchthon (1988), 128f.

[13] 'Ego ab initio, cum primum coepi nosse Ciconiam et Ciconiae factionem, unde hoc totum genus Anabaptistarum exortum est, fui stulte clemens. Sentiebant enim et alii, haereticos non esse ferro opprimendos. Et tunc Dux Fredericus vehementer iratus erat Ciconiae: ac nisi a nobis tectus esset, fuisset de homine furioso et perdite malo sumptum supplicium. Nunc me eius clementiae non parum poenitet. Quos ille tumultus, quas haereses postea non excitavit? Sic enim sentire debes: ut ex dentibus serpentis in fabula natam esse gentem armatam ferunt; ita ab uno Ciconia ortae sunt omnes istae factiones Anabaptistarum et Zinglianorum. Quare ita sentias, magistratum debere uti summa severitate in coercendis huiusmodi spiritibus. Vides quam contempta sit auctoritas magistratuum; quam sint securi improbi, quia lenitatem vel potius indulgentiam in imperio tantam esse vident.' Letter to Friedrich Myconius, February 1530, *MBW* no. 868, *CR*, II, 17.

[14] For Zwingli's theology in relation to the state, see Stephens (1986), 262–309, esp. 302f. for justification of civil disobedience.

up to 1530. I have described in the previous chapter how deep an impression the Anabaptists made on Melanchthon during the summer of 1527. Ever since then, Melanchthon was actively engaged in advocating the death penalty for the Anabaptists. Civil disobedience was what Melancthon felt very strongly against and actively engaged himself in refuting.[15] And it is in the light of this problem of civil disobedience that Melanchthon confronted the deviations of the Zwinglians.

In 1530 Melanchthon attended the Diet of Augsburg in order to defend the causes of Luther and of the evangelical princes in front of the Emperor. By then, the Roman Catholics had launched a new attack, identifying Luther's claims with those of the Anabaptists and the Zwinglians. Johannes Eck, one of Luther's oldest foes, had pre-empted the opportunity for a fair hearing for Luther by publishing a pamphlet listing 404 errant articles which Luther was alleged to have instigated.[16] The articles were taken from the writings not only of Luther, Melanchthon and Jonas, but also of Carlstadt, Müntzer, Zwingli, Oecolampadius and the Anabaptists. Eck firmly laid the blame for all these views at Luther's door. This meant that Luther was made responsible, for instance, for the following views:

403. It is proper and genuine by the Word of God to arouse seditions and troubles. Here I do not have a stronger proof that my teaching is from God, than that it encourages discord, dissensions and troubles. Luther. Hence many of them have often publicly testified to the common people that the Gospel calls for blood. Zwingli and others.[17]

In the wake of the attack of the 404 articles, it became necessary that a defence of Luther's teachings should articulate clearly his differences with other evangelicals, as well as his disagreement with the Roman Catholics. The result was the 'Augsburg Confession', a comprehensive statement of Luther's teachings.[18] In it Melanchthon included the following article:

[15] Skinner (1978), II, 65–71.

[16] Johannes Eck, *Articulos 404 partim ad disputationes ..., partim vero ex scriptis pacem ecclesiae perturbantium extractos, Coram divo Caesare Carolo V etc.* (Ingolstadt: G. and P. Apianus, 1530), Diiiir. For background and reactions to the 404 articles, see Manschreck (1958), 177–80.

[17] '303 [misnumbered, = 403] Proprium et genuinum est verbo dei, seditiones et tumultus excitare: hinc non habeo fortiorem probationem, doctrinam meam esse a deo, nisi quia suscitat discordias dissensiones et tumultus. Lutther. Vnde multi eorum saepe publice testati sunt ad plebem. Evangelium velit habere sanguinem. Zuinglius et alii.' Johannes Eck, *Articulos 404 partim ad disputationes ...*, Diiiv.

[18] For a theological analysis of the Augsburg Confession, see Maurer (1976–8), *passim*, esp. 17–27 for the background.

Of civil affairs they teach that legitimate civil ordinations are good works of God, that it is possible for Christians to carry on magistracy, to exercise legal justice, to judge matters from royal and other principal laws, to constitute petition of the law, to contest the law, to fight, dispute with the law, to hold property, to swear oaths before magistrates who ask for it, to take a wife, to be married.

They condemn Anabaptists, who forbid Chrsitians those civil duties. And they condemn those who do not think that evangelical perfection consists in the fear and faith of God, but rather in abandoning civil responsibilities since the gospel gives eternal justice to the heart. Meanwhile it does not diminish the government or economy, but seeks chiefly to preserve as much as possible the ordinations of God, and to exercise charity in such ordinances. And so Christians ought necessarily to obey their magistrates and laws, unless they command them to sin; and then they must obey God more than men.[19]

At a time when the need to defend Luther's position in dissociation from the evangelical radicals was growing, an important point of departure was thus the issue of civil obedience.

Melanchthon's concern to dissociate Luther's cause from the claims of the evangelical radicals was directly reflected in his writings on education. In an oration *De ordine discendi* delivered on 31 January 1531,[20] Melanchthon defended the necessity of both arts and religious studies and called on the magistrates to maintain such learning through their divinely appointed offices.[21] He promptly reminded the listeners what neglect of such studies might amount to:

We have also seen during these years several mad men theologizing profanely with fanatical opinions in this way pay the penalty for their error. For you remember Müntzer and the Anabaptists, and that breed and other monstrosities. In this way, judge as mad those who upset the chorus and concord of the arts having neglected and despised the lower arts (*inferioribus artibus*).[22]

He further points out that there were many theologians, lawyers and medics who lacked training in grammar, dialectic, rhetoric or the 'first elements of natural philosophy and moral philosophy' (*incuna-*

[19] 'The Augsburg Confession' (1530), as translated by R. A. Keen in Melanchthon (1988), 104.

[20] Delivered by Caspar Cruciger, *CR*, XI, 209–14; the date can be verified from Köstlin (1888), 20.

[21] *CR*, XI, 210, 213f.

[22] 'Et vidimus his annis quosdam ἀνοσίως θεολογοῦντας dementatos huiusmodi fanaticis opinionibus, erroris sui poenas dare. Meministis enim Monetarium et Anabaptistas, et hoc genus alia portenta. Ad hunc modum iudicate insanire eos, qui chorum et concentum artium perturbant, neglectis et contemptis inferioribus artibus.' *CR*, XI, 212.

bulis philosophiae naturalis ac moralis).[23] Here natural philosophy is part of a proper arts education. It is not clear, however, what exactly Melanchthon meant by an elementary kind of natural philosophy. He does, however, praise in the same oration how the second book of Pliny's *Historia naturalis* was taught well at Wittenberg.[24] In view of the role the second book of Pliny's *Historia naturalis* later played as an introductory textbook of natural philosophy, it may well have been intended as such already by this date,[25] but I have been unable to confirm this conjecture.

Melanchthon's defence of study in the arts faculty and of philosophy in particular became more pronounced with subsequent threats from the radical movement. Between 1534 and 1535, the city of Münster was taken over by Anabaptists who tried to live the 'New Jerusalem' under the rule of Jan Bockelson, alias John of Leyden (d. 1536).[26] An erstwhile friend of Melanchthon, Bernhard Rothmann (*c.* 1495–*c.* 1535), who initially worked in Münster to spread Luther's message, was converted to Anabaptism and became one of its ablest spokesmen.[27] Further, Melanchthon himself was directly involved in interrogating Anabaptists late in 1535 and early 1536.[28] With such fresh and bitter memories of Anabaptism, Melanchthon wrote and delivered on 27 April 1536 an oration entitled '*De philosophia*'.[29] In it he strongly promoted the study of philosophy against 'unlearned theology' which he defined as 'a confused teaching in which great things are not explained clearly, things which should be separated are mixed up, those which nature requires to be united are torn apart'.[30] Once again, the Anabaptists come up as an example of 'unlearned' men:

23 'Subito sicut fungi nascuntur nobis Theologi, Iurisconsulti et Medici, sine Grammatica, sine Dialectica, sine ratione dicendi, sine incunabulis Philosophiae naturalis ac moralis.' *Ibid.*

24 'Summa fide traduntur artes, quae continent rationem dicendi: elementa Philosophiae et Mathematum planissime proponuntur. In qua schola secundus liber Plinii tam perspicue enarratus est, ut hic enarratur?', *CR*, XI, 213.

25 See pp. 136f.

26 For this movement in Münster, see G. H. Williams (1962a), 362–86.

27 See Melanchthon's letter to Rothmann, 24 December 1532, *MBW* no. 1294, *CR*, II, 619f. For a brief biographical sketch of Rothman, see Bakker (1982).

28 Oyer (1964), 160f.

29 Delivered on the occasion of promoting the masters of arts under the deanship of Jacob Milich, *De philosophia* (1536), *CR*, XI, 278 and therefore the date can be verified from Köstlin (1888), 22.

30 'Primum enim omnino ilias malorum est inerudita Theologia. Est enim confusanea doctrina, in qua magnae res non explicantur diserte, miscentur ea quae oportebat seiungi, rursus illa quae natura coniungi postulat, distrahuntur ...' *De philosophia* (1536), *CR*, XI, 280.

And I call unlearned not only those who are ignorant of letters, as are the Anabaptists, but also those inept men who, although they may declaim magnificently, say nothing of the truth, both because they are not accustomed to method and also because they do not understand the sources of things (*fontes rerum*) sufficiently. Moreover, because they were not educated in philosophy, they understand sufficiently neither what theology should teach, nor how far it agrees with philosophy.[31]

In this oration, it is the study of philosophy in particular that Melanchthon promotes as an antidote to such unlearnedness:

In order to judge and explain intricate and obscure matters correctly and clearly, it is not sufficient to have known the common precepts of grammar and of dialectic, but a manifold erudition is necessary; indeed many things should be taken up from natural philosophy (*ex Physicis*), and many things from moral philosophy should be directed to Christian doctrine.[32]

Melanchthon then goes on further to explain how natural philosophy might help a theologian:

The theologian who does not know those most erudite discussions on the soul, on the senses, on the causes of volition and affections, on knowledge and on the will, lacks a great instrument. He who teaches dialectics will be behaving insolently if he does not know those divisions of causes which are taught only in natural philosophy (*in Physicis*) and cannot be understood except from natural philosophy (*a Physicis*).[33]

In the light of Melanchthon's earlier criticism of Aristotelian natural philosophy which was voiced in unison with Luther, this is a remarkable statement. The soul, the senses, appetites, affections, knowledge and the will are all topics which had traditionally been treated in the universities in reading Aristotle's *De anima* and the

[31] 'Et indoctos voco non solum rudes literarum, ut sunt Anabaptistae, sed etiam illos ineptos, qui cum magnifice declamitent, tamen certi nihil dicunt, et quia ad methodum non sunt assuefacti, et qui fontes rerum non satis tenent, propterea quia cum in Philosophia non sint instituti, non satis videant aut quid Theologica profiteatur, aut quatenus cum Philosophia consentiat.' *CR*, XI, 282.

[32] 'Nam ad iudicandum, et ad recte et dilucide explicandas res intricatas et obscuras, non satis est nosse haec vulgaria percepta Grammatices et Dialectices, sed opus est multiplici doctrina; multa enim assumenda sunt ex Physicis, multa ex Philosophia morali conferenda sunt ad doctrinam Christianam.' *CR*, XI, 280.

[33] 'Magno instrumento destitutus est Theologus, qui nescit illas eruditissimas disputationes, de anima, de sensibus, de causis appetitionum et affectuum, de noticia, de voluntate. Et arroganter faciet, qui se profitetur Dialecticum, si nescit illas causarum partitiones, quae traduntur tantum in Physicis, et intelligi non possunt nisi a Physicis.' *CR*, XI, 281.

ensuing *Parva naturalia*.[34] As was the case with Aristotle's moral philosophy, Melanchthon did not, however, mean the kind of reading the medieval theologians taught in order to support their own theology. Melanchthon's reading of the *De anima* was quite different.

From 1533 Melanchthon had indeed begun working on the topic of 'the soul'. On 8 November 1533, Melanchthon asked Johannes Naevius (1499–1574) for assistance with the topic 'on the soul' since the usual Aristotelian teaching was 'meagre, inept and useless for teaching'.[35] In addition, Melanchthon showed a keen interest in Galen.[36] A month later, Melanchthon informed Camerarius that Jacob Milich (1501–59), a lecturer at Wittenberg, was helping him with his '*physice*'. He further solicited Camerarius' advice on Galen's passages on the human body.[37] Work seems to have progressed steadily into the next year.[38] By April 1534, Melanchthon was satisfied with his revision of Aristotle, as he wrote to Leonhard Fuchs (1501–54) on 30 April 1534:

> You know that in the schools natural philosophy (*Physica*) which is called Aristotelian or Tartaretic or the like, is crammed with cold and stupid discussions. Therefore here we have begun to write a natural philosophy (*Physicam*) and we have finished some part of the work ... When we reach the nature of man and of the soul, I especially wish to include anatomy (ἀνατομίαν), natures of the parts, varieties of the temperaments, namely of

34 The requirement for the *De anima* to be heard by (usually) BA candidates can be found in virtually every university's statutes. See for instance, Thorndike (1975), 54, 65, 246, 279, 347, 353.

35 'Plurimum a vobis adiuvari possum in physicis adornandis. Vides enim illa Aristotelica, quae vulgo in scholis traduntur, nimis exilia et ieiuna esse.' Letter to Johann Naevius, 8 November 1533, *MBW* no. 1508, *CR*, IV, 1021. Cf. *MBW* no. 524 (January 1527).

36 *CR*, IV, 1021f.

37 'Venio ad Philosophiam nostram, Physicen adornamus, quam edet Milichius, habet illas communes disputationes, quae in scholis tradi solebant, sed elegimus elegantiores atque utiliores. Atque omnino do operam, ut plurimum habeat illecebrarum: cupio enim, ut scis, excutere veternum nostris hominibus, quibus possum modis: inserui suavissimas disputationes et dignas homine Philosopho. Cum autem in Galeno verseris, quo nos quoque utimur, te rogo, ut nobis impertias, si quos locos invenies, quos arbitrabere nobis profuturos, de Temperamentis, deque aliis, quae Physici magis quam Medici quaerunt. Cupimus inserere partes humani corporis, quas si collegisti, quaeso ut nobis communices.' Letter to Camerarius, 7 December 1533, *MBW* no.1384, *CR*, II, 687 (dated 5 December).

38 'Galeno valde delector. Tu quoque velim cum incides in locos venustos περὶ κράσεων, aut de humoribus, mihi eos indices.' Letter to Camerarius on 24 January 1534, *MBW* no. 1400, *CR*, II, 700 (dated 27 January); 'Itaque scribimus iam φυσικὴν, quae non solum illas usitatas scholarum praeceptiunculas contineat, sed sit referta eruditissimis disputationibus, sumptis cum ex Galeno, tum ex aliis litteris, quae et ad multas vitae partes prosunt, et bene institutis ingeniis pariunt voluptates suavissimas.' Letter to Arnold Burenius, 1 February 1534, *MBW* no. 1403, *CR*, II, 702.

mixtures, causes and species of human beings, none of which gets mentioned in common natural philosophy (*in vulgaribus Physicis*). Here your work would be very useful for us, if you would either publish it yourself or send us [the passages] concerning these [above] topics which will seem much worthy of knowing. For the booklet of Alexander Benedictus [*Anatomice, sive de historia corporis humani libri quinque*] is very slender and childish. I desire a well-founded work (*iustum opus*) to be constructed from the anatomical writings of Galen, by employing the nomenclature commonly used today ...[39]

Clearly Melanchthon was dissatisfied with the traditional treatment of Aristotle's *De anima*, and thus had been working on it himself, incorporating Galenic anatomy.

A year later in 1535, Melanchthon reported to Camerarius that he was having difficulty with the part entitled the *De anima* 'in which the whole nature of man is to be explained as much as we can'.[40] Five months later, however, he was enjoying working on the part on human anatomy.[41] Then other pressing political issues seem to have kept him from working on the topic for some time.[42]

In 1538 Melanchthon categorically expressed the importance of Galen.[43] It was not only for his medicine, but also for his *natural philosophy* (*physice*) that Galen ought to be cherished.[44] Melanchthon elaborated on Galen's importance in the following way:

[39] 'Scis in scholis Physica, quae sic vocantur 'Αριστοτέλεια vel potius Tartaretica aut similia, frigidis ac insulsis disputationibus referta esse. Nos igitur hic Physicam scribere instituimus, ac iam partem aliquam operis absolvimus ...Nunc cum ad hominis et animae naturam accedimus, magnopere cupio inserere ἀνατομίαν, et partium naturas, varietates temperamentorum, id est, κράσεων, humanarum causas et species, quarum rerum nulla fit mentio in vulgaribus Physicis. Hic tua nobis opera plurimum prodesse poterit, si vel edas ipse, vel nobis mittas de his locis ea, quae maxime videbuntur digna cognitione. Nam Alexandri Benedicti pertenuis et puerilis libellus est. Vellem ex anatomicis Galeni confici iustum opus, adhibitis etiam usitatis hoc tempore nomenclaturis ...' Letter to Leonhard Fuchs, 30 April 1534, *MBW* no. 1430, *CR*, II, 718f. Alexander Benedictus' *Anatomice* (Paris: H. Stephanus, 1514) was in the collection of the University Library of Wittenberg, see Kusukawa, forthcoming.

[40] 'Quaestiones habeo multas *Physicas*, de quibus utinam tecum et cum Medicis vestris confabulari liceret. Perveni enim iam ad eam partem, quae inscribitur de anima, in qua tota hominis natura nobis, quantum quidem possumus, exponenda sunt.' Letter to Camerarius on 24 January 1534, *MBW* no. 1400, *CR*, II, 878 (dated 27 January).

[41] 'Nostra φυσικὰ etiam satis pulchre procedunt, nunc etiam pervenimus ad Anatomen corporis humanis.' Letter to Camerarius, 3 October 1535, *MBW* no. 1638, *CR*, II, 951.

[42] 13 July 1537, *MBW* no. 1919, *CR*, III, 388.

[43] There does not seem to be a copy of Galen's Greek *Opera omnia* (1538 Basle edition) which contains this preface, despite Bretschneider's suggestion (*CR*, II, 489f.). See Nutton (1990), 156 note 57. The earliest sixteenth-century printing of this preface known to me is in Melanchthon's *Liber selectarum declamationum* (Strasburg: C. Mylius, 1541), 698–705, with the title 'Praefatio in Galenum', without date.

[44] 'Iam Galenus non modo propter *medicinam*, sed etiam propter pulcherrimam philosophiae partem, quae *Physice* dicitur, summorum Principum diligentia generi humano conservan-

For there is no author more fruitful on this part of philosophy which we call natural philosophy (*physicen*) than Galen, who covered the whole natural philosophy (*universam physicen*) most eruditely in the discussions in which he sought demonstrations about the powers in living beings, about the causes of generations, about temperaments, about organs of the senses, about the causes of actions in the senses, about the causes of illness and their remedies, about the resemblance of qualities and about the 'sympathy' of very many things in nature. No one except Galen alone discussed these matters. And so the natural philosophy (*physica*) begun by Aristotle was completed by Galen alone ... With great prudence and with a great mind he rejects attacks and word-battles, loves nothing confused or sophistical, but he seeks the simple truth everywhere and reveals it clearly, which is a great indication of the best mind and of a nature loving justice and truth. Just as that wisest Tragedian has said, 'What is noble is always clear' [Euripides, *Orestes* 397].[45]

Melanchthon revered Galen not only for perfecting Aristotle's natural philosophy but also for his clarity of style in defending the simple truth. Melanchthon thus yearns for a 'reborn Galen', because he will be useful for students for the study of truth and conducts. In fact Galen played a very important role indeed in Melanchthon's work on the soul, which began to be printed in June 1539 and was ready at the beginning of 1540 as the *Commentarius de anima*.[46]

THE *COMMENTARIUS DE ANIMA*

When Melanchthon's *Commentarius de anima* was first published in 1540, Erasmus Flock, a lecturer at Wittenberg, immediately began

dus est.' Preface to Francis I, 13 February 1538, *MBW* no. 1996, *CR*, III, 494f., my emphasis. See also Bylebyl (1990) for an analysis of the medical meaning of term '*physica*' in the twelfth and thirteenth centuries. Cf. Hooykaas (1980).

45 'Nullus enim extat autor uberior eius partis philosophiae, quam Physicen vocamus, quam Galenus, qui universam Physicen eruditissime complexus est in his disputationibus, in quibus quaerit demonstrationes de potentiis in animantibus, de generationum causis, de temperamentis, de sensuum organis, de causis actionum in sensibus, de morborum et remediorum causis, de qualitatum cognatione, de συμπαθεία, plurimarum rerum in natura. Haec praeter unum Galenum nemo disputat. Itaque inchoata ab Aristotele Physica, ab uno Galeno absoluta sunt ... Magna prudentia et magno animo cavillationes ac λογομαχίας repudiat, nihil perplexum aut sophisticum amat, sed ubique simplicem veritatem inquirit, et perspicue patefacit, quod magnum indicium est optimae mentis, et naturae amantis iustitiam et veritatem. Sicut ille prudentissimus Tragicus inquit: τὸ ἐσθλόν, σαφὲς ἀεί.' Preface to Francis I, 13 February 1538, *MBW* no. 1996, *CR*, III, 493f.

46 Letters to Camerarius, 25 June 1539, *MBW* no. 2232, *CR*, III, 727 (dated 26 June); to Camerarius, on 31 August 1539, *MBW* no. 2263, *CR*, III, 765; to Vitus Theodorus, 1 January 1540, *MBW* no. 2337, *CR*, III, 895.

to use it in his lectures.[47] It became one of the most frequently printed commentaries on the *De anima* in the sixteenth century, with fifteen printings during the next twenty years.[48]

In the prefatory letter to the *Commentarius de anima*, Melanchthon repeated his conviction that erudition is necessary to restore order and discipline in society and in the Church.[49] Despite its scholastic title, Melanchthon considered his commentary as necessary for explaining religion because it contained 'erudite' distinctions of the powers of the soul.[50] He has also explained matters that have been passed over by others.[51] Melanchthon acknowledges the help of Jacob Milich and awaits constructive criticism from Joachim Camerarius, both of whom we have already met as his close collaborators on this topic.[52] Furthermore, students would benefit by supplementing his incomplete 'hotch-potch' with the works of Juan Luis Vives, Johannes Bernhardi Velcurio and Jodocus Trutfetter.[53] Melanchthon concedes that he has retained several traditional statements on the topic, but he makes one point quite explicit: whenever the teaching of Aristotle and of the Church disagree, he has diverged from Aristotle.[54]

A Christian reading of Aristotle's *De anima* was not an anomaly. From the early Church Fathers such as Lactantius and Gregory of Nyssa,[55] theologians have interpreted Greek philosophy from a Christian perspective. It is true that Pietro Pomponazzi (1462–1525) had read Aristotle's *De anima* as philosophy separated from

[47] 'Decrevi igitur enarrare librum de anima hic editum, ac polliceor auditoribus diligentiam et fidem.' Erasmus Flock (1540), *Scriptorum publice propositorum a professoribus in Academia Witebergensi ab anno 1540 usque ad 1553*, Tomus primus (Wittenberg: G. Rhaw, 1560), B8r.

[48] *Lohr*, 256. For an overall survey of sixteenth-century commentaries of the *De anima*, see *Bibliographie der psychologischen Literatur des 16. Jahrhunderts*.

[49] *Commentarius de anima* (Wittenberg: P. Seitz, 1540), α2v.

[50] *Commentarius de anima*, α3v.

[51] *Commentarius de anima*, α5r. [52] *Commentarius de anima*, α5r, v.

[53] Cf. Vives, *De anima et vita* (Basle, 1538); Trutfetter, *Quam Iudocus Eysennaien tocius philosophie naturalis summam nuper elucubravit* ... (Erfurt, 1517); Velcurio, *Epitome physicae libri quatuor* (Basle, 1537). A modern study on Trutfetter's thought is yet to be undertaken; for Vives' thought, see Noreña (1970), esp. 228–74; for Velcurio, see pp. 109–13 below.

[54] 'Cunque nobis in Ecclesia quaedam paulo aliter dicenda sint, quam dicuntur ab Aristotele, peto mihi veniam dari, si interdum ab Aristotelica phrasi discessi.' *Commentarius de anima*, α5v.

[55] Gregory of Nyssa is mentioned in the *Commentarius de anima*, α4r. Melanchthon was probably referring to the *De natura hominis* of Nemesius of Emesa which circulated during the Middle Ages under the name of Gregory of Nyssa, see Wicher (1986), 39–68. See Temkin (1973), 81–92 for Nemesius' appropriation of Galen. For Gregory of Nyssa's philosophy on the soul, see Cavarnos (1976) and Ladner (1958).

theology,[56] and thus concluded that, philosophically speaking, man's soul is mortal. Yet it was still usual to read the *De anima* within a Christian framework.[57] Melanchthon, then, was reading the *De anima* in the way that many others before him had done, namely reading Aristotle for Christian purposes. The result of his reading, the *Commentarius de anima*, was, however, quite different from the commentaries of his predecessors.

At the outset of the *Commentarius de anima*, Melanchthon redefines the subject matter of his commentary: it is to be about the faculties (*potentiae*) and powers (*vires*) of the human soul and body, namely 'the whole nature of man'.[58] This is quite different from what Aristotle originally intended in his own *De anima*. Aristotle was investigating the nature of the soul as 'the first principle of *animated being*'.[59] Aristotle sought a principle common to the whole genus of 'animated beings', whilst Melanchthon's focus is on human beings.[60] It is the knowledge of man's soul, Melanchthon claims, which provides the basis of understanding the soul as a general principle for all living beings. For Aristotle, in contrast, whose starting point of the investigation of the soul is an examination of the concept according to his logical categories,[61] it would be simply impossible to

56 For Pomponazzi, see Pine (1986).

57 Lohr (1988b). See also Gentian Hervert's reaction to those who claim that the soul is mortal: 'Sed exorti sunt hodie ... nonnulli, qui hanc verissimam de immortalitate animae sententiam oppugnare conantur. Atque ij quidem sunt, qui quoniam omni penitus religionis, et pietatis nomini infesti sunt, ἀθεῶν cognomen iure sortiti sunt: qui non alia ratione se melius posse θεομαχεῖν iudicaverunt, quam si, quod in eis est, divinam sui partem prius penitus extinguerent.' Gentian Hervet, Preface (dated 1543), *Commentarius Ioannis Grammatici Philoponi Alexandrei in Aristotelis Stagiritae libros tres de anima* (Lyon, 1558), A2r. For Hervet, see *Lohr*, 187f.

58 'Nec vero locupletior, nec eruditior, nec dulcior ulla pars est *physices*, quam hae disputationes de Anima. Etsi enim substantia Animae non satis perspici potest, tamen viam ad eius agnitionem monstrant actiones. Itaque cum de actionibus dicendum erit, potentiae ceu vires discernentur, describentur organa, qua in re simul tota corporis, ac praecipue humani, natura explicanda est. Itaque haec pars, non solum de anima, sed de tota natura hominis, inscribi debebat.' *Commentarius de anima*, A1rf.

59 '... the soul is in a sense the principle of animal life,' Aristotle, *De anima*, I, i, 402a6f. In fact, the focus on the soul of 'animated beings' is precisely a point that Aristotle regards as new in his approach compared to others who confine their inquiry to the soul of man alone, see *De anima*, 402b4f.

60 'Magnam autem scientiae varietatem et copiam complectitur hominis natura. In superiori parte physices in genere dictum est de generationibus, hic in specie monstrandae erunt causae generationis, nutricionis, alteracionum in corpore humano. Magnam igitur lucem afferent haec exempla superiori parti physices, quae quidem sine hac parte pertenuis ac plane mutila est. Quanta varietas quam suavis cognicio, quam iucundum homini bene instituo a natura spectaculum est, sensuum actiones et earum causas et mirificam organorum oeconomiam considerare?' *Commentarius de anima*, A1v.

61 *De anima*, I, i, 402a23–403a3.

base on the special definition of man's soul the generic definition of the soul of animated beings, of which man is but one species. Melanchthon thus reorientated the focus of his *Commentarius de anima* from the soul of all animated beings to the 'whole nature of man'.

As a knowledge of the 'whole nature of man', Melanchthon's commentary contains discussions on both the human body and the rational soul. Although the anatomical part has been frequently passed over by modern scholars,[62] human anatomy, as I shall argue, formed quite an important part of Melanchthon's commentary on the soul. Melanchthon, of course, was not the first to claim that human anatomy was necessary for investigating the soul. Indeed Aristotle himself had given a positive role to the inquiry into the physical body in order to investigate the affections of the soul.[63] Furthermore, Magnus Hundt (1449–1519), for instance, had already juxtaposed anatomical knowledge (of Mundinus) alongside an Aristotelian discussion on the rational soul in the *Antropologium*.[64] The *Antropologium* was a humanist eulogy on the dignity of man – what wonderful things man can do. Melanchthon's *Commentarius de anima* differs from Aristotle or any other of his predecesssors in the reason why and the extent to which he regards human anatomy as important for a commentary on the soul. Melanchthon's *Commentarius de anima* was about the *human soul*, and it was, in fact, about the *Christian* soul.[65] Melanchthon, I believe, is making a novel claim when reading the *De anima*, that knowledge of human anatomy is necessary for understanding the Christian soul. Melanchthon indeed goes as far as to claim that knowledge of human anatomy is divinely ordained:

Since God alone applied so much skill in fashioning the human body (*in fabricando humano corpore*), He wished that His wondrous work be seen so that we may understand that those mechanisms created and arranged so

[62] For instance, *CR*, XIII, 120–78, with Keen (1984); *StA*, III, 307–72 and Melanchthon (1988), 239–89 contain only the latter half of the *Liber de anima*. See also the limited discussion of human anatomy (only on the humours) in Rump (1896), 19–29. But see now Nutton (1993) who notes the theological and moral significance of anatomy for Melanchthon.

[63] For Aristotle's philosophy on the relationship between soul and body, see further Sorabji (1979).

[64] Magnus Hundt (1449–1519), *Antropologium de hominis dignitate, naturae et proprietatibus ... de mentis partibus et membris humani corporis etc.* (Leipzig: W. Stöckel, 1501).

[65] For the difference from the Italian treatment of the *De anima* as preparatory for medical knowledge, see Nutton (1993), 24.

skilfully came into being by no means by chance, but that there is an eternal architectonic Mind.[66]

That a soul of a man is about both body and the rational soul was indeed the stance that Luther had taken against Eck in 1519. It was an error, Luther then argued, to presume that the 'spirit' and 'flesh' were two different substances in man and that the 'spirit' meant the rational soul.[67] For Luther, the whole human being, including body and soul, was the subject of grace. This is a stance that Luther also took in stark contrast with Erasmus.[68] Erasmus firmly believed that man was composed of both 'flesh' and 'spirit', the latter being the nobler part in which lay the power to know and incline towards good.[69] Man, for Erasmus, therefore had the capacity of Will to choose and strive towards God. Luther violently objected to this on the grounds that there was no inherent 'spirit' in man with which he could merit salvation.[70] Instead of the rational soul alone, man as a whole, both body and soul, became subject to salvation or damnation for Luther. Melanchthon's Christian soul in the *Commentarius de anima* should thus be understood in the light of this teaching of Luther's.

Having redefined the subject matter of his commentary about the soul, Melanchthon set out to define what the soul is. As Aristotle had characteristically done, Melanchthon lists various definitions of the

66 'Et cum Deus tantum adhibuerit artis in fabricando humano corpore, voluit profecto, tam mirum opus conspici, ut cogitaremus tam artificose fabricatas et distributas machinas nequaquam casu ortas esse, sed esse mentem aeternam architectatricem.' *Commentarius de anima*, α3v. For a machine metaphor of the body and the cognition of the Intelligence behind it, see Gregory of Nyssa (1967), 208–10. Cf. the idea of nature as 'craftsman', Solmsen (1963).

67 'Causa erroris est, quod subiectum gratiae dant solam animam eiusque nobiliorem parte, deinde quod carnem et spiritum distinguunt metaphysice tanquam duas substantias, cum totus homo sit spiritus et caro, tantum spiritus quantum diligit legem dei, tantum carum quantum odit legem dei.' 'Resolutiones Lutherianae super propositionibus suis Lipsiae disputatis' (1519), *WA*, II, 415. See also *Lectures on Galatians* (1519), *LW*, XXVII, 364.

68 For the background of the dispute between Luther and Erasmus, see Brecht (1981–7), II, 210–34 and Augustijn (1991), 119–45. For an analysis of the dispute between Luther and Erasmus, see further Boyle (1983) and Boisset (1962).

69 'Yet not all human desire is flesh, but there is that part of man which is called his soul, and that which is called his spirit, with which we strive after virtue, which part of the soul is called the reason (or "*hegemonikon*", that is, the "governing part") ... I shall make full use of the authority of the Fathers who say that there are certain seeds of virtue implanted in the minds of men by which they in some way see and seek after virtue, but mingled with grosser affections which incite them to other things. It is this flexible will which is called free choice.' Erasmus, *De libero arbitrio*, translated by E. G. Rupp in *Luther and Erasmus*, 76f. For Erasmus' dichotomy of 'flesh' and 'spirit', see further Augustijn (1991), 45–55.

70 Luther, *The Bondage of the Will* (1525), *LW*, XXXIII, 215, 222–9. Cf. Hägglund (1983).

soul by other philosophers. Melanchthon rephrases the question 'what is the soul?' (*Quid est anima?*) into 'what thing is the soul?' (*Quae res sit anima?*). Because Aristotle had evaded this question, Melanchthon says, he is going to turn to Galen for clarification.[71] Melanchthon recites Galen's tripartite division of the human soul, originally derived from Plato. There are three functions of the human soul which each have their seat in the bodily organs: the rational soul which regulates voluntary motions and supplies motions to the senses has its seat in the head; the sensitive soul which supplies motions to the sensitive appetites has its seat in the heart; and the nutritive soul which nourishes and gives growth to the human body has its seat in the liver.[72] Galen's division of the soul is thus linked with the functions of the human body. Melanchthon writes:

> for Galen, the soul, that is, especially the sensitive and vegetative soul, is either a temperament, or a vital spirit and natural spirit in animated beings; that is, a temperament or the vital spirit is the principle of life and motion in animated beings, or it is the thing moving the body. Thus Galen tried to point at something moving so that we could surmise what kind of a thing the soul might be.[73]

For Melanchthon, Galenic anatomy thus provides a clearer conception of what thing the soul might be.

Melanchthon then turns to Aristotle's definitions of the soul, that it is a 'first actuality (ἐντελέχεια) of a physical body possessed of organs, having the power of life', and that 'it is a principle by which we live, move and first understand'.[74] Melanchthon regards the first definition as obscure and confusing because it is a definition of a name, rather than of a thing. The second definition describes the soul only from its effect and not what thing it is nor that it is a

71 *Commentarius de anima*, 4v–5r. 72 *Commentarius de anima*, 5r–v.

73 'Ergo Galeno anima presertim sensitiva et vegetativa, aut temperamentum est, aut spiritus vitalis ac naturalis in animantibus, hoc est, aut temperamentum, aut spiritus vitalis est principium vitae ac motus in animantibus, seu est res movens corpus. Ita rem aliquam moventem Galenus digito monstrare conatus est, ut quae res esset anima suspicari possemus.' *Commentarius de anima*, 6v.

74 'Anima est actus primus corporis physici, organici, potentia vitam habentis. Addit et alteram, Anima est principium, quo vivimus, sentimus, movemur, et intelligimus primo.' *Commentarius de anima*, 7r. The first definition seems to be a combination of *De anima*, II, i, 412a29f and 412b5f. Precisely these passages are underlined in Melanchthon's own copy of Aristotle now in the British Library (British Library Classmark, c. 45. i. 14: *'ΑΡΙΣΤΟΤΈΛΟΥΣ 'ΑΠΑΝΤΑ*, edited by Desiderius Erasmus, Basle: J. Bebel, 1531), 169v. For the second definition, see the *De anima*, II, ii, 413b10–14.

principle of motion.[75] Melanchthon explains that Aristotle had not answered the question 'what thing is the soul?' because he had something else in mind, namely to divide everything in nature into 'form' and 'matter'.[76] The 'form' of all living beings was for Aristotle 'entelechy',[77] a kind of continuous agitation, in contradistinction from non-living beings. This is illustrated by Aristotle's eye-vision metaphor; the soul is to the body what vision is to the eyes.[78] Melanchthon then shows how Cicero's translation of 'entelechy' corroborates Aristotle's definition. Cicero correctly interpreted 'entelechy' as 'endelechy', a continuous motion rather than the perfected state aimed at by such motions.[79] Melanchthon ends the section on the definition of the soul by stating the Christian definition of the human soul as an intelligent spirit which is immortal.[80] This definition has no physical explanation, but is taken from Scriptures.[81]

In the section on the definition of the soul, there is no effort on Melanchthon's part to gauge the correctness of each classical author against one another. Instead, Melanchthon goes through Galen, Aristotle and Cicero attempting to ground the definition of the soul in the human body. To recapitulate, Melanchthon first moved from Aristotle to Galen for clarification about 'what thing' the soul might be; the Galenic definition of the *human* soul was grounded in the *human body*; Aristotle's soul related to the *body* as vision did to the eyes; the soul was a kind of continuous agitation; finally Melanchthon gave a Christian definition of the *human* soul. Although somewhat uneasily, supplemented by Galen and reinforced by Cicero, the section on the definition of the soul may be read as Melanchthon's attempt to reinterpret Aristotle's definition of the soul in the light of what Melanchthon wants to focus upon, namely the whole nature of a Christian man, both body and soul.

Melanchthon's concentration on the human body continues. Since the powers of the soul can be known only through its actions, it

75 *Commentarius de anima*, 7r. 76 *Commentarius de anima*, 8v.

77 *Commentarius de anima*, 10r.

78 *Ibid.* Aristotle, *De anima* II, i, 412b19f. Also underlined in Melanchthon's copy of *'ΑΡΙΣΤΟΤΈΛΟΥΣ ῞ΑΠΑΝΤΑ*, 169v.

79 *Commentarius de anima*, 13r–15r. For a brief but useful survey of humanist interpretations of the terms 'ἐντελέχεια' (Aristotle) and 'ἐνδελέχεια' (Cicero, *Tusculan Disputations* I. 22), see further Garin (1937), esp. 185f. for Melanchthon.

80 'Anima rationalis est spiritus intelligens, qui est altera pars substantiae hominis, nec extinguitur cum a corpore discessit, sed immortalis est.' *Commentarius de anima*, 15v.

81 'Haec definitio non habet physicae rationes, sed sumpta est ex Sacris literis ...' *Ibid.*

is necessary, Melanchthon argues, to include a description of the whole human body.[82] His discussion of the human body breaks away from traditional commentaries on the *De anima*[83] and, needless to say, also from the original discussion by Aristotle. Melanchthon first lists the Latin names of the parts of the body, with their Greek equivalents.[84] He starts from the head and works downwards: the head, its parts such as the crown, the temples, eyes, nose, the bone, mouth, teeth, then to the neck, trachea, arm, elbow, hands, fingers, and to the diaphragm, navel, loins, joints, hips, knees, feet, heels and fingers. Melanchthon's intention here was to show the variety of the parts of the body rather than to be exhaustive.[85]

Melanchthon then goes on to describe how students should study the internal structure of the human body:

> You should imagine that you are led into a temple or some sacred place, wherefore you should watch (*aspicere*) with all respect not only look at the material but much more so at the skill and consider the design (*consilium*) and diligence of the Maker. For the plan of the work itself testifies that man did not come into existence by chance, but that he originated from an infinite Mind, which arranged all the parts with wondrous planning and assigned them to certain ends (*ad certos fines*) and impressed in him knowledge and mind, which is the clearest footprint of divinity.[86]

The physical body is given the utmost respect as if it were sacred. As a creation of God, it reveals the greatness of the Creator. The greatness of the Creator is known because all the parts of the body

[82] *Commentarius de anima*, 20r–21r, 32r.

[83] Cf. for instance the medieval scholastic treatment of the *De anima*, which hardly contains any reference to anatomy, Jansen (1951).

[84] For Melanchthon's knowledge of contemporary terminology, see Nutton (1990), 147.

[85] 'Recensuimus appellationes exteriorum precipuas. Nam haec quamvis grammatica et brevis explicatio, tamen non solum affert aliquid lucis in lectione veterum scriptorum, ac praecipue philosophorum, sed etiam aditum patefacit ad considerandam cognoscendamque naturam multarum partium corporis humani. Nec vero omnia vocabula curiose undique conquisivimus, quod non erat difficile factu. Sed hic modus visus est aptior et utilior rudibus. Iam vero interiora membra breviter describemus. Etsi autem non omnes minutas particulas, omnes venarum, arteriarum ac nervorum propagines distribuemus, sed crassiores partes obiter spectandas proponemus, tamen haec ipsa explicatio ostendet mirificam naturae varietatem, multis de causis consideratione dignissimam.' *Commentarius de anima*, 44r–v.

[86] 'Vos vero velut in templum ac sacrarium quoddam, vos introduci putetis. Quare singulari reverentia aspicere non solum materiam, sed multo magis artem et considerare consilium et diligentiam opificis debetis. Nam ipsa opificij ratio testatur, homines non casu extitisse, sed ab aliqua infinita mente ortos esse, quae singulas partes mirabili consilio distribuit, et ad certos fines destinavit, quae impressit noticiam ac mentem, quae est clarissimum vestigium divinitatis.' *Commentarius de anima*, 44v–45r.

are designed for certain ends. It is thus not the material of the human body *per se*, but how it is arranged and what it is designed for, that should be studied through anatomy.

Melanchthon proceeds to explain human anatomy by the tripartite division of the venters. He begins with the lowest venter which serves generation and nutrition and includes organs such as the stomach, bowel, intestines and liver. The middle venter includes the heart, aorta and lung. It gives rise to motion and guards the body. The last and supreme venter includes the head, the *pia mater*, the brain, its ventricles, the *rete mirabile*, eyes, ears and nose. These serve cognition. The structure of each organ and its uses is further explained in detail over fifty pages.

After explaining the interior organs of the human body, Melanchthon goes on to explain the humours and the spirits. He repeats the traditional account that man's natural disposition is determined by the balance of the four humours, blood, yellow bile, black bile and phlegm.[87] A spirit is defined as a fine, flame-like vapour squeezed out from blood. Vital spirits carry the vital heat from the heart to the rest of the body and the arteries were made for these vital spirits to travel through them. There is also another kind of spirit, the animal spirit, which is refined in the brain and effects the actions of the senses by exciting the nerves. Melanchthon mentions a third kind of spirit, the natural spirit, which warms the blood in the liver and excites vapour in the blood, but following Galen, he doubts its existence because its use seems to overlap with that of the vital spirit.[88] Melanchthon is thus prepared to doubt the existence of things which are teleologically superfluous.

As Melanchthon is about to end the section on human anatomy, he reiterates that it is necessary to study these parts of the body because they have been assigned to necessary uses and actions and have been arranged with wondrous skill. Having completed this new part, he now turns to the topics traditionally treated in the reading of the *De anima*.[89]

After working up through the usual Aristotelian hierarchy of the level of the soul, namely the vegetative, sensitive appetitive and the

87 *Commentarius de anima*, 130v. 88 *Commentarius de anima*, 134r–135v.

89 'Haec [membra humani corporis, et humores, et spiritus] enim praecipue consideranda sunt in nostris corporibus, quia ad necessarios usus, atque actiones destinata sunt, et mira arte facta, ac distributa. Nunc redeo ad usitatas quaestiones, quae in scholis solebant tractari in libro de Anima.' *Commentarius de anima*, 135v.

locomotive, Melanchthon arrives at the rational soul. There are two distinctive faculties of the rational soul, the Intellect (*Intellectus*) and the Will (*Voluntas*). The Intellect is defined as 'a faculty of the mind, knowing, recording, judging, reckoning particulars and universals, having some innate knowledge or principles of great arts placed within it. Also having a reflexive act by which it distinguishes and judges its own actions.'[90] Melanchthon explains the working of the Intellect starting from the senses: singular objects are first perceived by the senses and from them universals or ideas are formed. By collation of such ideas, the Intellect distinguishes substance and accidents. Melanchthon then departs from Aristotle and strongly argues for the existence of innate knowledge. Melanchthon finds some basic innate knowledge necessary in resolving differences of opinion and in avoiding errors.[91]

Melanchthon distinguishes two kinds of innate knowledge: one is 'speculative', like knowledge of numbers, orders and syllogistic reasoning, the other 'practical' in the sense that it regulates human behaviour. Although the degree of certainty of the two kinds of knowledge may differ in man's cognition, Melanchthon states clearly that both kinds are equally certain:

Just like the speculative principles, the practical principles are certain and firm. But we more easily allow the practical ones to be weakened because of the infirmity and flexibility of our will. The statement 'Adultery is disgraceful' is certain and firm. But we do not comprehend this as firmly as we do that two times four is eight. However, the certitude in the thing itself is similar, not because evidence from outside affects our eyes, but because this belief has been placed in the mind by the divinity. Therefore we follow the word of Paul on this matter who testified that the knowledge that there is a God, and that we should obey him, was placed in the mind by the divinity. Similarly the distinction between good and bad, that is, the laws of nature (*leges naturae*), for he said 'The work of law embraces the hearts.'[92]

90 'Est potentia mentis cognoscens, recordans, iudicans et rationcians singularia et universalia, habens insitas quasdam noticias, seu principia magnarum artium. Habens item actum reflexum, quo suas actiones cernit et iudicat.' *Commentarius de anima*, 205r–v.

91 '... saepe in conferendo dissimilia iungunt homines, item in raciocinando contexunt non necessario coherentia, ideo saepe errant ac hallucinantur, ut Epicurus non recte confert magnitudinem solis ad corpora, quae prope aspicimus. Neque vero progredi ad raciocinandum possemus, nisi hominibus natura insita essent adminicula quaedam, hoc est artium principia, numeri, agnitio, ordinis, et proportionis, connexio syllogistica, geometrica, physica, et moralia principia.' *Commentarius de anima*, 208r.

92 'Ut speculativa principia, ita practica certa et firma sunt, sed practica facilius labefieri sinimus, propter voluntatis nostrae infirmitatem et mobilitatem. Certa est firma sententia. Adulterium est turpe. Sed non tam firmiter eam amplectimur, ut hanc bis 4 sunt 8. Re ipsa tamen certitudo similis est, non quia foris evidentia movet oculos, sed quia et haec sententia

Once again, Melanchthon asserts that man knows innately which external action is good and what is evil. These God-given moral principles, namely natural law, as I have indicated in the previous chapter, formed the basis of his claim for civil obedience.

Traditionally, innate knowledge about good and bad actions was called 'synteresis'.[93] Melanchthon is careful to point out, however, that the kind of innate knowledge he is talking about is nothing like the traditional idea of 'synteresis' which allowed man some power to avoid sin and aspire towards eternal life. Luther himself had discarded the idea of 'synteresis' because it did not effect salvation.[94] In Lutheran terms, Fallen man is so totally averse to God that he cannot save himself without the Holy Spirit. It is therefore only the knowledge limited to civil good or bad that Melanchthon admits to 'synteresis'. Melanchthon thus followed a Lutheran position in defining what 'synteresis' meant.

The discussion on the Intellect is followed by the section on the Will, which is defined as 'a pre-eminent power, supreme and freely acting on an object indicated (*monstrato objecto*) by the Intellect'.[95] However, before going any further as to what the object or the capacity of the Will might be, Melanchthon inserts a discussion on the image of God (*Quae est imago Dei in homine?*). A study of the rational soul, Melanchthon explains, lifts students to the knowledge of the Architect (*ad architecti agnitionem*).[96] This knowledge, *agnitio*, seems for Melanchthon to have a specific Christian, especially a Pauline connotation as a recognition of the divine by those who have faith in Christ.[97] Referring to Colossians 3. 10 and 1 Corinthians 13. 12, Melanchthon continues:

divinitus insita est menti. Itaque nos sequemur Pauli sententiam de haec controversia, qui testatur divinitus insita se esse mentibus has noticias, quod est Deus, quod Deo sit obediendum. Item discrimen honestorum et turpium, seu leges naturae. Ait enim ἔργον τὸν νόμον γὰρ γραπτὸν ἐν ταῖς καρδίαις αὐτῶν.' *Commentarius de anima*, 210r–v.

93 For medieval interpretations of 'synteresis', see Lottin (1948), II, 104–349; for medieval views on the relationship between synteresis and conscience, see Crowe (1977), 129–41 and Potts (1980).

94 Baylor (1977), 157–208.

95 'Voluntas est potentia appetens, suprema ac libere agens monstrato obiecto ab intellectu.' *Commentarius de anima*, 218r.

96 'Priusquam de obiecto, et de libertate dicam, monendi sunt studiosi, ut cogitantes praestantiam harum virium, intellectus et voluntatis, erigant animos ad architecti agnitionem. Nam in hoc opere praecipue lucent eius natura, sapientia, bonitas et voluntas erga nos. Per nos et in nobis innotescere voluit. Ideo nos condidit, ideo attribuit sui imaginem, dedit mentem, indidit aliquam noticiam divinitatis, addidit discrimen honestorum et turpium, adiunxit libertatem electionis.' *Commentarius de anima*, 219r.

97 For the Pauline references to 'agnitio', see for instance Colossians 1. 9; 2. 2; 3. 10; 1 Timothy 2. 4; Titus 1. 1.

> Paul therefore cries out and bids us to renew the image of God by a knowledge of Him (*agnitione ipsius*), in justice and in truth. Elsewhere he also said that the image of Him is renewed when Christ brings into us, as if into a mirror knowledge of Himself (*agnitionem sui*), and that true knowledge of Him shines in us and we recognise that He is not idle, but we are truly in His care, on account of His Son, we are truly heard and protected. Therefore the mind itself is an image of God, but insofar as the true knowledge of God (*noticia Dei*) shines in it and true obedience [shines] in the Will, that is, a blazing love of God, rejoicing trust in God, and freedom, which wholly submits to that knowledge (*noticiam*) and love of God.[98]

It is only after true faith is gained that the mind becomes a true image of God and that the true object of the Will could be acknowledged as God.

> For it is said to be an image because it shows the Archetype. Where there is no knowlegde of the Archetype it is not possible to show the Archetype. And the image should refer itself back to the Archetype as if to the greatest good ... if the image were complete it would be the case that God is the proper and greatest object of our will. Because there is the greatest similarity between the effigy and the Archetype, and the effigy understanding and yearning is moved especially towards that exemplar by which it was impressed. After this image was contaminated, it was renewed by the Word of God through the Holy Spirit who started in our minds a new light and new obedience through the Word of God.[99]

This treatment of the 'image of God' is markedly different from Melanchthon's Italian predecessors for whom the image of God was a powerful inspiration for praising the power and predominance of

98 'Clamitat igitur Paulus ac iubet renovare imaginem Dei, agnitione ipsius, iusticia ac veritate. Et alibi sic renovari inquit, cum transfundit Christus in nos, tanquam in speculo, agnitionem sui, et vera ipsius noticia luceat in nobis, et statuamus eum non esse ociosum, sed nos vere ei curae esse, propter filium, nos vere exaudiri ac servari. Est igitur imago Dei ipsa mens, sed quatenus in ea lucet vera noticia Dei, et in voluntate vera obedientia, hoc est ardens dilectio Dei et fiducia acquiescens in Deo, ac libertas, quae illi noticiae et amori Dei integre obtemperat.' *Commentarius de anima*, 220r.

99 'Ideo enim dicitur imago, quia ostendit archetypum. Iam ubi non est noticia archetypi, non potest eum ostendere. Et imago referre se debet ad archetypum, tanquam ad summum bonum. Ideo accedit amor Dei. Sic condita est imago, et insita divinitus noticia, dilectio Dei, et vera libertas, hoc est harmonia omnium virium. Ergo si esset integra imago, constaret Deum esse proprium, et summum obiectum nostrae voluntatis. Quia maxima est cognatio inter effigiem et archetypum, et effigies intelligens ac appetens, maxime ad illud exemplar, ex quo expressa est, ferretur. Postquam vero contaminata est haec imago, restituitur verbo Dei per Spiritum sanctum, qui novam lucem et novam obedientiam per verbum Dei in mentibus inchoat. Haec est vera et veterum quorundam de imagine sententia.' *Commentarius de anima*, 220r–v.

the human will.[100] Here, for Melanchthon, the 'image of God' provides the scriptural grounding for establishing the object of Will which is otherwise unknowable to Fallen man.[101] It is precisely because of the Lutheran position of the total spiritual incapacity of Fallen Man that Melanchthon can go on to explain the object and capacity of the Will only after he has established on scriptural grounds the true knowledge of the soul of man as the image of God.

If the nature of man were complete, Melanchthon writes, the object of the Will would be God.[102] Although even without Christ, pagans such as Cicero or Cato may have understood that the object of the Will is to desire 'the good' insofar as reason or the senses can determine, they mean only the good of human nature or of society.[103] Not only are they ignorant of the true object of their will, but also they are unable to yearn for that object. Even if the pagans know that there is a God, they still doubt His care and Providence and thus do not love God.[104] It is only when man recognizes God as a Providential God who sent His Son for us that we start loving God.

> Therefore, let us depart from the schools of the philosophers and let us know that for us called to the knowledge of the Gospel (*ad Evangelij agnitionem*) the object of the Will is infinite Good, and other good things to be desired in due order. For we are called to the instauration of nature and our Lord Jesus Christ the Son of God was offered to us, who testified that God is not idle, but indeed cares for us, receives us in grace, listens and liberates. When we know (*agnoscimus*) God as such, we begin to love Him, acquiesce in Him, expect good from Him, obey Him, we see Him in things rightly done, cherish virtue in Him, so that we submit to Him and beseech that we be guided by Him.[105]

To know God as the Providential Creator is thus the beginning of loving God and also the point of departure from pagan philosophy. To know the true object of the Will and to have desire for that object

100 For a study of the 'Image of God' as an inspiration for Italian humanists, see Trinkaus (1970).

101 Cf. St Augustine, *De trinitate*, XII, 11, 16, and Hassel (1962).

102 *Commentarius de anima*, 221v.

103 *Ibid.*

104 *Commentarius de anima*, 223r–v. A biblical allusion is made to Romans 1. 21. Cf. St Augustine, *De trinitate*, XIV, 19, 26.

105 'Discedamus igitur iam a scholis Philosophorum, et sciamus nobis vocatis ad Evangelij agnitionem obiectum esse voluntatis, Bonum infinitum, et cetera bona suo ordine appetenda. Vocamur enim ad instaurationem naturae, et proponitur nobis filius Dei Dominus noster Iesus Christus, qui testatur Deum non esse ociosum, sed vere nos curare, recipere in gratiam, exaudire, liberare. Cum sic agnoscimus Deum, incipimus eum amare, in eo acquiescere, ab eo bona expectare, ei obedire, et in recte factis ipsum intuemur, virtutem

is possible only through faith. Man is unable to do anything spiritual. In fact, without the Holy Spirit, he cannot help turning away from God.[106] Man has no freedom of Will to save himself.[107] Melanchthon reiterated thus the Lutheran position on the Will of Fallen Man. The section on the Will was in effect a summary of the Lutheran teaching of the Will.

The last section in the *Commentarius de anima* is on the immortality of the soul. The immortatlity of the soul, the most important issue for those who believe in salvation, life after death, is stated at once on scriptural grounds.[108] Melanchthon here seems quite oblivious to the contemporary and quite sophisticated debate in Italy about the immortality of the soul,[109] and it may reflect the disinterest on Melanchthon's part in proving theological tenets on the basis of philosophy. Some philosophers, such as Plato, have hit on the idea of the immortality of the soul.[110] Melanchthon also does not fail to cite the only passage in the *De anima*, a passage which he promptly underlined in his copy of Aristotle, which suggests that the rational soul is immortal.[111] Yet Melanchthon never uses philosophy in this section to prove the immortality of the soul. For Melanchthon the truth of the theological doctrine itself can only be grasped through faith. In other words, without faith one cannot gain a complete understanding of the human soul.[112] Hence, Melanchthon ends his *Commentarius de anima* with a characteristically Lutheran invocation:

I beseech God with all my heart that we may know the Archetype and we may honour it correctly, since He has made our souls in such a way that an image of Him impressed in our souls may shine through and since He gave us His son our Lord Jesus Christ for the restoration of that image so that He may renew in us those images by the Holy Spirit. I pray also that He may guide and promote the study of the young so that they may be useful for the

eo amplectimur, ut ipsi obtemperemus, ac ab ipso gubernari nos petimus.' *Commentarius de anima*, 223v–224r.

106 *Commentarius de anima*, 217v.

107 'De libero arbitrio', *Commentarius de anima*, 225r–v.

108 *Commentarius de anima*, 238r–244v.

109 Schmitt (1988a), 798.

110 *Commentarius de anima*, 244r–246v.

111 *Commentarius de anima*, 247r. *De anima* II, ii, 413b25–28. In the margin next to this passage, Melanchthon wrote in his copy of Aristotle, 'ἕτερον γένος/ψυχῆς/ Nota de immor/ talitate/ animæ.' (170r).

112 'Id argumentum de Dei agnitione valde fulsisset, si non accesissent tenebrae post delictum Adae. Vidisset enim natura integra mentem esse imaginem Dei, et futurum ut archetypi perfecta noticia frueremur . . . Nam et providentiam esse non dubium est, cum certum sit esse Deum. Et impossibile est optimam generis humani partem, tantum ad perniciem conditam esse.' *Commentarius de anima*, 245v–246r.

Church and illuminate the glory of our Lord Jesus Christ. Praise be to God.[113]

It was a Christian and indeed a Lutheran reading of Aristotle's *De anima*. Following Luther's view of 'the whole man' as an object of salvation, Melanchthon pursued, as much as he could, the discussion of the nature of the whole man in his *Commentarius de anima*. Galenic anatomy was used to demonstrate that the physical body was God's creation. Because the 'whole man' was Fallen, the rational soul was limited in its spiritual ability and clouded in its knowledge of the sacred. Although utilizing Aristotelian definitions, terminology and teleological arguments, Melanchthon's deviations from Aristotle's philosophy were many and several other classical authors were drafted in. The upshot was a reading of Aristotle's *De anima* which was Melanchthon's own, and a commentary about the soul which can only be made full sense of in terms of Lutheran theology.

If we see Melanchthon simply as a 'humanist' and read the *Commentarius de anima*, we will be disappointed because it is nothing like a philological exegesis on the meaning of Aristotle's original passages about the 'soul'. It is true that Melanchthon often collates opinions of others without committing himself to either position, perhaps an indication of his inheritance of an Augustinian 'sceptical tradition',[114] but it is equally important to note why on certain issues Melanchthon takes a definite and particular stance. If we seek in Melanchthon a 'philosopher' and read the *Commentarius de anima*, we will be equally disappointed because it is not a work which we, in modern times, would call 'original' philosophy, but rather a mixture of teleological and dogmatic statements of theological principles. But then, these are all misplaced expectations[115] about a work which was never *intended* as such. As Melanchthon himself made clear from the beginning, the *Commentarius de anima* was about the soul as the

[113] 'Precor autem Deum toto pectore, cum animas nostras ita condiderit, ut in eis luceret impressa ipsius imago, cunque ad eam restituendam donavit nobis suum Filium, Dominum nostrum Iesum Christum, ut Spiritu sancto has ipsas imagines in nobis renovet, ut archetypum agnoscamus et recte celebremus. Oro etiam ut iuventutis studia gubernet, et provehat, ut Ecclesiae prodesse possint, et illustrare gloriam Domini nostri Iesu Christi. δόξα τῷ θεῷ.' *Commentarius de anima*, 247r–v.

[114] For the influence of St Augustine's *Contra academicos* on Melanchthon, see N. Jardine (1979), 146–9. For Melanchthon's *De anima* as a source of Marin Mersenne's 'mitigated scepticism', see Dear (1984).

[115] For the anachronism of assessing the 'creativity' or 'originality' of renaissance philosophy, see Kristeller (1993).

whole nature of man and indeed it was a Lutheran soul he was trying to explain.

Why then, did Melanchthon use Aristotle at all, if his concern was merely to expound on the nature of the Lutheran soul? Luther himself, after all, did not use (in his *Bondage of Will*, for instance) Aristotle or Galen to explain the soul, nor did Melanchthon ever try to prove theological points about the soul in the *Commentarius de anima*. In the *Commentarius de anima*, theological points were all established on scriptural grounds. It would be too simplistic, however, to regard it as Melanchthon bringing a traditional university subject in line with Lutheran principles. We ought to remember instead that Melanchthon was deeply worried about civil disobedience when he began to work on the philosophy of the soul. It is indeed this issue that his *Commentarius de anima* ultimately addressed:

> Moral philosophy takes from natural philosophy this proposition: the nature of man was created for a certain purpose. This is demonstrated in natural philosophy, but not confirmed in moral philosophy. But it is accepted in moral philosophy like a hypothesis, namely a firm proposition, which is taken from elsewhere so that it may be the starting point of moral philosophy.[116]

Demonstration of the starting point of this moral philosophy was the task of natural philosophy. To prove that man was created by God for a definite purpose is indeed what Melanchthon did in his *Commentarius de anima*. For Melanchthon, the strength of Aristotle and Galen who supplemented him lay precisely in their teleological arguments: they demonstrated how each and every part of the human being was designed for a specific function. As I have argued in the previous chapter, Melanchthon developed his moral philosophy which was knowledge of Lutheran 'Law', in order to counter the problem of civil obedience. Amidst further threats from the evangelical radicals, Melanchthon had gone further to prove the starting point of this moral philosophy.

A LUTHERAN NATURAL PHILOSOPHY OF THE SOUL

The *Commentarius de anima* was an exposition of the Lutheran soul which provided the starting point of Melanchthon's moral phil-

[116] 'Philosophia moralis ex Physica assumit hanc propositionem: Natura hominis condita est ad certum finem. Id in physicis demonstratur, non confirmatur in Philosophia morali. Sed recipitur, tanquam hypothesis, id est, firma propositio, aliunde assumpta, ut sit inchoatio doctrinae moralis.' *Erotemata dialectices* (1547), *CR*, XIII, 650.

osophy. Taken as a whole, the *Commentarius de anima* can further be understood, I believe, as imparting a *Lutheran* type of knowledge. This means understanding the *Commentarius de anima* just as Melanchthon intended it to be, namely as a work on both the human anatomy *and* the rational soul. The anatomical part, which has frequently been passed over by historians, thus needs to be taken seriously as part of that knowledge which Melanchthon intended to impart.[117]

Human anatomy had been taught in the universities ever since the time of Mundinus (*c.* 1270–1326), and indeed the greatness of the Creator in creating and arranging every part of the human body for a certain purpose had frequently been praised in studies of human anatomy.[118] Wittenberg University Library, where Melanchthon is known to have been an avid reader, had a rich collection of anatomical works and commentaries of Mundinus and his followers such as Giampietro Ferrari, Gabriel de Zerbis and Dynus de Garbo.[119] There were also works of Galen and Hippocrates as well as of contemporaries such as Alexander Benedictus, Johannnes Dryander and Johann Guinther von Andernach.[120] There is further indication that Melanchthon had an extensive personal library containing medical works.[121] In other words, he was surrounded by all kinds of works on anatomy.

[117] Nutton (1993) has recently noted the theological and moral significance of anatomy for Melanchthon and his followers. Here, I should like to present a stronger claim that the kind of knowledge the *Commentarius de anima* presented as a whole was peculiarly Lutheran. I first learnt the importance of understanding anatomy as a 'faithful' enterprise in lectures given by Dr A. R. Cunningham in 1986/7. I am most grateful to him for subsequently allowing me to read his forthcoming work, *The Anatomical Renaissance*, on which this chapter heavily draws.

[118] For an introduction to the place of anatomical knowledge in medicine, see Siraisi (1990), 78–114. For the various kinds of the study of anatomy as a Christian enterprise, see Cunningham, *The Anatomical Renaissance*.

[119] In 1513, amongst others, the following books were purchased for the University Library: Giampietro Ferrari, *Practica*, for 12 gr.; Gabriel de Zerbis, *Anatomia*, for 1 fl. 5 gr.; and Dynus de Garbo, *Chyrugia* (in German), for 10 gr., Buchwald (1896).

[120] Works such as the following are known to have belonged to the University Library of Wittenberg: Mundinus, *Anathomia* (Strasburg: M. Flach, 1513); Alexander Benedictus, *Anatomicae sive historiae corporis humanis* (Paris: H. Stephanus, 1514); Johannes Dryander, *Anatomia capitis humani* (Marburg: E. Cervicornus, 1536); Guinther von Andernach, *Institutionis anatomis secundum Galeni sententiam libri IV* (Basle: R. Winter, 1536) ; Amidenus Aetius, *Opera* (Basle: J. Froben and N. Episcopius, 1535); Celsus, *Medicinae libri VIII* (Venice: A. Manutius and A. Torresanus, 1528). There were also works on Avicenna, the *Articella*, and many *Feldtbuchs*. For the catalogues of Wittenberg University Library, see Schwiebert (1940). For details of the contents of the University Library, see Kusukawa, forthcoming.

[121] When the library of a German medic and antiquarian, Georg Kloss (1787–1854), was sold by Sotheby's in 1835, Samuel Leigh Sotheby (1805–61) claimed that many of the books

In the *Commentarius de anima*, Melanchthon followed the traditional three-venter division and repeatedly praised the skill of the Creator in creating the human body for certain uses, but there is no positive evidence that Melanchthon followed any particular anatomist in the Mundinus tradition. Instead, in the *Commentarius de anima* Melanchthon quotes extensively from Galen in Greek.[122] As we may surmise from Melanchthon's correspondence, such passages of Galen may well have been provided by his friends Camerarius and Fuchs who were involved in editing the Greek edition of Galen.[123] Melanchthon certainly seems to have known his Galen very well.[124] It would be too simplistic, however, to regard Melanchthon as the humanist interested only in the original, Greek Galen, and not in the works of later commentators or anatomists.[125] At least on one occasion, Melanchthon had gone to the trouble of reading and then disappointedly rejecting a work on Galenic anatomy by Alexander Benedictus (*c.* 1450–1512), which was well embedded in the Mundinus tradition.[126] We also ought to remember that he did not intend to teach anatomical knowledge exhaustively or to promote a particular kind of dissection. Yet, of all the available readings of human anatomy, it is Galen himself that Melanchthon had chosen to follow. What then, were Melanchthon's reasons for following Galen specifically and deliberately?

In the same year as his *Commentarius de anima* appeared, Melanchthon wrote an oration on the life of Galen in which he praised Galen's human anatomy in the following way:

since it [anatomy] sets forth this wonderful construction of human limbs, it teaches that this nature did not come into being by chance, but was created by some eternal Mind which did not wish that it should have thus occupied

contained annotations by the Reformers, especially by Melanchthon, see Sotheby (1835), (1839) and (1840). Kloss objected to this 'Melanchthomanic' claim of Sotheby's in Kloss (1841) and most of Sotheby's claims are now regarded as unsound, see for instance Clough (1976). Sotheby himself bought a substantial part of Kloss' library which he believed to contain Melanchthon's marginalia, and kept them until his death, when they were dispersed. For the auction of Sotheby's library, see Bell (1862). I am indebted for most of this information to Professor Vivian Nutton and Mr John Symons, Chief Cataloguer at the Library of the Wellcome Institute, London.

122 For Melanchthon's reliance on the Greek text, see also Schmitt (1988a), 797.

123 For an analysis of Fuchs' commentaries on Galen, see Durling (1989).

124 Melanchthon's sources for Galen were the *De usu partium*, the *De anatomicis administrationibus*, and the *De Hippocratis et Platonis dogmatibus*, Nutton (1993), 22.

125 Melanchthon as seeker of 'truth' rather than a committed Hellenist, see Nutton (1993), 16.

126 See p. 84 above.

itself without purpose in creating man, but wished to signify that mankind was of great importance to it. Therefore Galen said most wisely that *the anatomical teaching is the beginning of Theology and the path to the knowledge of God (ad agnitionem Dei)*, and those books are to be that much more loved by those studious of philosophy because Galen added those things which were wanting in Aristotelian anatomy, corrected some [errors] eruditely, and added light to many topics of Aristotle.[127]

Melanchthon claims that Galen intended his anatomy to be the beginning of theology and the path to the *agnitio Dei*. The first claim occurs in Galen's *De usu partium* where the only use of the word 'θεολογία' in the whole Galenic corpus is recorded.[128] It is irrelevant here that some modern scholars regard this passage as a later interpolation,[129] since Melanchthon evidently believed that it was by Galen. The second reference to anatomy as the path to the *agnitio Dei* probably alludes to Galen's description of human anatomy as an initiation into the mysteries of God.[130] *Agnitio* in the New Testament certainly meant the knowledge of the divine mystery gained through faith in Christ.[131] The significance of Galen for Melanchthon is that Galen himself had said that his human anatomy taught the knowledge of God the Creator. Galen had said the following in the *De usu partium*:

when anyone looking at the facts with an open mind sees that in such a slime of fleshes and juices there is yet an indwelling intelligence and sees too the structure of any animal whatsoever – for they give evidence of the wise Creator – he will understand the excellence of the intelligence in the heavens.

Then a work on the usefulness of the parts, which at first seemed to him a

127 '(... inquit se scripsisse divinos illos libros anatomicos qui extant, qui quidem non solum Medicinae studiosis, sed omnibus Philosophiae amantibus in manibus esse debent; profecto enim praecipua pars est Philosophiae, doctrina de partibus humani corporis et earum officiis. Cumque sit plena suavitatis, ingentes etiam utilitates adfert, magnopere conducit singulis ad tuendam valetudinem: mores etiam regit, cum monet quid cuiusque partis natura postulet.) Denique cum hanc admirandam texturam humanorum membrorum proponit, docet hanc naturam non casu extitisse, sed ab aeterna quadam mente conditam esse, quae non frustra voluit esse adeo occupata in formando homine, sed significare, sibi genus humanum curae esse. Itaque sapientissime Galenus inquit, doctrinam anatomicam initium esse Theologiae, et aditum ad agnitionem Dei, suntque eo magis amandi hi libri studiosis Philosophiae, quia ea quae desiderantur in Aristotelica anatomia, adiecit Galenus, quaedam etiam erudite correxit, multis etiam locis Aristotelis lumen addidit.' *CR*, XI, 501.

128 Galen (1821–33), IV, 360. For a comprehensive account of classical teleology, including physiological teleology, see Pease (1941).

129 For instance, Siegel (1973), 29.

130 G. E. R. Lloyd (1973), 151.

131 Colossians 2. 2, for instance.

thing of scant importance, will be reckoned truly to be the source of a perfect theology, which is a thing far greater and far nobler than all of medicine. Hence such a work is serviceable not only for the physician, but much more so for the philosopher who is eager to gain an understanding of the whole of Nature.[132]

For Melanchthon, this Galen taught through anatomy precisely the kind of knowledge of God Melanchthon was interested in teaching in the *Commentarius de anima*, namely that every part of the human body was created for a sure purpose by God.

In his oration, Melanchthon further goes on to praise Galen as having 'faith': 'But since in the good Doctor (*in bono Doctore*) faith is required no less than erudition and industry, Galen should be loved especially, he, who as the thing itself shows, excelled not only in industry and dexterity, but also *in faith*.'[133] In an age when the nature of 'faith' was seriously debated, to declare Galen as 'faithful' and his anatomy a 'path to theology' is, surely, not a trivial point. Melanchthon could accord such high praise to Galen because, I believe, the kind of knowledge Galenic anatomy imparted for Melanchthon constituted a significant part of a *Lutheran* kind of natural philosophy.

Luther frequently explained the nature of faith through Law and Gospel. True knowledge of Law meant the recognition of the total spiritual incapacity of man, namely that man could claim nothing meritorious for himself. The knowledge of the Gospel on the other hand was to realize that faith in the crucified Christ alone sufficed for salvation. Law was not Gospel, but the former was necessary for the true understanding of the latter. Luther called this knowledge of Law also a self-knowledge, as he said 'the commandments . . . show us what we ought to do but do not give us the power to do it. They are intended to teach man to *know himself*, that through them he may recognize his inability to do good and may despair of his own inability.'[134]

It is this knowledge of Law, I believe, that Melanchthon's *Commentarius de anima* taught. This natural philosophy did not teach

[132] *De usu partium*, Book XVII, as translated by M. T. May in Galen (1968), II, 731.

[133] 'Cum autem in bono Doctore non minus fides quam eruditio atque industria requiratur, magnopere amandus est Galenus, qui, ut res ostendit, non solum industria et dexteritate excelluit, sed etiam *fide*.' *CR*, XI, 501, my emphasis.

[134] 'The Freedom of a Christian Man' (1520) translated by W. A. Lambert and revised by H. J. Grimm in *LW*, XXXI, 348. My emphasis.

the message of the Gospel in that all theological tenets were introduced on Scriptural grounds, not as something to be proven, but as a basis on which certain terms such as 'synteresis' or 'will' ought to be reinterpreted. Melanchthon's natural philosophy of the soul did teach, on the other hand, self-knowledge: in the *Commentarius de anima*, after the power of the Creator was understood through the fabric of the human body, in stark contrast, the spiritual incapacity of man was set forth in the discussion of the rational soul. The message was thus twofold: God is almighty but man is totally helpless. At the end of the *Commentarius de anima*, an invocation is made to God for restoring His image through Christ and the Holy Spirit, thus indicating the necessity of true faith for true knowledge of the divine. Thus, in the kind of knowledge about God and man that it imparted, Melanchthon's *Commentarius de anima* may well be understood as a knowledge of Law.

Strikingly, Melanchthon elsewhere calls anatomy a knowledge to 'know thyself'. In an oration in praise of anatomy delivered in 1550 by his collaborator in this subject, Jacob Milich, Melanchthon wrote:

> Since knowledge of the edifice of the human body has enormous use, in no way should the anatomical teaching be neglected. It is always a worthy matter for man to behold (*aspicere*) the nature of things and not to despise the consideration of this wondrous work of the world, which was so skilfully created that it reminds us about God and about His Will, as if we were watching a theatre. But it is most befitting and useful for us to see (*videre*) in ourselves the series of parts, figures, connections, powers and duties. It is said that there is an oracle 'know thyself' which although it advises many things, may here be taken to mean that we should earnestly behold (*aspiciamus*) those things which in ourselves are worthy of admiration and are the sources of most actions in life. And because men were created for the sake of wisdom and of justice, and true wisdom is knowledge of God (*agnitio Dei*) and consideration of nature (*consideratio naturae*), it should be acknowledged that anatomical teaching in which the causes of many actions and changes in us are seen, should be learned.[135]

135 'Cum igitur ingens sit utilitas nosse humani corporis aedificium, doctrina anatomica nequaquam negligenda est. Est omnino digna res homine, aspicere rerum naturam, nec aspernari considerationem huius mirandi opificii mundi, quod ideo tanta arte conditum est, ut tanquam theatrum aspiciatur, nosque de Deo, et de eius voluntate commonefaciat. Sed tamen maxime in nobis ipsis et decet, et prodest partium seriem, figuras, coagmentationem, vires et officia videre. Oraculum esse dixerunt, γνῶθι σεαυτὸν, quod etsi multa monet, tamen etiam huc accommodetur, ut illa, quae in nobis ipsis admiratione digna sunt, et quae sunt fontes plurimarum actionum in vita, studiose aspiciamus. Cumque

The above statement is also remarkable for the stark contrast it provides with Melanchthon's own earlier comment when he stressed the limits of pagan moral philosophy with respect to the message of the Gospel. There, Melanchthon claimed that pagan philosophy which taught 'know thyself' was ineffectual for salvation. With the development of his moral philosophy, as I have argued in the previous chapter, pagan philosophy gained a positive role as knowledge of Law. Here, pagan philosophy continues to have a positive meaning in enabling man to 'behold the things which *in ourselves* are worthy of admiration'. What was worthy of admiration in the *Commentarius de anima* was the greatness of the Creator.

The association of human anatomy with self-knowledge itself was not new. Magnus Hundt, for instance, quoted amongst numerous other classical passages the Delphic maxim of 'know thyself' to justify the knowledge of human body and soul.[136] Hundt, however, did not make a specific identification of the maxim with anatomy. For him, the maxim was one of the many classical references he could use in order to justify the knowledge of both the soul and body of man as a dignified creation of God. The ultimate source for the association seems to be Cicero, though he explicitly interprets the maxim as referring only to the soul and not the body.[137] The idea of anatomy as 'know thyself' gained wide currency in the sixteenth and seventeenth centuries.[138] Moreover, the motto 'know thyself' came to carry a wide range of meaning and could be used for a variety of purposes in various kinds of works, including poems and maps.[139] For Melanchthon, however, it had quite a specific meaning and significance. The *Commentarius de anima* taught knowledge of Lutheran Law, namely the spiritual incapacity of Fallen man and the greatness of the Creator. Human anatomy was an essential and integral part of this teaching. At Wittenberg, it was thus in the

homines ad sapientiam et iusticiam conditi sint, ac vera sapientia sit, agnitio Dei, et naturae consideratio, fatendum est et doctrinam anatomicam cognoscendam esse, in qua causae multarum actionum et mutationum in nobis conspiciuntur.' *CR*, XI, 945f.

136 Magnus Hundt, *Anthropologium*, Aiijvf. For the early German interest in this motto, see Wells (1964). Cf. also Vives (1782), 298.

137 Cicero, *Tusculan Disputations* I. xxii. 50–2. Cf. A. C. Lloyd (1964) for philosophical analysis of classical theories of self-awareness of thought under the phrase '*nosce teipsum*'.

138 Schupbach (1982).

139 See the map in Greenblatt (1992), plate 10. For the literary use of the motto, see Wilkins (1929).

lectures in the arts faculty on the *De anima* that human anatomy was taught as to 'know thyself'.[140]

Thus the *Commentarius de anima* not only was a commentary on the soul re-interpreted through Lutheran doctrine, but also the kind of knowledge of God and Fallen man it taught was in itself a Lutheran one. The *Commentarius de anima* taught the self-knowledge of Lutheran Law which was not Gospel. It taught the the spiritual incapacity of Fallen man and the greatness of the almighty Creator. This natural philosophy was developed in order to prove the starting point of moral philosophy, which was itself knowledge of Lutheran Law. The premise of Melanchthon's natural philosophy of the soul itself was also Lutheran. That God's power to create, plan and preserve could be perceived through physical and created things at all was a Lutheran position to hold on Providence. As I have argued at the beginning of this chapter, whether God is present *in* this world or presides *over* this world was a point of difference which became manifest between the differing interpretations of the Lord's Supper by Luther and by Zwingli.[141] The presence of (the power of) God in this physical world is hence in essence a theological point which underpins Luther's view of Christ as the incarnate Word and a point which perhaps received adequate elaboration only when the necessity to do so arose. Thus, in its aim, the kind of knowledge it imparted and the premise on which it rested, the *Commentarius de anima* was a Lutheran natural philosophy of the soul.[142]

140 See the motto 'know thyself' on the anatomical fugitive sheet dated 1601 in Nutton (1993), 19. A similar sheet was printed in Wittenberg even in 1625. For the use of the motto in anatomical fugitive sheets, see Lint (1924), 79–89.

141 See for instance Luther against Zwingli: 'It is God who creates, effects, and preserves all things through his almighty power and right hand, as our Creed confesses. For he dispatches no officials or angels when he creates or preserves something, but all this is the work of his divine power itself. If he is to create or preserve it, however, he must be present and must make and preserve his creation both in its innermost and outermost aspects. Therefore, indeed, he himself must be present in every single creature in its innermost and outermost being, on all sides, through and through, below and above, before and behind, so that nothing can be more truly present and within all creatures than God himself with his power.' 'That These Words of Christ, "This is My Body" etc. Still Stand Firm Against the Fanatics' (1527), as translated by R. H. Fischer in *LW*, XXXVII, 57f.

142 It is precisely because of this Lutheran orientation and the importance of understanding the soul as a Christian one that I have refrained from calling Melanchthon's natural philosophy an 'anthropology' or 'psychology', though it seems to be standard practice in current scholarship, see for instance Park and Keßler (1988) and Bornkamm (1961). The traditional view that Melanchthon was the first to use the term (based on Bretschneider's remark in *CR*, XIII, 1f.) has been challenged in Lapionte (1973), 140–2. The term

A natural philosophy of the Christian soul will necessarily be shaped by how one understands man, Creation and God, as well as by how one believes knowledge of the sacred to be possible. And naturally, people with different beliefs wrote different kinds of commentaries on the *De anima*. We may catch a glimpse of this in two other natural philosophy textbooks on the soul written by men who had once taught the *De anima* at Wittenberg.

The first example is a work written by Vitus Amerbach (1503–57) who had been teaching natural philosophy at Wittenberg for some time in the late 1530s.[143] Amerbach published his *Quatuor libri de anima* in 1542, deliberately, it seems, in opposition to Melanchthon's *Commentarius de anima*.[144] The first book explains Aristotle's definition of the soul as 'entelechy' which, Amerbach says, has to be immobile because it is a principle.[145] Amerbach then goes on to argue in the rest of the first book that Cicero's reading of 'entelechy' as 'endelechy', a continuous agitation, was *not* what Aristotle meant.[146] The second book deals with the nutritive and sensitive souls with minimal reference to the physical body. In the third book, Amerbach deals with the Intellective soul. He is not interested at all in drawing a clear distinction between the natural state of Fallen man and knowledge gained through faith. He simply defines the free will as 'a capacity of reason or will by which good is chosen with the assistance of grace and bad chosen with the departure of grace'.[147] Nor is he interested in the value of the human body as a creation of God, or as 'self-knowledge'. For Amerbach, to 'know thyself' is to know what man can or cannot do in learning, in making things and in actions.[148] There is no indication that such a self-knowledge

'psychology' in either its Latin or Greek form started to be used towards the end of the sixteenth century. Cf. the works by later Lutherans: Otto Casmann (1562–1607): *Psychologia anthropologica, sive animae humanae doctrina* (Hanau, 1594) and *Anthropologiae pars II, hoc est, de fabrica corporis* (Hanau, 1596); Johannes Magirus (d. 1596), *Anthropologia, hoc est commentarius eruditissimus in aureum Philippi Melanchthonis libellum de anima etc.* (Frankfurt, 1603).

143 *Urkundenbuch*, 163. He also published the *Liber de meteoris, cum interpretatione Viti Amerbachii* (Strasburg: C. Mylius, 1539).

144 For a comparison of the use of Greek between Melanchthon and Amerbach, see Nutton (1990), 146.

145 Amerbach, *Quatuor libri de anima*, (Strasburg: C. Mylius, 1542).

146 *Quatuor libri de anima*, 65–87; Keßler (1988), 517.

147 'Liberum arbitrium est facultas rationis aut voluntatis, qua bonum eligitur, gratia assistente, vel malum, ea desistente.' *Quatuor libri de anima*, 247.

148 'Atque hoc est, quod veteres periti rerum dixerunt, γνῶθι σεαυτὸν. Vere enim is se cognovit, qui didicit, quid possit vel in discendis, vel agendis, vel faciendis rebus, et quid non possit efficere.' *Quatuor libri de anima*, 175.

should lead to a knowledge of God. Amerbach states at the end of the third book that the human body is simply an instrument of the locomotive soul. The fourth books deals with some topics from the *Parva naturalia*.

This work seems to have angered several people at Wittenberg.[149] Some time in 1542 Amerbach left Wittenberg, taught at a Latin school in Eichstätt for a while, and then moved to Ingolstadt in 1543.[150] At Ingolstadt he re-converted to Catholicism and succeeded Johannes Eck, one of Luther's fiercest foes, who had died earlier that year.[151]

It seems that Melanchthon was not too offended by Amerbach's *De anima*.[152] What was more crucial, it seems, was that Amerbach was refusing to accept the particle *sola* of Luther's *sola fide*, and was arguing that faith signifies knowledge only and not trust in grace.[153] Amerbach's difference with Melanchthon seems to go back earlier than his composition of the *Quatuor libri de anima* in 1542. In 1537 Caspar Cruciger was reported to have called Amerbach 'Thersites', the deformed and foul-mouthed man who spoke against Agamemnon (*Iliad* I, 225–42), because Amerbach had in his own lecture on the *Physica* slandered Melanchthon.[154] The nature of Amerbach's criticism is not known, but it may have been the case that for Amerbach a point of difference had, through his writing of the *De anima*, developed into a point of departure, a departure which ultimately meant leaving the Lutheran faith. Amerbach's *De anima* may be understood as a commentary which, although coming out from Wittenberg, the heart of the Reformation, displayed no characteristic elements of a Lutheran commentary. The author himself did not understand the essence of Lutheran faith.

Another natural philosophy text written by a Wittenberg man, and which had a curious *fortuna*, is the *Epitome* of Johannes Bernhardi (d. 1534) published posthumously in 1537 and used frequently

149 'Constat aliquos veterum philosophorum ad insaniam versos, quos imitatus Amerbachius pro philosophari debacchari incoepit, inque convitia prolapsus pro scientia de anima docet inania, quae confixerat somnia . . .' *CR*, V, 232.

150 Friedensburg (1917), 226.

151 See Luther to Anton Lauterbach, 9 February 1544, *WBr*, X, 527f.

152 Letter to Vitus Theodorus, 25 October 1543, *MBW* no. 3356, *CR*, V, 207 (dated 22 October).

153 'De iustificatione displicet ei [Amerbach] particula sola, et disputavit fide significari tantum noticiam, non fiduciam misericordiae.' Letter to Georg Pontanus, 19 November 1543, *MBW* no. 3377, *CR*, V, 233, my interpolation.

154 Friedensburg (1917), 226.

by others. Johannes Bernhardi was better known as Johannes Velcurio after his home town Feldkirch, in order to distinguish him from his brother, Bartholomaeus Bernhardi (1487–1551).[155] Having been one of the students to live through the excitement of Luther's revolt from its earliest times, Johannes Velcurio seems to have actively supported Luther's cause. In 1520 he defended Luther's denial of the papal supremacy in the *Confutatio pro D. M. Luthero* in response to an attack by Augustine Alveld (*Libellus quo ostendere conatur, divino iure hoc institutum esse, ut totius ecclesiae caput sit romanus pontifex*).[156] Both Melanchthon and Luther regarded Velcurio highly. Luther warmly praised Velcurio's faith in a consolation speech at the latter's deathbed in 1534.[157] Melanchthon recommended Velcurio as a tutor,[158] and arranged for the posthumous publication of Velcurio's commentary on Erasmus' *De duplici copia verborum*.[159]

Velcurio, an active supporter of Luther's cause, whose faith and scholarly integrity were approved of by the Reformers, seems also to have been a lecturer on natural philosophy. His work on natural philosophy appeared posthumously in Basle in 1537 as the *In philosophiae naturalis partem omnium praestantissimam, hoc est, Aristotelis de Anima libros, Epitome longe doctissima, per D. Welcurionem, clarissimum quondam philosophiae in Academia Witenbergensi professorem conscripta, et nunc primum in lucem edita*. It was printed with a commentary on Aristotle's *Metaphysica* by an Italian, Marcus Antonius Flaminus.[160] The printers were a printing partnership in Basle, Balthassar Lasius and Thomas Platter, for whom the future famous printer Johann Oporinus, then a Latin teacher at Basle, acted as a binder and technical advisor.[161]

As was often the case in this partnership, Oporinus wrote the

155 Kropatscheck (1901), 456, *CR*, I, 166 note*. The name Velcurio itself was a further source of confusion until 1523 because Johannes Dölsch was called Velcurio after his prebendary precinct.

156 The two parts were printed together, see *VD* A2106 (Cologne: H. von Neuss, 1520). There seems no positive evidence to suggest that Velcurio's *Confutatio* was mainly written by Melanchthon, as claimed by Bretschneider in *CR*, I, 166f. See also his letter to Johann Hess, 8 June 1520, *MBW* no. 95, *CR*, I, 201.

157 For the speech, see Buchwald (1884).

158 Letter to Johannes Velcurio, 1525, *MBW* no. 434, *CR*, I, 777f.

159 Cf. Melanchthon's letter to the printer, Petrus Brubach, August 1534, *MBW* no. 1455, *CR*, II, 784f. For a brief discussion of the place of Velcurio's commentary in renaissance ideas of commonplaces, see Lechner (1962), 176–9.

160 Lohr, 149.

161 Steinmann (1967), 8–11.

prefatory letter to the reader. The letter is dedicated to Du Bellay de Langey, French ambassador to the Empire, who was accompanied by Wilhelm Bigot who helped edit the original manuscript, according to Oporinus.[162] Bigot had stayed in Tübingen for a while where he taught philosophy until he was forced to resign the chair and went to Basle in 1536, because of his disagreement with other professors over introducing Melanchthon's philosophy.[163]

In the prefatory letter, Oporinus says that he knows nothing of the author Velcurio other than the fact that he was at one time a teacher of natural philosophy of Wittenberg.[164] Velcurio had composed an epitome of natural philosophy in four parts. The first part comprised Aristotle's *Physica*, the second part the *De caelo et mundo*, the *De generatione et corruptione* and some others, the third part the *Meteora* and the fourth part the *De anima*. Although last in order, Oporinus says that he has produced the fourth part on the soul first because it was most ready for publication. He hopes to publish the remainder in due course.[165] Even this fourth part, which Bigot seems to have edited, is not complete as it lacks the last chapters on the origin and immortality of the soul. Despite its deficiencies, we can readily notice that Velcurio's work has several features in common with Melanchthon's. For instance, Velcurio, like Melanchthon, stresses the importance of natural philosophy for moral philosophy, theology and medicine. 'Synteresis' is regarded as an innate practical principle useful for regulating civil conduct. This commentary on the soul by Velcurio does not, however, contain any part on human anatomy.

In the following year, 1538, there appeared in Erfurt an enlarged edition of Velcurio's commentary, *Epitomae physicae libri quatuor, authore Ioanne Veltkirchio, clarissimo quondam apud Vittenbergenses philosophiae professore, nunc primum in lucem editi.* This contained all the four parts with the last three chapters of the fourth book augmented as well. This was edited apparently by a student of Velcurio, Caspar Cerameus.[166] Cerameus dedicated this work to the patron and members of the Saxon college of the University of Erfurt.

162 Velcurio, *Aristotelis de Anima ..., Epitome* (Basle: T. Platter and B. Lasius, 1537), A3r.
163 Hoffmann (1982), 212.
164 'Caeterum de autore ipso illud solum nobis constat, insignem quondam VVittenbergensis Academiae in Philosophia professorem fuisse ...' *Aristotelis de Anima ..., Epitome,* A3r.
165 *Aristotelis de Anima ..., Epitome,* A3r–v.
166 See Cerameus' preface, *Epitomae physicae libri quatuor* (Erfurt: M. Saxo, 1538), A2v–A3r.

Interestingly enough, in this augmented edition we can see that Velcurio had some interest in human anatomy. In the third book, after having dealt with the animal books of Aristotle, he devotes the last five chapters to human anatomy. The last chapter is on the parts of the human body and he promises to explain human anatomy with descriptions and a picture of the internal and external parts of the body. The works of some medics, Velcurio says, such as the first Fen of Avicenna, Alexander Benedictus' *Libri quinque de anatomia* or *De historia corporis humani* and Berengario da Carpi's *Isagoge anatomie corporis humani*, should exhibit to the eyes what should be seen.[167] However, only the headings of the chapters on the human body are printed in this commentary. It is not clear whether this is due to the condition of the manuscript or a deliberate and/or practical editorial omission. This edition, however, seems to preserve several elements of what was once a work of a Lutheran.

In 1539, at Tübingen, another edition, the *Commentarii in universam physicam Aristotelis*, was published. Although hardly different from the Erfurt edition, it is this Tübingen edition which was reprinted most frequently, nineteen times until 1595.[168] At the request of the printer Ulrich Morhard, this edition seems to have been edited by Sebald Hawenreuther (1508–89), father of Johann Ludwig Hawenreuther (1548–1618), who wrote the *Synopsis, compendium librorum physicorum Aristotelis* for the Strasburg Academy.[169] Sebald Hawenreuther matriculated in the University of Wittenberg in 1531 and had heard Velcurio's lectures. In 1535 he moved to the newly reformed University of Tübingen.[170] As its printing record indicates, the text seems still to have been in use even after Hawen-

[167] '... item absolvuisse volo, caput tricesimumquartum, de corpore hominis, in quod congerere potest studiosus ea quae de moribus et affectionibus corporum, item de complexionibus et qualitatibus corporis humani Physicis medicisque produntur. Item absoluisse volo caput tricesimumquintum de partibus corporis humani, quarum internarum scilicet, et externarum in corpore humano, anatomiam et descriptionem, adeoque picturam diligenter cum alij Medici, tum imprimis Avicenna in primo Tomo, et post cum Alexander Benedictus libris quinque de anatomia, vel de historia corporis humani, et Iacobus Carpus Bononiensis in Isagoge anatomiae corporis humani etiam oculis spectandam praebuerunt.' *Epitomae physicae libri quatuor*, c4v.

[168] *Lohr*, 474.

[169] *Lohr*, 183f. See also Johan Sturm's letter to Sebastian Hawenreuther dated 1578 in Johann Ludwig Hawenreuther, *Synopsis, commentarii in universam physicam Aristotelis* (Cambridge: J. Legatt, 1594), a5v.

[170] *Die Matrikeln der Universität Tübingen*, I, 280; for the reformation of the arts faculty at Tübingen, see Hoffmann (1982); for Melanchthon's role in reforming Tübingen, see Harrison (1978).

reuther had left Tübingen where Jacob Schegk (1511–87), a medic and polemicist, was teaching natural philosophy.[171]

Jacob Schegk is better known for his bitter dispute with Petrus Ramus (1515–72) over the value of Aristotelian logic and philosophy from around 1569 until the latter's death in the St Bartholomew's Day Massacre.[172] Schegk also conducted a medical controversy with Simon Simonius (1532–1602) between 1571 and 1573.[173] After Camerarius had left for Leipzig in 1541,[174] and Leonhart Fuchs had died in 1553, Schegk seems to have dominated the teaching of Aristotelian logic, philosophy and medicine at Tübingen. It may well have been the case that Schegk was responsible for the continued use of the Velcurio text at Tübingen.[175] Schegk is known to have supported a Zwinglian interpretation of the Lord's Supper,[176] and he was a lecturer on logic, natural philosophy and medicine until he finally retired owing to his complete loss of eyesight in 1577.[177]

Although a study of the teaching of natural philosophy at Tübingen doubtless deserves a full study of its own, I should like to draw attention to the likelihood that Velcurio's commentary on natural philosophy, which differed most from that of Melanchthon in that it did not contain human anatomy, was used as a text by a Tübingen lecturer on natural philosophy who was a Zwinglian. Schegk was a Zwinglian in the sense that he denied the real presence of Christ in the Lord's Supper. It seems to be a striking contrast that a Zwinglian would be content to use a textbook on the soul which did not contain details of human anatomy while a Lutheran natural philosophy on the soul considered such knowledge integral.[178] The

171 Schegk lectured on natural philosophy from 1536 to 1552 and on a summary course on natural philosophy (*Lectio physices sive compendii physices*) between 1546 to 1552, Hoffman (1982), 246. For Schegk, see also Sigwart (1889), Hoffmann (1982), 138–40, and the biobibliographic entry in the *Cambridge History of Renaissance Philosophy*, 836.

172 For the relevant sources, see Ong (1958), 374–80.

173 For Schegk's medical theory on formative virtue, soul and heat, see Pagel (1969–70), 9: 26–30. For Simonius, see Mandonia (1988).

174 Schegk too was invited to Leipzig but refused to go owing to his poor eyesight. Sigwart (1889), 261, 263.

175 Schegk himself seems to have disliked compendium forms, though he was probably not against such forms for introductory texts, Sigwart (1889), 265.

176 For Schegk as espousing a Zwinglian interpretation of the Lord's Supper, see Sigwart (1889), 274–6.

177 Sigwart (1889), 278f.

178 The *De anima* of Conrad Gessner, who was a Zwinglian, confined its anatomical discussion to the brain and its functions, and had little use of the new Galen or anatomy. Nutton

one does not need the Providence of God to rule in the world, for the other it is crucial that God is present in this world.

At times when it was imperative to dissociate Luther's cause from the evangelical radicals, Melanchthon had developed a natural philosophy of the whole man which demonstrated the starting point of his moral philosophy of civil obedience. As many had done before him, Melanchthon turned to Aristotle's *De anima* in order to discuss the Christian man. The way he did it, however, was new. Because of the Lutheran reorientation of the meaning of man's spirituality, (Galenic) human anatomy was included for the first time. By teleologically proving the presence of the power of the Creator God in man, and contrasting it with man's Fallenness, Melanchthon developed a distinctive Lutheran knowledge of Law which was different from, but was necessary for understanding the message of the Gospel. It was, I hope to have shown, a distinctively Lutheran kind of natural philosophy. It is also in this light that Melanchthon's well-known adoption of Vesalian anatomy ought to be understood.

VESALIUS AND THE *LIBER DE ANIMA*

At the beginning of the year 1552, Melanchthon was staying at Nuremberg awaiting the Elector Maurice of Saxony's instructions for whether to proceed to attend the Council of Trent or not. On the day of the conversion of Paul, namely 25 January in 1552, Melanchthon wrote a poem entitled *De humani corporis consideratione*. It seems to have been printed at Nuremberg the same year, but I have so far been unable to locate any printing dating from 1552.[179] The autograph copy of this poem was attached to Melanchthon's own copy of Andreas Vesalius' *De humani corporis fabrica libri septem* (Basle, 1543) (Fig. 6).[180] And it is according to this work by Vesalius that Melanchthon was revising his *Commentarius de anima*, as he wrote to Johann Stigelius:

Paul Eber has sent you leaflets which contain some stuff recited in [his] explanation of the *De anima*. I shall be sending you through other messengers descriptions of others who have corrected more accurately some

(1990), 151. For Gessner in general, see Wellisch (1984), and for his Zwinglian faith, see Serrai (1990), 52–69.

179 See also *Hartfelder*, 608.

180 Melanchthon's copy of the *Fabrica* is now in the Surgeon-General's Library, National Library of Medicine, Bethesda, Maryland, USA, see *A Bio-Bibliography of Andreas Vesalius*,

errors in anatomy. The work of Vesalius was not yet published when I was collecting those elements from Galen and Carpi [Berengario da Carpi]. And the teaching of Carpi is more confused. Therefore, even if with fair diligence I picked out the principal parts, yet later when I saw it, correction became necessary. And if I may live, I shall renew the whole book. For it is necessary that there is in the Church a fairly well explained teaching about the distinction of the powers of the soul. And although this work was of use to many, second thoughts may bring some light.[181]

As early as 1540, Melanchthon had been thinking of revising his *Commentarius de anima*. Leonhart Fuchs seems to have been one of his earlier correctors in anatomical matters.[182] It seems, however, that it was only after ten years that Melanchthon finally got around to doing so. Some time after 1550,[183] Melanchthon sent a copy of his work on the soul to Joachim Camerarius the younger (1534–98).

You remember the verse in which the rhythm is that of a Greek poet, but its sense is God's: 'Good qualities descend to the sons of the pious, but not to those of the ungodly' [Theocritus, *Idylla*, XXVI, 32]. Your parents have worshipped God with true invocation and have supported the Church and your father has adorned the Church with distinguished monuments. Therefore his family will be in God's care and I wish you to heed the examples of your parents. As it is necessary for you at this age to learn the elements of philosophy (*philosophica elementa*), I am sending you some pages of the book of the *De anima* (*pagellas libri de Anima*) intended to be taught to young men, as often explained in the book itself. I wanted to inscribe these verses in the booklet but there was not enough space:

Your good father and I, although two bodies we are, our souls agree [as one] in God. Thus my mind is not so different from yours. Receive it, and may you profit from this small gift.[184]

80f. For Vesalius, the standard biography is C. D. O'Malley (1964). Cf. Cunningham, forthcoming.

181 'Paulus Eberus mittit tibi pagellas, quae continent quaedam recitata in enarratione sylvulae περὶ ψυχῆς. Mittam autem per alios nuntios aliorum descriptiones, qui emendarunt quaedam σφάλματα in Anatomia accuratius. Nondum erat editum Wesalii opus, cum ego haec initia colligerem ex Galeno et Carpo. Et confusior est Carpi doctrina. Etsi igitur mediocri diligentia excerpsi praecipua, tamen postea vidi, opus esse emendatione. Et si vivam, retexam totum libellum. Necesse est enim in Ecclesia exstare mediocriter explicatam doctrinam de discrimine potentiarum animae. Et quanquam haec sylvula profuit multis, tamen δευτέραι φροντίδες aliquid lucis adferent.' Letter to Johann Stigelius, 29 June 1552, *CR*, VII, 1015. For Berengario da Carpi, see French (1986).

182 Letters to Fuchs, 14 December 1540 and 25 December 1540, *MBW* nos. 2579 and 2598; *CR*, III, 1211, 1246.

183 The following letter is dated as 25 January 1550 in *CR*, VII, 539. The original autograph letters are now in the Vatican Library (Chigi J VIII-294, 299r).

184 'Meministi versum in quo numeri sunt graeci poetae, sed sententia divina est
ἐυσεβέων παιδέσσι τὰ λωϊα, δυσσεβέων δ'οὔ.

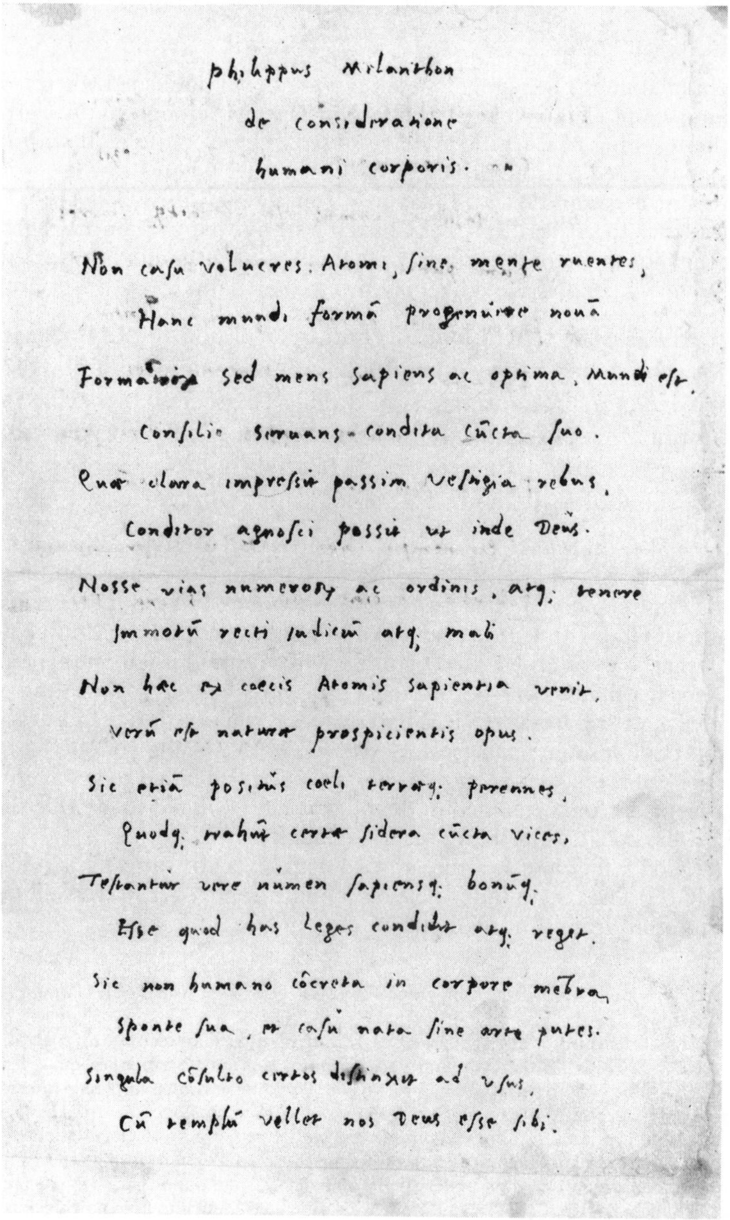
Philippus Melanthon
de consideratione
humani corporis.

Non casu volucres Atomi, sine mente ruentes,
Hanc mundi formã progenuere nouã
Formatorq; sed mens sapiens ac optima, mundi est,
Consilio seruans condita cũcta suo.
Quae clara impressit passim vestigia rebus,
Conditor agnosci possit ut inde Deus.
Nosse vias numerorũ ac ordinis, atq; tenere
Immotũ recti iudiciũ atq; mali
Non haec ex coecis Atomis sapientia venit,
Verũ est naturae prospicientis opus.
Sic etiã positus coeli terraq; perennes,
Quodq; trahũt certas sidera cũcta vices,
Testantur vere numen sapiensq; bonũq;
Esse quod has leges condidit atq; reget.
Sic non humano cõcreta in corpore membra,
Sponte sua, et casu nata sine arte putes.
Singula cõsulto certos destinxit ad usus,
Cũ templũ vellet nos Deus esse sibi.

6 *The Fabric of the Human Body*. Autograph poem by Melanchthon (1552), from the fly-leaf of his copy of Andreas Vesalius' *De humani corporis fabrica libri septem* (Basle: Johannes Oporinus, 1543)

Divina in cerebro radios sapientia spargit

Cum verbo mentes Luce suaque regit.

At cor Iusticiae domus est, sentitque dolores,

Cum punit sontes vindicis ira Dei.

Adflatuque dei purgatū gaudia sentit

Et vita fruitur non pereunte Dei.

Formatū ad tantos corpus cū videris usus

Factorē agnoscas & venerere Deū.

Ipsius & templū non labes ulla prophanet,

Pollutū abyciat ne gravis ira Dei.

Noribergae Die

conversionis Pauli

1590.

Most probably on the same day, Melanchthon wrote to the father for his approval of the text.[185] It is difficult to believe that Melanchthon had been waiting for Camerarius Sr's approval of the *Commentarius de anima*, a work printed more than ten years ago. Thus we may well conjecture that Melanchthon's commentary was undergoing some revision by the early 1550s. Judging from the location of Melanchthon's autograph manuscript for the *Liber de anima*, it may well have been the case that some substantial revision was done during Melanchthon's stay at Nuremberg. The revised edition came out as *Liber de anima recognitus* later in 1552.[186] Significant additions, revisions and omissions occurred in the *Liber de anima*.[187] Several changes are direct results of Melanchthon's reading of Vesalius' *De humani corporis fabrica*. For example, he adopts Vesalius' distinction of the functions of glottis and epiglottis, which were not properly distinguished from each other by Galen.[188] Vesalius is also cited for Melanchthon's adoption of the correct shape of the liver. Melanchthon's rejection of the existence of the *rete mirabile* may also be due to his reading of the *Fabrica*.[189]

Melanchthon, however, possibly saw in Vesalius something more substantially important than a mere corrective to Galen. After discussing the structure and use of the heart Melanchthon wrote:

> seeing this wonderful variety of work and these arrangements of God, looking from without and through a thick darkness, we are dumbfounded, and grieve that we cannot examine nature deeply and see the causes. But then, at least, when we see the 'Idea' (*Ideam*) of nature in the divine mind, we shall look at this whole machine as from within, and understand the

Parentes autem tui vera invocatione colunt Deum et Ecclesiam adiuvant, et pater ornat eam multis egregiis monumentis. Ideo et familia eius Deo curae erit, teque volo intueri parentum exempla. Cum autem necesse sit te hac aetate discere philosophica elementa, mitto tibi pagellas libri de Anima, qui quo consilio tradatur adolescentibus, saepe in ipso libro exponitur. Hos autem versus inscribere pagellis volebam, sed spacii tantum non erat.

σώματα μὲν δυό ἐσμὲν, ὁμοφρονέουσα δε ψυχὴ
ἐν θεῷ, ἀυτος ἐγὼ σὸς τε πατὴρ ἀγαθός
τὴν δ'ἐμõυ οὖν ψυχὴν ὀυκ ἀλλοτρίαν σοι ἐοῦσαν
δεξάμενος δῶρον τοῦδε ὄναιο μικροῦ.'

Letter to Joachim Camerarius Jr. 25 January, early 1550s, *CR*, VII, 539.

185 Letter to Joachim Camerarius Sr., Vatican Library, Chigi JVIII-294, 387r. This letter does not occur in *CR*. *MBW* has not reached this year by the time of going to press.

186 The Nuremberg Stadtarchiv owns an autograph manuscript of the *Liber de anima recognitus*, prepared for the 1552 edition, *Iter Italicum*, III, 664. For Melanchthon's stay in Nuremberg, see *CR*, VII, xiv.

187 Nutton (1990), 150f.

188 *Liber de anima*, *CR*, XIII, 62.

189 For details, see Nutton (1990), 149.

plans of the Creator and the causes of all the divine works. Now by this incomplete consideration, we acknowledge that God is the Architect and we should be inflamed with the desire for that perfect wisdom.[190]

This passage, which does not occur in the *Commentarius de anima*, echoes the scriptural passage on the yearning for the complete knowledge of God in 1 Corinthians 13. 12: 'For now we see through a glass, darkly; but then face to face: now I know in part; but then shall I know even as also I am known.'[191] Through anatomy, as if through a clouded glass, Melanchthon was reaching out for the knowledge of the Architect. The agreement in sentiment with the following passage from Vesalius is striking. After conceding that the production of the animal spirit in the ventricles of the brain does not explain much about the working of the rational soul, Vesalius had written:

singing songs of praise to God, the Universal Creator, we shall render thanks to Him that He has bestowed on us a Rational soul which we have in common with angels (and so, not to forget even ill-used philosophers, Plato himself intimated). If only to this good gift of God we add Faith, we shall enjoy that eternal felicity, when the seat of the Soul and its substance need be sought neither by dissection of the body nor by our reason oppressed and fettered by the body. For He who is True Wisdom will teach us, not as beings formed of this substance which comes into being and passes away, but [as beings formed] of a spiritual substance which resembles His own. But since up to now we are that which frail Reason declares us to be, we shall explore the ingenuity of the Artificer of the Universe, as shown in the remaining parts of the brain, according to our powers as men.[192]

Both agree on the reason why human anatomy is necessary (because man's natural cognition is clouded) and both agree on what is to be seen through anatomy (God the Creator and His skill). In short, they are in complete agreement on what anatomy should mean for a Christian man.

We may recall how important Galen was for Melanchthon in the

190 'Hanc mirificam operis varietatem, et haec Dei consilia, foris et per densam caliginem aspicientes, obstupescimus, ac dolemus, nos non penitus introspicere naturam, et causas videre posse. Sed tunc demum, cum ideam naturae in mente divina cernemus, totam hanc machinam velut intus aspiciemus, et opificis consilia et causas omnium operum divinorum intelligemus. Nunc inchoata hac consideratione Deum Architectum agnoscamus, et illius perfectae sapientiae desiderio accendamur.' *CR*, XIII, 57.

191 For this theme in literature, see Nolan (1990).

192 As translated in Singer (1952), 40.

Commentarius de anima. Galenic anatomy demonstrated teleologically the existence of God the Creator in the human body. Galen pointed to the presence of God the Creator in the physical body. Perhaps Vesalius was the 'reborn Galen' Melanchthon had been hoping for.[193] Melanchthon and Vesalius saw the human body in the same way and also understood the importance of human anatomy in the same way. This is why Melanchthon praises Vesalius so highly and why Vesalius' work was incorporated in the *Liber de anima*.

What is most striking about the *Liber de anima* is, as noted by Walker, that Melanchthon now sees the working of the Holy Spirit (as well as of the evil spirits) as physical reality in the human body:

> and [the spirits, vital and animal], by their light excel the light of the sun and all the stars; and, what is still more marvellous, in pious men the divine spirit itself is mixed with these very spirits, and makes them shine more brightly with divine light, so that their knowledge of God may be clearer, their ascent to Him more resolute, and their feelings towards Him more ardent. Conversely, when devils occupy the heart, by their blowing they trouble the spirits in the heart and brain, impede judgement and produce manifest madness, and drive the heart and other limbs to the cruellest movements; as when Medea killed her children, or when Judas killed himself. Let us therefore look to our nature and diligently rule it and let us pray to the Son of God that He may drive the devils away from us, and may pour the divine spirit into our spirits.[194]

It is unclear whether it was directly due to his reading of Vesalius that Melanchthon began to see the Holy Spirit as physical reality. The above passage seems to signify, however, what Melanchthon wanted to see all along in the human body, namely the presence of the power of God. In the *Liber de anima*, with a renewed conviction in the use of anatomy, this vision of the Providence of God was now a reality for Melanchthon.

The title-page of the *Liber de anima* shows a brazen serpent, a famous device of the Reformation printers at Wittenberg (Fig. 7).[195] It was also Melanchthon's coat of arms. The brazen serpent is an Old Testament episode (Numbers 21) in which Israelites who spoke against God were bitten by serpents. Moses interceded with God on behalf of the Israelites and was ordered to make a bronze serpent and set it on a pole, so that anyone bitten by the serpents would be

[193] See p. 84f. above. For Vesalius as following Galen, see Cunningham, forthcoming.
[194] *Liber de anima*, *CR*, XIII, 88f., as translated in Walker (1984), 228, interpolation by Walker.
[195] Ehresmann (1966/7), 33.

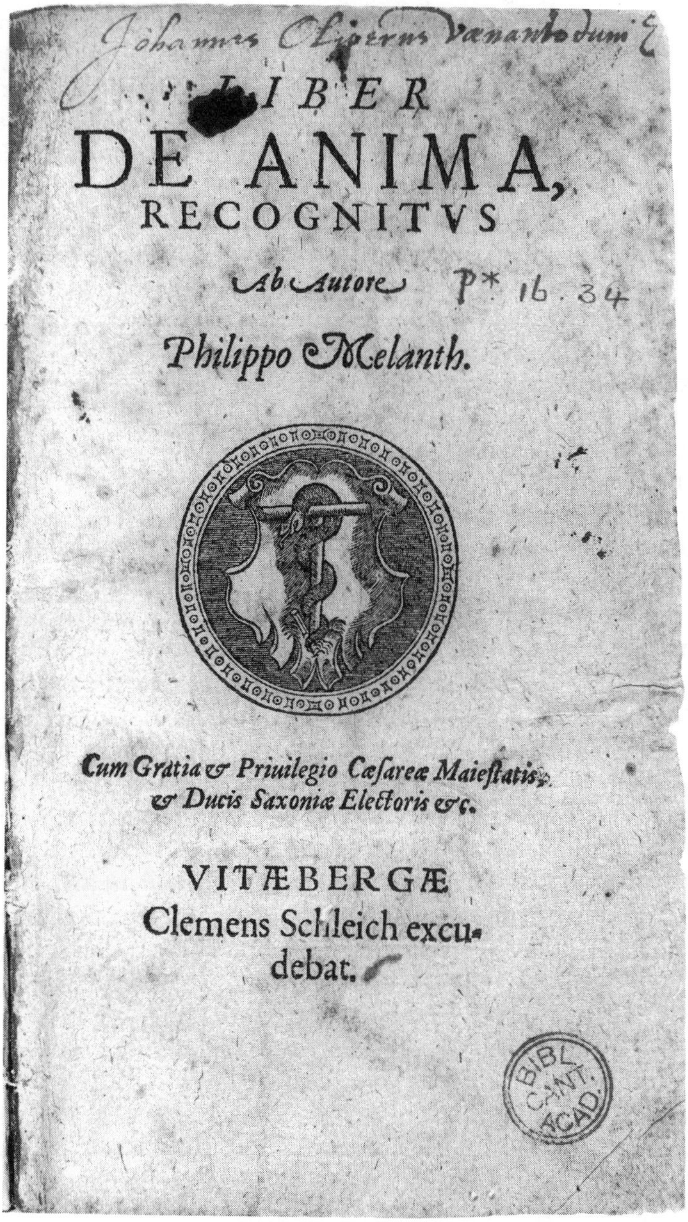

7 The Brazen Serpent. Title-page of the *Liber de anima recognitus* (Wittenberg: Clemens Schleich, 1552)

saved just by looking at it. As Ehresman has clearly shown, although an Old Testament episode, Luther attached special significance to the brazen serpent episode as an illustration of faith and idolatry.[196] Luther rejected all images except for the Crucifixion as representation of faith. But he needed to clarify that it was not the image that brings salvation, but only faith in God's promise which the image symbolizes. By choosing an image of the same object which afflicted the Israelites, God allows no possiblity that the object itself will be interpreted as the source of the healing power. Instead, God demands faith in His Word that the serpent will heal, a faith symbolized in the act of looking at the brazen serpent. It is not the image but faith in the Word that brings salvation. The brazen serpent thus became a powerful example by which the true nature of faith could be understood.

It is around the same time as Luther began to understand the brazen serpent as a significant symbol of the crucified Christ that Melanchthon took it up as his coat of arms.[197] It is also around this time that Melanchthon re-evaluated the significance of philosophy teaching, specifically in order to refute the civil disobedience of those he considered to be Anabaptists. Civil disobedience also became the issue through which Melanchthon dealt with the deviations of the Zwinglians, who had been identified with Luther and himself by the Roman Catholics. In an effort to draw a clear distinction between Luther and the evangelical radicals, and in order further to fortify his argument against civil unrest, Melanchthon began to interpret from a Lutheran perspective a pagan philosopher's philosophy of the soul and a classical medic's human anatomy. In this process other authors, ancient and modern, were freely drawn upon. Though Melanchthon's commentary on the soul may well be characterized as 'eclectic' in this respect, it has to be remembered that Melanchthon's principle of choice was distinctively Lutheran. He was not trying to revive or relive the philosophy of the ancients, but he was using them in order to provide an exposition of a *Lutheran* concept of soul. As a knowledge of Lutheran Law, this natural philosophy did not teach the message of the Gospel, but nevertheless it taught the self-knowledge of Fallen man and the greatness of the Creator. Thus, it seems to me that the

[196] Here, I have paraphrased the excellent argument in Ehresmann (1966/7).
[197] Ehresmann (1966/7), 34, 45.

title-page of the *Liber de anima* aptly signifies what Melanchthon was doing in his natural philosophy of the soul: pagan (i.e. non-Christian) material was re-interpreted in a Lutheran framework in order to demonstrate a specifically Lutheran point.

CHAPTER 4

The Providence of God

All the world's a stage.

William Shakespeare, *As You Like It* II. ii

THE COMET OF 1531

But there were false prophets also among the people, even as there shall be false teachers among you, who privily shall bring in damnable heresies, even denying the Lord that bought them, and bring upon themselves swift destruction ... And turning the cities of Sodom and Gomorrha into ashes [he] condemned them with an overthrow (καταστροφή), making them an ensample unto those that after should live ungodly. (II Peter 2. 1, 6)

From 1530 on, both Luther and Melanchthon could clearly see in this passage a parallel of their times.[1] At the Marburg Colloquy Luther refused to compromise with the Zwinglians whom he regarded as 'false brethren'.[2] Melanchthon also refused to acknowledge the Zwinglians as brethren.[3] When at the Diet of Augsburg Eck identified Luther with other evangelical radicals including Zwingli, it became imperative to dissociate themselves from the Zwinglians and the evangelical radicals. Melanchthon painstakingly pointed out their differences with the Zwinglians in the *Augsburg Confession*. It is during the Diet of Augsburg that Melanchthon began using the Greek word 'καταστροφή' ('catastrophe') to mean a mounting threat of an impending disaster.[4] When the Emperor

[1] It was after 1530 that Luther saw in the second epistle of St Peter contemporary parallels, see his preface to that letter, *LW*, xxxv, 392.

[2] For Luther's identification of his opponents (including the Zwinglians) with 'false brethren', see Edwards (1975).

[3] Manschreck (1958), 171.

[4] See for instance, letters to Hieronymus Baumgarten, 21 May 1530, *MBW* no. 912, *CR*, II, 58; to Vitus Theodorus, 1 September 1530, *MBW* no. 1059, *CR*, II, 336; to Camerarius, 12 November 1530, *MBW* no. 1098, *CR*, II, 439 (dated 13 November). The word 'καταστροφή'

rejected the Protestant princes' case at Augsburg, both Melanchthon and Luther developed an acute sense not only of the imminent outbreak of war, but also of an impending catastrophe, namely, the End of the World.

Luther was vividly living the Last Days.[5] The practice of indulgences and the Turkish menace were apocalyptic signs.[6] Most significantly, Luther found the Anti-Christ in the Pope who oppressed and persecuted the Word of God.[7] Luther did not, however, believe in an active pursuit of the Millennium, as some others did.[8] For Luther, the Reformation could only be implemented by God Himself on the Last Day, and man could only endure, persevere and eagerly await the Last Day.[9] The persecution of the Word of God will necessarily precede the Last Judgement, and in preparation for the Last Day, the Word of God should be proclaimed as prophesied in Matthew 24. 14.[10] At the Diet of Augsburg, it became Melanchthon's task to proclaim the Word of God in the *Augsburg Confession.* After Augsburg, he was further engrossed in defending that Confession through numerous revisions and the *Apologia.*[11] Being constantly overworked, Melanchthon soon began to see the end of his own life.[12]

Under such circumstances Melanchthon saw a comet for the first time in his life. In a letter to the astrologer Johann Carion (1499–1537) dated 17 August 1531, Melanchthon sought the former's opinion as to what the comet might signify.[13] In it, Melanchthon lists predictions given by various astrologers as to how the princes might move. On the following day, Melanchthon wrote to Camerarius about the sighting of the comet and wondered whether it was

is used in the New Testament in the same sense as in the above passage, II Peter 2. 1, 6 and 2 Timothy 2. 14, *Computer-Konkordanz zum Novum Testamentum Graece*, 1016.

5 For a biography of Luther as vividly living the Last Days between the Devil and God, see Oberman (1989).

6 Oberman (1989), 70f.; Quanbeck (1961), 122.

7 The identification of the Pope with the Anti-Christ itself was not new. For the difference between the Bohemian and Lutheran views of Pope as Anti-Christ, see Althaus (1970), 420.

8 Althaus (1970), 418f. Cf. the popular millenarian movement, see Cohn (1970).

9 For the difference of attitude towards the Last Day between the medieval tradition and Luther, see Althaus (1970), 420f., and now Barnes (1988).

10 Oberman (1989), 72.

11 Stupperich (1966), 82–92. For sixteenth-century printing of the various editions of the *Confessions* and its *Apologia*, see Neuser (1987).

12 'Ego laboribus et curis miserrimis conficior, ut recte responderit vester Astrologus, me morti vicinum esse, quam ego quidem mihi saepius quam vitam opto.' Letter to Camerarius, 26 July 1531, *MBW* no. 1167, *CR*, II, 515.

13 This letter was first printed in Warburg (1919), 72–5; 7–9 (German translation).

the same kind of comet that Pliny the Elder had called the 'dagger' (ξιφίας).[14] In the ensuing correspondence, Melanchthon further tried to find out over how wide an area the comet could be seen and especially what other astrologers made of its significance.[15] He was soon convinced that something terrible was about to happen.

The appearance of a comet usually signified an ill portent. If something drastic was to happen, this comet of 1531 indeed turned out to precede tragic events especially for the Swiss camp.[16] Zwingli died a violent death in the battle of Kappel in October. On hearing the news, Melanchthon was now quite convinced of the imminent 'catastrophe'.[17] Oecolampadius died two months after Zwingli, and Melanchthon suspected that he was not saved.[18] There is no direct evidence that either Melanchthon or Luther took the appearance of this comet as an Apocalyptic sign,[19] but the destruction of the 'false brethren' that followed it certainly confirmed their belief in an impending catastrophe.

During the same month as he sighted this comet, Melanchthon wrote a eulogy on the study of astrology and astronomy. It was prefixed to an edition of Sacrobosco's *De sphaera*, a standard university textbook on astronomy based on Ptolemy, Macrobius and Arabic commentators such as al-Battani and al-Fraghani.[20] Melanchthon addressed it to Simon Grynaeus (1491–1541), his school friend and gifted Hellenist.[21] This 1531 edition of Sacrobosco was frequently re-printed at Wittenberg.[22]

[14] Letter to Camerarius, 18 August 1531, *MBW* no. 1178, *CR*, II, 518f. For 'ξίφιας' see Pliny, *Historia naturalis*, II, xxii, 89.

[15] See for instance letters to Camerarius, *MBW* no. 1184, *CR*, II, 537f.; *MBW* no. 1190, *CR*, II, 545f.; *MBW* no. 1201, *CR* II, 551f; and to Johannes Brenz, *MBW* no. 1193, *CR*, II, 547.

[16] For the significance of the comet of 1531 amongst different denominational camps, see Rauscher (1911).

[17] 'Egregium habent homines ἄθεοι praetextum hoc tempore, qui nullas volunt habere religiones, qui volunt omnia vincula excutere, simulant se recipere ῥωμαικὴν διδαχὴν abiecta nostra, sed Deus his rebus remedium ostendet. Hic annus afferet, ut ego spero vel καταστροφὴν, vel παρασκευὴν τῆς καταστροφῆς.' Letter to Joachim Camerarius, 6 November 1531, *MBW* no. 1201, *CR*, II, 551f. (dated 2 November).

[18] Letter to Camerarius, 13 January 1532, *MBW* no. 1210, *CR*, II, 563.

[19] Though Luther understood the falling of the star at the end of the World (Apocalypse 8. 10, 9. 1) to mean a comet after 1530. Quanbeck (1961), 122. For the eschatology of the reformers, see further Kunz (1980).

[20] For Sacrobosco's *De sphaera*, see Thorndike (1949).

[21] For a brief but concise biography of Grynaeus, see *Contemporaries of Erasmus*, II, 142–6. Melanchthon's preface itself had a chequered history, being removed by censors, Pantin (1987), 94f. A similar fate was suffered by another prefatory letter of Melanchthon's to Grynaeus, prefixed to the latter's Latin version of Proclus' commentary on the first book of Euclid's *Elements*, Thomas-Stanford (1926), 8.

[22] Of the twenty-four printings during the next fifty years, fifteen were printed in Wittenberg, *General Bibliography of Astronomy to the Year 1880*, II, I, 508.

As usual, Melanchthon's eulogy follows an epideictic form of oration to praise the study of astrology and astronomy. Referring to Plato, Melanchthon gives a strong reason why the study of astronomy is necessary:

Plato should be judged to have said not only eruditely but also in conformity with religion (*religiose*) that eyes were given to us for the sake of astronomy [*Timaeus* 47a, *Republic* VII, 530d]. For eyes were certainly given especially for this reason: that they may be guides to seeking some knowledge of God. Therefore, *of the philosophers, those alone who despised astronomy were deliberate atheists* (*ex professo fuerunt* ἄθεοι): by having removed providence they have also undermined the immortality of our souls. If these men had dealt with this doctrine they would have discovered the manifest footprints of God in nature; by heeding [those footprints] they would have been forced to admit that this totality of things (*hanc rerum universitatem*) was both made and is governed by a certain Mind. But if anybody asks for the authority from Scriptures which commends this study, he has the weightiest testimony in Genesis where it is written 'let them [the lights] be for signs and for seasons, and for days and years' [Genesis 1. 14].[23]

The force of Melanchthon's statement here is remarkable. The Scriptures guarantee that astronomy ought to be studied, but Melanchthon is here claiming that the study of astronomy is as basic to human beings as it is to use their eyes for what they were made for. Thus, those who deny the validity of this study are '*deliberate* atheists' by denying something basic and natural to human beings.

It should be noted that the word 'atheist' in the sixteenth century did not have the modern connotation of someone who explicitly professed a disbelief in the existence of any God. There was no such person who would openly profess to deny the existence of a God at that time.[24] The word 'atheist' was used against unbelievers rather than disbelievers in the sixteenth century.[25] Yet for the sixteenth-

[23] 'Quare Astronomia confirmat hanc de DEO opinionem in animis hominum, Plato non solum erudite, sed etiam religiose dixisse iudicandus est, astronomiae causa nobis oculos datos esse. Sunt enim certe ob hanc causam praecipue dati, ut ad quaerendam aliquam DEI notitiam duces essent. Proinde ex Philosophis soli isti, qui Astronomiam aspernati sunt, ex professo fuerunt ἄθεοι, et sublata providentia etiam immortalitatem animorum nostrorum sustulerunt: qui, si attigissent hanc doctrinam, manifesta Dei vestigia in natura deprehendissent, quibus animadversis coacti fuissent fateri, mente aliqua hanc rerum universitatem et conditam esse et gubernari. Sed si quis etiam auctoritatem requirit ex sacris literis, quae haec studia commendat, habet in Genesi testimonium gravissimum ubi scriptum est: Erunt in signa, tempora et annos.' Letter to Grynaeus (1531), *MBW* no. 1176, *CR*, II, 531f.

[24] Kristeller (1968) and Buckley (1987), 46f.

[25] Febvre (1982). Cf. also Walker (1955), 255–9.

century people who accused somebody else of being an 'atheist' the word carried the force of 'Godlessness',[26] denoting someone who denied an essential element of faith: the 'atheist' denied something so basic and so fundamental to the notion of God or of faith that its denial amounted to no God or belief at all from the accuser's point of view. For Melanchthon, Providential government of God was just one such basic and fundamental issue. Because astronomy teaches this Providence, deniers of the validity of that study were therefore called 'deliberate *atheists*'.

Melanchthon further goes on to label contemporary theologians who despise astronomy as 'Epicureans'.[27] Indeed it is the Epicureans who are soon singled out as 'atheists'.[28] Melanchthon had earlier called Epicureans 'atheists' alongside others such as the Stoics, Democriteans and Aristotle, on account of their misguided use of human reason.[29] From 1530 onwards, Melanchthon's Epicurean–atheist identification seems, however, to indicate a renewed emphasis on a single issue. Unlike Luther's use of Epicurus/Epicurean as an *ad hominem* insult to Erasmus,[30] Melanchthon uses the term in order to denote anybody who denied the Providence of God. The denial of the Providence of God was of course frequently regarded as a characteristic of Epicurean philosophy,[31] but it was by no means its only distinguishing feature. Their hedonistic and degenerate lifestyle was common enough to be identified with the hedonism described in Luke 12. 19.[32] Although there was a precedent in Cicero for regarding Epicurus as an atheist,[33] it was not Epicurus who was entered as a prime classical example under lexical definitions of the word 'atheos', but Diagoras whom Cicero had

[26] Copenhaver (1988), 109. For a survey of fifteenth-century usage of the term, see also Bianca (1980).

[27] Letter to Grynaeus, August 1531, *CR*, II, 533.

[28] '...ex Philosophis soli Epicurei fuerunt ἄθεοι, quia haec illustra de Deo testimonia, videlicet certissimas motuum leges, et mirabilem harmoniam aspicere noluerunt.' In *arithmeticen prefatio* (1536), *MBW* no. 1176, *CR*, XI, 289.

[29] *Adversus Rhadinum pro Luthero oratio* (1521), *StA*, I, 76, see p. 44 above.

[30] For Luther's usage of the word 'Epicurus' as applying to Erasmus, see Boyle (1981), 67–95.

[31] See for instance the treatment of Epicurus by the Church Fathers, Jungkuntz (1962), and for a historical survey of the changing views on Epicurean philosophy, see now Jones (1989), 94–213.

[32] See *LW*, XXXV, 392 note 40. Here I am referring to what sixteenth-century people tended to associate with the term Epicurus or Epicurean, rather than giving an accurate explanation of what Epicurean philosophy was. For an exposition of Epicurus' own philosophy on Providence, see Rist (1972), 14–162, 172.

[33] *De natura deorum*, I, 44, 123. Cf. *ibid.*, III, 1, 3f.

explicitly labelled as an atheist.[34] Against this background of various possible connotations for an 'atheist' or an 'Epicurean', Melanchthon made a specific identification between 'Epicurus' and an 'atheist' on specific grounds, namely their denial of Providence.[35] From 1530 onwards, Melanchthon's focus was on Divine Providence.[36]

The study of astronomy was valuable for Melanchthon because it taught about Providence. In his letter to Grynaeus, Melanchthon goes on to praise Peurbach and Regiomontanus as gifted restorers of the study of Ptolemy, a *locus classicus* in contemporary German accounts of the history of astronomy.[37] Although Melanchthon concedes that the Arabs have powerfully pursued these arts, he is not much impressed with the 'curious nation' which also pursued sorcery and various kinds of predictions not based on proper causes (ἀναιτιολόγητα), as if 'not content with Ptolemaic astrology'.[38]

Melanchthon then moves on to defend astrology. He brushes aside the famous attack on astrology by Giovanni Pico della Mirandola (1463–94)[39] as contrary to experience, and cites two well-known sources favourable to astrology for support, namely Aristotle's *Meteora* (339a19) and Hippocrates' *Airs Waters Places* (ii). Melanchthon then elaborates on how astrology is not detrimental to Christian teaching. There are, he writes, three kinds of sources for man's actions: inclinations, divine interventions and the influences of the Devil. By inclinations, Melanchthon means certain tendencies in actions which follow the quality of the temperaments. By divine interventions Melanchthon means miraculous events such as the drying up of the Red Sea (Exodus 14), Peter's delivery from

34 For instance, 'Atheos ... is est qui deos negat: ut Diagoras fertur cognominatus. Nam componitur ex a quod negationem importat et theos deus.' Johannes Tortellius, *De orthographia* (Rome: S. N. Lucensis, 1471). Cicero, *De natura deorum*, i. 2. 63.

35 Cf. Melanchthon's criticism of Lorenzo Valla's ethics as 'Epicurean', but he does not call Valla an 'atheist', *CR*, xvi, 31–7. For Valla's Christian use of Epicurus, see Jones (1989), 145–8.

36 By 1555 'Epicureans' have come to mean enemies of the Church in general, see the reference to Stephen Gardiner in Melanchthon's Exposition of Psalm x, *Commentary on Psalms* (1555), *CR*, xiii, 1034.

37 '... haec doctrina, cum aliquot seculis sine honore iacuisset, nuper in Germania refloruit, restituta a duobus summis viris Purbachio et Regiomontano, quorum alter ex Norico, alter ex Francis vicinis ortus est. Hos heroas singulari quadam vi divinitus ad has artes illustrandas excitatos esse, res testatur ipsa.' Letter to Grynaeus, August 1531, *CR*, ii, 532. See Thorndike (1923–58), v, 332, for the *locus classicus*.

38 Letter to Grynaeus, August 1531, *CR*, ii, 532f.

39 For an examination of Pico's critique of astrology, see Rabin (1987), 40–126.

prison (Acts 12) and Paul's conversion (Acts 9). These should correctly be attributed to God. On the other hand, the Devil can easily affect man's actions, as the preposterous desires and murders of tyrants like Nero exemplify.[40] To distinguish amongst such different kinds of actions is a wisdom worthy of a Christian.[41] Melanchthon reminds his students that they should not sneer at astrology simply because they are unfamiliar with it. If proper judgement is exercised, it will be understood that this astrology should be regarded as part of the '*physice*', just as medical predictions are.[42]

At first sight, a defence of astrology for an astronomy textbook may strike us as strange. It should be remembered, however, that astronomy and astrology were not so readily separable in this period and several people used the terms astrology and astronomy interchangeably.[43] Melanchthon, however, made a clearer distinction in that astronomy meant the study of celestial motions and astrology that of celestial effects, but the two were nevertheless inseparable:

> It should be understood that those most beautiful bodies of the stars were not created to no purpose (*frustra*), especially when that order and course accords with the highest reason such that it seems as if a government in heaven has been depicted, as if in a poem. Indeed the Sun which seems to rule, travels in the middle orb, attended by senators, a warrior and an orator. It also has its stewards, the moon and Venus, for these especially dominate in exciting the humours by which bodies are maintained.[44]

[40] Letter to Grynaeus, *CR*, II, 534f.

[41] 'Ac prudentia digna Christiano est diiudicare, quae sint communes actiones Dei et naturae, quae sint propriae Dei, supra naturam positae.' Letter to Grynaeus, *CR*, II, 534.

[42] 'Et si quis adhibebit iudicium, intelliget, alteram partem artis, divinatricem videlicet, perinde esse partem Physices, sicut medicorum praedictiones pars quaedam Physices esse existimantur.' *CR*, II, 536.

[43] Garin (1983), 1–28, and Lemay (1978), 343f. See for instance contemporary dictionary entries: 'Astronomia ... dici potest astrorum regula. Nam νόμος graece latine regula et norma dicitur. Astrologia ... dici potest astrorum sermo vel ratio.' Johannes Tortellius, *De orthographia* (Rome: S. N. Lucensis, 1471); 'Astronomia ... astrorum regula νόμος latine lex et regula ... Astrologia ... astrorum sermo vel ratio. Astrologia de cursu astrorum loquitur. Astronomia de iudiciis ad vitam fortunamque pertinentibus, hic astrologi et astronomi qui astrorum scientiam profitentur.' Ambrosius Calepinus, *Dictionarium* (Reggio: D. Berthochus, 1502), f3r; 'Astrologia, ... Scientia de sideribus sive quae de cursu astrorum tractat ... Astronomia, astronomiae, ... Scientia est quae de iudiciis ad vitam fortunamque pertinentibus loquitur.' *Thesaurus linguae latinae* (Lyon: J. Tinghuis, 1573), I, 269r.

[44] 'Neque enim illa pulcherrima corpora siderum frustra condita esse sentiendum est, praesertim cum ille ordo atque cursus summa ratione constet, adeo ut quaedam quasi politia in coelo, velut in poemate, depicta esse videatur. Sol enim, qui regnare videtur, in medio orbe vehitur, stipatus senatoribus bellatore atque oratore; habet et oeconomas, Lunam et Venerem. Nam hae praecipue dominantur in ciendis humoribus, quibus aluntur corpora.' *CR*, II, 536.

This should not be taken as Melanchthon's endorsement of heliocentrism, but rather as his attempt to depict the orderly governance of the heavens, perhaps in the spirit of Macrobius.[45] God's governance of heaven, however, was undoubtedly through celestial motions *and* effects. As knowledge of God's government of the heavens, the studies of astronomy and astrology were thus inseparable for Melanchthon.

In the preface to Sacrobosco, Melanchthon thus defended the validity of the studies of both astronomy and astrology in very strong terms, namely as knowledge about God's Providential government of the heavens. This is precisely why Melanchthon claims that these studies are worthy for Christians. This preface to Sacrobosco, I believe, marks a departure in emphasis and in content from Melanchthon's earlier recommendations of the study concerning stars.

There are two earlier remarks by Melanchthon which refer to studies of the stars. One is a preface to a 1521 edition of the Greek astro-meteorological poem, *Phaenomena* by Aratus (late fourth century to first half of third century BC).[46] Melanchthon had taught Aratus earlier on at Tübingen at the instigation of his teacher, Johannes Stöffler (1452–1531), and again at Wittenberg in 1522.[47] Melanchthon commended Aratus for his elegant style founded on things themselves and describing the Greek knowledge of nature, the '*physiologia*', which the Latin poets had imitated.[48] Here, '*physiologia*' refers to an ancient knowledge (*prisca eruditio*) of the Greeks concerning the positions and courses of planets. Melanchthon's

45 For the use of heliocentric imagery (without necessarily endorsing the physical theory) in a political setting, see Hutchison (1987).

46 *Aratus solensis phaenomena* (Wittenberg: M. Lotter Jr, 1521), *VD* A3188. I have not been able to see the original. For Aratus, see Hutchinson (1988), 214–36.

47 Preface addressed to Johannes Schöner in 'De artibus liberalibus Oratio' (July 1517), *MBW* no. 18, *CR*, I, 16; Letter of Albertus Burerius to Beatus Rhenanus, 27 March 1522, *Briefwechsel des B. Rhenanus*, 304.

48 'Nam efficacissime commendari linguae studium utilitate iudico. Idem mihi consilii fuit in Arato edendo, auctore ad rerum naturalium inquisitionem adprime utili. Arcebat Horatius theatris versus rerum inopes nugasque, ut vocat, canoras. Quanto magis in scholis praestandum est, ut eiusmodi scriptores exhibeantur, qui simul et linguam et mentem expoliant... Proinde in Arato periculum faciemus, qui plane amoenissimam τῆς φυισιολογίας partem carmine persecutus est. Argumentum certe dignissimum est liberalibus ingeniis, et quod naturae studium per sese honestissimum est, et quia Latinis poetis multum hinc lucis accedit. Nam hunc fere in iis quae ad siderum positus ac meatus pertinent sequuntur. Quod si non extincta iam olim iaceret omnis prisca eruditio per eos qui pro *scientia* naturae Sorbonica sophismata docuerunt, haud dubie omnium iam manibus tereretur Aratus.' *MBW* no. 196, T-1, 421; *CR*, I, 517f.

praise of Aratus for his elegance of style and foundation in things follows the literary taste of the humanists of his times.[49] In the same humanist vein, Melanchthon is here concerned with recovering the ancient knowledge about nature of the Greeks, which he terms '*physiologia*'.

'*Physiologia*' is a word used again in a second reference by Melanchthon to a study concerning stars. To the readers of the 1524 edition of Giovanni Gioviano Pontano's (1426/9–1503) meteorological verse, the *Meteora*,[50] Melanchthon wrote:

> Here, it is prudently agreed that those who teach '*physiologia*' instead of the disgusting commentaries which had previously dominated the schools, should interpret, besides other good writers, Pontano's *Meteora* too ... I would wish these booklets by Pontano to be called into the physical schools (*physicas scholas*) wherever the barbaric [teaching] has finally been exploded. For, it has such elegance of style that it can rival the ancients, and the things in themselves are taught in it most prudently.[51]

Here again, just as in the preface to Aratus' *Phaenomena*, Melanchthon praises Pontano's poetical elegance and foundation in the things themselves. Here also Melanchthon seems to be using '*physiologia*' to denote a pure study of nature in the same humanist vein as he did in the preface to Aratus. Except for two later instances, we do not know how frequently this work by Pontano was taught at Wittenberg.[52]

By '*physiologia*' Melanchthon thus seems to have meant a study about nature different from that taught with traditional commentaries, which he regarded as sophistical and barbaric. The term implies a pure and pristine classical knowledge of the ancients concerning nature. A typical definition found in other contemporary dictionaries is 'discussion about nature' derived etymologically

[49] Copenhaver (1988), 109. Cf. also the case of the classical period when Aratus was the authority on astronomical and astrological matters in schools which placed great importance on rhetorical elegance, see Marrou (1956), 185f.

[50] *Pontani meteora* (Wittenberg: J. Klug, 1524), *VD*, P4218. I have not seen the original. For Pontano's meteorological verse, see Trinkaus (1985).

[51] 'Prudenter hic constitutum est, ut hi, qui physiologian tradunt, pro rancidis commentariis, qui paulo ante in scholis regnabant, interpretentur praeter alios bonos scriptores, et Pontani μετέωρα, ... optarim in physicas scholas ubique explosa tandem barbarie, accersi hos Pontani libellos, quando ea est elegantia carminis, ut facile opponi vetustati possit, et res ipsae prudentissime docentur.' Preface to the reader, *MBW* no. 365, *CR*, XX, 793f.

[52] See Vitus Amerbach, *Liber de meteoris, cum interpretatione Viti Amerbach* (Strasburg: C. Mylius, 1539), and Sebastianus Theodoricus, lecture advertisement (1548), *Scriptorum publice propositorum ... tomus primus*, 211r, see p. 182 note 43.

from '*physis*' (nature) and '*logos*' (reason, speech).[53] Melanchthon's use of the term '*physiologia*', however, mostly applies to discussions about the working of nature in classical verse form. Both Aratus and Pontano deal in verse form with heavenly motions and their effects. Later on, Virgil's *Georgics* are also understood by Melanchthon as teaching this '*physiologia*' with a definite connotation of 'effects' in nature.[54] Melanchthon's usage of '*physiologia*' is perhaps closer to that of Cicero when the latter used it in the Greek form to denote knowledge of the Greeks on which divination was based.[55] What is important to note is that in both instances where Melanchthon uses the term '*physiologia*' to denote the poetic, pristine knowledge of the Greeks, there is no exaltation of that study as knowledge about God valuable to Christians.

In the Grynaeus letter of 1531, in contrast, Melanchthon used the term '*physice*' (a Latin transcription of the Greek adjective meaning 'natural' (φυσικῆ) in the feminine singular form).[56] Probably a noun denoting some kind of knowledge (τέχνη, ἐπιστήμη) is understood after the adjective. It is as part of this '*physice*' that Melanchthon defended the compatibility of astrology with Christian teaching.[57] Melanchthon frequently used the term '*physice*', but never '*physiologia*' when referring to his own work on natural philosophy. It seems that Melanchthon began using the word '*physice*' when the study of nature had become immediately and directly pertinent to the Christian man, whilst '*physiologia*' simply denoted the pristine knowledge

53 For instance, 'Physiologia ... naturae ratio'. Nizolius, *Observationes* (Basle: J. Hervagius, 1548), Ll2r; 'physiologus, physiologi. De naturis disserens.' *Linguae latinae thesaurus* (Paris: R. Stephanus, 1531), 642v; 'phisiologus/gi qui loquitur vel tractat de naturis rerum et dicitur a phisis quae est natura et logos sermo vel ratio ...', *Ortus vocabulorum alphabetico ordine etc* (London: W. de Worde, 1528), fo. ccc, iiii, v. Cf. the adoption of Hellenistic ideas of 'physiologia' into a Christian perspective in the medieval bestiary, *Physiologus*, see Curley (1980).

54 'Accedunt obiter descriptiones affectuum in rebus gerendis, item locorum et temporum, et morborum vulnerum, remediorum, quae pertinent ad φυσιολογίαν.' Preface to *Virgilius cum Philippi Me. Scholis*, 1530, *MBW* no. 856, *CR*, II, 23, see also *CR*, XIX, 313. Cf. Luther's definition of '*physiologia*' as knowledge which 'discovers the powers and processes of nature', p. 45 above.

55 'Divitiacum Aeduum ... cognovi, qui et naturae rationem, quam φυσιολογίαν Graeci appellant, notam esse sibi profitebatur et partim auguriis, partim conjectura, quae essent futura, dicebat.' Cicero, *De divinatione*, I, xli, 90.

56 In 1534 Melanchthon glossed as 'φυσικῆ' what Cicero had called a study 'on the nature of things (*de natura rerum*)' (*Orator*, IV, 16), in the *Scholia in Ciceronis oratorem*, first printed in 1534, *CR*, XVI, 774.

57 'Sicut igitur aliae partes Physices non laedunt religionem Christianam: ita neque Astrologia (nam hanc quoque partem Physices esse sentimus) officit pietati, si quis in loco utatur.' Letter to Grynaeus, August 1531, *CR*, II, 535.

about nature of the Greeks. The use of different terms such as '*physiologia*' and '*physice*' by Melanchthon perhaps suggests that the terms had different shades of meaning for him, although their usage was probably not mutually exclusive.[58]

What is important to note is that it is in the Grynaeus letter that Melanchthon commends for the first time the study of astrology and astronomy for an explicitly Christian reason: astrology and astronomy ought to be studied because they teach the knowledge of God's Providential governance, which is necessary for a Christian man.

ASTRONOMY, ASTROLOGY AND MATHEMATICS

Although Melanchthon's active promotion of mathematical studies has been recognized,[59] it has never been explicitly noted that the letter to Grynaeus marked a significant change of the *reason* for commending such studies. As I shall argue further, the *whole* of Melanchthon's ensuing activity to promote mathematical studies, including the works of his collaborators, was in fact motivated by the same reason, that is, to know God's governance of the heavens.

As was the case with Galenic anatomy, Camerarius shared Melanchthon's interest in astrology, and his works and advice were instrumental to Melanchthon's promotion of the studies of astrology and astronomy. By the end of 1531, Camerarius had written a treatise on the significance of comets, *Norica sive de ostentis libri duo*, for which Melanchthon wrote a prefatory letter, likening accurate astrological predictions to writing history.[60] In 1532 Camerarius wrote a eulogy of astrology, the *Astrologia*, partly in Greek, justifying its value on the basis of classical sources.[61] Camerarius was soon engaged in editing a Greek text of Ptolemy's astrological treatise, the

58 For instance 'Et quam multa sunt in aliis Physiologica, cum disserunt de partibus et officiis animae.' *De philosophia*, 1536, *CR*, XI, 559. This seems to be a usage of the term 'physiologia/ physiologein' which parallels one of Aristotle's when he refers to Plato as doing '*physiologia*' in discussing the soul in the Timaeus (*De anima*, 406b26f.).

59 For instance, Gilbert (1960), 84f., Westman (1975) and (1980b), Pantin (1987) and Hammer (1951). For a classic study of the humanist contribution to the revival of mathematics in Italy, see Rose (1975).

60 'Extat enim carmen quoddam tuum, in quo insunt vaticinia de futuris Europae motibus, quae ita comprobavit eventus, ut non solum προγνωστικὸν, sed etiam historiam harum rerum multo ante scripsisse videaris.' Prefatory letter to Lucas Gaurico in *Norica, sive de ostentis libri duo*, February 1532, *MBW* no. 1223, *CR*, II, 570 (dated March 1532). Cf. Gaurico's own use of astrology in Zambelli (1986).

61 See Camerarius' dedicatory letter to Jacob Milich, *Astrologia*, fos. *iir–*iiir.

Tetrabiblos, based on a manuscript previously owned by Regiomontanus.[62] Melanchthon seems to have been kept abreast of Camerarius' progress. The Melanchthon–Camerarius correspondence abounds with astrological discussions, including the reading of horoscopes and interpretations of passages from the *Tetrabiblos* and the *Centiloquium*.[63]

Coinciding with the publication of Camerarius' edition of the *Tetrabiblos* in 1535, Melanchthon began lecturing on it for the first time.[64] Melanchthon proposed to read the *Tetrabiblos* in a 'grammatical' way, meaning probably that it was in his capacity as a Greek professor that he was teaching the *Tetrabiblos*.[65] It may also have meant that Melanchthon was not going to deal with any mathematics. Two years earlier he had written to Camerarius that he did not regard himself as an '*artifex*' (master, skilled practitioner) on Ptolemy.[66] He refrained from passing judgement and referred matters to Jacob Milich, whom he frequently praised for his mathematical teaching.[67] Ptolemy's *Tetrabiblos* is indeed a highly descriptive treatise about the validity of astrology and details of the planetary effects.[68]

Melanchthon taught Ptolemy continually until 1545, mostly from the *Tetrabiblos*, except for one instance in 1541 when he taught the *Almagest*.[69] Both the astrological and astronomical treatises of Ptolemy were important to Melanchthon. Melanchthon wrote a Greek poem for an edition of the *Almagest* in which he held Ptolemy

62 Baron (1978a), 204.

63 Virtually every letter to Camerarius of this period includes something on the topic, e.g. *CR*, II, 545f. (*MBW* no. 1190); 551 (*MBW* no. 1201); 554f. (*MBW* no. 1207). See letter to Camerarius, September 1531, *MBW*, no. 1189, *CR*, II, 548. They were consulting the translation made by Pontano. For the *Centiloquium* as a university textbook for astrology, see also Lemay (1978), 344f.

64 *Hartfelder*, 560.

65 '... institui interpretari Ptolemaei librum de Iudiciis, in quo nihil nisi grammaticam interpretationem polliceor, cuius certe non sum plane rudis.' To the Students, 14 October 1535, *CR*, II, 954, For a classical definition of grammarian as teaching a broad range of literary topics, see Gwynn (1926), 92.

66 'De Ptolemaeo, etsi mihi quaedam venerunt in mentem, tamen quia non sum artifex, reieci rem ad Μειλίχιον.' Letter to Joachim Camerarius, 20 July 1533, *MBW* no. 1347, *CR*, II, 659.

67 See below p. 136.

68 For an analysis of Ptolemy's own astrology and astronomy, see now Taub (1993).

69 Melanchthon taught the *Tetrabiblos* in 1535, 1536, 1537, 1543, 1544 and finally in 1545, *Hartfelder*, 560–6. For Melanchthon's edition of the Latin translation of Ptolemy's *Tetrabiblos*, see *CR*, XVIII, 1–118. For its editions, see *A Checklist of Melanchthon Imprints*, 202f.

in high esteem because his works led to the knowledge of God the Creator and Ruler in the heavens.[70]

In addition to Camerarius, Melanchthon had another close collaborator at Wittenberg, Jacob Milich. Like Camerarius, it was not only in the area of medicine and anatomy that Milich collaborated with Melanchthon. To Milich Melanchthon had referred mathematical matters concerning Ptolemy. He also praised Milich for his mathematical works.[71] It was also on the occasion of Milich's promotion to the master of arts that one of the first recorded disputations on astrology at Wittenberg took place.[72] Milich seems to have been such a close collaborator in Melanchthon's cause that even his contemporaries mistook Milich's commentary on the second book of the *Historia naturalis* (*Commentarii in librum secundum historiae mundi C. Plinii*) as a work by Melanchthon himself.[73] Melanchthon's authorship of this commentary has now been challenged.[74] It is true that Melanchthon had taught the *Historia naturalis* once in 1521 when he stepped in to lecture on it after Aesticampianus' death.[75] Which book he then taught is unknown and Melanchthon's only publication related to the *Historia naturalis* dating from 1527 bears no similarity to Milich's commentary.[76] Melanchthon also mentioned in 1525 that Johannes Longicampius, Milich's predecessor in lecturing mathematics, wished to teach the second book of the *Historia naturalis*, though Melanchthon himself regarded that book as an awkward text to teach.[77] In 1531, when

70 Preface to *Ptolemaei mathematicae constructionis liber primus graece et latine editus, additae explicationes aliquot locorum ab Erasmo Reihnolt, Salveldensi*, *CR*, VII, 405. For the theological *and* ethical orientation of Ptolemy, see Taub (1993), 138–53.

71 See for instance Melanchthon's reference to Milich, 'Iacobus Milichius utilius consilio coniunxit libellos Arithmeticos et Geometricos aptissimos scholis, scriptos a praestantibus artificibus, et in ea Academia, quae aliquot seculis praecipuum fuit domicilium harum artium.' Melanchthon to Johannes Reiffenstein (Preface to Johann Vögelin's *Libellus de geometricis elementis*, August 1536), *MBW* no. 1780, *CR*, III, 114 and further, *CR*, III, 536, 538. Milich also seems to have collaborated in translating Ptolemy, see Melanchthon's letter to Joachim Camerarius, 29 September 1531, *MBW* no. 1189, *CR*, II, 548.

72 *De dignitate astrologiae*, *CR*, XI, 261–6.

73 'Editi commentarii Iacobi Milichii in secundum librum Plinii, cuius laboris maximam partem docti viri Philippo soliti ascribere.' Martinus Mylius, *Chronologia scriptorum Phil. Melanchthonis* (Görlitz: A. Fritschius, 1582), D1r. Also *Hartfelder*, 592.

74 Nauert (1980), 384.

75 Friedensburg (1917), 120. See also Melanchthon's reluctant attitude to teaching Pliny's *Historia naturalis* (book unspecified) in his letter to Spalatin, 13 June 1520, *MBW* no. 96, *CR*, I, 202f. (dated 25 June). Cf. p. 41 above.

76 *Plinianae praefationis παράφρασις*, (1527), *CR*, XVII, 639–50.

77 'Logicampius praelegere coepit. Ego volui, ut mathematum elementa traderet, verum adduci non potuit, maluitque Plinii Secundum librum enarrare, ubi obiter rudimenta

Milich was teaching mathematics, Melanchthon reported proudly how the second book of the *Historia naturalis* was taught clearly at Wittenberg.[78] In 1534, Milich published a commentary on the second book of Pliny's *Historia naturalis*, based on his own lectures. The second book of Pliny's *Historia naturalis* had frequently been read as an introduction to astrology,[79] but Milich's commentary, in contrast, states clearly that it is intended for beginners in the '*physice*' and is conducive to knowing God.[80] Milich's goal in his commentary is similar to what Melanchthon had begun advocating, namely to trace 'providential design and the usefulness of nature for man'.[81] In 1538, when Melanchthon wrote to the University of Prague to borrow a manuscript of Pliny the Elder on behalf of Caspar Borner (d. 1547), Melanchthon stated quite explicitly that Pliny's *Historia naturalis* taught about the nature of things (*de rerum natura*) and led the mind to the appreciation of the work of God and of Providence.[82] It seems reasonable to conclude, then, that it was Milich who read the second book of the *Historia naturalis* in a way that Melanchthon would have had it, and that Melanchthon in turn, on seeing Milich's work, came to regard Pliny highly for the teaching of the '*physice*'. In 1545, the second book of Pliny's *Historia naturalis* became a set text for the natural philosophy lectures for beginning students.[83]

promisit se traditurum esse. Utinam esset paulo tractabilior.' Melanchthon to Spalatin, October 1525, *CR*, I, 763.

78 'Summa fide traduntur artes, quae continent rationem dicendi: elementa Philosophiae et Mathematum planissime proponuntur. In qua schola secundus liber Plinii tam perspicue enarratus est, ut hic ennarratur?' *De ordine discendi* (1531), *CR*, XI, 210. Cf. the first date Nauert gives (i.e. 1534) for Milich's teaching of the second book of the *Historia naturalis* in Nauert (1980), 384. Milich taught mathematics from 1529 until he proceeded to the medical faculty in 1536, Friedensburg (1917), 228; *Urkundenbuch*, 163; *CR*, IV, 1028.

79 See for instance Georgius Valla, *Commentationes. In Ptolemei quadripartitum inque Ciceronis partitiones et Tusculanas quaestiones ac Plinii naturalis historie librum secundum* (Venice: A. Firmanus, 1502), Nauert (1980), 350f. Note also that the oration *De dignitate astrologiae* was added at the end of the 1538 edition of Milich's commentary on the second book of Pliny's *Historia naturalis*. Thorndike (1923–58), V, 386 note 1. For a renaissance reading of Plinian astronomy in the second book of the *Historia naturalis*, see Eastwood (1986), 219f.

80 Nauert (1980), 385. I have not seen Milich's 1534 edition.

81 French (1986), 263.

82 'Toties iam editus est liber Plinii de natura rerum, seu, ut alii titulum addunt, naturalis historiae ... Nec profecto unus auctor extat ullus apud Graecos et Latinos locupletior. Equidem illum legens in plantis videor mihi non tantum in horto aliquo amoenissimo versari, sed intueor animo totam naturam ac admiror illam infinitam varietatem opificii, rerum συμπάθειας, utilitates, quarum cogitatio me de opificis sapientia et de providentia admonet.' Letter to the University of Prague, 9 December 1538, *MBW* no. 2129, *CR*, III, 616. The edition came out from Basle (H. Froben and N. Episcopius) in 1539, *VD*, P3540.

83 *Urkundenbuch*, 267.

By lecturing himself on Ptolemy, and with the help of Camerarius and Milich, Melanchthon was thus actively engaged in promoting the studies of astrology and astronomy in the university. By July 1536, however, such an active promotion seems to have come under attack.[84] Some historians conjecture that the attacker might have been Luther, though we have no direct evidence for this.[85] Melanchthon nevertheless stepped up his defence in response, extending his promotion of studies to mathematics.

In a declamation on arithmetic delivered by Rheticus in 1536, Melanchthon wrote:

In the Phaedrus [*Phaedrus* 246c], Plato represented two kinds of souls, one of which he said was winged and the other, he said, had lost its wings. He further said that the winged ones float to heaven, enjoying the encounter and colloquy with God and the most beautiful spectacle of the courses of the heavens and they consider the causes of all changes in the lower nature, in the air, in the bodies of animals, in the studies and manners of men, in the varied fates of empires and states. And these souls floating in the whole heaven, captured by the beauty of divine things and of their wonderful order and by the pleasure of teaching virtue, they yearn to enjoy forever this singular pleasure, but they do not burden their minds with obscene pleasures which upset the harmony of virtue in the soul and throw up a fog, so that they cannot see the heavens. But those souls from which wings have fallen away wander on the ground and seek impure pleasures from earthly things, and they cannot see that most beautiful light of celestial things (*lucem rerum coelestium*). Even though Plato understood the wings as heroic impetuses of geniuses, yet, those impetuses alone do not carry souls upward, and those arts by which those impetuses themselves are elevated are necessary. Therefore, Arithmetic and Geometry are the wings of the human mind.[86]

84 See Letter to Joachim Camerarius, July 1536, *CR*, III, 105.

85 For a study of Luther's attitude towards astrology, see Ludolphy (1986).

86 'Plato in Phaedro fingit duplices animas, quarum alteras ait alatas esse, altera, inquit, decidisse alas. Porro alatas ait volitare in coelum, fruentes congressu colloquioque Dei, et pulcherrimo spectaculo cursuum coelestium, et considerare causas omnium mutationum in inferiore natura, in aëre, in animantium corporibus, in hominum studiis et moribus, in variis imperiorum et civitatum casibus. Atque hae animae toto volitantes coelo captae pulchritudine divinarum rerum, et illius admirandi ordinis et suavitate doctrinae et virtutis, hac una voluptate perpetuo frui cupiunt, nec onerant animos obscoenis voluptatibus, quae perturbant harmoniam virtutis in anima, et obiiciunt caliginem, ne coelestia aspicere possint. At illae animae, quibus alae deciderunt, humi vagantur, et quaerunt voluptates impuras ex rebus terrenis, nec enim illam pulcherrimam lucem rerum coelestium aspiciunt. Etsi autem Plato alas intelligit heroicos impetus ingeniorum, tamen ne illi quidem impetus soli animos subvehunt, sed opus est etiam artibus, quibus illi ipsi impetus attollantur. Sunt igitur alae mentis humanae, Arithmetica et Geometria.' *Praefatio in Arithmeticen* (1536), *CR*, XI, 288.

Here Melanchthon uses a Platonic metaphor to exalt the importance of studying about the heavens. Plato was stressing the need for a kind of divine frenzy, in contrast with a rational kind of learning, in order to gain a vision of the Idea of Beauty.[87] Melanchthon, however, turns around the meaning of the passage and claims that such 'frenzy' is not sufficient.[88] Geometry and arithmetic are necessary to acquire such a learning. Although using Platonic metaphor, the point Melanchthon wishes to make is thus his own: as preparatory studies for the study of the heavens, both geometry and arithmetic are 'wings' necessary for knowing God.

In this oration, Melanchthon acknowledges the utility of arithmetic traditionally ascribed to it, namely its usefulness for preparing the mind for syllogism.[89] For Melanchthon, however, arithemetic has a greater use: without it, a student cannot reach 'that most important part of Philosophy about celestial matters' (*ad illam praestantissimam Philosophiae partem de rebus coelestibus*).[90] The prime utility of and reason for studying arithmetic was thus defined by Melanchthon as a necessary preparation for knowing God the Creator and Ruler.

Also in 1536, Melanchthon spelt out the importance of geometry in a letter prefixed to Johannes Vögelin's *Libellus de geometricis elementis*, an introductory textbook on geometry. Geometry is a discipline previously ignored, Melanchthon claims, which has to be defended by churchmen and magistrates in order to root out absurd and confused opinions.[91] For Melanchthon geometry is useful on didactic grounds because it explains things clearly like a picture to the eyes.[92] What is more, geometry signifies the governance of God:

I hope you ... blaze with the desire of knowing that most beautiful teaching of celestial motions and effects. This step should be made through geometry. You will believe that you should thank God when you devote yourself to these studies. For it was said by Plato most gravely: 'God always geometrizes', that is, as I understand it, He governs everything and with

[87] See Tigerstedt (1969), 53f.

[88] Cf. Ficino's reading of the same passage in Allen (1984), 86–112.

[89] *CR*, XI, 291; cf. other types of praises of the utility of mathematics of this period in Dear (1988), 43–7.

[90] '... hac arte opus sit, tum vero sine ea ad illam praestantissimam Philosophiae partem de rebus coelestibus nullus pateat aditus'. *CR*, XI, 291.

[91] *Praefatio in Geometricam* (1536), *MBW* no. 1780, *CR*, III, 110.

[92] 'Nec vero sine causa doctissimi homines delectati sunt Geometricis similitudinibus. Incurrunt enim in oculos velut picturae. Quare, cum intelliguntur, valde illustrant disputationes, et multa monent admiratione digna.' *CR*, III, 113.

the surest law regulates the heavenly courses and the whole of nature. Hence it is hardly doubtful that he approves the study of those who, as if observing the lines of the courses of the heavens, know and worship (*agnoscunt et venerantur*) the Ruler Himself.[93]

Here Melanchthon is perhaps alluding to a traditional identification of God the Providential Creator with a geometer, as typified in iconographic traditions of the illuminations of the Book of Genesis. Although not a biblical notion, God creating the universe was often represented with a pair of dividers.[94] What is striking is that for Melanchthon, geometry quite literally became a way to know the God who geometrizes. And thus again, as he did for the study of arithmetic, Melanchthon exalts the study of geometry as a path to 'that most important philosophy about celestial matters' (*ad illam praestantissimam Philosophiam de rebus coelestibus*).[95] Undoubtedly in both prefaces on arithmetic and geometry, the 'most important philosophy of celestial matters' refers to the studies of astrology and astronomy.

In fact the very goal of philosophy is defined elsewhere in the following way:

Plato said gravely ... that the goal of philosophy always consists in the knowledge of God (*agnitionem Dei*), as he said in a letter [(pseudo-) Platonic Epistle VI: 323D]; 'we will philosophize correctly if we know (*agnoscemus*) God as the Father of the whole of nature (*universae naturae*), its cause and governor, and we living justly, will obey Him.'[96]

The quote from Plato is a very loose translation of part of the original sentence.[97] This again highlights Melanchthon's choice of

93 'Spero autem te ... flagrare cupiditate cognoscendae illius pulcherrimae doctrinae de motibus et effectibus coelestibus. Ad hanc gradus faciendus est per Geometriam. Putabis autem te etiam Deo gratum facere, cum his studiis operam dabis. Suavissime enim a Platone dictum est: θεὸν ἀεὶ γεωμετρεῖν, hoc est, ut ego quidem interpretor, gubernare omnia, et certissima lege cursus coelestes et totam naturam regere. Quare haud dubie probat studium eorum, qui, quasi observantes illius cursus lineas, gubernatorem ipsum agnoscunt et venerantur.' *CR*, III, 114.

94 For the (neo-)Platonic and rabbinic origin of this iconography, see Friedman (1974).

95 '... haec ars [geometria] aditum patefacit ad illam praestantissimam Philosophiam de rebus coelestibus', *Praefatio in Geometriam*, *CR*, III, 109.

96 'Disputat [Plato] enim graviter ... Philosophiae finem ubique constituit *agnitionem Dei*, sicut inquit in quadam epistola: ita recte philosophabimur, si Deum agnoscemus universae naturae patrem, causam et gubernatorem esse, eique iuste viventes obtemperabimus.' *De Platone* (1538), *CR*, XI, 424.

97 Cf. '... with an earnestness that is not out of tune combined with playfulness that is sister to earnestness, swear by the God that is Ruler of all that is and that shall be, and swear by the Lord and Father of the Ruler and Cause, Whom, if we are real philosophers, we shall all know truly so far as men well-fortuned can.' Plato, *Epistle*, VI, 323D, translated by R. G. Bury.

Plato rather than his adherence to Plato's words.[98] In other words, Melanchthon saw in Plato what he believed, namely that philosophy is to know God the Creator and Ruler. It is precisely because the study of astrology and astronomy taught this very knowledge of God the Creator and Ruler that Melanchthon could call them philosophy.

It is because he considered the study of astrology as philosophy that Melanchthon considered it to be aiming at a goal beyond the scope of medical astrology:

> it remains the case that this teaching of divination is a physical view of nature (*physicam ac naturae aspectionem*) in which temperaments and inclinations are determined and referred to celestial causes as much as possible. Medics consider these very same matters (*res*) but refer them back to nearer causes (*ad causas propiores*), namely to matter (*materiam*). Yet it is often necessary for both the nearer and more remote (*remotiores*) causes to be considered (*aspici*). Such a physical view of nature is not superstitious, because it is a knowledge of the Divine Works (*cognitio divinorum operum*) . . .[99]

Medical astrology was perhaps the main reason why astrology, and to some extent astronomy, had been taught at universities.[100] Melanchthon had rendered astrology (and astronomy) philosophical by positing a goal which, on his own admission, exceeded the scope traditionally ascribed to medical astrology.

Melanchthon's defence of the studies of astrology and astronomy did not waver, nor did attacks on him cease.[101] Melanchthon continued writing numerous prefaces for mathematical, astronomical and astrological textbooks. There is no room or necessity to

98 Bellucci (1988) has presented a study of Melanchthon's idea of astrology as mainly neo-Platonic, by comparing Melanchthon's writings with those of Pico della Mirandola and of Lucius Bellantius (d. 1499). It should be noted, however, that although by inspiration or for metaphorical purposes Melanchthon frequently alludes to Plato, he is reading Plato for his own purposes.

99 'Relinquitur ergo, hanc divinatricem doctrinam esse physicam ac naturae aspectionem, in qua temperamenta et inclinationes, quantum fieri potest, iudicantur et ad causas coelestes referuntur: quas easdem res et medici considerant, sed referunt ad causas propiores, scilicet ad materiam. Saepe autem opus est utrasque causas propiores et remotiores aspici. Talis autem physica naturae aspectio non est superstitiosa, cum sit consideratio divinorum operum . . .' *Praefatio in libros de iudiciis nativitatum Iohannis Schoneri* (1545), *CR*, v, 822.

100 For the role of astrology in medicine, see L. White (1975) and Siraisi (1990), 68f., 135f.; and for the astrological orientation of astronomy instruction, see Lemay (1976). For the implication of this transformation of astrology by Melanchthon, see further Kusukawa (1993).

101 For further attacks, see letters to Petrus Vincentius and Joachim Camerarius, 16 February 1554, *CR*, vii, 225ff.

examine in detail all of his writings on these topics here.[102] Melanchthon's message was always the same: the studies of astrology, astronomy, arithmetic and geometry are necessary because they all aim at the same goal of knowing God the Ruler and Creator; the inseparable studies of astrology and astronomy had to be studied because they were the knowledge of God's government of the heavens; geometry and arithmetic had equally to be learnt because they were necessary preparations for this knowledge of God's government.

Melanchthon also showed active interest in classical authors who had dealt with celestial motions and effects. For instance, Melanchthon recommended Hesiod's (eighth-century BC) *Works and Days* to be read alongside the *De sphaera*, Aristotle's *Meteora* or the *De caelo*, because Hesiod 'has commented with wondrous diligence on the course of times, rise of planets, and interval of days, and he also seems to be among the first Greeks to attain astronomy (*astronomia*)'.[103] Aratus was also a favourite poet for both Melanchthon and Camerarius. Camerarius affixed a Latin verse on Aratus' *Phaenomena* to the *Mathematicarum disciplinarum tum etiam astrologiae encomia*, a compilation of Melanchthon's prefaces which praised the value of mathematics, astronomy and astrology.[104] Melanchthon too sent an excerpt on the comet from the *Phaenomena* to Spalatin in 1535.[105] By 1536, he seems to have read virtually all translations of Aratus then available.[106] Two passages from Aratus' *Phaenomena* seem to have been particularly appealing to Melanchthon. These two excerpts come from the part on 'signs', and describe, significantly, how the

102 See, for instance, the prefatory letters to the Fugger brothers in Regiomontanus' *Tabulae directionum*, dated 24 February 1552, *CR*, VII, 950–3; to Erasmus Ebnerus in *Quadripartitum, graece et latine, libri IV*, dated March 1553, 1554, *CR*, VIII, 61–3; to Hieronymus Commerstaedt, *Procli paraphrasis in quatuor Ptolemaei libros de Siderum effectionibus*, dated 1 September 1554, *CR*, VIII, 337–41.

103 '... posterior [libelli] ortus et occasus siderum et pleraque φυσικὰ continet. Et quia solent in Scholis quidam technici libelli de natura rerum proponi, quales sunt vel de Sphaera commentarius, vel Aristotelis μετέωρα, vel de coelo; videtur mihi in his etiam aliquis locus Hesiodo tribuendus esse, quia temporum vices, ortus siderum, dierum spacia, mira diligentia annotavit, videturque inter primos apud Graecos Astronomian attigisse.' *Praefatio in Hesiodum* (1533), *CR*, XI, 249.

104 According to Baron (1978a), 207, this poem was originally published in Camerarius' *Erratum* printed in 1535, a compilation of errors starting from Homer to demonstrate that Erasmus, with whom Camerarius had a dispute, was wrong.

105 Letter to Georg Spalatin, 22 April 1535, *MBW* no. 1561, *CR*, II, 872 (dated May 1535), and the accompanying poem in *CR*, X, 544. This excerpt was one of the passages reprinted numerous times.

106 See Brandis (1917), 212.

heavenly phenomena attest to the Creator.[107] For Melanchthon, 'signs' in the stars in fact meant signs of Providence:

Plato said in the *Epinomis* that the famous grace of God is dispersed among the stars and in the teaching of stars (*doctrina astrorum*), which is expressed most pleasingly in this most ancient distich:

Stars themselves are full of images of the Godly Providence (πρόνοια)
The extraordinary teaching about the stars, even more so.

The stars are indeed the surest signs of God; and its teaching teaches very certainly (*certius*) that God exists.[108]

During 1538 Melanchthon also lectured on Ovid's *Fasti*, a poetical treatise on the Roman calendar.[109] Melanchthon's *Scholia* on it came out in 1539, and later he compiled a calendar showing the movements of the planets by collating information extracted from classical authors such as Aratus, Ptolemy, Pliny, Ovid and Columella.[110]

Melanchthon's active interest in the classical authors (such as Hesiod, Aratus, Pliny, Ovid and Columella) may well be regarded as a humanist reverence for classical literature and knowledge of the ancients. Yet in a didactic context, the use of such authors could have a specific role to play:

Since there are only four kinds of speech, demonstrative, deliberative, judicial and didactic, and none of them is more suitable in teaching than the last didactic kind because by a certain dialectical method of sure questioning, it explains the proposed matter simply (*nude*), briefly and perspicuously, and for this reason, it should especially be exercised in schools. It seems a good idea to me at the beginning to propose that the whole succinct idea (*imaginem*) of astrology should be seen (*spectandum*) and

107 The two excerpts are from the *Phaenomena* lines 768–72 and 1090–3. For a history of their publication, see *CR*, XIX, 271f.

108 'Plato in Epinomide ait, gratam de Deo famam in astris et doctrina astrorum sparsam esse, quae sententia hoc venustissimo disticho expressa est:

'Αστρα μὲν ἀυτὰ πέλει θείας σημεῖα προνοίας
μᾶλλον δ'ἥ ἄστρων θεσπεσίη διδαχή

Astra quidem sunt ipsa Dei certissima signa
At doctrina Deum certius esse docet.' *CR*, x, 662.

Again, Melanchthon seems to be paraphrasing the general idea of the *Epinomis* (perhaps of 984A).

109 The lectures lasted from 11 October 1537 till 23 December 1538, *CR*, XIX, 473f.

110 *Ovidii Fastorum libri VI cum scholiis Phil. Melanchthonis. Accedunt Claudii Ptolemaei in errantium stellarum significationes per Nicolaum Leonicum e Graeco translatio* (Halle, 1539), *A Checklist of Melanchthon Imprints*, 200.

later that the testimony of learned men should be added *for the sake of persuading more efficaciously*.[111]

Perhaps because of increasing attacks, Melanchthon considered it necessary to defend the teaching of astrology by resorting to the authority of learned men. Melanchthon's active interest in the classical authors who had written on celestial motions and effects may thus be understood, in a didactic context, as an attempt to defend astrology more effectively. This interest was shared by his best friend and collaborator, Camerarius. As Baron has argued, Camerarius had resorted to classical authors in order to build a 'learned' astrology in opposition to the kind of astrology professed by Faustus, the historical 'Doctor Faust'.[112] That 'learnedness' should mean conversance with classical authors may indeed be a humanist value, but we should also remember that it was part of Melanchthon's defence of the study of astrology.

Taken as a whole, Melanchthon's promotion of the studies of astronomy, astrology, geometry and arithmetic was thus motivated towards a single goal, namely knowledge about God as Creator and Ruler. It was amidst mounting attacks that geometry and arithmetic became important as preparation for such studies and that classical authors were utilized to persuade people more efficaciously of that importance. As a knowledge of God the Creator and Ruler, astrology and astronomy became philosophy. And, as I shall now argue, it was natural philosophy that they became.

INITIA DOCTRINAE PHYSICAE

In 1533 Melanchthon wrote a poem 'De initiis doctrinae physicae'. Alluding to his favourite line from Virgil,[113] Melanchthon empha-

111 'Quum autem quatuor omnino sint dicendi genera, demonstrativum, deliberativum, judiciale et διδακτικόν, nullumque illorum docendo sit accomodatius postremo illo genere didactico, quod methodo quadam dialectica per certas quaestiones rem propositam nude adeoque breviter ac perspicue explicat, eamque ob causam in scholis praecipue usurpandum est, visum est mihi initio succinctam totius Astrologiae imaginem ... spectandum proponere: postea, ad persuadendum efficacius, testimonia doctorum virorum ... subjicere.' *Artis divinatricis, quam astrologiam seu iudiciariam vocant, encomia et patrocinia* (1549), as quoted in Pantin (1987), 101.

112 Baron (1978a).

113 Virgil, *Georgics*, II, 490ff.:

'Felix, qui potuit rerum cognoscere causas,
atque metus omnis et inexorabile fatum
subiecit pedibus strepitumque Acherontis avari.'

The first line is often found in Melanchthon's declamations, for instance, in *Contra empiricos medicos* (1531), *CR*, XI, 208, *Praefatio in Arithmeticen* (1536), *CR*, XI, 292, *De physica* (1542) *CR*, XI, 556.

sized the importance of causal investigation.[114] The 'physical teaching' (*doctrina physica*) is a knowledge about the Creator in terms of His government in the heavens and His image in the nature of man.[115] By 1549, Melanchthon had written a full textbook entitled the *Initia doctrinae physicae dictata in Academia Vvitebergensi*. This was most probably based on Melanchthon's Ptolemy lectures.[116] A hitherto unstudied manuscript indicates how Melanchthon's promotion of the studies of astrology and astronomy became an integral part of the *Initia doctrinae physicae*. The manuscript is entitled *Physicae seu naturalis philosophiae compendium*, now in the Vatican Library,[117] and dates from 1543.

The *Compendium* is undoubtedly a prototype of the *Initia doctrinae physicae* in form and in content. The obvious formal similarities between the two are that both are divided into three books; each section is headed by a question or topic; both contain a list of *loci*, principal topics to be learnt. Moreover, the definitions of natural philosophy (*Quid est physica (doctrina)?*) are virtually identical:

It is a science which inquires and reveals the causes of generations, corruptions, and of other motions, and qualities in the bodies [and] of the whole nature of things insofar as the human mind can reach and comprehend those causes. (*Compendium*)

It is what inquires into and reveals the connection, qualities, motions of all bodies and species in nature, and the causes of generations and of corruptions and other motions in the elements and in other bodies, which arise from the mixture of the elements, insofar as is allowed to this weakness of the human mind . . . (*Initia doctrinae physicae*)[118]

In both the *Compendium* and the *Initia doctrinae physicae*, a brief outline of the history of Greek philosophy of nature follows the definition of natural philosophy: there are two kinds of causes of

114 Note also that a typical way to counter 'atheism' by reason is by way of producing 'design-arguments', Walker (1955), 268–73.

115 See the poem 'De initiis doctrinae physicae' (1533), *CR*, x, 539.

116 To my knowledge, Melanchthon was never specifically paid to teach natural philosophy, or Aristotle's *Physica*.

117 Pal. Lat. 1038, first listed in *Iter Italicum*, II, 392. The text itself is not written by Melanchthon but perhaps by his *famulus*, Johann Koch. The title-page and corrections are in Melanchthon's handwriting.

118 'Quid est Physica? Est sientia [*sic*] quae inquirit et patefacit causas generationum; corruptionum et aliorum motuum et qualitatum in corporibus totius rerum naturae quatenus illas causas humana mens assequi et deprehendere potest.' *Compendium*, fo. 3v. 'Quid est physica doctrina? Est quae seriem, qualitates, et motus omnium corporum et specierum in natura, et causas generationum, corruptionum et aliorum motuum in

change in inferior (i.e. sublunary) bodies, one universal or celestial and the other proximate causes.[119] Accordingly there were two traditions of natural philosophy (*physice*) in Greek philosophy. The one was started by Thales of Miletus and inquired into both the motions and the effects of the stars which caused various changes in the elements and in those which consist of such elements. In the *Compendium* Melanchthon calls this branch of inquiry astrology.[120] The other branch, commonly called '*physice*', investigates causes inside the matter of the bodies such as temperaments and qualities. Empedocles and Democritus, though imperfectly, dealt with this branch and then it was corrected by Hippocrates, polished up by Aristotle and perfected by Galen.[121]

After this section, only in the *Compendium* there follows a somewhat awkward sentence which seems to read that there is a great connection between astrology and what is usually called natural philosophy (*physice*) and that one subserves the other because it is necessary to seek all kinds of causes for the sake of the whole cognition of things.[122] Melanchthon goes on to say that when Aristotle said that the sublunary world is governed by the superior world, he most wisely recalled natural philosophy back to astrology.[123] The *Compendium* further goes on to discuss the different natures of inquiry between what is usually called a natural philosopher and an astrologer:

For the natural philosopher (*physico*) it is enough to say that the matter (*materiam*) of a comet has a sticky and long-lasting nature (*habitus*) forced together by motion and then set on fire. Its effect is dryness and winds

elementis et aliis corporibus, quae ex elementorum commixtione oriuntur, inquirit et patefacit, quantum in hac caligne humanae mentis conceditur ...' *Initia doctrinae physicae*, *CR*, XIII, 179.

119 *Compendium*, fo. 2v.

120 'Fuisse duas quasi scholas Physicorum in Graecia, manifestum est. Thales enim et Anaxagoras disserentes de natura rerum, non solum propinquas causas a materia, videlicet ab elementis et mixtis corporibus ortas considerabant, sed longuis progressi ab hac instabili materia, adiunxerunt doctrinam de motibus et effectibus celestibus, et ostenderunt materiae vices et mutationes, aliquo modo regi a celestibus causis.' *Initia doctrinae physicae*, *CR*, XIII, 182.

'Hanc Physicus [*sic*] speciem si quis velit Astrologiam vocare non repugnabo ...' *Compendium*, fo. 4r.

121 *Compendium*, fo. 4r, *CR*, XIII, 182.

122 'Astrologica illa ut haec quam usitate vocant φυσικὴν diversae professiones existimantur tum magna eorum cognatio est et altera subserviunt alteri, quod ad integram rerum cognitionem opus est omnia causarum genera conquirere.' *Compendium*, fo. 4r.

123 'Et prudentissimus Aristoteles revocat φυσικὴν ad Astrologiam, quum ait hunc inferiorem mundum a superiori gubernari.' *Compendium*, fo. 4r.

because flames are dispersed in the air. Those which are dissipated give rise to winds and because these are dry, they dry up and desiccate the air over a wide area. Here you see the natural philosopher (*physicus*) engaged with truths in materials from their particular causes.

The astrologer (*astrologus*) seeks efficient causes, what power confines the mass into one place in the air. Likewise what reasons there are, why this mass resists at one time, but is moved at others, and not even in the same way. Which stars set it aflame, which ones impel or attract it. Then he inquires into the longer-lasting effects, why comets are said to threaten pestilence, great movements of tribes and the like. And here natural philosophy (*Physica*) subserves (*subservit*) astrology because from the cognition of qualities one can investigate how sticky temperaments of the air cause diseases.[124]

What is commonly called natural philosophy thus subserves astrology for Melanchthon because the latter investigates more general causes from which causes of the former can be deduced.

The last half of Book One of the *Compendium* goes on to reproduce Melanchthon's defence of astrology as produced in the Grynaeus letter of 1531. In fact, the whole aim of Book One of the *Compendium* is to provide an epitome of astrology.[125] It is thus quite clear that Melanchthon's own natural philosophy will have to include both astrology and what others have called natural philosophy.

In the *Initia doctrinae physicae*, on the other hand, the terms astrology/astrologer fare less prominently. In the first book we read, instead:

Although the joining (*adiunctio*) of the teaching on celestial motions and effects to this consideration of inferior matter is useful ... and the combination of the two arts brings light, nevertheless, because each art is great and ranges widely, it is now customary (*usitatum*) to call natural philosophy (*physicen*) this teaching which reveals the immediate causes of changes in mixtures which arise from the motions and qualities of this inferior matter,

124 'Physico satis est dicere cometae materiam esse viscosos ac lentos habitus motu coactos ac tandem inflammatos. Effectus vero esse siccitates et ventos, quia sparguntur in aere fumi. Qui dissipant ventos excitant et quia sicci sunt aerem late urunt et dissiccant Hic vides Physicum veris versari in materialibus ex proprioribus causis.

Astrologus quaerit efficientes causas, quae vis tantam molem in unum aëris locum contrahat. Item quae causae sunt cur alias resistat haec moles alias moveatur, ac nequidem eodem modo, quae stellae inflamment, quae impellant aut trahant. Deinde effectus eciam longiores quaerit Cur Cometae dicantur minari pestem, motus publicos gentium et similia. Atque Hic Physica Astrologiae subservit cum de qualitatum cognitione disputandum est quomodo viscosa aeris temperamenta pariunt morbos.' *Compendium*, fo. 6r–v

125 '... nos eam [Astrologiam] deo volente in primo libro huius Epitomes exponemus.' *Compendium*, fo. 4r, my interpolation.

just as a medic (*medicus*) when healing pleurisy considers the motion and quality of the matter in sick bodies and understands that the blood flows to the affected place . . .[126]

It can readily be seen that this is a rephrasing of what Melanchthon said about what is commonly called natural philosophy and astrology in the *Compendium*. The term astrology is replaced with the description 'doctrine of celestial motions and effects' in the *Initia doctrinae physicae*. The point remains unaltered, however, that Melanchthon's natural philosophy includes astrology (now the doctrine of celestial motions and effects) and what is commonly called natural philosophy (the doctrine of inferior matter).

Melanchthon then goes on in the *Initia doctrinae physicae* to remind the students that Aristotle believed in the continuity between the superior and sublunary worlds, and admonishes them to remember Aristotle's statements on that topic, in the *De generatione et corruptione*, the *Meteora*, the *De caelo* and the *Physica*. Melanchthon then proceeds to explain planetary motions and effects, following, perhaps, the format of the first books of Ptolemy's *Tetrabiblos*. In this section, Melanchthon corrects Ptolemy by utilizing recent findings, such as the Copernican correction of the apogees of the sun and the superior planets.[127] Melanchthon was clearly aware, however, that inclusions of such material on celestial motions and effects deviated from the customary treatment of the subject, as he ended the first book of the *Initia doctrinae physicae*:

Such a lengthy exposition of celestial motions in this place could be seen by some as inopportune, as it is taught elsewhere more accurately and is regarded as separate from the teaching of the natural philosophy. But we had many reasons, which we shall omit here, why we considered this discussion on the laws of motions ought to be attached to this part of natural philosophy. We commend the young to strive to draw out a fuller knowledge (*cognitionem*) of this most important part of natural philosophy from the Great Work [*Almagest*] of Ptolemy, which includes the sources of

126 'Quanquam autem adiunctio doctrinae de motibus et effectibus celestibus ad hanc considerationem inferioris materiae, utilis est, ut infra suo loco dicetur, et collatio artium utrique lumen adfert, tamen quia utraque ars magna est, et latissime patet, usitatum nunc est physicen vocare hanc doctrinam, quae causas mutationum in mixtis propinquas, quae oriuntur ab huius materiae inferioris motu et qualitatibus, patefacit, ut medicus in curanda pleuritide, materiae motum et qualitatem in aegro corpore considerat, intelligit adfluere sanguinem ad locum adfectum . . . Hanc vocari nunc usitate physicen sciendum est. Loquor autem non de Democriti atomis, sed de vera doctrina, qualis est Aristotelica sumpta ex Hippocratis fontibus.' *Initia doctrinae physicae*, *CR*, XIII, 183f.

127 *CR*, XIII, 225, 241, 262.

this teaching and is now publicly and faithfully explained in this university.[128]

Thus in essence, what Melanchthon meant by natural philosophy remained unchanged since 1543. For Melanchthon it comprised both the traditional sort which dealt with sublunary matter *and* what he considered to be proper astrology. The disappearance of the terms astrology/astrologer from the *Initia doctrinae physicae* may perhaps be explained as a further attempt to render astrology 'learned'. Although astrology indeed formed an important part of the medieval Aristotelian world-view,[129] and Aristotle himself had claimed the celestial bodies as legitimate subject matters of natural philosophy (*Physica* II, VII, 198a21–5), it is important for our present purpose that we can trace by way of the Vatican manuscript Melanchthon's own efforts in reaching a position which he felt was different from the traditional treatment of natural philosophy. A comparison between the first books of the *Compendium* and the *Initia doctrinae physicae* shows that Melanchthon's earlier defence of astrology and astronomy was incorporated into his idea of natural philosophy and that astrology and astronomy came to form an integral part of Melanchthon's natural philosophy. Although a further comparison between the *Compendium* and the *Initia doctrinae physicae* would undoubtedly be fruitful, I shall now concentrate on what Melanchthon published as a finished textbook on natural philosophy, the *Initia doctrinae physicae*, partly because Melanchthon's idea of natural philosophy remained unchanged in essence between 1543 and 1549 and partly because the *Compendium* is somewhat patchy and repetitive in its arguments.

As we have seen above, Melanchthon began the *Initia doctrinae physicae* by defining natural philosophy as an inquiry into 'the series, qualities, motions of all bodies and species in nature and the causes of generations and corruptions'. This included astrology and astronomy. Melanchthon then goes on to claim that in natural philosophy certainty may be attained through dialectical rules and therefore

128 'Videri autem poterit aliquibus intempestiva hoc in loco motuum coelestium tam prolixa expositio, quae alibi traditur accuratius, et a physica doctrina censetur seiungenda. Sed nos multas causas habuimus, cur hanc narrationem de motuum legibus huic physicae parti attexendam esse duceremus, quas hic omittimus, et hortamur adolescentes, ut pleniorem huius suavissimae partis physicae cognitionem ex Ptolemaei magno opere haurire studeant, quod huius doctrinae fontes continet, et nunc in Academia hac publice fideliterque explicatur.' *CR*, XIII, 292.

129 See North (1986).

totally rejects Pyrrhonian scepticism.[130] The criteria by which certainty may be achieved in natural philosophy are the three rules developed in his dialectics as early as 1528.[131] They are innate knowledge (principles), experience, and conclusions drawn by syllogistic reasoning from principle and experience. It is these criteria which guarantee certainty, not the authority of a single philosopher, such as Aristotle or Plato, since they all have made mistakes.[132]

Melanchthon then proceeds to the discussion of the use of this natural philosophy. Strikingly, Melanchthon starts by saying:

> The whole nature of things is like a theatre [for] the human mind, which God wished to be watched (*aspici*) and for this reason He placed in the minds of men the desire of considering things and the pleasure which accompanies this knowledge (*agnitionem*). These reasons invite healthy minds to the consideration of nature, even if no use followed. Just as vision delights, even if no use followed, so the mind also, by its own nature, is led to beholding things (*aspiciendas res*). Therefore these are the reasons of this study, especially because to consider nature is to follow one's own nature, and consideration *per se* leads to the most pleasant joy, even if other uses did not follow.[133]

Perhaps alluding to Aristotle (*Metaphysica* I, 980a), Melanchthon thus considered natural philosophy worthy in its own right. Nature is like a theatre in which God acts out his Providential design. Watching this theatre was worthwhile even if no use followed. A similar point was made when Melanchthon first defended astronomy and astrology in his Grynaeus letter in 1531. Now natural philosophy, of which astronomy and astrology were parts, Melanchthon claims, is knowledge that man ought to study by nature.

130 'Explodatur ergo illa pyrrhoniorum et similium dubitatio, et opponantur cum regulae certitudinis, quas, dixi, principia et universalis experientia, tum vero etiam testimonium doctrinae coelestis et voluntas Dei.' *Initia doctrinae physicae*, *CR*, XIII, 187. The main source of classical scepticism at this point is Cicero's *Academica*, see Schmitt (1972). For the history of Pyrrhonian scepticism after the publication of Sextus Empiricus, see the definitive work of Popkin (1979) and for a survey of the historiography of scepticism, see further Schmitt (1987).

131 *Initia doctrinae physicae*, *CR*, XIII, 186f.

132 *CR*, XIII, 188.

133 'Tota natura rerum velut theatrum est humani ingenii, quod Deus vult aspici, ideo indidit hominum mentibus cupiditatem considerandarum rerum, et voluptatem, quae agnitionem comitatur. Hae causae invitant sana ingenia ad considerationem naturae, etiamsi utilitas nulla sequeretur. Ut visio delectat, etiamsi utilitas nulla sequeretur, ita et mens sua natura ducitur ad aspiciendas res. Sint igitur hae causae huius studii, quia maxime secundum naturam est considerare naturam, et consideratio per sese adfert dulcissimas voluptates, etiamsi aliae utilitates non sequeretur.' *CR*, XIII, 189.

Melanchthon's natural philosophy, however, does have some positive use for other branches of knowledge. Because it distinguishes between elements, qualities, the varied nature of humours in the human body, temperaments and so on, natural philosophy is the basis of the medical art. Furthermore, to know the parts of man and the difference between the cognitive and appetitive powers is necessary for explaining Christian teaching. It is also useful to refute the errors of the Epicureans and Stoics.[134]

Melanchthon then lists the *loci*, principal topics to be mastered by the students (Fig. 8). Though Melanchthon mainly excuses his diversion from Aristotle's order of argument for didactic reasons,[135] his ordered list of *loci* shows how he mapped out the entire subject matter of natural philosophy. Starting from God and Providence, Melanchthon lists the universe, planets, elements, causes, sublunary meteorology, plants and minerals, ending with the human body, the human soul and man's goal (*de fine hominis*). Thus Melanchthon's natural philosophy deals with the whole physical universe beginning with God and ending with man. The last three *loci*, the human body, the human soul and man's goal, we may remember, were precisely what Melanchthon's *De anima* dealt with. The *Initia doctrinae physicae* therefore deals with what is left – the physical universe beginning with God and leading up to man.

In book one Melanchthon thus begins with the topic God, though he is at pains to point out that it is not the same knowledge of God as gained through the Gospel. On the basis of Romans I. 18–20, however, Melanchthon asserts the validity of a natural knowledge of the existence of God. Nine proofs are given: order in nature presupposes an intelligent Mind; man, who has reason, must have been created by a Mind; natural knowledge such as distinction between good and bad actions must have been given by God; by nature, man knows that there is a God; conscience of criminals which feels guilt must have been given by a Mind; the impossibility of an infinite regress of efficient causes demonstrates the necessity of a primary cause; since all things in nature are designed for sure uses, there must have been an architectonic Mind; that signs of future events are given presupposes a foreseeing Mind.[136] All these proofs are *a posteriori* ones, proceeding from the effects in nature to the primary cause. It is, in fact, a demonstration of the existence of a God who is

[134] *CR*, XIII, 190–3. [135] *CR*, XIII, 195. [136] *CR*, XIII, 200–2.

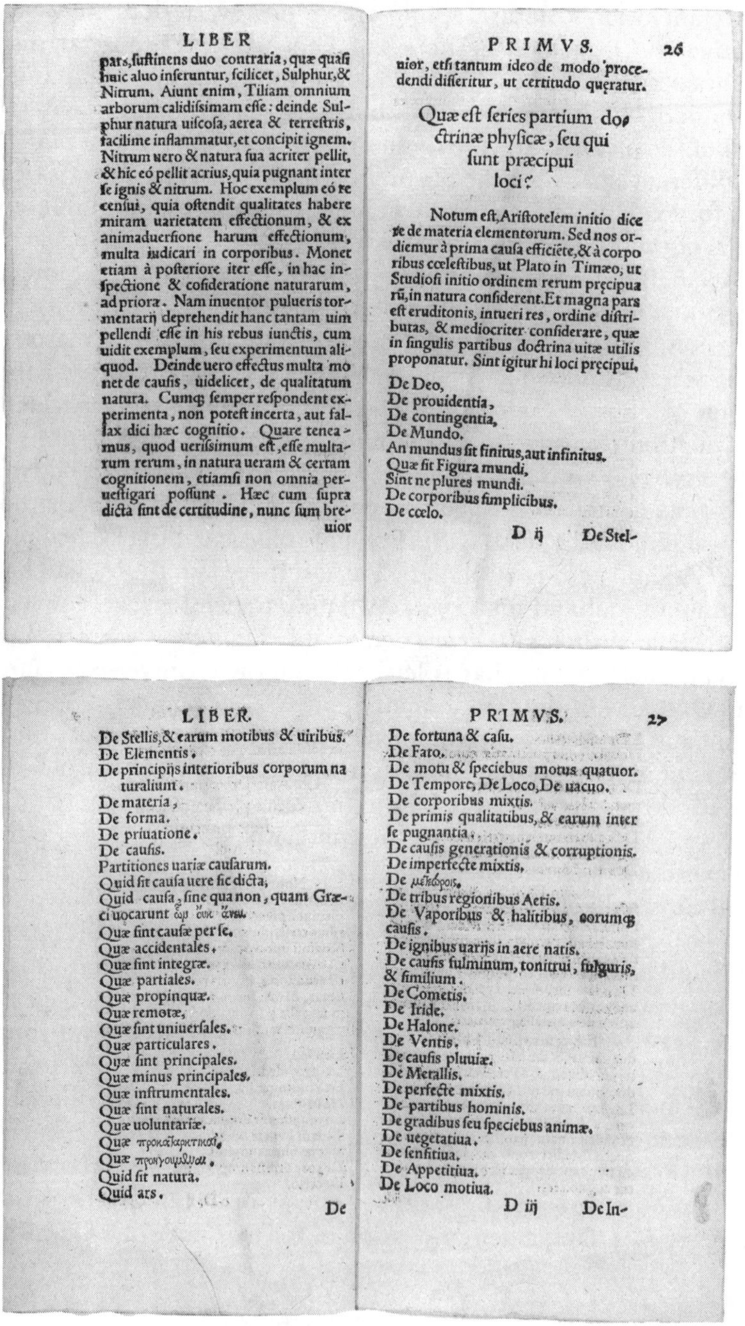

LIBER

pars, sustinens duo contraria, quæ quasi huic aluo inseruntur, scilicet, Sulphur, & Nitrum. Aiunt enim, Tiliam omnium arborum calidissimam esse: deinde Sulphur natura uiscosa, aerea & terrestris, facilime inflammatur, et concipit ignem. Nitrum uero & natura sua acriter pellit, & hic eó pellit acrius, quia pugnant inter se ignis & nitrum. Hoc exemplum eó re censui, quia ostendit qualitates habere miram uarietatem effectionum, & ex animaduersione harum effectionum, multa iudicari in corporibus. Monet etiam à posteriore iter esse, in hac inspectione & cosideratione naturarum, ad priora. Nam inuentor pulueris tormentarij deprehendit hanc tantam uim pellendi esse in his rebus iunctis, cum uidit exemplum, seu experimentum aliquod. Deinde uero effectus multa monet de causis, uidelicet, de qualitatum natura. Cumq; semper respondent experimenta, non potest incerta, aut fallax dici hæc cognitio. Quare teneamus, quod uerissimum est, esse multarum rerum, in natura ueram & certam cognitionem, etiamsi non omnia peruestigari possunt. Hæc cum supra dicta sint de certitudine, nunc sum breuior

PRIMVS. 26

uior, etsi tantum ideo de modo procedendi disseritur, ut certitudo quęratur.

Quæ est series partium doctrinæ physicæ, seu qui sunt præcipui loci?

Notum est, Aristotelem initio dicere de materia elementorum. Sed nos ordiemur à prima causa efficiēte, & à corporibus cœlestibus, ut Plato in Timæo, ut Studiosi initio ordinem rerum pręcipuarū, in natura considerent. Et magna pars est eruditonis, intueri res, ordine distributas, & mediocriter considerare, quæ in singulis partibus doctrina uitæ utilis proponatur. Sint igitur hi loci pręcipui,

De Deo,
De prouidentia,
De contingentia,
De Mundo.
An mundus sit finitus, aut infinitus.
Quæ sit Figura mundi.
Sint ne plures mundi.
De corporibus simplicibus.
De cœlo.

D ij De Stel-

LIBER.

De Stellis, & earum motibus & uiribus.
De Elementis.
De principijs interioribus corporum naturalium.
De materia,
De forma.
De priuatione.
De causis.
Partitiones uariæ causarum.
Quid sit causa uere sic dicta,
Quid causa, sine qua non, quam Græci uocarunt ὧν οὐκ ἄνευ.
Quæ sint causæ per se.
Quæ accidentales.
Quæ sint integræ.
Quæ partiales.
Quæ propinquæ.
Quæ remotæ,
Quæ sint uniuersales.
Quæ particulares.
Quæ sint principales.
Quæ minus principales.
Quæ instrumentales.
Quæ sint naturales.
Quæ uoluntariæ.
Quæ προκαταρκτικαί.
Quæ προηγούμεναι.
Quid sit natura.
Quid ars.

De

PRIMVS. 27

De fortuna & casu.
De Fato.
De motu & speciebus motus quatuor.
De Tempore, De Loco, De uacuo.
De corporibus mixtis.
De primis qualitatibus, & earum inter se pugnantia.
De causis generationis & corruptionis.
De imperfecte mixtis,
De μετέωροις.
De tribus regionibus Aeris.
De Vaporibus & halitibus, eorumq; causis.
De ignibus uarijs in aere natis.
De causis fulminum, tonitrui, fulguris, & similium.
De Cometis.
De Iride.
De Halone.
De Ventis.
De causis pluuiæ.
De Metallis.
De perfecte mixtis.
De partibus hominis.
De gradibus seu speciebus animæ.
De uegetatiua.
De sensitiua.
De Appetitiua.
De Loco motiua.

D iij De In-

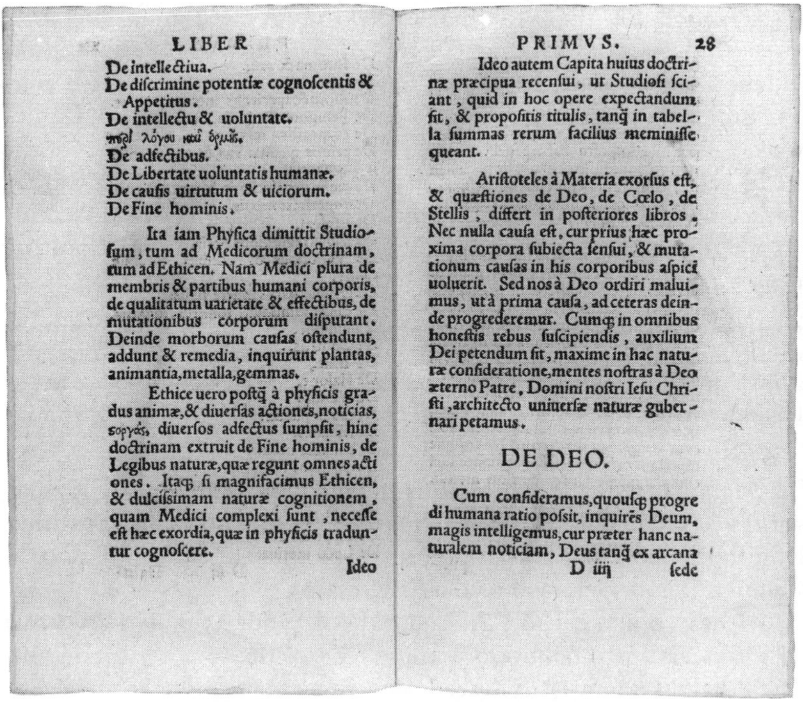
LIBER

De intellectiua.
De discrimine potentiæ cognoscentis & Appetitus.
De intellectu & uoluntate.
περὶ λόγου καὶ ὁρμῆς.
De adfectibus.
De Libertate uoluntatis humanæ.
De causis uirtutum & uiciorum.
De Fine hominis.

Ita iam Physica dimittit Studiosum, tum ad Medicorum doctrinam, tum ad Ethicen. Nam Medici plura de membris & partibus humani corporis, de qualitatum uarietate & effectibus, de mutationibus corporum disputant. Deinde morborum causas ostendunt, addunt & remedia, inquirunt plantas, animantia, metalla, gemmas.

Ethice uero postq̃ à physicis gradus animæ, & diuersas actiones, noticias, στοργάς, diuersos adfectus sumpsit, hinc doctrinam extruit de Fine hominis, de Legibus naturæ, quæ regunt omnes actiones. Itaq; si magnifacimus Ethicen, & dulcissimam naturæ cognitionem, quam Medici complexi sunt, necesse est hæc exordia, quæ in physicis traduntur cognoscere.

Ideo

PRIMVS. 28

Ideo autem Capita huius doctrinæ præcipua recensui, ut Studiosi sciant, quid in hoc opere expectandum sit, & propositis titulis, tanq̃ in tabella summas rerum facilius meminisse queant.

Aristoteles à Materia exorsus est, & quæstiones de Deo, de Cœlo, de Stellis, differt in posteriores libros. Nec nulla causa est, cur prius hæc proxima corpora subiecta sensui, & mutationum causas in his corporibus aspici uoluerit. Sed nos à Deo ordiri maluimus, ut à prima causa, ad ceteras deinde progrederemur. Cumq; in omnibus honestis rebus suscipiendis, auxilium Dei petendum sit, maxime in hac naturæ consideratione, mentes nostras à Deo æterno Patre, Domini nostri Iesu Christi, architecto uniuersæ naturæ gubernari petamus.

DE DEO.

Cum consideramus, quousq; progredi humana ratio posit, inquirẽs Deum, magis intelligemus, cur præter hanc naturalem noticiam, Deus tanq̃ ex arcana

D iiij sede

Principal topics of natural philosophy. List of *Loci* from the *Initia doctrinae physicae* (Wittenberg: Johannes Lufft, 1549), fos. 25v–28r

the primary cause of the physical world. Seven out of the nine proofs are taken from the Stoic proofs for the existence of God in Cicero's *De natura deorum.*[137] Of all the available classical proofs for the existence of God and Providence, the Stoic arguments were probably most congenial to Melanchthon who wanted to establish God's government in the physical world, since compared to Aristotle's prime mover or Plato's demiurge the Stoic deity is emphatically immanent in the universe.[138]

Melanchthon next defines Providence as a knowledge by which God foresees everything and a government by which He protects His

137 Meijering (1983), 128–30. The source for the others is Xenophon's *Memorabilia*.

138 See Solmsen (1963), esp. 496. For a survey of classical proofs for the existence of God, see Dragona-Monachou (1976). Melanchthon's concept of Providence *in* nature is also noted in Barnes (1988), 148.

whole creation.[139] Five proofs given earlier for the existence of God are repeated for the Providence of God. As I shall argue in a moment, this was a Lutheran concept of Providence.[140] What should be noted here is that the first two *loci* of the *Initia doctrinae physicae*, God and His Providence, set forth quite clearly the Christian framework of the work.

Melanchthon then defines the world (*mundus*), following the *De mundo*, as 'a structure of celestial and inferior bodies skilfully distributed and including animals and other natures which procreate or exist in each part'.[141] Significantly, Melanchthon then adds:

> this great and wondrous work (*opus*) was created by God so that it might be the dwelling place of human nature, in which God wished to be known and beheld, and the goodness of God and His immense love towards mankind should frequently be pondered upon because such a labour was begun for our own sakes.[142]

For Melanchthon the world thus meant God's Creation and that world was created for the sake of man. Although utilizing Aristotle's definition, man thus was the centre of the entire world, which Melanchthon understood as God's Creation.

As I have noted earlier, the rest of Book One of the *Initia doctrinae physicae* deals with the motions and effects of the sun, the moon and the planets. Ptolemy is followed with some corrections from recent Copernican data. It is an exposition of the orderly motions and effects of the heavens, thereby demonstrating the government of God.

In the second book of the *Initia doctrinae physicae*, Melanchthon proceeds to what he regards as commonly called natural philosophy, namely 'consideration of matter, of the qualities in matter and their effects, which are the causes of changes in the bodies, such as generation, nutrition, alteration and corruption'.[143] Such an

139 'Usitatum est vocare providentiam, et cognitionem, qua Deus omnia cernit et prospicit, et gubernationem, qua naturam universam servat . . .' *Initia doctrinae physicae*, *CR*, XIII, 203.

140 See below, pp. 160–5.

141 'Mundus est compages coelestium et inferiorum corporum arte distributorum, continens animantia et alias naturas, quae in singulis partibus procreantur, aut existunt.' *Initia doctrinae physicae*, *CR*, XIII, 213f.

142 '. . . conditum esse hoc tantum et tam mirandum opus a Deo, ut sit domicilium humanae naturae, in qua Deus innotescere et conspici voluit, ac saepe cogitanda est bonitas Dei, et erga genus humanum, ingens amor, quod vere nostra causa tantus labor institutus est.' *CR*, XIII, 214.

143 '. . . estque consideratio materiae et qualitatum in materia, et earum effectionum, quae sunt causae mutationum in corporibus, ut generationum, nutritionum, alterationum,

inquiry, Melanchthon claims, would lead the mind to seeking more remote causes, and ultimately God. Causal investigation leads man from God's footprints in nature to knowledge about God Himself. Melanchthon thus regards the different kinds of causes as a 'pointer to God' (*monstratrix Dei*).[144]

The causes that a natural philosopher should investigate, Melanchthon points out, are different from those of the medics:

From [fire, air, water and earth] medics compose mixtures and into these elements they resolve mixtures. Nothing beyond can be discerned by the eyes.

Therefore, somebody may ask, because these are the primary elements subject to the eyes, why doesn't a natural philosopher rest with these [elements]? What necessity is there to investigate into something beyond this matter which is not discerned by the eyes, except insofar as these elements are discerned?

By explaining this question, it can be more easily understood what the natural philosophers' matter is.

Therefore I respond thus: natural philosophers not only understand bodies mixed from the elements but also seek the causes, why elements can be mixed among themselves and transformed, because they examine the causes of generation and corruption in nature.[145]

Melanchthon now defines a natural philosopher as an investigator into the invisible causes of nature, a point which parallels that he had made earlier on about the difference of traditional medical astrology and the astrology he was promoting.[146]

Two-thirds of Book Two of the *Initia doctrinae physicae* is taken up by an explanation of the kinds and classification of causes (*per se*). Under the section '*De causis per accidens*', Melanchthon elaborates his idea of causal investigation as a 'pointer to God'. Following Aris-

corruptionum, deinde et partium in corporibus, et causarum propinquarum et remotarum, quantum acie humanae mentis in hac infirmitate perspici natura potest.' *CR*, XIII, 291.

144 *CR*, XIII, 292f.

145 'Ex his [Ignis, Aër, Aqua, Terra] Medici componunt mixta, et in haec resolvunt. Nec alia extrema oculis cerni possunt.

Quaerat igitur aliquis, cum haec sint prima corpora oculis subiecta, cur non in his resistit Physicus? quid opus est quaerere ultra haec materiam, quae non cernitur oculis, nisi quatenus ipsa elementa cernuntur?

Hac quaestione explicata facilius intelligi poterit, quid sit apud Physicos materia.

Sic igitur respondeo: Physici non solum gignunt mixta corpora ex elementis, sed quaerunt etiam causas, cur elementa inter sese misceri, ac transmutari possint, quia causas generationum et corruptionum in natura scrutantur.' *CR*, XIII, 294f.

146 See p. 141 above.

totle, Melanchthon defines accidental causes as causes by which an effect does not necessarily follow but may or may not follow. They are divided into two kinds, fortune and chance.[147] Fortune is an accidental cause in agents with deliberation, whose actions are concomitant with other events and thus unforeseen and unintended, and could be good or bad for the agent. Melanchthon firmly points out, as Aristotole had done, that it is not that there are no causes but that they are indeterminable or unknown to us.[148] Chance on the other hand is an accidental cause in agents without deliberation. Whilst nature produces a given effect always or most of the time, chance or fortune happens only sometimes.[149]

After reciting these Aristotelian definitions, Melanchthon diverges from Aristotle's *Physica* and gives the biblical example of David's sufferings and delivery as God's doing.[150] This is given as the example that fortuitous events can be reduced to causes *per se*. Melanchthon then enumerates six causes to which fortuitous events could be reduced: God; His angels; evil spirits; temperaments and planetary effects; man's own behaviour; and the instability of matter.[151] Miracles such as Peter's liberation from prison by an angel should rightly be attributed to God and His angels. God is also a cause *per se* when He punishes wicked deeds by physically inexplicable events, such as the destruction of the city of Sodom or of Oedipus. Tyrannical wicked deeds should rightly be attributed to the working of the Devil. Planets are causes *per se* of fortuitous events because they give rise to the prominent qualities in the temperaments which are either good or bad. Melanchthon gives examples of horoscopes of eminent men, demonstrating characteristics such as boorishness, poetic gift and ostentation. By man's own behaviour, Melanchthon means that wicked deeds such as unjust massacres are causes *per se* of the death of the murderers because God is moved by such deeds to punish the perpetrators. The wide variety and mobility of matter of inferior bodies are also causes *per se* of fortuitous events. For instance it rains in one place but it does not in another because wind has blown away the clouds.[152] By thus claiming that

[147] *CR*, XIII, 316–21. Cf. *Physica*, II, iv–vi. [148] *CR*, XIII, 319f. Cf. *Physica*, II, v, 197a7–10.
[149] *CR*, XIII, 320. [150] *CR*, XIII, 321f.
[151] 'Eventus autem fortuiti referri magna ex parte ad has sex causas possunt: ad Deum et pios Angelos eius ministros, ad malos spiritus, ad temperamenta, ad varias inclinationes a stellis ortas, ad suos cuiusque mores, denique ad materiae fluxibilitatem.' *CR*, XIII, 322.
[152] *CR*, XIII, 322–8.

all fortuitous events are reducible to causes per se, Melanchthon eliminated the possibility of accidental events, a conclusion that Aristotle also reaches in his *Physica* II, vi. Such a reduction of fortuitous events to causes *per se* implies the existence of a Mind, as Melanchthon summarized his argument:

It was demonstrated above that there is an architectonic mind of this world, because it is impossible for this most beautiful order of things (*corporum*) and of celestial motions, position of elements and conservation of species, mind and knowledge ruling life in man, to have come into being by chance or to subsist (*manere*) by chance.[153]

Melanchthon's defence of astrology is repeated under the section 'Physical Fate', with a notable addition of a list of people Melanchthon condemns as having meddled with magic by a pact with the Devil.[154] The rest of the second book deals with the principal topics in the *Physica* such as motion, rest, place, vacuum, time and continuity. Melanchthon ends by identifying the prime unmoved mover with God and refuting Aristotle's claims that the world is eternal.[155]

In Book Three Melanchthon deals with the four elements and the causes of various changes in matter, the subject matter of the *De generatione et corruptione*. The nature of elements, primary and secondary qualities, mixtures, generations, alterations, augmentations and putrefactions is discussed. These changes in inferior bodies are not only useful to know for the medics, but it also helps to consider the wonderful skill of the Creator because those numerous and varied changes are governed by a few primary qualities, namely hot, cold, wet and dry.[156] Thus, by seeking order in various changes in the inferior bodies, God's governance of physical change in inferior matter is discussed in the Third Book. Although there are several *loci* in the list which Melanchthon did not treat in the *Initia doctrinae physicae*, the message of this work is very clear: it is to demonstrate

[153] 'Supra demonstratum est, esse mentem architectatricem huius mundi, quia impossibile est, casu extitisse, aut manere casu, hunc pulcherrimum ordinem corporum et motuum coelestium, positum elementorum, conservationem specierum et mentem, et noticias in homine regentes vitam.' *CR*, XIII, 346.

[154] *CR*, XIII, 335–9. [155] *CR*, XIII, 375–80.

[156] 'Non solum Medicis necessaria est doctrina, quae numerum primarum qualitatum, et proprias singularum actiones quaerit, sed etiam aliis omnibus in regenda valetudine, et in multis aliis rebus iudicandis, haec consideratio valde utilis est. Deinde iuvat etiam considerare admirandam Dei opificis artem.' *CR*, XIII, 381.

God's Providence throughout the physical world in an Aristotelian way. Thus Melanchthon ends his *Initia doctrinae physicae* by writing:

These last sentences in Aristotle's book *De generatione et corruptione* are most memorable: 'the cause of the perpetual generation and corruption is the motion of the sun and the planets in the Zodiac'. He therefore affirms that there is some universal action of the stars in nurturing nature, both in conserving this inferior matter and in exciting remarkable changes of matter. Therefore he added also that there are fixed periods of life for all living beings. But when the mind considers this wondrous order of nature, namely those laws of motions, the fixed species of planets and animated beings and their modes of generation and the periods of their duration, it is necessary to infer (*ratiocinari*) a prior and knowing (*intelligentem*) cause, namely God the Creator, by whose design this whole order is both established and governed as well as conserved, just as the teaching about God in the Church clearly teaches.[157]

The *Initia doctrinae physicae* followed the form of an Aristotelian natural philosophy in that it dealt with the topics treated in Aristotle's *De caelo*, *Physica* and *De generatione et corruptione*. More significantly, Melanchthon utilized Aristotelian notions of causality in order to demonstrate that nothing came into existence or is sustained by chance. Yet Melanchthon did not follow Aristotle strictly. Aristotle's views are stressed and amplified in some places, passed over in silence in others and sometimes refuted rigorously. Furthermore, several discussions alien to Aristotle are included. The astronomical and astrological parts of Book One are derived from Ptolemy's *Tetrabiblos* and the *Almagest*, and there are several references to Plato, Galen, Cicero and other classical authors. To attempt to characterize Melanchthon's philosophy as Platonic in inspiration or Aristotelian in foundation would be to concentrate only on partial aspects of Melanchthon's philosophy.[158] Underlying the *Initia doctrinae physicae*, there was a single concern of Melanch-

[157] 'Postremae sententiae in libro Aristotelis de Generatione maxime memorabiles hae sunt: Causa perpetuitatis generationum et corruptionum est motus Solis et Planetarum in Zodiaco. Adfirmat igitur aliquam esse actionem stellarum universalem, in fovenda natura, et in conservanda hac inferiore materia, et ciendis insignibus mutationibus materiae. Ideo addit: etiam omnium viventium certas vitae periodos esse. Sed cum mens hunc mirandum naturae ordinem considerat, videlicet ipsas motuum leges, et certas planetarum et animantium species, et modos generationis et periodos durationis, necesse est ratiocinari, aliam esse priorem et intelligentem causam videlicet, Deum conditorem, cuius consilio totus hic ordo et institutus est, et gubernatur et conservatur, sicut doctrina de Deo in Ecclesia clarius docet.' *CR*, XIII, 410ff.

[158] For Melanchthon the 'Platonist', see Maurer (1967–9), vol. I and Bellucci (1988); and for Melanchthon the Aristotelian, Petersen (1921), 48–101.

thon's: to demonstrate that absolutely everything was made and ruled by God, as the title-page of the *Compendium* reads: 'it is necessary that an effect is effected by an active efficient cause; the effect should cease when the cause ceases'.[159]

The *Initia doctrinae physicae* thus demonstrated the Providence of God in this physical universe whose centre was man. In the *Commentarius de anima* Melanchthon had already proved that man was created for a certain purpose. Even earlier, Melanchthon had argued that that certain purpose was to obey civil governments. We may thus understand in the order of Melanchthon's publications on philosophy (*Epitome moralis philosophiae*, 1536; *Commentarius de anima*, 1540; *Initia doctrinae physicae*, 1549) the unity of Melanchthon's philosophy, designed ultimately for a single goal. The very reason for which Melanchthon had first re-evaluated philosophy – to counter the problem of civil disobedience – was also the goal of natural philosophy. Melanchthon's following testimony for a student succinctly summarizes what he thought natural philosophy ought to be about:

> Since he [the student] attached himself to this natural philosophy (*physice*) and saw that consideration of matter (*considerationem materiae*) is useless unless that higher cause is also considered which moves and excites matter, namely, the motion of the heaven and stars, he diligently worked on that most pleasing part of all which inquires into the movements and effects of the stars, which is indeed worthy of knowing for the sake of many other uses and also to be more studiously studied because it reminds the human mind about the Work of God and clearly testifies that that nature of things did not arise by chance, but that it was established and arranged by some eternal and architectrical mind thinking about and taking care of the order (*ordinem intelligente et tuente*). This statement about God is the beginning of the greatest virtues.[160]

Not without design (*Non casu* ...) – Melanchthon's poems on natural philosophy, anatomy, astrology and astronomy all begin in

159 'Agente Causa efficientj, effectum fieri ne*cesse* est. Cessante causa cesset effectus.' *Compendium*, title-page.

160 'Cumque ad haec Physicen adiungeret, videretque inutilem esse considerationem materiae, nisi etiam illa superior causa aspiceretur, quae materiam movet, et ciet, videlicet motus coeli et siderum, diligenter elaboravit, in ea parte omnium dulcissima, quae motus et effectus siderum inquirit, quae quidem cum propter alias multas utilitates cognitione digna est, tum vero eo studiosius consideranda est, quod hominum mentes de Deo opifice commonefacit, ac perspicue testatur, hanc naturam rerum non casu extitisse, sed ab aeterna quadam mente architectatrice ordinem intelligente et tuente conditam et distributam esse. Quae sententia de Deo maximarum virtutum est initium.' Testimony for Ioannes Prunsterer, May 1546, *CR*, VI, 125.

the same way and these poems alone begin with these words.[161] Teleological arguments of Greek philosophy furnished Melanchthon with philosophical proof for the Providential design of God the Creator.[162] Knowledge of God's Providence was the single aim of Melanchthon's whole philosophy.[163] It was a knowledge of God's Providence which was distinctively Lutheran.

LUTHERAN PROVIDENCE – FROM LAW TO GOSPEL

In his *Loci communes* of 1521, Melanchthon clearly distinguished between Luther's justification by faith alone and justification by works. Melanchthon rejected as hypocritical the scholastic view that 'imperfect' faith was granted to everyone, and that through love and good works it could be made perfect. For Melanchthon, on the other hand,

> to have faith is to believe the promises, that is, to trust the mercy and goodness of God against the wickedness of the world, sin, death, and even the gates of hell ... 'the assurance of things hoped for' [Hebrews 11. 1] is called 'faith'. Therefore, those who do not hope for the promised salvation do not believe.[164]

Faith is to place absolute trust in the promised salvation. In terms of understanding Creation, faith is thus to believe in the absolute power of God in His Creation and government of the world.[165] Although trust in the Providence of God is thus an important corollary to justification by faith alone, it is an issue that does not fare prominently in the first edition of the *Loci communes*. This is because, in 1521, Melanchthon was mainly preoccupied with establishing Luther's *sola fideism* against the Roman Catholic teaching of works righteousness.

As I have already discussed, the Lutherans began from the late

[161] *In Ethica Aristotelis* (1532), *CR*, x, 537f. (see Chapter 2 note 248); *De consideratione humani corporis* (1552), *CR*, x, 610 (see Fig. 7); *De venis metallicis* (1552), *CR*, x, 611; *De motu astrorum in Theoricas Planetarum* (1542), *CR*, x, 578; Greek poem on Ptolemy (1549), *CR*, VII, 465. For an index of incipits of Melanchthon's poems, see *CR*, XXVIII, 317–24.

[162] For an analysis of Greek teleological arguments, see Pease (1941), and for the idea of nature as 'craftsman' in Greek thought, see Solmsen (1963). See Walker (1955) for teleological arguments as a powerful weapon against atheism.

[163] That natural philosophy should be a knowledge of Providence may well be Augustinian in inspiration. For Melanchthon's debt to Augustinian theology, see Maurer (1959).

[164] Melanchthon (1969), 97, *StA*, II, 98.

[165] Melanchthon (1969), 98, *StA*, II, 99f. The same view is expressed in *In obscuriora aliquot capita Geneseos annotationes* (1523), *CR*, XIII, 763.

1520s to dissociate their teachings not only from those of the Roman Catholics but also from those of the Zwinglians. The confrontation at Marburg in 1529 highlighted the differences amongst the evangelicals. On 29 September 1529, Zwingli preached at Marburg (in German) in front of Philip of Hesse on the Providence of God. Luther and Melanchthon did not hear it, as they arrived only the next day. Zwingli's sermon, however, was subsequently printed in Latin under the title *Sermonis de providentia Dei Anamnema*.[166] Although exceptionally philosophically orientated, this work is ultimately a theological exposition of a central tenet of Zwingli's theology, God's Providence.[167]

For Zwingli, God's Providence has an entirely different meaning. In the *Providentia Dei*, Zwingli begins with the notion of God as the absolute Good, as derived from Scriptures. He argues that God as absolute Good has, by necessity, to be all-knowing and all-powerful, and thus, as a corollary, there must be Providence, God's activity which is an application and confirmation of God's wisdom (*sapientia*).[168] Providence is defined as 'the perpetual administering and immutable rule over all things'.[169] God holds absolute sovereignty over creatures. The question why, if all things depend on God, law was given to man brings into stark contrast the difference between God and man. Man, although the most noble creature of God, has a twofold nature: the mind, which strives for love of God; and the body, a dirty mass, which holds back the soul from its spiritual quest. Law is necessary for the soul's struggle with the flesh. Why, on the other hand, did God create man in such a sorry state if He is absolutely Good? Zwingli answers that precisely because God is by nature Good, he cannot show unrighteousness Himself. Thus the angel and man fell. Zwingli's idea of the absolute Providence thus leads him to a supralapsarian position.[170]

The Providence of God forms the basis of predestination, or

166 At the request of Philip of Hesse, Zwingli produced the Latin version, *Ad illustrissimum Cattorum principem Philippum, sermonis de providentia Dei Anamnema*; the text is in *CR*, XCIII-III, 1–230.

167 Stephens regards the philosophical language as due to the context from which the tract arose, namely a disputation. Stephens (1986), 93. For a summary of this sermon in the context of Zwingli's whole theology, see *ibid.*, 84–107.

168 *CR*, XCIII-III, 70–81.

169 'Providentia est perpetuum et immutabile rerum universarum regnum et administratio.' *CR*, XCIII-III, 81.

170 *CR*, XCIII-III, 115–24. I follow Stephens in reading the soul for 'animus', Stephens (1986), 145. *CR*, XCIII-III, 124–40.

Election, as Zwingli preferred to call it. Because God's Providence is absolute, no action on man's part will alter God's decision. In other words, Election, defined by Zwingli as 'the free disposition of the divine will in regard to those that are blessed',[171] is predetermined. This Election is not merely derived from the righteousness of God, but also from His Goodness which is the most universal essence of God. Election precedes faith and faith is a sign of Election.[172] Zwingli defines faith on the basis of Hebrews 11. 1. as 'the essence of things hoped for and the evidence of the invisible things'.[173] By 'essence', Zwingli means 'the essential thing (*rem*) to the soul, not a cursory notion that pops lightly into a mind that wavers and believes or thinks now this, now something else, like uncertain things'.[174] Zwingli understands by the 'things hoped for' a periphrasis of the whole Will of God and by 'evidence' he means an unshaken confidence similar to 'essence'.[175] By 'the invisible', Zwingli understands a periphrasis for God in contradistinction with the 'visible' creatures by quoting Romans 1. 20 and, significantly, II Corinthians 4. 18 ('for the things which are seen are temporal; but the things which are not seen are eternal').[176] It is due to this strong conviction in the invisible God that Sacraments which use creaturely elements should be regarded only as memorial by the faithful.[177] In other words, for Zwingli the invisible God remains invisible precisely because of His absolute Providence over creatures. It is only as a result of the Providence of God that man is elected, and faith is a sign of that election. Zwingli gives some examples of the Providence of God from the Bible and nature in the final chapter.[178]

The sermon ends with a claim that God's Election remains immutable and firm, and therefore even the Elects' wicked deeds are rendered good.[179] This is a point that Philip of Hesse, to whom it was addressed, would have favoured.[180] As a 'godly prince' he had ruthlessly quashed the rioting peasants, and he was willing to take

171 *CR*, XCIII–III, 156. 172 *CR*, XCIII–III, 184. 173 *CR*, XCIII–III, 169.
174 Stephens (1986), 162.
175 *CR*, XCIII–III, 170f. 176 *CR*, XCIII–III, 171–6. 177 *CR*, XCIII–III, 175.
178 *CR*, XCIII–III, 192–217.
179 'Sic omnibus bene utitur tam recte quam male factis, quamvis interim hoc discrimine, ut electis, etiam quae nequiter faciunt, omnia tamen bene vertant, repudiatis contra ... Iam si electio et redemptio coaetaneae sunt, firma manet electio, etiamsi electus in tam immania scelera prolabatur, qualia impii et repudiati designant; nisi quod electis causa sunt resurgendi, repudiatis autem desperandi. Testes sunt David, Paulus, Magdalene, latro, alii.' *CR*, XCIII–III, 217, 222.
180 Potter (1976), 323.

up force in order to fulfil his great ambition to challenge the rule of the House of Habsburg.

Zwingli had thus proved from the biblical notion of God His absolute Providence over creatures. This formed the basis of a strong election which guaranteed the absolute goodness of the Elects' actions. Faith was a sign of this Election. In Zwingli's theology which was centred on the absolute Providence of God, the divinity was understood in opposition to creatures. In contrast, Luther saw God's divinity in precisely that creatureliness. Behind Zwingli's interpretation of the Lord's Supper and of Providence there thus was a whole evangelical theology which, as became blatantly obvious at Marburg, was at odds with Luther's theology of Christ.

It is true that Melanchthon did not hear Zwingli's sermon on the Providence of God but it was he who debated with Zwingli over the Lord's Supper at Marburg.[181] It could not have been clearer to Melanchthon at Marburg that the difference between Luther's theology of Christ and Zwingli's theology of the Providence of God was irreconcilable. Later on, at Augsburg, Melanchthon had to dissociate Luther's theology from that of Zwingli against the Roman Catholic identification of the two. This inevitably meant the need for a comprehensive and much clearer exposition of Luther's theology.

After 1531, therefore, all the major theological works of Melanchthon underwent substantial revision. The *Loci communes*, which was primarily concerned in 1521 with establishing Luther's doctrine of justification by faith alone against the then prevalent Catholic doctrine of works righteousness, was revised in 1535 with a greater concern for providing an accurate and systematic explanation of the Lutheran doctrine as a whole.[182] It was not so much a change of basic tenets as a redirection and expansion of arguments. For instance, the doctrine of the Trinity is discussed for the first time in the 1535 edition.[183] In the 1521 edition, Melanchthon had deliberately refrained from such discussion on the grounds that there were more important topics to be discussed such as the message

[181] Manschreck (1958), 170.

[182] For instance, compare the preface to the *Loci communes* of 1521 in Melanchthon (1969), 18f. and that of 1555 in Melanchthon (1965), XLIII–li. For a more comprehensive study on the development of Melanchthon's theology, see further Herrlinger (1879), Schwarzenau (1956) and Engelland (1961).

[183] Meijering (1983), 109–23.

of Christ.[184] Creation and Providence are also discussed independently for the first time in the 1535 edition. Proofs (*demonstrationes*) for the existence of God and His Providence, which were explicitly rejected as a matter of human curiosity in the 1521 edition,[185] also appeared in 1535. These proofs had appeared for the first time in Melanchthon's revised commmentary on Romans, *Commentarii in Epistolam Pauli ad Romanos*, of 1532.[186] These were the proofs which were subsequently incorporated into the *Initia doctrinae physicae*.

Melanchthon's idea of Providence was different from that of Zwingli in that Melanchthon believed that there is God's Providence *in* this physical world which could be known by man. For Melanchthon, Providence meant the government of God who created and sustains this world for the sake of man, because He cares for man:

> It is customary to call providence both the knowledge (*cognitio*) by which God discerns and foresees everything, and the rule (*gubernatio*) by which He protects the whole nature, namely the order of motions, changes of seasons, fruitfulness of the earth and animated beings, and He cares for and protects mankind, guards political society, authorities, courts, justice, punishes atrocious crimes which oppose the law of nature, in which He shows His will to us, and finally He liberates those unjustly oppressed. This is a kind of knowledge of law about God which affirms that God is not idle, but with paternal love, He nurtures mankind, punishes atrocious crimes and frees the innocent. These are perceived to be done not always in the same way. For occasionally when whole groups are wiped out by diseases, floods, fire, ruins of wars, the evil and the good perish at the same time, and frequently extremely vicious tyrants attack with impunity the good, and the good seem to be deserted and cast out by God . . .[187]

Melanchthon proved the existence of Providence in five *a posteriori* ways: the order of celestial motions implies a Creator who cares for mankind; the innate knowledge of the distinction between good

184 See *Loci communes* (1521), Melanchthon (1969), 21f.

185 *StA*, II, 42f.

186 Melanchthon's commentary on Romans can readily be compared with those of his contemporaries in Parker (1986).

187 'Usitatum est vocare providentiam, et cognitionem, qua Deus omnia cernit et prospicit, et gubernationem, qua naturam universam servat, id est, ordinem motuum, vices temporum, foecunditatem terrae et animantium, et curat et servat genus humanum, custodit politicam societatem, imperia, iudicia, iusticiam, punit atrocia scelera pugnantia cum lege naturae, in qua voluntatem suam nobis ostendit, et tandem iniuste oppressos liberat. Haec est quaedam de Deo legis noticia, quae adfirmat Deum non esse ociosum, sed paterna στοργῇ genus humanum fovere, punire atrocia scelera, et liberare innocentes. Haec non semper eodem modo fieri cernuntur. Interdum enim cum totae gentes delentur morbis, diluviis, incendiis, aut bellorum cladibus, pereunt simul boni et mali, saepe crudelissimi

and bad in the human mind implies obedience to God; history testifies that crimes will be punished; geniuses who restore the empire and the arts are divinely inspired; and significations and predictions of future events are signs of God's care for us.[188] The first proof implies that this world is ordered by God and therefore should not be upset; the second proof guarantees that man has the faculty to distinguish between good and bad actions, and therefore should be performing good actions; the third proof confirms that no crime or injustice will escape the notice of God, and hence, that if people act badly, they are most certainly going to be punished; the fourth proof provides divine sanction for promoting studies conducive to enhancing civil obedience and the fifth proof signifies that God gives guidance to us. All these proofs can be understood as aiming to establish civil obedience.

Thus, Melanchthon's Providence is understood from the world he is surrounded by, unlike Zwingli's Providence which was derived logically from the Goodness of God. Unlike Zwingli who had (theo)logically proved Providence over creatures from the Goodness of God which sanctioned civil disobedience for the Elect, Melanchthon demonstrated a physical Providence in his natural philosophy in order to prove that the order in this world was instituted by God and hence to disrupt it was wrong. In short, the ideas of Providence of Melanchthon and of Zwingli were quite different: they were demonstrated differently and they implied different moral consequences. Their notions of Providence were different because their beliefs were different. For Melanchthon, the Providence of God was visible in this world; for Zwingli, by definition, it was invisible. As the Lord's Supper controversy had highlighted, Zwingli's was a theology altogether different from that of Luther and Melanchthon. Melanchthon's efforts in philosophy and the *Loci communes* after 1530 may thus be understood as a systematic effort, based on Lutheran principles, to dissociate Luther's claims from Zwingli's.

Melanchthon's natural philosophy not only was developed in dissociation from Zwingli's theology of the absolute Providence of God, but also was shaped into a distinctive Lutheran formula. As Melanchthon was often at pains to point out, natural philosophy

tyranni impune grassantur in bonos, et boni videntur deserti a Deo ...' *Initia doctrinae physicae*, *CR*, XIII, 203.

188 *Initia doctrinae physicae*, *CR*, XIII, 204f.

was a knowledge of Law.[189] It was, in fact, a distinctively *Lutheran* Law. This Law is not Gospel: Law does not teach the remission of sins, but it has a civil function to hinder crimes, preserve peace and order through God-instituted offices of governnments, parents and teachers and civil law.[190] Law and Gospel are, however, inseparable because Gospel presupposes Law and Law has to be interpreted through the Gospel.[191] The true function of Law is to lead to the Gospel. Lutheran Law awakens in man a self-knowledge as sinner and helpless before God and then leads man to the understanding of justification through faith in Christ alone.

Melanchthon's natural philosophy demonstrated the existence of God the Creator and Ruler in this physical universe, but it did not teach that God sent His son to be crucified for our own sakes. In this sense Melanchthon's natural philosophy was Law and not Gospel. Melanchthon's natural philosophy was designed to demonstrate the basic principles of moral philosophy, which in turn demonstrated civil obedience. In this sense natural philosophy fulfils a civil function of Law. What natural philosophy demonstrated was the Providence of God in this physical universe. Absolute trust in the Providence of God presupposes denial of works righteousness, and the notion of Providence *in* the physical world did not allow the moral implication of Zwinglian Providence. The Providence of God in this physical universe could be understood only through Lutheran faith. In this sense Law was understood through the Gospel. Furthermore, demonstration of God as Maker and Sustainer of absolutely everything implies that man has made and sustains absolutely nothing.[192] In this sense, natural philosophy can be regarded as a demonstration of self-knowledge. Such a knowledge of man's spiritual incapacity, when man turns to the question of salvation, eliminates any possibility of merit by man's own power

[189] See for instance, 'Ut autem in doctrina Ecclesiae, necesse est saepe commonefieri homines de discrimine Legis et Evangelii, ita hic praemoneo auditores, *physicam de Deo noticiam, esse Legis noticiam, non Evangelii* ... Etsi autem ad confirmandas mentes, ut certo statuant esse Deum mentem aeternam, conditricem rerum, iudicem humanorum factorum, et Vindicem scelerum, maxime conducunt illustria et manifesta testimonia, quibus se Deus patefecit, ... tamen ad hanc communem de providentia sententiam multum prodest, etiam semper in conspectu habere demonstrationes, ex natura sumptas, quae ideo diligentius colligendae sunt, ut conspici possit Epicureos cum ipsa voce naturae pugnare, cum negant esse Deum, et Deo curae esse res humanas.' *Initia doctrinae physicae*, *CR*, XIII, 198–200. My emphasis.

[190] Althaus (1970), 254; Ebeling (1970), 125–40.

[191] Althaus (1970), 257–60.

[192] Althaus (1970), 112 note 27.

and works. Trust in Providence leads to trust in the Redeemer God: the knowledge that God has made absolutely everything and sustains everything leads to the assurance that God is able to achieve the eternal purposes of his love as they are revealed in His promises.[193] For Melanchthon, who was living the Last Days like Luther, trust in the Providence of God pointed to the assurance of the (Second) Coming of Christ, the ultimate message of the Gospel.[194] Through the Providence of God, Law (natural philosophy) thus points to the Gospel (the Coming of Christ). It is thus as a Lutheran Law that we may best understand what natural philosophy meant for Melanchthon.

It would be misleading, I believe, to regard this natural philosophy of Melanchthon's as natural theology simply because of his preoccupation with the Providence of God.[195] For Melanchthon his natural philosophy could not have been any form of theology because the former does not and cannot teach the message of the Gospel. This is precisely why Melanchthon called his own philosophy a knowledge of Law. In this sense, Melanchthon can be seen as showing a significant break from his teacher Stöffler for whom astronomy was natural theology.[196] Although Melanchthon may well have inherited from Stöffler the possibility of knowing some aspects of God through astronomy, the important point here is that the kind of knowledge Melanchthon sought, his reasons for doing so and the status he gave to that knowledge were a creation of his own, based on his Lutheran conviction. Natural theology, in fact, emerged as a discipline later on in the sixteenth century, from metaphysics.[197]

NATURAL PHILOSOPHICAL ASTROLOGY

We finally return to the significance of the comet of 1531. Of all the astrologically significant events, it was the appearance of the comet

[193] Althaus (1970), 110f.

[194] Thus astrological signs in particular may also function as 'consolation' for man at times of hardship, *CR*, XIII, 339. For Melanchthon's conception of the End of the World and astrology, see further Caroti (1982) and Barnes (1988), 60–99. Cf. the use of philosophy as 'consolation' by fourth-century patristics in Gregg (1975).

[195] See for instance Maurer (1962).

[196] '... ideo astronomia haud indigne naturalis theologia nominatur.' Johannes Stöffler, *Procli diadochi* (Tübingen: U. Morhard, 1534), 2r. Cf. Petrus Alliaco, *Concordantia astronomiae cum theologia* ... (Augsburg: E. Ratdolt, 1490).

[197] For the emergence of natural theology as a branch of knowledge from metaphysics, see Lohr (1988a), 629f. For classical precedents of natural theology, see Jaeger (1947). See also pp. 204f. below.

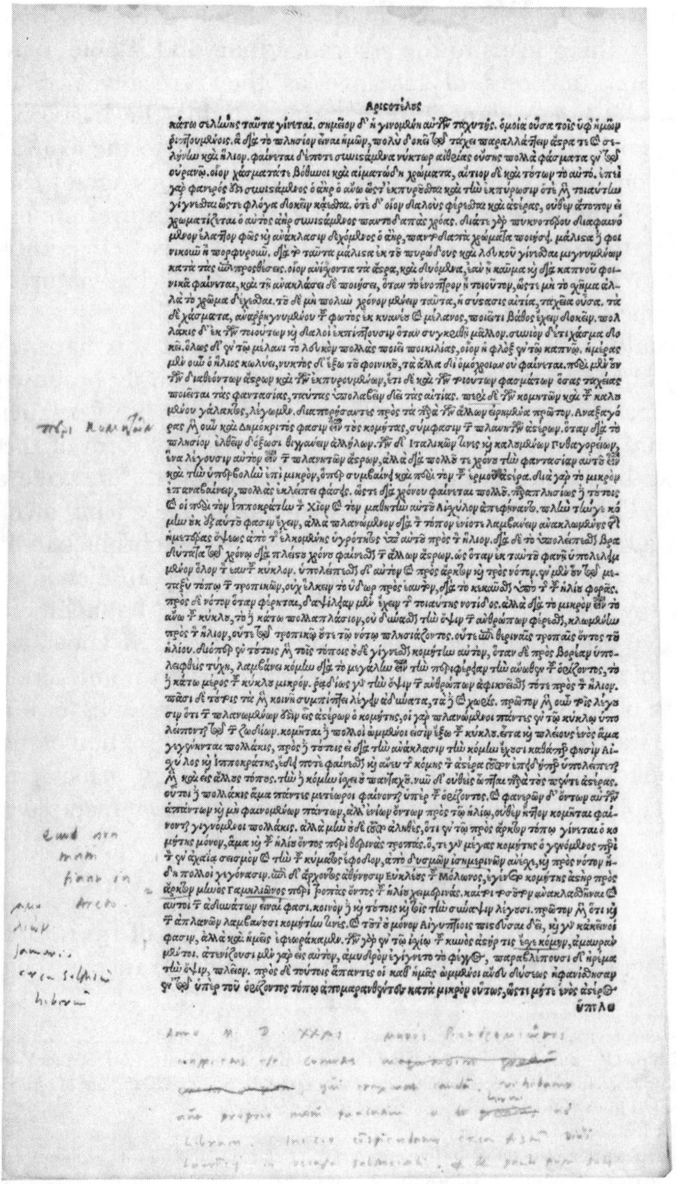

9 The comet of 1531. Melanchthon's copy of ᾿ΑΡΙΣΤΟΤΈΛΟΥΣ ῞ΑΠΑΝΤΑ ed. Desiderius Erasmus (Basle: Johannes Bebel, 1531), fos. 143v–144r

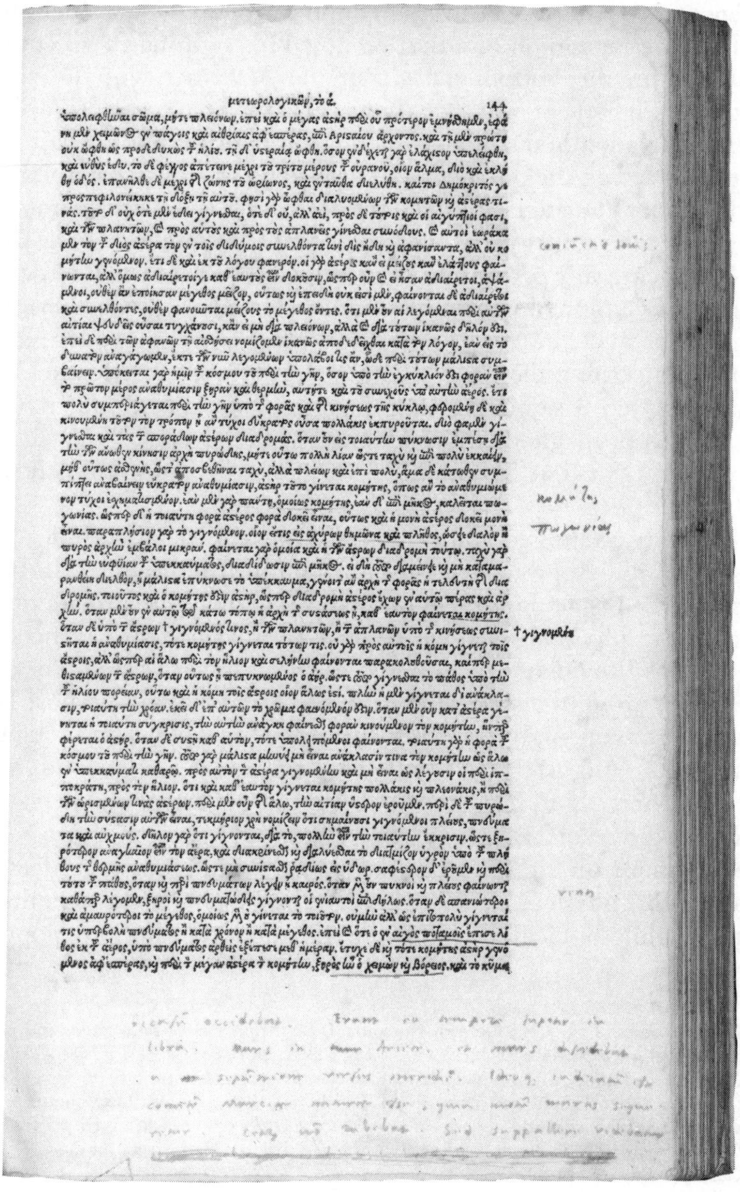
μετεωρολογικῶν, τὸ α.
144
κομήτης
πωγωνίας

of 1531 that signalled the beginning of Melanchthon's vigorous defence of the studies of astronomy and astrology. The comet made such an impression on him that he noted his sighting in his copy of Aristotle (in the bottom margin of the *Meteora* I, VII, the comet section) (Fig. 9). It was not, however, the first comet to appear during Melanchthon's lifetime, though it is probably the case that he missed seeing the one in 1527 because he was busy conducting a visitation in Thuringia.[198] Even more striking is how little immediate impact the controversy over the Great Conjunction of 1524 had on Melanchthon's promotion of astrology.[199] He certainly knew of the Great Conjunction since he often referred to it. Furthermore, his teacher at Tübingen, Johannes Stöffler, was embroiled in the debate concerning the Great Conjunction of 1524.[200] Melanchthon himself played a significant role in using astrological and natural portents to propagandize the message of the Gospel.[201] Yet it was only after 1530 that Melanchthon began to promote the study of astrology.

Astrology, as studied in the university was for Melanchthon a part of natural philosophy. Melanchthon's natural philosophy, in turn, was about a particular aspect of divinity, namely the Providence of God in the physical universe. It was after 1530 that the need to defend this Providence of God and to strengthen the claim for civil obedience arose in dissociation from the Zwinglians. The Last Day was also drawing nigh. It is thus within the theological and religious context of August 1531 that we can best understand why Melanchthon began his defence of the study of astrology then.

The study of astrology in a university constituted for Melanchthon an integral part of natural philosophy in demonstrating the physical Providence of God. I choose to call this a natural philosophical astrology in distinction from the popular

198 For the comet of 1527, see Gerardi Noviomagi, *De terrifico cometa, cui a condito orbe similis visus non est, qui apparavit anno MDXXVII, mense octobri, epistola ad Carolum V Impe. Caes. Aug. P.F. Victorem Gall. P.* without place or date, in *Annales typographici*, IX, 146, no. 391. During this time Melanchthon was probably in Thuringia, where he was busy conducting a visitation and hence could not see the comet, see editor's note in *CR*, I, 519. For a list of German meteorological events in the sixteenth century, see Hellmann (1921).

199 Caroti (1986).

200 For Stöffler's involvement in this dispute, see Thorndike (1923–58), V, 178–233.

201 For Melanchthon's views on popular astrology, see Caroti (1982) and (1986). For Lutheran uses of popular astrological literature, see Robinson-Hammerstein (1986) and Scribner (1981), esp. 123–7.

practice of horoscope-casting and fortune-telling.[202] By making this distinction I do not wish to imply that there existed two mutually exclusive kinds of astrology. As the skill of horoscope-casting was necessary for both types of astrology for Melanchthon, the two were very much interdependent. In fact, that the planets and stars had an effect on the sublunary world in one way or another was a belief that was part of everyday life.[203]

Melanchthon was not, of course, the first to include astrology in a system of natural philosophy. Indeed, even in the initial introduction of Aristotle's *libri naturales* to the West, historians have detected an astrological interest (gained through the *Introductorium in astronomiam* of Abu Ma'shar).[204] That planets affected in one way or another the sublunary world became part of an Aristotelian world-view in universities. As we have seen, however, on his own admission, Melanchthon felt that he was doing something different from what was commonly called natural philosophy or medical astrology, when he began promoting his own astrology. What I have tried to show in this chapter was that Melanchthon incorporated astrology into natural philosophy in his own particular way for his own particular reasons.

It is within the context of this natural philosophical astrology, I believe, that Melanchthon's adoption of Copernicus is best understood. It has been pointed out, though never sufficiently explained, that Melanchthon promoted a reading of Copernicus in such a way that Copernicus' predictions about the angular position of a planet were accepted but his cosmological claims ignored, and that Melanchthon thereby hindered the full consideration of 'the realist and cosmological claims of Copernicus' great discovery'.[205] This is a judgement pronounced by modern historians for whom Copernicus is important because he made realist claims about a heliocentric universe.[206] From this point of view, Melanchthon's reading of Copernicus exhibits at best a 'pragmatic' attitude.[207] What this view

202 See also distinction between 'high' and 'low' astrology made in Field (1984). For recent studies in this area, see Clulee (1988) for the practice of this kind of natural philosophical astrology by John Dee, Schaffer (1987) for Newton's astrology and Curry (1989) for the *fortuna* of popular astrology.

203 Garin (1983). See also Melanchthon's astrological and other 'superstitious' beliefs in everyday life compiled in Hartfelder (1889).

204 This is Lemay's main thesis in Lemay (1962) and (1987).

205 Westman (1975), 168.

206 For a reassessment of Copernicus, however, see now Westman (1990).

207 Westman (1975), 174.

presupposes is that cosmological systems and how to establish the validity of those systems were central and meaningful questions in Melanchthon's natural philosophy. However, for Melanchthon himself, it seems to me that the importance of Copernicus lay elsewhere.

In a famous letter to Mythobius, Melanchthon referred to Copernicus' cosmological claims that the earth moved around the sun as absurd.[208] As has been argued convincingly by Wrightsman, Melanchthon's criticism of Copernicus' cosmological claims is on a par with his criticism of those who claimed knowledge for their own glory.[209] It is at best incidental. What should be noted is that Copernicus' heliocentric claims could not have had a meaningful place in Melanchthon's system of philosophy. Melanchthon had first re-evaluated and developed moral philosophy for the sake of demonstrating what actions were correct for man. He further developed a natural philosophy in order to prove the starting point of this moral philosophy. Thus the goal of Melanchthon's natural philosophy was man, as the list of *loci* in the *Initia doctrinae physicae* indicated. This goal was demonstrated through the physical Providence of God in nature. Hence in order for Melanchthon's natural philosophy to be what it was intended to be, the earth, man's habitation, *had* to be the centre of the physical universe, i.e. the centre of God's Creation, as his definition of *mundus* clearly stated. Copernicus' heliocentric claims were a far cry from what Melanchthon intended to achieve in his natural philosophy. In other words, the question of which cosmological system to choose was not the foremost question that Melanchthon needed seriously to address in his natural philosophy. What the world should be like was already determined so far as Melanchthon was concerned. That is why Melanchthon brushed aside Copernicus' cosmological claim. It is also why Melanchthon did not have to deal with Copernicus' cosmological claim in the *Compendium* of 1543, when he already knew about it.

Instead Copernicus was important for Melanchthon because of

208 'Vidi dialogum, et fui dissuasor editionis. Fabula per sese paulatim consilescet; sed quidam putant esse egregrium κατόρθωμα rem tam absurdam ornare, sicut ille Sarmaticus Astronomus, qui movet terram et figit Solem.' Letter to Burkhard Mythobius dated 16 October 1541, *MBW* no. 2830, *CR*, IV, 679. The dialogue referred to here is that of Johannes Lening which defended bigamy.

209 Wrightsman (1970), 341–59, esp. 344f.

his contribution to natural philosophical astrology. Copernicus calculative improvements implied better accuracy in predicting planetary positions, a crucial point for astrology.[210] It is precisely those data that improved the prediction of planetary positions such as the apogees of the sun and the three superior planets that were adopted in the *Initia doctrinae physicae*. Morevoer, Copernicus may well have been known to Melanchthon and his friends as a skilled astrologer quite a while before Copernicus' cosmological claims were known. In 1535 Camerarius prepared a horoscope for Duke Albrecht of Prussia and, together with predictions for the coming three years, it was sent to Duke Albrecht via his chancellor, Johannes Apel.[211] On sending these predictions to the Duke, Apel praised Camerarius as a skilled mathematician but warned the Duke not to show them to Johann Poliander, the Duke's chaplain.[212] The reason for this warning against Poliander, a Lutheran theologian, is unclear.[213] What Apel says next is quite significant. Since Camerarius uses a 'different method', for further interpretations one should consult the 'old canon in Frauenburg'.[214] It is difficult not to equate this reference with Copernicus. If we take Apel's claim to mean that Camerarius had utilized Copernicus' calculatory improvements or indeed the latter's tables for 1535/6, it is equally likely that Melanchthon knew of Copernicus at least indirectly through Camerarius. Thus, it may well have been the case that Copernicus was important for Melanchthon and his friends primarily as a skilled astrologer.

It may at best be a 'pragmatic' attitude from our modern point of view, but for Melanchthon, he read and used Copernicus in the particular way that he did, because Copernicus was useful for his natural philosophical astrology.

210 Lemay (1978), 350. 211 Baron (1978a), 204f., and Lemay (1978), 353.

212 *Briefwechsel der berühmtesten Gelehrten des Zeitalters der Reformation*, 111f.

213 Baron (1978a), 205.

214 *Briefwechsel der berühmtesten Gelehrten des Zeitalters der Reformation*, 112.

CHAPTER 5

The construction of orthodoxy

FAUSTUS: Think, Faustus, upon God, that made the world.
Christopher Marlowe, *Doctor Faustus* VI. 76

Melanchthon's works on philosophy set the trend of sixteenth-century 'textbooks'.[1] Instead of staying close to Aristotle's order of argument, Melanchthon followed a list of *loci*, selected and ordered with didactic clarity in mind. The list did not necessarily cover all the problems or arguments in Aristotle and it also included topics which were alien to Aristotle. Instead of trying to resolve exhaustively by way of logical reasoning (as in the *quaestio* method), Melanchthon proceeded by *loci*: each section began with a question such as '*Quid est physica?*', '*Quid est anima?*' and '*Quid est mundus?*', followed by a direct and clear answer. Classical and contemporary authors were cited primarily in order to endorse these answers. No attempt was made on Melanchthon's part to reconcile differences among authorities or to follow a single classical author. This was perhaps due to his recognition that most classical authors have erred in one way or another and that human knowledge was always fallible.[2] Melanchthon simply selected what was useful for his purposes.

It was not simply for didactic purposes that the *loci* were arranged in a certain way but, as I have argued, it was mainly in order to facilitate demonstration of the Providence of God in the physical world. Strikingly, Melanchthon never explained how and why certain *loci* were selected and ordered in the particular way that they were. Even in his dialectics textbooks where he explains the finding part of the *loci*, Melanchthon is reticent about the *order* or *choice* of

[1] For a survey of the textbook tradition, see Schmitt (1988a), and Reif (1969) for the first half of the seventeenth century.

[2] *Initia doctrinae physicae*, *CR*, XIII, 185.

appropriate topics. His textbooks proceeded through a list of *loci* in a simple question-and-answer form, without any explanation or discussion of the underlying principle of the order of the list. What such textbooks amounted to was a way of drilling students into getting the right answer to a given question without having them question the underlying principles or goal of natural philosophy.[3] As Schmitt rightly observed, Melanchthon's textbooks were 'catechetical' in nature.[4]

Melanchthon had created a natural philosophy in order to dissociate his and Luther's claims from those of their evangelical opponents. Through the textbooks he produced, he sought to make uniform the students' understanding of the subject. In the area of natural philosophy, as I shall now argue, Melanchthon's aim was quite effectively understood.

NATURAL PHILOSOPHY IN THE UNIVERSITY

In 1545 Melanchthon composed a new set of statutes for the philosophy faculty and a set of regulations for the studies and behaviour of the listeners.[5] From these two sets of regulations, we may understand what Melanchthon thought should be taught and learnt in the philosophy faculty and, in particular, what the teaching of natural philosophy meant within the learning of a university.

According to these regulations, there were ten lecturers who constituted the philosophical college, of whom five were to deal with Latin grammar, Latin literature, Hebrew, dialectics and rhetoric.[6] The rest of the faculty was dedicated to teaching natural philosophy, moral philosophy and mathematics. Two lectures were assigned to natural philosophy: one 'inspector' of the college taught natural philosophy (*physicen*) and the second book of Pliny's *Historia naturalis*, and the other, a '*physicus*', lectured on Aristotle's *Physica* and Dioscorides, and pointed out herbs.[7] Although not treated

[3] For Melanchthon's dialectics as a means to establish uniform understanding of knowledge, see Kusukawa, '*Vinculum concordiae*', forthcoming.

[4] Schmitt (1988a), 798.

[5] *Leges academiae Witebergensis de studiis et moribus auditorium*, *Urkundenbuch*, 255–61, and *Leges collegii facultatis liberalium artium, quas philosophia continet*, *Urkundenbuch*, 266–77.

[6] *Urkundenbuch*, 267.

[7] 'Duo inspectores collegii, quibus cura locationis mandata est, quorum alter dialecticen et rhetoricen tradat, alter physicen et secundum Plinii [tradat] ... Octavus physicus, qui Aristotelis physica enarret et Dioscoriden ac monstrator sit herbarum.' *Urkundenbuch*, 267.

comprehensively in Melanchthon's natural philosophy textbooks, Dioscorides and the study of the properties of plants had become a legitimate part of natural philosophy since around 1540, as I shall point out later.[8] There were also two lecturers assigned to mathematics. One was to teach Euclid's *Elementa*, arithmetic and the *De sphaera*, while the other was to teach the *Theorica planetarum* and the *Almagest*. A Greek lecturer was to teach the Greek language and Homer, Hesiod, Euripides and other authors, in addition to some Pauline epistles. He was also to be the ethics teacher, and explain Aristotle's *Ethica* verbatim in Greek.[9] This wide-ranging definition of the Greek lecturer's responsibility is probably due to the fact that Melanchthon occupied the post most of the time, reflecting the wide range of his own teaching. There were thus five lecturers appointed to the teaching of subjects about the study of God's Providence in His Creation, or knowledge of Law.

From a student's point of view, a beginning student who had a fair knowledge of Latin first learnt some further Latin, dialectic, rhetoric and the whole of Christian teaching.[10] Those who wished to apply themselves to the study of philosophy further heard publicly the lectures on the *De sphaera*, arithmetic, natural philosophy (*physica*), the second book of Pliny's *Historia naturalis* and Aristotle's *Ethica*.[11] In addition to these lectures, Euclid, the *Theorica planetarum* and the *Almagest* had to be heard for a master's degree.[12] A student in his final years of the arts course would thus be hearing in his lectures predominantly about the Providence of God.

Such knowledge of Law was learnt alongside the Gospel. Every morning, after rising, students were to read a chapter of the Old Testament, and when they came back to their chamber in the evening, they were to read a chapter of the New Testament. Such readings were to be accompanied by prayers based on the reading. On feast days students were required to go to chapel and learn where to join in their prayers.[13] After these public assemblies, they

[8] See below, pp. 181–3. [9] *Urkundenbuch*, 267f. [10] *Urkundenbuch*, 256, 271f.

[11] '[P]ublice vero omnes, qui versantur in studiis philosophicis, audiant has praelectiones, in quibus traduntur elementa doctrinae de circulis coelestibus collecta a Johanne de Sacrobusto [*sic*], arithmetica, physica, secundus liber Plinii et Aristotelis ethica.' *Urkundenbuch*, 256f.

[12] '[I]lli vero, qui magisterii philosophici gradum petituri sunt aut alioqui locupletiorem cognitionem philosophiae adpetunt, adjungant ad praelectiones, quarum jam mentio facta est, Eucliden, theoricas planetarum et magnam constructionem Ptolemaei.' *Urkundenbuch*, 257.

[13] *Urkundenbuch*, 272f.

were to recite the catechism of Christian doctrine and respond to questions concerning articles of faith and important topics such as the difference between Law and Gospel, what sin is, what faith is, and what the correct use of the Sacrament should be.[14] Thus at Wittenberg Law and Gospel were taught and learnt alongside each other.

Once again, we may discern the Lutheran formulation of Law and Gospel in Melanchthon's plan of teaching in the philosophy faculty. Law, in a true Lutheran sense, should point to the message of the Gospel and, as such, Melanchthon saw the role of the philosophy faculty as teaching human knowledge which was drawn to the support of the message of the Gospel:

Since this philosophical assembly should also be a part of the Church of God, we wish all who are received into this college to embrace the pure teaching of the Gospel which our church teaches unanimously and univocally with the universal Church of God. They should recognize God and His Son our Lord Jesus Christ, and teach philosophy in such a way that they do not corrupt the teaching of the Gospel nor with curiosity or obtuseness either sow, prove or defend abusive and profane opinions against God, just as many philosophers in schools of other nations wish to be allowed to do so because they dare to defend Epicurean or other madnesses ... Indeed [sincere minds] should hear the Word of God sounding from heaven and admonishing that we should pay attention to the teaching of His Son. We should embrace His teaching brought forth from the bosom of the eternal Father and confirmed with so many clear testimonies, and we should take it to be the special directress of our opinions and life, and we should restrain our minds, as Paul said [We destroy arguments and every proud obstacle to the knowledge of God] 'taking every thought captive to obey Christ [II Corinthians 10. 5]'.[15]

[14] 'Privatim vero diebus festis post publicas conciones domestici praeceptores catechesin doctrinae christianae recitare discipulos cogant et interrogent eos ordine de articulis fidei et doctrinae locis praecipuis: quod sit discrimen legis et evangelii, quid intersit inter invocationem ethnicorum et verae ecclesiae dei, quid sit peccatum, quomodo detur remissio peccatorum, quid sit fides, quae sint in invocatione necesaria, quae sint sacramenta et quis sit eorum usus, quae sit ecclesia dei et quomodo sit agnoscenda.' *Urkundenbuch*, 273.

[15] 'Cum hic philosophicus coetus etiam pars esse debeat ecclesiae dei, volumus omnes, qui recipiuntur in hoc collegium, amplecti puram evangelii doctrinam, quam ecclesia nostra uno spiritu et una voce cum ecclesia dei catholica profitetur. agnoscant deum et filium ejus, dominum nostrum Jesum Christum, et ita doceant philosophiam, ut non corrumpant doctrinam evangelii nec aut curiositate aut petulantia ingeniorum serant aut probent aut defendant prophanas opiniones contumeliosas adversus deum, ut multi in gymnasiis aliarum gentium hac una re perhiberi volunt philosophi, quia ausint Epicurea aut alios furores defendere ... immo vero audiant vocem dei sonantem de coelo ac praecipientem, ut filium docentem audiamus. hujus doctrinam prolatam ex sinu aeterni patris et confirmatam tot illustribus testimoniis amplectamur et praecipuam rectricem opinionum et vitae

The teaching in the philosophy faculty was to assist students in reaching a *unanimous* and *univocal* understanding of the Church. To lead every human thought to Christ was thus what was ultimately aimed at. In order to ensure that this aim was reached, the dean of the philosophy faculty controlled and inspected the content of lectures, disputations and declamations and he also appointed lecturers and domestic tutors who directly supervised the religious duties of the students in practice.[16]

Statutes and regulations, however, are at best indications of what was intended or expected of institutions and therefore do not necessarily provide us with a fair picture of the practice of the teaching of natural philosophy. From disputation records, lecture announcements and other material which indicate the actual practice of the teaching at Wittenberg, however, it is quite clear that much of what Melanchthon propounded was understood, repeated and sometimes expanded.[17]

For instance, it is known from disputation records that topics concerning the soul, such as temperaments, powers of the soul, formation of the foetus and nutrition, were already disputed upon in the arts faculty from 1536, some time before Melanchthon completed his *Commentarius de anima*.[18] Once the *Commmentarius de anima* was published, it was immediately put to use in the lecture room.[19] The utility of knowledge of the whole human body for moral

esse ducamus et frenemus ingenia, ut Paulus inquit: αἰχμαλτίζοντες πᾶν νόημα εἰς τὴν ὑπακοὴν τοῦ Χριστοῦ [II Corinthians 10. 5].' *Urkundenbuch*, 268.

16 *Urkundenbuch*, 269f.

17 Records of some of the several ordinary disputation topics in the arts faculty are available from 1536 onwards. Records for the years 1503–35, 1543–50, 1557–81 are missing. The earliest lecture advertisements in printed form date from 1540. I have used the *Scriptorum publice propositorum a professoribus in Academia Witebergensi ab anno 1540 usque ad 1553, tomus primus* (Wittenberg: G. Rhaw, 1560); *Scriptorum publice propositorum a gubernatoribus studiorum in Academia Witebergensi, tomus quartus complectens annum 1559 et duos sequentes usque ad festum Michaelis* (Wittenberg: G. Rhaw, 1561); *Scripta quaedam in Academia Witenbergensi a rectoribus, decanis et alijs eruditis quibusdam viris publice proposita* (Wittenberg: J. Klug, 1545); *Scripta quaedam in Academia Witenbergensi publice proposita, digesta in duos libros*, I (Wittenberg: J. Klug, 1549).

18 'De temperamentis' (Winter 1536, by Melchior Fendius); 'de formatione foetus' (21 December 1538, by Paul Eber); 'de potentiis animae' (13 September 1539, by Joannes Turstennius); 'de nutritione' (13 March 1539, by Hieronymus Oderus). Köstlin (1888), 26; (1890), 22f.

19 'Decrevi igitur enarrare librum de anima hic editum, ac polliceor auditoribus diligentiam et fidem.' Erasmus Flock (1540); 'Et quia libellus de anima clarissimi praeceptoris nostri D. Philippi Melancthonis, videtur conducere scholasticorum studijs, decrevi eum enarrare.' Jacob Milich, *Scriptorum publice propositorum a professoribus in Academia Witebergensi ... tomus primus* (Wittenberg, 1560), B8r; 8v.

purposes, the theological use of the knowledge about the human soul and the importance of anatomy were clearly understood by the lecturers.[20] It also became a tradition at Wittenberg to use fugitive anatomical sheets based on Vesalius for the lectures on the *De anima*.[21] Students also continued to dispute upon such topics as nutrition, against the Stoic theory of pain, innate knowledge, difference of powers in man, and parts of the human body.[22]

Aristotle's *Physica* seems also to have been taught twice a week alongside the *De anima*.[23] We have already noted that Melanchthon himself taught Ptolemy's *Tetrabiblos*. Once the *Initia doctrinae physicae* was published, it too was used in the lectures.[24] There were disputations on astrology, the powers of the planets, and on some topics from the *Centiloquium*.[25]

As for the mathematics lectures, lecturers frequently declared the importance of their subjects in terms very similar to those of Melanchthon. For instance, Georg Joachim Rheticus advertised in 1540 that he would teach al-Fraghani because 'the doctrine of celestial motions is useful for many aspects of life' and it leads to the knowledge of God (*ad agnitionem Dei*).[26] Rheticus regarded Ptole-

20 See for instance the lecture advertisements in the *Scriptorum publice propositorum a professoribus in Academia Witebergensi . . . tomus primus* (Wittenberg, 1560), by Erasmus Flock (1540), B5v; Jacob Milich, 9v; Paul Eber (1545), 112v–114r; Sebastianus Theodoricus (1546–7), 177r–178r, 194v–195r. In the *Scriptorum publice propositorum a gubernatoribus studiorum in Academia Witebergensi, tomus quartus* (Wittenberg, 1561), see Erasmus Rudinger (1559, 1561), 13r–14v, n6v–n8r; Albertus Lemeigerus (1560), T7r–v1r.

21 Lint (1924), 79–89.

22 'Contra Stoicos de dolore' (1540, by Sigismund Ferrarius); 'de principiis natura notis' (1540); 'de differentibus in homine potentiis' (15 December 1554, by Caspar Peucer); 'de partibus humani corporis et methodo' (December 1556, by Henricus Paxmannus). Köstlin (1890), 23; (1891), 30.

23 For instance, '. . . biduum libro de Anima et deinde biduum Physicis tribuemus et operam dabimus', P. Eber (1545), *Scriptorum publice propositorum a professoribus in Academia Witebergensi . . . tomus primus* (Wittenberg, 1560), 113v; see also Theodoricus (1546), *ibid.*, 161v–162r.

24 V. Theodoricus (1552), *Scriptorum publice propositorum a professoribus in Academia Witebergensi . . . tomus primus* (Wittenberg, 1560), 421r; see also *Scriptorum publice propositorum a gubernatoribus studiorum in Academia Witebergensi, tomus quartus* (Wittenberg, 1561), Y2r–Y3r (anonymous, 1560).

25 'De astrologia' (29 May 1540, by E. Floccius); 'de viribus stellarum' (1541, by Ioannes Berchtoldus); 'de anni ratione, ex centiloquio Ptolemaei' (25 June 1554, by Caspar Peucer). Köstlin (1890), 23; (1891), 30.

26 'Constat enim, doctrinam de motibus coelestibus multis vitae partibus prodesse, ut alias saepe dictum est. Et naturae non monstrosae fatentur, nihil hac philosophia dulcius ac iucundius esse. Quia enim traducit nos ad agnitionem Dei, et aspiciendas res perpetuas, et ad causas mutationum in natura, quarum cognitionem vehementissime expetit humana mens, adfert mirificas voluptates.' Rheticus (1540), *Scriptorum publice propositorum a professoribus in Academia Witebergensi . . . tomus primus* (Wittenberg, 1560), C5r–v.

my's *Almagest* as comprising the entire doctrine of celestial motions.[27] For justification of this study, Rheticus refers to Genesis 1. 14.[28] We know from a student note now in Paris, that between 1536 and 1538, Rheticus also taught Proclus, al-Fraghani and how to interpret horoscopes by using nativities of eminent men.[29] During 1536 Erasmus Reinhold began to teach Euclid and the *Theorica planetarum*, claiming that geometry was the beginning of 'that part of philosophy called *Physica*'.[30] After finishing the *Theorica*, Reinhold intended to teach the students the rules of the horoscope so that they could compute one correctly.[31] He commends the teaching of the motions and significations of planets because it leads them to understand that they were made for the knowledge of God (*ad agnitionem Dei*) and immortality.[32] Disputations on the topics of astronomy, comets, the horizon and the distinction of feasts were regularly held.[33]

As for the lectures on the second book of Pliny's *Historia naturalis*, several people are known to have taught them since Milich. Paul Eber, Sebastianus Theodoricus and Bartholomaeus Schonborn all repeat at the beginning of their lectures what Milich had stated before – that this book is for beginners, that it is part of the '*physices*' and that it leads to the knowledge of God.[34] Schonborn's commen-

27 'Vt igitur excitemus studia ingeniosorum enarrabimus (Deo iuvante) scriptum, quod pene ausim dicere, omnium humanorum operum longe pulcherrimum esse τὴν μεγάλην σύνταξιν Ptolemaei, quae complexa est doctrinam de motibus coelestibus integram.' *Scriptorum publice propositorum a professoribus in Academia Witebergensi ... tomus primus* (Wittenberg, 1560), c7r–v.

28 *Scriptorum publice propositorum a professoribus in Academia Witebergensi ... tomus primus* (Wittenberg, 1560), c7v.

29 Baumeister (1968), I, 6f., 30f.

30 'Nam illa pars Philosphiae, quae vocatur Physica, sumit initium a Geometria ... decrevi aliquot libros Euclidis explicare, et inchoabo primum librum de Iovis proxima. Hoc absoluto, postea per intervalla singulis septimanis tribuam aliquos dies Euclidi, aliquos Theoricis.' *Scriptorum publice propositorum a professoribus in Academia Witebergensi ... tomus primus* (Wittenberg, 1560), D2rf.

31 'Absolutis Theoricis, Deo dante, adijciam praecepta, die figuris geneseon constituendis, ut syderum positus in qualibet genesi recte computare studiosi possint.' *Scriptorum publice propositorum a professoribus in Academia Witebergensi ... tomus primus* (Wittenberg, 1560), D1r.

32 'Quare doctrina de motibus, et de significationibus consideranda est, qua quidem ut recte utamur, etiam studiosos adhortari debemus, videlicet, quod et motus et significationes de Deo opifice nos admoneant, ut cogitemus, nos ad agnitionem Dei, et ad immortalitatem conditos esse.' *Scriptorum publice propositorum a professoribus in Academia Witebergensi ... tomus primus* (Wittenberg, 1560), D1v.

33 'De astronomia' (May 1537, by Reinhold); 'de cometis' (21 June 1539); 'de horizonte' (20 December 1539); 'de distinctione dominiorum' (7 February 1540 by Nicholaus Reinholt). Köstlin (1888), 26; (1890), 23.

34 See *Scriptorum publice propositorum a professoribus in Academia Witebergensi ... tomus primus* (Wittenberg, 1560), 78r–v (Eber, 1544); 86v–87v (Eber, 1545); 283r–v (Theodoricus,

tary on the second book of the *Historia naturalis* also stays very close to that of Milich.[35] What is important to note is that this Pliny was clearly understood as an *introduction* to, rather than a replacement for, natural philosophy which was based on Aristotle and Ptolemy.[36]

Although records are somewhat patchy about the individual theses of disputations, we have on one occasion a full list of the topics that were disputed. At the end of the 1548 edition of the *Commentarius de anima*, twenty-five disputation theses dated 7 June are listed.[37] The theses cover virtually all the crucial points in Melanchthon's philosophy: God gave man innate knowledge; this innate knowledge is very useful for man; true philosophy is built on demonstrations; the Epicureans, the Stoics and the New Academicians should be refuted; moral philosophy is part of Divine Law; but the difference between Law and Gospel should be retained.[38] There is not one thesis that Melanchthon had not promoted before. Given the catechetical nature of the textbooks we may not be too amiss in surmising that the kind of arguments presented in support of these theses closely followed Melanchthon's lines of argument.

Texts not stipulated in the statutes were also taught. In an undated notice, Melanchthon advertised that he was going to teach Nicander (second century BC) because the latter dealt with many erudite descriptions of herbs. For Melanchthon, knowledge of plants (*consideratio plantarum*) was an important part of philosophy and it was quite necessary for knowing the remedial uses of herbs.[39] Again, it is God's Providence that is found through such a study of plants:

> For there is no doubt that there is a wonderful power in plants, placed there by the divinity for the sake of maintaining the health of the human body . . . this virtue and variety of things show that nature did not come into being

1549); 319r (Eber, 1550); *Scriptorum publice propositorum a gubernatoribus studiorum in Academia Witebergensi, tomus quartus* (Wittenberg, 1561), Y2r–Y3r (anonymous, 1560), N1v–N2v (Schonborn, 1561). For Milich, Eber, Schonborn, see also Nauert (1980), 384f., 400–2.

35 Eastwood (1986), 234 note 132.

36 See a contemporary testimony on Milich: '. . . quam fideliter et utiliter servit Scholae, et quantum navaverit atque effecerit ad posteritatem, testatur enarratio Secundi Plinij, in qua ex doctrinae Ptolemaicae et Aristotelicae fontibus nodi ac Labyrinthi astronomici et Physici plerique ita sunt explicati et illustrati, ut difficultas, quae visa fuit rudiori saeculo superiori inesse maxima, evicta atque discussa omnis videatur.' Eusebius Menius, *Oratio de vita Jacobi Milichii* (Wittenberg: G. Rhaw, 1562), B7r.

37 Melanchthon, *Commentarius de anima* (Wittenberg: J. Lufft, 1548), X4r–X6r.

38 Melanchthon, *Commentarius de anima* (1548), X4r, X4v–X5r, X6r.

39 'Nicandrum ideo enarrare decrevi, quia plurimas habet herbarum descriptiones plenas frugiferae eruditionis. Est autem non infima pars philosphiae consideratio plantarum. Cum

by chance but was arranged by some eternal mind for human use, and this knowledge (*consideratio*) admonishes us about Providence.[40]

This lecture may perhaps be identified with the ones held in 1539 which Valerius Cordus (1515–44) attended.[41] The text used then was the *Alexipharmaca*, a hexameter poem on snake-bites and remedial uses of herbs for such wounds. Cordus himself is known to have taught Dioscorides at Wittenberg in 1540.[42] The stipulation of the natural philosophy lecturer to teach Dioscorides in the 1545 statutes should thus be regarded as a confirmation of what had already been taught. The following advertisement of 1546 by Sebastianus Theodoricus[43] who taught Dioscorides would suffice as an ample illustration of a natural philosophy lecturer's conviction, in complete agreement with Melanchthon, that the physical world is a manifest testimony of Providence:

On Thursdays and Fridays I shall explain Dioscorides, so that the young students may learn in some way about the names and natures of herbs and grains. And I shall point out (*monstrabo*) those herbs that grow in this region and add the customary names in the vernacular language. I shall begin the explanation from the names of grains. For it is a shameful negligence to be ignorant of the nature and names of those very grains and olives on which we feed. The whole doctrine on plants is not only delightful and useful for other reasons but *is also very worthy of consideration because it is a manifest testimony of Divine Providence*. For since the multitude and variety of herbs is so great, and sure (*certae*) powers have been given to each so that some would be remedies for certain diseases, it is manifest that this nature of things did not come into existence by chance, but that there was an

enim describuntur earum naturae, cum usus ostenditur in remediis, multa physica commemorare simul necesse est. Est utilitas in promptu.' To students (no date) *CR*, x, 82.

40 'Non enim dubium est, mirificam plantis vim inesse, divinitus insitam ad salutem corporis humani tuendam ... Cumque haec efficacia et rerum varietas ostendat, non casu extitisse naturam, sed ab aliqua aeterna mente ordinatam ad usus humanos, admonet nos haec consideratio de providentia.' *Ibid.*

41 'In familiaritatem eius [Cordus] deveni ante annos viginti cum uterque nostrum audiret Philippum Melanchthonem explicantem Nicandri Alexipharmaca.' A letter by Johannes Crato to Conrad Gesner dated 1559, in Cordus, *Annotationes in P. Dioscordis de medica materia libros V* (Strasburg: J. Rihelius, 1561), biir.

42 Dannenfeldt (1972), 227.

43 In May 1546, Theodoricus was teaching Aristotle's *Physica* and Pontanus' *Meteora*, *Scriptorum publice propositorum a professoribus in Academia Witebergensi ... tomus primus* (Wittenberg, 1560), 161v–162r; in September the same year he was teaching the *De anima*, *ibid.*, 177r–178r; in October 1549 he was teaching the *De anima* again, *ibid.*, 190–2, *Urkundenbuch*, 299 note 1; and in 1552 he was teaching the second book of Pliny's *Historia naturalis* and a 'libellus physicae'. *Scriptorum publice propositorum a professoribus in Academia Witebergensi ... tomus primus* (Wittenberg, 1560), 283r–v, 421r–v.

Artificer-like mind which foresaw the purposes (*fines*) and wished to take care of the life of men (*vitae hominum consulere voluerit*).[44]

By understanding the uses for which they were made, plants were studied as a manifest testimony of the Providence of God. The study of plants was thus also a part of natural philosophy.

It is unclear whether these natural philosophy lecturers pointed out herbs in botanical gardens. Caspar Cruciger, who had also taught Dioscorides, built two gardens outside the town of Wittenberg.[45] He was also an avid collector of plants. Cruciger is reported to have said that he could discern the presence of God in nature, a God who had skilfully created things with sure purposes.[46] It is not known how the gardens at Wittenberg were designed, though by the end of the sixteenth century 'Paradise' was sought in gardens by Lutherans like Laurentius Scholz.[47] It may thus have been the case that, at Wittenberg, gardens were yet another place to seek the Providential design of God.

Providence was also sought in '*geographia*', a study of the distance, size and boundaries of lands.[48] Although the importance of Providence in Lutheran geography has been repeatedly noted, it would

[44] 'Die vero Iovis et Veneris enarrabo Dioscoridem, ut herbarum, et fruticum appellationes et naturas aliquo modo discant iuniores. Nam et herbas ipsas, quas gignit haec regio, monstrabo, et nomina usitata in lingua vernacula addam. Et quidem inchoabo enarrationem a frumentorum appellationibus. Est enim turpis negligentia horum ipsorum frumentorum et olearum, quibus vescimur, naturas et nomina ignorare. Est autem tota doctrina de stirpibus cum ob alias causas iucunda et utilis, tum vero ideo etiam digna consideratione, quia manifestum testimonium est providentiae divinae. Cum enim tanta sit herbarum multitudo, et varietas, et singulis certae vires inditae sint, ut medeantur aliae alijs morbis, manifestum est, hanc naturam rerum non casu extitisse, sed mentem fuisse Architectatricem, quae fines prospexerit, et vitae hominum consulere voluerit.' *Scriptorum publice propositorum a professoribus in Academia Witebergensi ... tomus primus* (Wittenberg, 1560), 211r–v. For the use of the vernacular in the study of plants, see also Longeon (1976).

[45] Pressel (1862), 10.

[46] 'Ac talis cum esset, vestigia Dei in natura etiam libenter considerabat, ac saepe dictum Platonis repetebat, gratam de Deo famam in artibus sparsam esse. Et illud Paulinum: Tam prope adesse Deum, fere ut manibus contrectari possit. Cernere se inquit praesentiam Dei in natura, qui prorsus ut artifex certo concilio singulis membris auxilia attribuit, et adversus singularia morborum genera peculiaria praesidia et remedia condidit. Convinci etiam homines dicebat, ne casu existiment hunc mundum ex chao temere confluxisse: quia ordo in numeris, in discrimine honestorum et turpium, in motibus coelestibus, in vicibus temporum testaretur mentem aeternam architectatricem esse.' Melanchthon, 'Caspar Cruciger', *CR*, XI, 838.

[47] For Scholz, see Fleischer (1979), and for early seventeenth-century Heidelberg, see Patterson (1981). For botanical gardens in general as Paradise re-created, see Prest (1981). For the assimilation of classical images and allegories of gardens into the ideal of the discovery of the Paradise, see Comito (1971).

[48] *CR*, XI, 293.

be misleading to treat this '*geographia*' as an independent discipline.[49] Reinhold taught Ptolemy's *Geographia* in his mathematics lecture in 1540.[50] Melanchthon himself seems to have taught '*geographia*' around 1536 alongside astronomy and astrology.[51] '*Geographia*' should thus also be understood as a part of natural philosophy. There is also some indication that the study of the properties of metals was also undertaken for the same purpose.[52]

Plants, the earth and metals are topics that were listed by Melanchthon as topics of natural philosophy but remained undiscussed in the *Initia doctrinae physicae*. When studies of these topics were undertaken, the same kind of knowledge about the Providence of God – *agnitio Dei* – was sought. These studies were legitimate parts of Melanchthon's natural philosophy, a natural philosophy that set out to prove that absolutely everything in this creation is created and ruled providentially by God.

From some incidental remarks made by the lecturers we may further catch a glimpse of the manner of teaching at Wittenberg. For instance, Melanchthon expected each of his students to have a copy of the text of the *Tetrabiblos*.[53] Erasmus Reinhold asked his students to get a copy of an arithmetic textbook by Gemma Frisius (probably the *Arithmeticae practicae methodus facilis*), and attach to it an epitome of arithmetic by Henricus Glareanus (*De sex arithmeticae practicae ... Epitome*).[54] On the other hand, manuscript copies either of the lecturers' notes or of the text circulated among students.[55] A celestial globe also seems to have been used in lectures. In 1543 the librarian asked the Elector to purchase a celestial globe 'over 4 cubits wide and decorated with twelve heavenly signs, not readily available but

49 For the importance of Providence in the study of Lutheran geography, see Büttner (1975) and (1979). For geography of the sixteenth and seventeenth centuries as an internally incoherent system dependent on extrinsic needs and interests, see Livingstone (1988).

50 *Scriptorum publice propositorum a professoribus in Academia Witebergensi ... tomus primus* (Wittenberg, 1560), D5v.

51 *CR*, XI, 293. 52 Thorndike (1923–58), V, 396f.

53 'Interim ut adolescentes invitentur ad Physicen, et alias Philosophiae partes, rursus incipiam enarrationem Quadripartiti, ac proximo die veneris inchoabo praefationem primi libri, Interim scholastici, qui codices non habent, et haec studia amant, libros emant.' Melanchthon, c. 1544, *Scripta quaedam in Academia Witenbergensi ...* (Wittenberg, 1545), D(8)r.

54 Erasmus Reinhold (1540), *Scriptorum publice propositorum a professoribus in Academia Witebergensi ... tomus primus* (Wittenberg, 1560), D5r.

55 'Tamen quia audio futurum, ut his proximis mensibus physica hic excudiantur, eam editionem expectandam esse censui, Erit enim emendatior, et locupletior ijs libellis, qui nunc manu scripti circumferuntur.' *Scripta quaedam in Academia Witenbergensi publice proposita, digesta in duos libros* (Wittenberg, 1549), A7v.

which Master Melanchthon regarded as necessary to be bought for the youths and [their] daily instruction'.[56] As a result it was recommended that the mathematics lecturer rather than the librarian buy the globe on the grounds that it might be broken or under-used if left in the library.[57]

Melanchthon's natural philosophy was thus actively taught at Wittenberg by Melanchthon himself and others. Lecturers clearly understood that natural philosophy was a knowledge about the Providence of God in the physical world and that mathematics, astronomy and astrology all led to this knowledge; they used Melanchthon's textbooks in their lectures; they extended his idea of natural philosophy to areas which Melanchthon had not dealt with himself; and topics on natural philosophy were disputed upon, following closely Melanchthon's own arguments. Knowledge about the Providence of God in the physical world, the knowledge of Law, was thus actively taught at Wittenberg.

As for how these lectures were heard or understood by the students, an extensive survey of German archives and textbook marginalia would first be necessary. There were, however, numerous Wittenberg students who moved to other universities, and taught and recommended what they had learnt. For instance, Johannes Mercurius Morsheimus taught at Heidelberg the first part of the *Tetrabiblos*, arithmetic and the *De sphaera*. In his tract on judicial astrology, he paid tribute to Melanchthon for the treatment of the same subject in the *Initia doctrinae physicae*, and to Caspar Peucer for his works on divination.[58] Bruno Seidel, an ex-student from Wittenberg who went on to study medicine at Padua, wrote a commentary on the human soul and body following Melanchthon, Galen and Vesalius.[59] Petrus Monedulatus Lascovius, another student at Wittenberg, repeated in his *De homine magno ... libri II* that it was important to 'know thyself' through knowledge about the faculties of the soul and anatomy. At Jena and Greifswald, the *De anima* was also taught in Melanchthon's spirit.[60] Michael Buether, a history lecturer who graduated from Wittenberg, recommended the

[56] '... über 4 Ellen breit und mit den 12 himmlischen Zeichen bemalt, nich[t] gern aus der Hand lassen, wiewohl Melanchthon den globum selber zu gut der jugent zu teglicher weisung gern kaufte und nötig were.' 13 November 1543, Librarian (Lukas Edenberger) to the Elector, *Urkundenbuch*, 234.

[57] *Urkundenbuch*, 236 [58] Thorndike (1923–58), v, 402.

[59] *Commentarius didascalius* (Hanover: G. Antonius, 1594).

[60] See Nutton (1993), 22–4.

second book of the *Historia naturalis* alongside Aristotle's *Meteora* and Ptolemy's *Geographia* to the Strasburg Council, when in 1567 they sought his advice on curricular reforms of the Strasburg Gymnasium.[61] Melanchthon's direct involvement in curricular reforms of other reformed universities and gymnasiums is well known.[62] For instance, the statutes of the University of Rostock of 1565 explicitly prescribe the use of Melanchthon's natural philosophy textbooks.[63] Numerous other recommendations by Melanchthon's students on the study of natural philosophy survive.[64] Wittenberg students who shared Melanchthon's view of astrology are well catalogued by Thorndike[65] and a long list of Lutheran botanists has been compiled by Dannenfeldt.[66] Melanchthon's natural philosophy was thus spread beyond Wittenberg.

Amongst Melanchthon and his students what was ultimately seen and understood in natural philosophy was one and the same thing – the Providence of God in the physical world. Material to be considered in natural philosophy might vary and expand, but it was always the same goal that was reached. The format of Melanchthon's textbooks was such that students were effectively drilled into this goal. Hence a verdict such as the following, passed forty years after Melanchthon's death, holds also for Melanchthon's natural philosophy:

> To Philip and the school of Wittenberg for a long time by God's grace this praise was peculiar, that he both instructed the minds of the students in varied knowledge and especially formed the judgement of youth as to true opinions concerning things and eminently prepared them for public

61 *Les statuts et privilèges des universités françaises* . . ., IV, i, 123.

62 Petersen (1921), 109–27, Engelland (1960), Ahrbeck (1961) and Harrison (1978). Cf. also Benrath (1970) and Freedman (1985).

63 Freedman (1984), 38 and Petersen (1921), 118f.

64 See for instance, Schonborn, *Oratio de studiis astronomicis recitata a decano collegij philosophici, magistro Schornborn* (Wittenberg: J. Crato, 1564); Eber, *Oratio de doctrina pysica [sic], recitata a Paulo Ebero die quartodecimo Augusti Anno 1550* (Wittenberg: V. Creuzer, 1550); and plans of studies by Eber and Victorinus Strigelius in the *Institutiones literatae, sive de discendi atque docendi ratione Tomus tertius* (Torun: A. Contenius, 1588), 210f., 219–23.

65 Thorndike (1923–58), v, 380–405. See also a contemporary list of 'astrologers' beginning with Adam and ending with Copernicus and Reinhold in Casper Peucer, *Elementa doctrinae de circulis coelestibus* (Wittenberg: I. Luft, 1553), A1r–A7v.

66 Dannenfeldt (1972). Although I am not claiming that Lutherans were solely responsible for the emergence of botanical studies and gardens in the sixteenth century, it is noteworthy that the Universities of Basle and Montpellier took up studies of plants in a language very similar to Melanchthon, when they became reform-minded. For the cases of Montpellier and Basle and the humanist background to the the renaissance studies of plants, see Reeds (1991).

service. Hence it came about that all who were true disciples of Melanchthon employed a very similar style and form of oration in speaking and writing, moulded and turned out in imitation of their most erudite preceptor.[67]

With respect to natural philosophy, a univocal understanding of its goal was reached.

During times of religious discord, to claim oneself as faithful was not sufficient. Agreement had to be reached on what 'faith' meant and how to behave 'faithfully'. St Paul had taught that agreement had to be reached by focusing on the message of Christ:

Now I beseech you brethren, by the name of our Lord Jesus Christ, that ye all speak the same thing, and that there be no divisions among you; but that ye be perfectly joined together in the same mind and in the same judgement. (1 Corinthians 1. 10)

By 1555, Melanchthon could see a parallel of his times in the same passage.[68] Melanchthon duly sought to reach agreement about the message of the Gospel through education. At Wittenberg, Law was taught alongside the Gospel. Melanchthon's natural philosophy was knowlege of Law in the sense that as self-knowledge it led to the message of the Gospel and it confirmed the Providence of God in this physical world. A univocal understanding of the goal of this natural philosophy was indeed reached among lecturers and students at Wittenberg. As Melanchthon wrote in the regulations of the philosophy faculty, human knowledge was to be captivated to Christ and this aim was indeed realized at Wittenberg, and to some extent, beyond. It is perhaps due to the same concern to captivate every human knowledge to Christ that the Faust legend – the moral story of the demise of Faust who pursued knowing for its own sake – was first begun in Wittenberg.[69]

What such an education amounted to was the generation of a

67 As quoted and translated in Thorndike (1923–58), v, 378.

68 'Talis erat eius [Pauli] temporis confusio profecto non levis, nec minor, quam fuerunt multae nostro tempore ... Multa vidit haec aetas exempla similia, ideo haec facilia sunt intellectu. Paulus igitur in primo capite initio obiurgat auditores, quod excitent dissidia. Deinde ut radicem dissidiorum evellat, reprehendit admirationem propriae sapientiae, et curiositatem, propriam levibus ingeniis ...' *Commentarius in Epist. Pauli ad Corinthos* (1555), *CR*, xv, 1065f. My interpolation.

69 For the role of the Reformers in the making of the Faust legend, see Baron (1978b). For the interpretation of the first Faust story as written by a Lutheran to a university audience, see Conerman (1973). Cf. also a survey on the idea of attainability of knowledge in the motto 'noli altum sapere' in the sixteenth and seventeenth centuries in Ginzburg (1976).

group of people who thought in the same way and saw the same goal. In other words, a tradition was begun in which there was a well-recognized consensus as to what was true, correct and right of given problems. We may justly call this a construction of orthodoxy.[70]

For historians of science, this orthodox, Lutheran tradition of natural philosophy is of particular significance. It is a tradition against which Johannes Kepler's (1571–1630) claim that he was a Lutheran astrologer[71] can be understood meaningfully. Kepler learnt from Jacob Heerbrand (1521–1600), Melanchthon's pupil, the notion of astronomy as a praise of God.[72] He called his *Astronomia Nova* an 'αἰτιολόγητα', an investigation into proper physical causes. As argued by Simon, Kepler's career of an astronomer was inseparable from that of an astrologer.[73] In his astronomy, Kepler sought to explain the movements of the planets by dynamical causes and their disposition to the sun by harmonic ratios. His 'reform' of astrology mirrored this enterprise in seeking physical causes of relations between the terrestrial and the celestial, and the harmonic theory of efficiency of planetary aspects.[74] Thus both astronomy and astrology for Kepler complemented each other in his quest to understand the Divine Harmony of God which permeated the world. By Kepler's time the immediacy with which to counter civil disobedience may have receded into the background, but the quest for the Providential design through natural philosophy in which astronomy and astrology were essential seems to carry a distinctive Lutheran stamp.

HEARING, SEEING AND BELIEVING

It remains to be explained why, despite the fact that Luther did not need natural philosophy, I choose to call this natural philosophy of Melanchthon's a Lutheran one. As I hope to have shown, in order to counter a problem which (in his eyes) was jeopardizing Luther's cause, Melanchthon had developed a natural philosophy in order to

70 For the importance of learning in maintaining purity of doctrine, see *De coniunctione scholarum cum ministerio Evangelii*, *CR*, XI, 606–18. For studies on this 'orthodox' tradition, see Zeeden (1985) and H. W. Weber (1969).

71 'I am a Lutheran astrologer, throwing away the nonsense and keeping the kernel', as quoted in Field (1984), 220.

72 For Kepler and Heerbrand, see J. Hübner (1975).

73 Simon (1979).

74 For Kepler's programme for the reform of astrology, see his *De fundamentis astrologiae certioribus*, which is translated in Field (1984), 225–68.

dissociate his and Luther's cause from the evangelical radicals. His *Commentarius de anima* was about the self-knowledge of the Lutheran soul, whilst the *Initia doctrinae physicae* demonstrated a distinctively Lutheran concept of Providence. As knowledge of Law, natural philosophy demonstrated the starting point of moral philosophy. It was also taught alongside the Gospel at Wittenberg. Melanchthon's natural philosophy cannot be understood adequately without the Lutheran theology that shaped it. Yet, there is *no intrinsic reason* within Lutheran theology that necessitates the development of natural philosophy.

Luther did not write a natural philosophy. In fact, he did not need any philosophy at all.[75] When we turn to Luther's reaction to the same people whose claims were the very reasons for Melanchthon's developing his natural philosophy, we find a totally different behaviour – there was no recourse to philosophy. Luther simply behaved like St Paul with whom he had so much in common. He identified his conditions with those of Paul, likening himself to Paul and his opponents to those of Paul. That sufficed. The conviction with which Luther set forth his views and which appeared as downright dogmatic and arrogant to his opponents was that of Paul.[76]

It was a conviction gained through his personal inner struggle which was essentially an 'aural' experience.[77] Hearing the Word (*fides ex auditu*) became central to Luther's Christology, as Wilhelm Pauck has put it:

> One could read a thing many times over and yet fail to understand it and apply it to himself. But when another person spoke the same thing with a living voice, then the hearer could know that he was the one being addressed. As this was true of language in general, so it was particularly true of the Gospel. God had so constructed man that the Gospel and the Law could reach him most effectively through the medium of the living voice.[78]

75 See for intance the difficulty of trying to draw out a systematic philosophy of nature from Luther's writings in Nitschke (1971). Cf. Gerrish (1962).

76 For Luther's reaction to the evangelical radicals by way of identifying himself with Paul, see Edwards (1975), 116–26.

77 'Do not look for Christ with your eyes but put your eyes in your ears', *WA*, XXXVII, 202; 'The Kingdom of Christ is a hearing Kingdom, not a seeing Kingdom', *WA*, LI, 11. For the centrality of '*fides ex auditu*' in Luther's theology and its intrinsic importance to the 'Turmerlebnis', see Bizer (1958) and Meinhold (1958).

78 *LW*, LV, 64.

The recognition of the fact that Christ has died *for you* is essentially an 'aural' experience: 'In holy and divine matter it is more necessary to hear than to see, to believe than to understand, to be embraced than to embrace, to be grasped than to grasp . . .'[79] This aural experience runs through the whole of Luther's theology: the importance of preaching as proclamation of the Word, the Kingdom of God as a 'hearing' Kingdom,[80] and above all, his idea of 'vocation' as a preacher and theologian.[81]

The importance of 'hearing the Word' extends to the importance of music in Lutheran worship. Music is an area in which Luther himself was the major driving force in establishing a new tradition, to which Johann Sebastian Bach, for instance, belonged.[82] Luther gave music the highest place after theology.[83] Following what was originally an Augustinian view, Luther believed music to be a divine gift to man before the Fall.[84] It was a gift unique to man by which he should praise God:

> the gift of language combined with the gift of song was only given to man to let him know that he should praise God with both word and music, namely by proclaiming [the Word of God] through music and by providing sweet melodies with words.[85]

For Luther the world is full of sound and harmony and music is the divine gift by which man should praise God the Creator. It also has a didactic role in controlling human emotions.[86] Of all the arts, Luther expected music in particular to be put to the service of God.[87] As Blume has put it:

> On the one hand, it [music] is the constantly resounding praise of God and His Creation; on the other, it leads the man who practises it to God, teaches him to understand better God's Word (it is primarily sacred vocal music that Luther had in mind), and prepares him for the reception of divine

79 *LW*, LV, 53 note 82. Cf. *WA*, XXXVII, 202. 80 See *LW*, xxii, 222.
81 'Against Infiltrating and Clandestine Preachers' (1532), *LW*, XL, 386f. (see pp. 57f. above). For the idea of vocation, see further Wingren (1958).
82 For Luther's role in music, I follow Blume (1975). Cf. Etherington (1962). See Robinson-Hammerstein (1989) for vocal music as a promotor of Reformation ideas. For Bach as an orthodox Lutheran and his music as preaching, see Leaver (1982). For Lutheran church music, see also the essays in *Das protestantische Kirchenlied*.
83 'Preface to Georg Rhau's *Symphoniae iucundae* (1538), *LW*, LIII, 323.
84 Blume (1975), 9.
85 Translated by U. S. Leupold, Preface to Georg Rhau's *Symphoniae iucundae* (1538), *LW*, LIII, 323f.
86 *LW*, LIII, 323. 87 Blume (1975), 14.

grace, while making him a better man and a happy Christian and driving out the devil and all vices.[88]

For Luther music thus seems to have taken the place which natural philosophy took for Melanchthon.

For Melanchthon, on the other hand, seeing was as important as hearing, even in matters of faith. Thus he spoke of the sacramental rites in the following way:

these rites contain the mandate of God and the promise of His grace, which is special to the New Testament. Indeed when we are baptized, when we eat the body of the Lord, and when we are absolved, the rites should establish in the heart that God forgives us through Christ. And God moves the heart through the Word and through the rite at the same time so that they may believe as well as receive faith, just as St Paul said, 'faith comes from what is heard [Romans 10. 17]'. But just as the Word strikes the ears and thus strikes the heart, so a rite itself strikes the eyes and thus moves the heart. The effect of the Word and of the rite is the same, as was clearly said by Augustine: the sacrament is the visible Word because the rite is received through the eyes as if it is a picture of the Word, signifying the same thing as the Word. Hence they have the same effect.[89]

For Melanchthon who knew he was no theologian of Luther's stature or conviction, the worship of God took an 'ocular' form: 'Not by chance did the most beautiful bodies of the world come into being, but are governed by a Mind and by the counsel of God ... Seeing this with your eyes and knowing this with your mind, you recognize the Maker and worship God.'[90] It is not only the mental eye but also the physical eye by which God is known and worshipped. For Melanchthon, the physical eyes were also the most impor-

88 *Ibid.*

89 '... hi ritus habent mandatum Dei, et promissionem gratiae, quae est propria novi Testamenti. Certo enim debent statuere corda, cum baptizamur, cum vescimur corpore Domini, cum absolvimur, quod vere ignoscat nobis Deus propter Christum. Et corda simul per verbum, et ritum movet Deus, ut credant, et concipiant fidem, sicut ait Paulus. Fides ex auditu est. Sicut autem verbum incurrit in aures, ut feriat corda, Ita ritus ipse incurrit in oculos, ut moveat corda. Idem effectus est verbi et ritus, sicut praeclare dictum est ab Augustino, Sacramentum esse verbum visibile, quia ritus oculis accipitur, et est quasi pictura verbi, idem significans, quod verbum. Quare idem est utriusque effectus.' *Apologia Confessionis Augustanae*, *CR*, XXVII, 570.

90 'Non ferri casu pulcherrima corpora mundi,
Verum mente regi, consilioque Dei:
...
Haec cum suspiciens oculis ac mente notabis,
Autorem agnoscas, et venerere Deum ...'
De motu astrorum in Theoricas Planetarum (1542), *CR*, X, 578.

tant sensory organs.[91] Furthermore, of the quadrivial arts, music had the least significance in Melanchthon's educational programme.[92]

When Melanchthon depicted the natural world as theatre at the beginning of the *Initia doctrinae physicae*, he was thus not simply employing the epideictic style but was also conveying the essence of his natural philosophy: to watch the unfolding of God's Providential design in Creation.

To try to explain further why Melanchthon had an 'ocular' perception of God, it seems to me, is quite problematic. The growing importance of visual perception in general during the renaissance has been noted in various ways by several historians, though they have perhaps not fully explained why that was the case. In his classic work on the growing importance of visual arts and art theory in the renaissance, Panofsky has traced the importance of the Platonic 'Idea' of beauty in this movement.[93] For Melanchthon, however, a Platonic idea meant a self-contained concept within the mind (rather than emanating from the *Idea*) and was identifiable with Aristotle's concept of demonstration.[94] In contrast Summers has underlined the importance of Aristotelian concepts relating to the mental faculty for the rise of renaissance aesthetics.[95] Melanchthon, as we have seen, extensively used Aristotle's *De anima*, but not for the sake of discussing artistic style. It was instead the humanist form of biographical narration that was recommended by Melanchthon and used by Camerarius in order to praise the talent of Albrecht Dürer, whom they both regarded as a gifted artist with faith.[96] Ong

91 *Liber de anima* (1558), *CR*, XIII, 72.

92 But see *CR*, VIII, 94–7, and a poem on music in Hartfelder (1892), 192f.; see also a somewhat apologetic account of the absence of music in the Wittenberg curriculum in Carpenter (1958), 260–71.

93 Panofsky (1975).

94 As noted in Panofsky (1975), 6. 'Id quod Plato ideas vocat, Aristoteles demonstrationes appellat.' Melanchthon, *Scholia in Ciceronis oratorem* (1534), III, §10. *CR*, XVI, 773; 'Certum est Platonem ubique vocare ideas perfectam et illustrem notitiam, ut, Apelles habet in animo inclusam pulcherrimam imaginem humani corporis, Archimedes imaginem αὐτομάτων motuum coelestium.' *Enarrationes aliquot librorum ethicorum Aristotelis* (1529), *CR*, XVI, 290. Cf. Tigerstedt (1974), 32–5.

95 Summers (1987).

96 For Camerarius' biography of Dürer, see Parshall (1978), and for Melanchthon's appreciation of Dürer's 'faithful' style, see Kuspit (1973). See also a contemporary testimony: 'De Durero D. Philippus piae memoriae solebat dicere, Pictoriam, qua antecelluit citra controversiam omnibus suae aetatis artificibus, fuisse in eo minimam, tanti fecit prudentiam et iudicij gravitatem in alijs rebus.' Eusebius Menius, *Oratio de Vita Jacobi Milichii* (Wittenberg: G. Rhaw, 1562), B4vr.

10 Melanchthon as St Basil.
Melanchthon, by Lucas Cranach the Younger

has stressed the invention of printing as a major force for the increasing emphasis on visual perception.[97] However, not only Luther and Melanchthon, but also many others understood the propaganda value of cheap print and cartoons.[98]

It thus seems unfeasible to explain away Melanchthon's natural philosophy by recourse to a single tradition or strand of thought which intellectual historians have identified in this period. From all the cultural and intellectual heritage that was available to him, Melanchthon selected several things and made them into something of his own. What made Melanchthon peculiarly Melanchthon was how he reacted to events in his life, and what he read, heard and felt strongly about. Without considering what mattered to him in his life, it would be impossible to understand the force of the statements he made, or why he bothered to write those words.

If the polemical attitude of the 'hearing' theologian, Luther, is best described by the figure of St Paul, that of the 'seeing' Greek teacher, Melanchthon, may best be depicted through St Basil the Great (*c.* 330–79). We thus turn to Melanchthon's last portrait, painted by Lucas Cranach the younger (Fig. 10).[99] There, Melanchthon holds a book in his hand. A passage from St Basil is quoted in Greek on the left-hand side of the book with the inscription 'BASILIVS pagina 388', the location of the quoted text in the 1532 Basle edition edited by Erasmus.[100] At the bottom of this page, '1559', the year of the composition of the portrait, is inscribed. On the right-hand page, a Latin translation of the same passage is written.[101] The passage is from Basil's homily on humility in which Basil quotes Paul on justification by faith alone (1 Corinthians 1. 30f.).[102] The same passage was cited in Greek in a speech composed by Melanchthon and delivered by the dean of the faculty of philosophy on the commemoration day of the saint the previous year.[103] In it Melanchthon likened his present-day condition to that of Basil:

For his [St Basil's] was also a turbulent time, full of atrocious disagreements. A great host of Arians led by the tyrant, the Emperor Valens, fell on him. Now similar things are happening. We too are opposed by many

97 Ong (1958). 98 Scribner (1981), Park and Daston (1981), 25–34, and Kurze (1958).

99 For a study of portraits of Melanchthon, see Thulin (1961).

100 Basil, *Opera*, Basle: ex off. Frobeniana, edited by Desiderius Erasmus.

101 To my knowledge, Melanchthon never systematically translated Basil's works, but see his oration below. For Melanchthon's usage of Patristic sources, see Fraenkel (1961a) *passim*.

102 Basil (1857), XXXI, 530. 103 *CR*, IX, 442f.

enemies who are armed both with the power of princes and by the teachings of unlearned men ...

It is very useful to keep in mind Basil's teaching and thence seek support. For he constantly defended the Nicean Creed. He indeed spoke expressively of justification by faith, using in our manner the particle 'by faith alone'.

These are his words:

'The Apostle tells us: "He that glorieth may glory in the Lord", saying "Christ was made for us, wisdom of God, justice and sanctification and redemption; that, as it is written: He that glorieth may glory in the Lord." Now, this is the perfect and consummate glory in God: not to exult in one's own justice, but, recognizing oneself as lacking true justice, to be justified by faith in Christ alone.'

... they [people at the assembly] may very gladly realize, if they ponder upon it, that this very Basil is the encourager, that philosophic teaching should not be neglected. For his writing survives on the reading and selecting of statements from poets and philosophers: because true statements are the words of the Law (*voces Legis*). For he wished to distinguish between the Law and the Gospel.[104]

St Basil vigorously defended the Nicean orthodoxy, endeavoured to unite orthodox Christians against the Arians and utilized Greek philosophy for Christian purposes.[105] In his *Letter to Young Men*, Basil also argued that classical literature should be read for Christian use, especially for moral purposes. As if following Basil's advice, Melanchthon utilized numerous pagan writers in his natural philosophy in order to provide a theoretical proof of moral principle. Melanchthon invigorated the teaching of Latin and Greek classics in response to the 'unlearned' Anabaptists and theologians. His educational programme was aimed at reaching agreement about Christian teaching. There, in the portrait, we see Melanchthon holding a book of St Basil on *sola fideism*, one half in Greek, the other half a

104 'Fuit enim et ipsius aetas turbulenta et plena atrocium dissidiorum. Et in ipsum incurrit magna phalanx Arianorum, instructa Valentis Imperatoris tyrannide. Nunc similia accidunt. Oppugnamur et Nos a multis inimicis, qui armati sunt et principum potentia et factionibus indoctorum ...

Plurimum autem prodest mente intueri doctrinam ipsius, et inde testimonium petere. Constanter defendit Nicenum Symbolum. De iusticia fidei etiam loquitur expresse, nostro more utens particula sola fide. Verba enim haec sunt [Greek passage, see note 102 above] ... Quod eo libentius facient, si cogitabunt, hunc ipsum Basilium hortatorem esse, ut doctrina philosophica non negligatur. Extat enim eius Scriptum de legendis et eligendis sententiis Poetarum et Philosophorum: quia verae sententiae sunt voces Legis. Discerni tamen vult legem et Evangelium.' *CR*, IX, 442. Translation of the passage of Basil's homily is by M. M. Wagner in Basil (1950), 479.

105 See Callahan (1958), esp. 31–51.

11 *Memorial of the Reformation.* Altar-piece by the Cranach Workshop (1547)

Latin translation. The text itself undoubtedly was meant to declare the 'authenticity' of his faith, which had come under much attack during his last years.[106] To the end of the Latin text is appended the following invocation: 'O Gospel, be with us and set our hearts afire with thy flame.'[107] In the figure of St Basil, we may thus see a life-portrait of Melanchthon.

In the figures of St Paul and St Basil, we see how Melanchthon and Luther differed in their concerns and preoccupations. Paul defended true faith through preaching and proclaiming the Word; Basil defended it with Greek philosophy. Their difference meant that they achieved different goals.

In 1547, Lucas Cranach the Elder completed an altar-piece, commissioned after Luther's death by the Wittenberg magistrates as a 'memorial' to his achievements (Fig. 11).[108] In it Melanchthon is depicted as baptizing an infant,[109] an explicit refutation of Anabaptism. Luther, in the garb of Junker Jörg, implying his abandonment

106 Especially from the gnesio-Lutherans headed by Flacius Illyricus, Stupperich (1966), 134–40.

107 Schade (1980), 103. 108 Thulin (1955), 35. 109 Christensen (1979), 134f.

of the monk's habit, is receiving the cup, a cup that was denied to the recipients of the Mass in the Catholic Church, but a cup restored by Luther.[110] It is a firm indication of the administration of the sacrament in both kinds. Bugenhagen, pastor of the Wittenberg church, is seen holding the two keys of St Peter, hitherto the symbol of the authority of the Papacy, now reinterpreted by Luther as the keys of 'binding' and 'loosing', namely the offices of repentance and absolution.[111] In the predella where a saint's most significant episode or action was usually depicted, Luther points to the crucified Christ – the most important of his teachings: justification by faith alone. The whole altar-piece thus signifies Luther's break with the Roman Catholic Church and his dissociation from the evangelical radicals.

The association of baptism with Melanchthon and of the Eucharist with Luther in this panel is quite apt. Luther's greatest output besides the question of justification was on the topic of the Lord's Supper.[112] He vigorously defended his interpretation of the real presence of Christ against Carlstadt and Zwingli. In contrast Melanchthon's educational progamme was ultimately a response to the Anabaptists. Against them, he constantly asserted the efficacy of infant baptism. In response to his experience of Anabaptism in Thuringia, Melanchthon re-evaluated philosophy and developed a natural philosophy which was knowledge of Law in every Lutheran sense of the word. Significantly, on the title-page of his copy of Homer, Melanchthon wrote in Greek: 'Buried together with the Lifegiver, let there be resurrection', an unmistakable reference to baptism (Frontispiece).[113] In the whole achievement of the Lutheran Reformation then, as depicted in the Wittenberg altar-piece, Luther and Melanchthon occupied different places.

By pointing out and contrasting their difference, it has not been my intention to imply that there existed a deliberate division of labour between Melanchthon and Luther. Nor do I wish to claim that each pursued his interests to the exclusion of the other's. I have pointed out the difference between the two in order to illustrate that the two acted and reacted differently because they pursued different vocations. That is ultimately why Melanchthon needed natural

[110] For a survey of Luther's portraits, see Strahl (1982).
[111] See 'The Keys' (1530), *LW*, XL, 325–77.
[112] Althaus (1970), 225.
[113] 'Συνθαφθεὶς τῷ ζωποιῷ ἴστῶ ἀναβιώση'. Cf. Romans 6. 4, Colossians 2. 12.

philosophy and Luther did not. That Melanchthon was preoccupied with the knowledge of Law in contrast with Luther's Gospel does not imply that Melanchthon's endeavours were any the less Lutheran.

In the preceding chapters I have tried to show how and why Melanchthon's natural philosophy was shaped by Lutheran theology, and in the previous section I have tried to point out how natural philosophy played an important part in his educational programme which was aimed at constructing Lutheran orthodoxy. Natural philosophy was indeed developed for reasons extrinsic to the system of Lutheran theology itself, but it was firmly based on Lutheran theology, and more importantly, it was deemed vital for the survival of Luther's message. This is why I call Melanchthon's natural philosophy a Lutheran one and also why I believe the aims of Luther and Melanchthon essentially agree.

The predella of the Wittenberg altar-piece shows Luther pointing to the crucified Christ (Fig. 11), a gesture with which he was often depicted[114] and a gesture which he shares with John the Baptist. Pointing was one of the traditional gestures ascribed to John the Baptist. For Luther, however, its meaning had become blurred.[115] Luther, referring everything to Christ as usual, renewed emphasis on the role of John the Baptist as the forerunner of Christ.[116] Thus the gesture pointing to Christ became *the* gesture of John the Baptist. As Luther wrote: 'John the Baptist had the office of pointing to the son of God. He was chosen to be Christ's forerunner, to point to Him with his fingers and his words, lest the world pass Him by, as the Jews did, who neglected to meet Him and still cannot find Him today.'[117] This concentration on John the Baptist as a figure pointing to Christ is best seen in Cranach's pictures. In the Law and Gospel panel now in Gotha (Fig. 2), most probably ideated by Melanchthon and/or Luther,[118] we see John the Baptist pointing to the crucified Christ, rather than to the traditional Lamb. As was so often the case, Cranach used a traditional motif, but changed the emphases and invested it with different meanings.[119] Saints or other

[114] See for instance Scribner (1981), plates 165 and 167, and Thulin (1955), plate 65.

[115] 'Sermons on the Gospel of St John' (1537), *LW*, XXII, 164.

[116] For a similar shift of emphasis in the depiction of John the Baptist in contemporary spiritual plays, see Thulin (1930).

[117] *LW*, XXII, 462.

[118] Schuchardt (1851–70), I, 81.

[119] See Christensen (1979), 160–2; and Hayum (1989), 95 for the pointing of John the Baptist as a testifying witness in Grünewald's Isenheim Altarpiece.

12 Double portrait of Melanchthon and Luther, from the binding of Martin Luther, *Leviticus, Das dritte buch Mose* (Wittenberg: 1574)

elements responsible for confusion are eliminated. Facing the soul of man (depicted naked in the picture), John the Baptist now quite clearly points to the crucified Christ. It is now impossible to miss the message: Christ died for you.

Melanchthon saw Luther as John the Baptist because both pointed to the Saviour, Christ.[120] On the other hand, Luther had called classical studies 'a sort of John the Baptist' because he saw them as a necessary preparation for 'Christ', namely theology.[121] This 'John the Baptist' was what Melanchthon taught. I have already discussed how the Providence of God in natural philosophy

[120] 'Revocavit igitur Lutherus hominum mentes ad filium Dei, et *ut Baptista, monstravit agnum Dei*, qui tulit peccata nostra, ostendit gratis propter filium Dei remitti peccata, et quidem oportere id beneficium fide accipi. Hic monstravit Legis et Evangelii discrimen, hic refutavit errorem, qui tunc in scholis et concionibus regnabat, qui docet mereri homines remissionem peccatorum propriis operibus, et homines coram Deo iustos esse disciplina, ut Pharisaei docuerunt.' 1 January 1546, preface to the second volume of Luther's works, *CR*, VI, 160f. My emphasis.

[121] See p. 57 above.

led to the message of the Gospel. In the most important Lutheran gesture of John the Baptist, then, we see a correspondence in what Luther and Melanchthon were doing in their respective vocations. As Luther spoke of John the Baptist from Christ's point of view:

> John came and, in answer to your inquiry, directed you to Me. He baptized you for repentance and led you to Me. And now that I am present, you should, in view of all this, be convinced of My identity as the Messiah and look at Me, especially since John was My forerunner. This should be a sign to which you should direct your diligent attention; for John warned you, saying that I would follow on his heels; yes, he pointed to Me with his fingers.[122]

Several double portraits of Melanchthon and Luther survive to this day (Fig. 12).[123] They are double portraits because they form a pair, but they are not complete with only one of them. Just like Law and Gospel, the two were different but each needed the other.[124] Two different men pursued two different careers, acted and reacted differently, but what they were doing most expressively agreed in their 'gesture', to point to Christ. Together they defended their belief in the theology of Law and Gospel.

122 *LW*, XXII, 239, translated by M. H. Betram.
123 Many double portraits were produced from the Cranach workshop, Posse (1942), 64.
124 Pauck (1984), 53.

Conclusion: a transformation of natural philosophy

> One last word. Wanting to make the sixteenth century a skeptical century, a free-thinking and rationalist one, and glorify it as such is the worst of errors and delusions. On the authority of its best representatives it was, quite to the contrary, an inspired century, one that sought in all things first of all a reflection of the divine.
>
> Lucien Febvre, *The Problem of Unbelief in the Sixteenth Century: The Religion of Rabelais*, trans. by Beatrice Gottlieb

Philip Melanchthon transformed the natural philosophy which was traditionally taught by the Schoolmen at universities into a Lutheran one. The late medieval Schoolmen frequently commented upon Aristotle's books on nature with the *quaestio* method and appealed to the authority of Aristotle, the Schoolmen and the Church. As part of university learning, natural philosophy contributed towards knowledge of God and alongside metaphysics it was an essential area of knowledge for theologians. The system of thought of the Schoolmen, tightly knit together by means of logic, was ultimately based on a conviction that rational knowledge about God was possible and necessary. Hence natural philosophical arguments were legitimately used to prove, elucidate and maintain theological points.

In contrast, Luther denied the validity of human rational knowledge as a support for theology. Human reason on its own could not affirm theological truths. Natural philosophy of the late medieval Schoolmen was therefore rejected by Luther and Melanchthon – it could not teach the message of the Gospel. Instead, Melanchthon's natural philosophy was knowledge of Law in the sense that it provided the theoretical foundation of his moral philosophy of civil obedience. For his natural philosophy, Melanchthon indeed used Aristotle's books on nature but he reinterpreted them on Lutheran principles and utilized many other authors, both ancient and modern. Melanchthon's natural philosophy was knowledge of Law also in the sense that it taught self-knowledge and the greatness of the Providential Creator.

Nature was a theatre in which God's Providence unfolded, but this Providence was only discernible through Lutheran faith, not through Roman Catholic or Zwinglian faith. To be able to glorify the Providence of God presupposed denial of works righteousness. That this Providence of God was visible through this Creation was due to the Lutheran conviction that spirituality lay in material things. That the Providence of God *ought* to be seen was due to the fact that natural philosophy was taught in a university where a correct understanding of the teaching of the Church had to be reached univocally. Instead of systematically resolving questions by logical distinctions, definitions and syllogisms, Melanchthon proceeded by providing definitions of pre-selected and pre-ordered *loci*, in order effectively to teach the Providential design of God in this physical world.

Melanchthon's natural philosophy never rationally proved the central tenets of Lutheran theology. Theological points were introduced always with Scriptural grounding. Melanchthon's natural philosophy offered *a posteriori* arguments in order to confirm a single point about the divinity, that God created and sustains everything in this physical universe with Providential design. Yet, for Melanchthon, natural philosophy was a strong defence for Luther's cause in that it provided a powerful argument against civil disobedience, an issue which Melanchthon believed with personal conviction to be jeopardizing their quest for Reform. Law was not Gospel, but it was necessary for establishing the message of the Gospel.

Melanchthon transformed the scope of natural philosophy by orientating it towards a civic and ethical value. It could now contribute to defending faith by way of actively supporting or demonstrating a Christian but human value such as the essence of the obedient Christian.[1] Some may see in this 'moralizing' aspect of natural philosophy a revival of the Hellenistic enterprise of cos-

[1] It should be noted that the 'secularization of theology' which proved a rich background for seventeenth-century natural philosophy, as argued in Funkenstein (1986), is paralleled by this extension of scope of natural philosophy itself.

mology as primarily subservient to moral and political theory.[2] Others may regard it as an extension of renaissance Ciceronianism which valued philosophy as useful for the *vita activa*.[3] The philologically sophisticated knowledge of a broader range of classical philosophy and the practical value of speculative philosophy are part of the unique and considerable achievements of the earlier humanists. These may well be regarded as necessary conditions of knowledge and of possibilities of what philosophy could offer, for Melanchthon to have been able to write the natural philosophy that he did. They are, however, not sufficient for understanding the uniqueness of Melanchthon's philosophy. From all the sources, ideas, canons of knowledge and cultural values that were available to them, people select certain things and not others, modify them and add other things, thus creating something of their own. It is the specificity of their choice from their heritage and learning, and the uniqueness of their creation that I have been interested in. That is why I have tried, perhaps *ad nauseam*, to determine how and why Melanchthon used certain words such as *physiologia* and *agnitio Dei*. As I have tried to indicate on several occasions, both Melanchthon and Luther wrote in the language of the Bible, rather than that of modern science, and that Bible itself they read in a particular way.

When we recognize the particular and concrete issues that mattered to people in the past and the immediate problems they were confronting – issues which in the sixteenth century turn out to be mainly Christian and theological – we may gain a fruitful understanding about the uniqueness and specificity of the way people in the past wrote and what they meant by what they wrote. Without his reactions to the disturbances of the Wittenberg Movement, the Anabaptists in Thuringia, the rift with the Zwinglians, his vocation as a classics teacher, and his Lutheran faith, it is impossible to understand why Melanchthon wrote at all about natural philosophy. This is precisely why, I believe, traditional accounts of 'Protestantism and science' which have concentrated on an internal analysis of Protestant theology have been unfruitful.[4] Logical compatibility between reading the Bible and making 'scientific' claims about the physical universe cannot explain sufficiently why a par-

[2] For the intrinsic relationship between classical cosmology and political theory, see Cornford (1937) and Vlastos (1947).
[3] For Melanchthon's Ciceronianism, see Tuck (1993), 18–20.
[4] See for instance Dillenberger (1961) and Gerrish (1968).

ticular type of natural philosophy, with its peculiar readings of Vesalius and Copernicus, was needed at all for Lutherans. Such an analysis assumes that there is an identifiable systematic body of doctrine, as well as taking as unproblematic what 'scientific' explanations of the natural world ought to be about. Indeed in this kind of account, the significance of the ethical orientation of Melanchthon's natural philosophy would be lost completely, and with it the very reason for the existence of natural philosophy. Moreover, what we may today easily identify as Lutheran, Calvinist or Roman Catholic doctrine did not suddenly appear as complete systems of theological doctrine. For the authors of the Reformation, theology was a living issue resulting as much from reaction to concomitant events as from action led by conviction and belief. Melanchthon's transformation of natural philosophy was part of such a process.

Instead of drawing an artificial line between 'science and religion' onto sixteenth-century natural philosophy, it is, I hope to have shown, far more fruitful to take heed of a distinction sixteenth-century people recognized. Law and Gospel is precisely such a distinction which embodies the Lutheran essence of Melanchthon's natural philosophy as a whole. Natural philosophy could not teach the message of the Gospel, but, as Law, it could provide theoretical grounding of a moral philosophy of civil obedience, which in turn was necessary to defend Luther's cause.

For the Lutherans in the 1570s, philosophy became necessary in a different way. The issues that they now faced were quite different from those that concerned Melanchthon in the late 1520s and 1530s. It was the controversy with the Calvinists over the two natures of Christ that occupied these Lutherans most and they saw metaphysics as a powerful tool with which to conduct the controversy.[5] It is in commentaries on the *Metaphysica* that we often find statements of Lutheran thinkers of this period about the nature and limits of philosophy and its relationship to theology.[6] Nicholas Taurellus, for instance, intended to establish proper procedures of philosophy in his *Philosophia triumphans* by using Schegk's idea of demonstration and Melanchthon's three criteria for certain knowledge. He believed that proper philosophy supplied foundations for belief, and

[5] Lohr (1988a), 625f.

[6] For the Lutheran appropriation of metaphysics, see Sparn (1976), and its teaching at Lutheran institutions, see Leinsle (1988).

could be useful for refuting unbelievers and for leading them to faith.[7] For Taurellus, despair of the limitation of human being was the end of philosophy and the beginning of faith.[8] The limitation of philosophy in religion was always a concern for Lutherans. Thus the Lutherans in Strasburg condemned Johannes Hasler's attempt to defend the doctrine of the Trinity with Aristotle's *Metaphysica*: he had overstepped the scope of philosophy legitimately assigned to it.[9]

Just as different conceptions of faith lead to different understandings of the Church, ministry and worship,[10] so different beliefs lead to the emergence of different kinds of knowledge.[11] Calvin too understood that all the works of God clearly demonstrated their Creator,[12] but he differed from Melanchthon in insisting that human reason is so impaired by sin that it misperceives God's revelation.[13] That is, there was no reliable natural knowledge of God for Calvin. This meant that there could not be a natural philosophy based on pagan philosophy and directed towards a Christian purpose. What little use Calvin found in Aristotle was motivated theologically.[14] Calvin saw no need for a natural philosophy, nor did he see a valid foundation for such a discipline. For him, in fact, it was only through faith and Scriptures that human reason could 'reclaim' creation as a reliable source of knowledge of God.[15] This is precisely how Lambert Daneau (*c.* 1530–95) wrote a *Physica Christiana*, a natural philosophy based on descriptions of the workings of nature as found in the Scriptures. Daneau scrupulously

[7] Taurellus, *Philosophia Triumphans, hoc est Metaphysica philosophandi methodus* ... (Basle: S. Henricpetri, 1573), *2rf., *4r.

[8] 'Hic est ultimus Philosophiae gradus, principiumque Theologiae Desperatio nimirum: Nam praeter hasce rationes conscientia torquet, ut gravissimum Dei iudicium expectemus.' Taurellus, *Philosophia Triumphans, hoc est Metaphysica philosophandi methodus* ..., 372. Lohr (1988a), 622f.

[9] Burchill (1988).

[10] For different beliefs leading to different systems of Church, ministry and ethics, see Loescher (1981) and for different forms of worship, Eire (1986).

[11] For an assessment of the ways in which the Book of Genesis could be commented upon in this period, see A. Williams (1948).

[12] Calvin's distinction between knowledge of God the Creator and God the Redeemer was inherited by his followers, see Muller (1979).

[13] Calvin's unique standpoint on knowledge of God through Creation in the Protestant tradition is briefly but clearly summarized in Steinmetz (1991). It should be noted that Steinmetz sees this kind of knowledge as essentially natural theological, rather than natural philosophical.

[14] For Calvin's limited use of Aristotle's physical arguments, see Kaiser (1988); for his attitude towards classical philosophy, see also Partee (1977); for his idea of education, see Bouwsma (1988), 113–27; 150–61.

[15] Steinmetz (1991), 153.

enumerated the correct statements by classical authors about the Creator, but his primary concern was to establish the true and correct teaching about Creation according to the Word of God.[16] In his *Ethices Christianae libri III*, Daneau also argued that even moral actions depended upon God's Will.[17] Just as Daneau sought to establish the authority of the Church over against secular authority in his ministry,[18] so in the realm of knowledge he tried to establish the authority of the Scriptures and God over human and pagan knowledge.

Meanwhile, a different kind of Calvinist natural philosophy was emerging at the Strasburg Gymnasium, on which the Genevan Academy was modelled.[19] When Johan Sturm reorganized the Latin schools in Strasburg into a single Gymnasium in 1538, its purpose was to educate good citizens and prepare students for the secular world as good Christians.[20] Bucer had established a *Collegium praedicatorum* in 1534 for training ministers of the Church.[21] Neither institution seems to have regarded natural philosophy as an essential area of knowledge, until Hieronymus Zanchi, an ex-Thomist theologian, gave extraordinary lectures on Aristotle's *Physica* in 1554, at the request of Sturm.[22]

In the prolegomena to the Greek text of Aristotle's *Physica*, Zanchi claims that natural philosophy is worthy for Christians because human beings are the only creatures to stand upright, so that they can lift their eyes to God, and it is their duty to give thanks to God by appreciating His works.[23] Natural philosophy is useful in three ways: in order to know and admire God through His Creation 'as if' ascending a ladder of creatures; to help understand metaphors in Scriptures taken from nature; and to lead students to piety.[24] True philosophy is well founded in the things themselves, while false

16 I have used the English edition, Daneau, *The Wonderful Woorkmanship of the World* (London: [J. Kingston] for A. Maunsell, 1578), trans. Thomas Twyne, Aiijr–Aivr.

17 Fatio (1981), 117. For Daneau's ethics, see further Fatio (1976), 177–89.

18 Fatio (1981).

19 See Borgeaud (1900).

20 *Les statuts et privilèges des universités françaises* ..., IV, i, 22. For Sturm's educational programme, see Sohm (1912) and Mesnard (1966). For the Academy, see Schindling (1977). For the Reformation in Strasburg, see Chrisman (1967).

21 *Les statuts et privilèges des universités françaises* ..., IV, i, 28.

22 For Zanchi, see Burchill (1984), and for his Thomism, Gründler (1964). Zanchi was converted by Peter Martyr Vermigli, another ex-Thomist, McNair (1967), 227–30.

23 Zanchi, *De naturali auscultatione* (Strasburg: W. Rihelius, 1554), avv–aviiiir.

24 Zanchi, *De naturali auscultatione*, biiiv–bvr.

philosophy is a construct of human imagination. It is the latter which St Paul condemned in Colossians 2. 8.[25] Zanchi also follows Melanchthon in preferring Aristotle to Plato for didactic reasons. The Platonic way of writing has recently been abused by the Anabaptists, while Aristotle teaches methodically.[26] In order to recover the 'fount' from which so many philosophical compendiums were cut off, Zanchi proposes to teach the Greek text of Aristotle's *Physica*.[27] Evidently, Zanchi was acquainted with Melanchthon's writings, as similar points and arguments about natural philosophy were made. There was, however, no attempt on Zanchi's part to prove systematically the Providence of God in the physical universe, homing in on the nature of the soul or body of man, in order to demonstrate the starting point of moral philosophy. Nor was there any effort to delineate the limits of philosophy with respect to theology. In fact, Zanchi's theology was based on the Thomist conviction that knowledge of God was possible through analogical reasoning, by way of using Aristotelian arguments of causation.[28]

Zanchi left Strasburg in 1563 after a dispute over predestination with the Lutheran pastor Johannes Marbach.[29] Zanchi's textbooks were in use even after his departure.[30] The natural philosophy lecture at Strasburg became the responsibility of medics such as Johannes Guinther von Andernach and Andreas Planer.[31] Zanchi himself became a well-known Calvinist theologian, modelling his works on Thomas Aquinas' *Summa theologiae* and using extensively Aristotelian categories and causality arguments.[32] At Heidelberg, he also defended the Trinity against the Arians by pointing out the logical fallacies of the latter's claims by following Aristotle's *Sophistici Elenchi*.[33] As is noted by historians,[34] it was this Thomist conviction in the active use of Aristotelian philosophy in theology that became central to Calvinist institutional philosophy.

Melanchthon's philosophy quickly became part of the philosophical culture of the sixteenth century, which was a rich background for many thinkers who in turn created their own philosophy. At the end of the sixteenth century, for instance, Melanchthon's philosophy

[25] Zanchi, *De naturali auscultatione*, bvir, bviir.
[26] Zanchi, *De naturali auscultatione*, bviiirf.
[27] Zanchi, *De naturali auscultatione*, ciir. [28] Gründler (1964).
[29] For how this dispute was resolved politically, see Kittleson (1977).
[30] Burchill (1988), 295f. [31] Schindling (1977), 247–52, 322–41.
[32] For Zanchi's Thomist background, see Gründler (1964).
[33] Burchill (1984), 202. [34] Donnelly (1976) and McLelland (1976).

could still play an important part in Andreas Libavius' effort to establish chemistry as a didactic subject.[35] The extent to which Protestant thinkers such as Schegk, Keckermann and Hawenreuther derived their inspiration and material from their philosophical background (which included Melanchthon) and how they reformulated such knowledge in creating their own natural philosophy needs further investigation.[36] Within the Reformed tradition, it is also necessary to understand how Petrus Ramus' dialectics, which appealed to many Huguenots and Puritans, affected the nature of natural philosophy.[37] It is only after such individual studies have been undertaken, that we may be in a proper position to examine whether there might be a general characteristic of a 'Protestant' natural philosophy.

Furthermore, if we are to gain a fairer picture of what natural philosophy in universities meant, it is necessary to take into account the efforts of the Counter-Reformation by those such as the Jesuits, the Dominicans and the Coimbra commentators.[38] University natural philosophy of the sixteenth century was in no way a monolithic and regressive commitment to Aristotle. If anything, it was very much alive, constantly being remoulded in order to accommodate the needs and counter the problems people deeply cared about. The exact nature of the various reformulations that natural philosophy underwent at the hands of these people still needs close examination. It may be reasonably surmised, however, that in an age of Confessionalization, several universities had a clear sense of their brief as maintaining and reinforcing orthodox views.[39] Natural philosophy was necessarily affected by this brief, as well as by the intellectual heritage and contemporary issues of the individual. It is then also

[35] Hannaway (1975).

[36] For literature on Schegk, see p. 113 above. For Keckermann as a Calvinist philosopher, see Muller (1984); for a study on Hawenreuther's appropriation of Zabarella's logic, see Backus (1988). For Keckermann's teacher, Clemens Timpler, there is now a comprehensive study by Freedman (1988).

[37] For Ramus, see Ong (1958) and Hooykaas (1958), but see also the recent studies in *Pierre de la Ramée*, esp. Vasoli (1986). For Ramus' idea of university reform, see Sharratt (1976) with Farge (1985) on the Reformation and the University of Paris. For Ramus' reception in Germany, see now Freedman (1993).

[38] See Vona (1968) for Counter-Reformation philosophy in general. For Jesuit education, the literature is enormous, but see esp. Martin (1988) for France, Hengst (1981) for Germany and Dear (1988) for the early seventeeth century. For a difference in the treatment of Aquinas between the Jesuits and the Dominicans, see Feldhay (1987). For the Coimbra commentators, see Stegmüller (1959).

[39] For the role of education in establishing 'ideology', see Kelley (1981), 131–67.

further necessary to compare such 'Confessionalized' enterprises with those south of the Alps such as at Padua.[40]

One also ought to remember that universities were not the only places where knowledge about nature was sought in this period. Knowledge of nature and mechanical arts received active patronage from princes such as Wilhelm IV of Hesse-Kassel and Rudolph II in Prague.[41] Some princes were expert practitioners themselves, while others saw the usefulness of the novel allegorical value of natural knowledge for promoting political authority.[42] Recent studies have shown how such patronage indeed affected the nature, method and content of the knowledge of nature and the mathematical arts. For instance, Galileo's *Sidereus Nuncius* can be read as the work of a mathematician who needed cognitive legitimation for making a claim on physical reality (the realm hitherto reserved to philosophers), seeking the patronage of an absolutist Medicean prince who might provide the authority for that legitimation.[43] The nature of patronage could also determine the kind of problem that was investigated, just as mathematicians of the mid-seventeenth century worked on squaring the circle, which allegorically implied a solution to the Habsburg problem of good governance.[44]

I do not mean to imply that there were two types of knowledge of nature such as university natural philosophy and patronized knowledge of nature which were mutually exclusive. University men such as Galileo and Kepler, for instance, pursued patronage, thus bridging the two realms. Furthermore, Paracelsus' medicine, clearly pitched against institutional knowledge and inspired by radical reform and popular protest,[45] would defy characterization by either type. What is important to note is that although there was to a great extent a common cultural and intellectual heritage, the *forum* for the knowledge of nature did affect the kind of knowledge that was pursued. Unless that forum for which knowledge of nature was produced is taken into account, it will be impossible to understand why these people wrote about knowledge of nature in the way that

[40] For Padua, see now N. Jardine, 'Keeping Order in the School of Padua', forthcoming, for the clash between Piccolomini and Zabarella as a clash between different perceptions and understanding of the office of teaching philosophy. I thank Professor Jardine for allowing me to read a draft version of this article. Cf. Ingegno (1988) for other philosophies of nature.

[41] For Wilhelm IV, see Moran (1980), and for Rudolph II, see Evans (1973).

[42] For a historical overview of patronage and knowledge, see Moran (1991).

[43] Biagioli (1990). [44] Ashworth (1991). [45] Webster (1993).

they did and, indeed, what it was that they were doing with such knowledge.

Melanchthon's transformation of natural philosophy may indeed have been only a part (though a significant one) of the many transformations that were taking place in natural philosophy in that period.[46] It would be of benefit to historians of science to understand the exact nature of the transformation that the understanding of the workings of the natural world underwent in the sixteenth century. This can be profitably done, I believe, by further asking questions as to what natural philosophy or knowledge of nature meant to others in the sixteenth century, and what it was that they were trying to achieve. The questions are yet to be answered because they are yet to be asked. It is the fruitfulness of reorientating the questions that I have tried to illustrate in this book.

46 For an overview of the reformulation of knowledge and institutions of this period, see Giard (1991).

Bibliography

WORKS OF REFERENCE

A. BIBLIOGRAPHICAL

Allgemeine deutsche Bibliographie, 56 vols., Leipzig, 1875–1912.
Contemporaries of Erasmus: A Biographical Register of the Renaissance and Reformation, ed. P. B. Bietenholz, 3 vols., Toronto, 1985–7.
Dictionary of National Biography, 63 vols., Oxford, 1885–1900.
Dictionnaire de biographie française, Paris, 1933–.

B. OTHERS

Annales typographici, ed. G. W. Panzer, 11 vols., Nuremberg, 1793–1803.
Bibliographie der psychologischen Literatur des 16. Jahrhunderts, by H. Schüling, Hildesheim, 1967.
A Bio-Bibliography of Andreas Vesalius, by H. W. Cushing, New York, 1943.
Biographical and Bibliographical Dictionary of Italian Humanists and of the World of Classical Scholarship in Italy, 1300–1800, ed. M. E. Cosenza, Florence, 1962–7.
A Checklist of Melanchthon Imprints Through 1560, ed. R. A. Keen, Sixteenth Century Bibliography 27, St Louis, 1988.
'A Chronological Census of Renaissance Editions and Translations of Galen', by R. J. Durling, *Journal of the Warburg and Courtauld Institutes* 24 (1961): 230–305.
Les Collèges français 16e–18e siècles, ed. M.-M. Compère and D. Julia, 2 vols., Paris, 1984–, in progress.
Computer-Konkordanz zum Novum Testamentum Graece, Institut für Neutestamentliche Textforschung und vom Rechenzentrum der Universität Münster, Berlin, 1980.
General Bibliography of Astronomy to the Year 1880, by J. C. Houzeau and A. Lancaster, rev. edn by D. W. Dewhirst, 3 vols., London, 1964.
Geschichte und Bibliographie der astronomischen Literatur in Deutschland zur Zeit der Renaissance, ed. E. Zinner, Stuttgart, 1964.

The Greek Myths, by R. Graves, 2 vols., London, 1955.

Iter Italicum: A Finding List of Uncatalogued or Incompletely Catalogued Humanistic Manuscripts of the Renaissance in Italian and other Libraries, ed. P. O. Kristeller, 6 vols., London, 1963–92.

Latin Aristotle Commentaries II. Renaissance Authors, ed. C. H. Lohr, Florence, 1988 (*Lohr* in notes).

Lexikon zu den philosophischen Schriften Cicero's, ed. H. Merguet, 3 vols., Jena, 1887–94.

Lexikon zu den Reden des Cicero, ed. H. Merguet, 4 vols., Jena, 1887–94.

Lexicon scholasticum philosophico-theologicum in quo termini, definitiones, distinctiones et effata a J Duns Scoto exponuntur, declarantur, ed. M. Fernández García, repr. edn, Hildesheim, 1974.

Die Melanchthonforschung im Wandel der Jahrhunderte, ed. W. Hammer, 3 vols., Heidelberg, 1967–81.

The Mennonite Encyclopedia, 4 vols., Scottdale, Pa., 1955–9.

New Catholic Encyclopedia, The Catholic University of America, Washington DC, 1967–79.

The New Testament Octapla: Eight English Versions of the New Testament in the Tyndale-King James Tradition, ed. L. A. Weigle, Edinburgh, 1962.

Verzeichnis der im Deutschen Sprachbereich erschienenen Drucke des XVI. Jahrhunderts, 19 vols., Stuttgart 1983–, in progress.

Die Widmungsvorrede im Buch des 16. Jahrhunderts, by K. Schottenloher, Münster, 1953.

PRIMARY SOURCES

A. MANUSCRIPTS

Melanchthon, Philip

His copy of the ’ΑΡΙΣΤΟΤΕΛΟΥΣ ῞ΑΠΑΝΤΑ, ed. Desiderius Erasmus (Basle: J. Bebel, 1531), now in the British Library, c.45.i.14.

His copy of the *Iliad* (Venice: Aldus Manutius, 1504), now in Cambridge University Library, Adv.d.13.4.

His copy of the *Odyssey* (Venice: Aldus Manutius, 1517), now in Columbia University Library.

His copy of Andreas Vesalius’ *De fabrica corporis humani libri septem* (Basle: J. Oporinus, 1543), now in the National Library of Medicine, Bethesda, Md.

‘Physicae seu philosophiae naturalis compendium’, 1543, Bibliotheca Apostolica Vaticana, Pal. Lat. 1038.

‘Miscellaneous Letters’, Bibliotheca Apostolica Vaticana, Chigi JVIII-294.

Volmar, Johannes

‘Tabulae resolutae et quarta pars summa Astrologiae’, Thüringer Universitäts- und Landesbibliothek Jena, MS El. F. 77.

‘Altera pars Astrologiae’, Thüringer Universitäts- und Landesbibliothek Jena, MS El. Phil. 9. 3.

B. PRINTED SOURCES

Album Academiae Vitebergensis, ed. C. E. Foerstemann, 3 vols., Leipzig, 1841–1905.

Alliaco, Petrus, *Concordantia astronomiae cum theologia*, Augsburg: E. Ratdolt, 1490.

Amerbach, Vitus, *Liber de meteoris, cum interpretatione Viti Amerbachii*, Strasburg: C. Mylius, 1539.

Quatuor libri de anima, Strasburg: C. Mylius, 1542.

Aratus, 'Phaenomena', in *Callimachus: Hymns and Epigrams, Aratus*, trans. G. R. Mair, The Loeb Classical Library, London, 1955.

Aristotle, *The 'Art' of Rhetoric*, trans. J. H. Freese, The Loeb Classical Library, London, 1962.

The Metaphysics, trans. H. Tredennick, 2 vols., The Loeb Classical Library, London, 1933–5.

Meteorologica, trans. H. D. P. Lee, The Loeb Classical Library, London, 1952.

The Nicomachean Ethics, trans. H. Rackham, The Loeb Classical Library, London, 1926.

The Physics, trans. P. H. Wicksteed and F. M. Cornford, 2 vols., The Loeb Classical Library, London, 1929–34.

On the Soul, Parva Naturalia, On Breath, trans. W. S. Hett, rev. edn, The Loeb Classical Library, London, 1957.

Augustine, St, *The Trinity*, trans. S. McKenna, Washington 1963.

Basil, St, *Opera*, ed. D. Erasmus, Basle: ex off. Frobeniana, 1532.

(1857). *Opera omnia*, 4 vols., Patrologiae cursus completus, series graeca vols. 29–32, Paris.

(1950). *Saint Basil: Ascetical Works*, trans. M. M. Wagner, Washington.

Bell, John Gray (1862). *Catalogue of a Singularly curious collection of Early printed Books, with Autograph Annotations by the Great Reformers Luther and Melanchthon, carefully selected from the important and interesting library of the late S. Leigh Sotheby*, Manchester.

Briefwechsel der berühmtesten Gelehrten des Zeitalters der Reformation mit Herzog Albrecht von Preussen, ed. J. Voigt, Königsberg, 1841.

Calepinus, Ambrosius, *Dictionarium*, Reggio: D. Berthochus, 1502.

Cicero, *Brutus, Orator*, trans. G. L. Hendrickson and H. M. Hubbell, The Loeb Classical Library, London, 1939.

De natura deorum, Academica, trans. H. Rackham, The Loeb Classical Library, London, 1933.

De oratore, trans. E. W. Sutton and H. Rackham, 2 vols., The Loeb Classical Library, London, 1942, 1960.

De senectute, De amicitia, De divinatione, trans. A. W. Falconer, The Loeb Classical Library, London, 1923.

Tusculan Disputations, trans. J. E. King, The Loeb Classical Library, 1989.

Cordus, Valerius, *Annotationes in Pedacij Dioscordis ... de medica materia libros v*, Strasburg: J. Rihelius, 1561.

Daneau, Lambert, *The Wonderful Woorkmanship of the World*, London: [J. Kingston] for A. Maunsell, 1578, trans. Thomas Twyne.

Eber, Paul, *Oratio de doctrina pysica [sic] recitata a Paulo Ebero die quartodecimo augusti anno 1550*, Wittenberg: V. Creuzer, 1550.

'Ratio studendi generalis scholasticis olim praescripta', in *Institutiones literatae, sive de discendi ratione tomus tertius*, Torun: A. Contenius, 1588.

Eck, Johannes, *Articulos 404 partim ad disputationes Lipsicam, Baden, et Bernen attinentes, partim vero ex scriptis pacem ecclesiae perturbantium extractos, coram divo Caesare Carolo V*..., Ingolstadt, [G. & P. Apianus], 1530.

Erasmus, Desiderius (1956–68). *Opus epistolarum Des. Erasmi Roterodami*, ed. H. M. Allen and H. W. Garrod, 12 vols., Oxford.

(1974–). *Collected Works of Erasmus*, vol. 1–, Toronto, in progress.

Galen, Claudius (1821–33). *Claudii Galeni opera omnia*, ed. C. G. Kühn, 20 vols., Leipzig.

(1968). *On the Usefulness of the Parts of the Body*, trans. M. T. May, 2 vols., Ithaca, NY.

Gregory of Nyssa (1967). *Saint Gregory of Nyssa: Ascetical Works*, trans. V. W. Callahan, Washington.

Hawenreuther, Johann Ludwig, *Compendium librorum physicorum Aristotelis*, Cambridge: J. Legatt, 1594.

Hervet, Gentian, *Commentarius Ioannis Grammatici Philoponi Alexandrei in Aristotelis Stagiritae libros tres de anima*, Lyon: J. Guinta, 1558.

Hesiod, *The Homeric Hymns and Homerica*, trans. H. G. Evelyn-White, The Loeb Classical Library, new edn, London, 1936.

Hippocrates, *Hippocrates vol. I. Ancient Medicine, Airs Waters Places, Epidemics I and III, The Oath, Precepts, Nutriments*, trans. W. H. S. Jones, The Loeb Classical Library, London, 1923.

Hoffer, Johannes, *Icones catecheseos, et virtutum ac vitiorum illustratae numeris*, Wittenberg: J. Crato, 1558.

Homer, *The Iliad*, trans. A. T. Murray, 2 vols., The Loeb Classical Library, London, 1924–5.

The Odyssey, trans. A. T. Murray, 2 vols., The Loeb Classical Library, London, 1919.

Honorius of Autun (1854). *Honorii Augustodunensis opera omnia*, Patrologiae cursus completus 172, ed. J.-P. Migne, Paris.

Horace, *Satires, Epistles, Ars poetica*, trans. H. R. Fairclough, rev. edn, The Loeb Classical Library, London, 1929.

Hundt, Magnus, *Anthropologium de hominis dignitate natura et proprietatibus de elementis partibus et membris humani corporis de iuvamentis nocumentis accidentibus vitijs remedijs. De spiritu humano eiusque natura partibus et operibus. De anima humana et ipsius appendicijs*, Leipzig: W. Stöckel, 1501.

Kloss, G. (1841). 'Über Melanchthons angebliche Handschriften, welche in dem Catalogue of the library of Dr. Kloss verzeichnen sind', *Serapeum* 2: 369–77.

Köstlin, J. (1888). *Die Baccalaurei und Magistri der Wittenberger philosophischen Fakultät 1518–1537 und die ordentlichen Disputationen 1536–1537 . . .*, Halle.

(1890). *Die Baccalaurei und Magistri der Wittenberger philosophischen Fakultät 1538 bis 1546 und die öffentlichen Disputationen derselben Jahre . . .*, Halle.

(1891). *Die Baccalaurei und Magistri der Wittenberger philosophischen Fakultät 1548–1560 und die öffentlichen Disputationem derselben Jahre . . .*, Halle.

Lascovius, Petrus Monedulatus, *De homine magno illo in rerum natura miraculo et partibus eius essentialibus libri II*, Wittenberg: J. Crato, 1585.

Linguae Latinae Thesaurus, Paris: R. Stephanus, 1531.

Lucian, *Lucian, vol. I. Phalaris, Hippias, Dionysius, Heracles, Amber etc.*, trans. A. M. Harmon, The Loeb Classical Library, London, 1913.

Luther, Martin, *Dr Martin Luthers Werke, kritische Gesamtausgabe*, 63 vols., Weimar, 1883–1987 (*WA* in notes).

Dr. Martin Luthers Briefwechsel, 17 vols., Weimar, 1930–83 (*WBr* in notes).

Luther's Works (English translation), ed. J. Pelikan and H. T. Lehmann, St Louis, 1955–76 (*LW* in notes).

Marlowe, Christopher, *Doctor Faustus*, ed. J. D. Jump, London, 1965.

Die Matrikeln der Universität Tübingen, ed. H. Hermelink, 3 vols., Stuttgart, 1906–54.

Melanchthon, Philip, *Corpus reformatorum Philippi Melanthonis opera quae supersunt omnia*, ed. C. B. Bretschneider and H. E. Bindseil, 28 vols., Halle, 1834–52, Brunswick, 1853–60 (*CR* in notes).

Melanchthons Briefwechsel: kritische und kommentierte Gesamtausgabe, im Auftrag der Heidelberger Akademie der Wissenschaften, ed. H. Scheible, Stuttgart 1977–, in progress (*MBW* in notes).

Melanchthons Werke in Auswahl, ed. R. Stupperich, 5 vols., Gütersloh, 1963 (*StA* in notes).

Commentarius de anima, Wittenberg: P. Seitz, 1540.

Commentarius de anima, Witteberg: J. Lufft, 1548.

De dialectica libri quatuor, Wittenberg: J. Klug, 1531.

Initia doctrinae physicae, Wittenberg: J. Lufft, 1549.

Liber selectarum declamationum, ed. N. Gerbelius, Strasburg: C. Mylius, 1541.

Mathematicarum disciplinarum, tum etiam astrologiae encomium, Lyon: S. Gryphius, 1540.

Selectarum declamationum Philippi Melanthonis, quas conscripsit et partim ipse in schola Vitebergensi recitavit, partim alijs recitandas exhibuit, 3 vols., Strasburg [S. Emmel *et al.*], 1558–9.

(1910–26). *Supplementa Melanchthoniana: Werke Philipp Melanchthonis die im Corpus Reformatorum vermisst werden*, ed. O. Clemen, 6 vols., Leipzig.

(1962). *Selected Writings*, ed. C. L. Hill, E. Flack and L. J. Satre, Augsburg.

(1965). *Melanchthon on Christian Doctrine: Loci communes of 1555*, trans. C. L. Manschreck, New York.

(1969). *Loci communes* (1521), trans. L. J. Satre and revised by W. Pauck, in *Melanchthon and Bucer*, London.
(1988). *A Melanchthon Reader*, trans. R. A. Keen, New York.
(1989). *Paul's Letter to the Colossians*, trans. D. C. Parker, Sheffield.
Menius, Eusebius, *Oratio de vita Jacobi Milichii medicae artis doctoris ac professoris in hac academia fidelissimi viri optimi et integerrimi* ..., Wittenberg: G. Rhaw, 1562.
Mylius, Johann Christoph, *Memorabilia bibliothecae academicae Jenensis*, Jena: J. C. Croekerus, 1746.
Mylius, Martinus, *Chronologia scriptorum Philippi Melanchthonis*, Görlitz: A. Fritschius, 1582.
Nizolius, Marius, *Observationes, omnia M. T. Ciceronis verba, ... complectentes*, Basle: J. Hervagius, 1548.
Ortus vocabulorum alphabeticus, London: W. de Worde, 1528.
Ovid, *Metamorphoses*, trans. F. J. Miller, rev. G. P. Goold, 2 vols., rev. edn, The Loeb Classical Library, London, 1977, 1984.
Peucer, Caspar, *Elementa doctrinae de circulis coelestibus, et primo motu, recognita et correcta*, Wittenberg: J. Lufft, 1553.
Plato, *Charmides, Alcibiades, Hipparchus, The Lovers, Theagnes, Minos, Epinomis*, trans. W. R. M. Lamb, The Loeb Classical Library, London, 1927.
Euthyphro, Apology, Crito, Phaedo, Phaedrus, trans. H. N. Fowler, The Loeb Classical Library, London, 1914.
Republic, trans. P. Shorey, 2 vols., The Loeb Classical Library, London, 1930.
Timaeus, Critias, Cleitophon, Menexemus, Epistulae, trans. R. G. Bury, The Loeb Classical Library, London, 1929.
Pliny, the Elder, *Natural History*, trans. H. Rackham, W. H. S. Jones, D. E. Eichholz, 10 vols., The Loeb Classical Library, London, 1938–62.
Polich, von Mellerstadt, Martin, *Exquisita Cursus Physici collectanea*, Leipzig: M. Lother, 1514.
Ptolemy, *Tetrabiblos*, ed. and trans. F. E. Robbins, The Loeb Classical Library, London, 1980.
Rhenanus, Beatus, *Briefwechsel des Beatus Rhenanus*, ed. A. Horawitz and K. Hartfelder, Leipzig, 1886.
Schonborn, Bartholomaeus, *Oratio de studiis astronomicis recitata a decano collegij philosophici, magistro Bartholomaeo Schonborn* ..., Wittenberg: J. Crato, 1564.
Scripta quaedam in Academia Witenbergensi a rectoribus, decanis et alijs eruditis quibusdam viris publice proposita, Wittenberg: J. Klug, 1545.
Scripta quaedam in Academia Witenbergensi publice proposita, digesta in duos libros, vol. 1, Wittenberg, 1549.
Scriptorum publice propositorum a professoribus in Academia Witebergensi ab anno 1540 usque ad annum 1553, tomus primus, Wittenberg: G. Rhaw, 1560.
Scriptorum publice propositorum a gubernatoribus studiorum in Academia Witebergensi, tomus quartus, Wittenberg: G. Rhaw, 1561.

Seidel, Bruno, *Commentarius didascalius, valde eruditus et perspicuus de corpore animato, ac potissimum quidem de corpore et anima hominis, accomodatus ad faciliorem intelligentiam librorum Aristotelis et interpretum ejus, ut et P Melanchthonis De anima, item Galeni, Vesalii, et aliorum qui de fabrica scripserunt, in usum physicae et anatomicae studiosorum recognitus a Rod. Goclenio, et nunc primum in lucem editus*, Hanau: G. Antonius, 1594.

Seneca, *Natural Questions*, trans. T. H. Corcoran, The Loeb Classical Library, 2 vols., London, 1971–2.

Sotheby, Samuel Leigh (1835). *Catalogue of the Library of Dr. Kloss, of Franckfort a. M. Professor; including many original and unpublished Manuscripts and Printed Books with Ms. Annotations, by Philip Melanchthon*, London.

(1839). *Observations upon the Handwriting of Philip Melanchthon. Illustrated with facsimiles from his marginal annotations, his commonplace-book, and his epistolary correspondence*, London.

(1840). *Unpublished Documents, Marginal Notes, and Memoranda in the Autograph of Philip Melanchthon and of Martin Luther*, London.

Les statuts et privilèges des universités françaises depuis leur fondation jusqu'en 1789, tome 4, 1: Gymnase, Académie, Université de Strasbourg, ed. M. Fournier and C. Engel, Paris, 1894.

Stöffler, Joannes, *In Procli Diadochi sphaeram mundi commentarius*, Tübingen: U. Morhard, 1534.

Strigelius, Victorinus, 'De ratio discendi', in *Institutiones literatae, sive de discendi ratione, tomus tertius*, Torun: A. Contenius, 1588.

Tartaretus, Petrus, *Commentarii Petri Tatareti in libros philosophie naturalis et metaphysice Aristotelis*, Paris: F. Regnault, 1514.

Taurellus, Nicolaus, *Philosophia triumphans, hoc est, metaphysica philosophandi methodus, qua divinitus inditis menti notitijs, humanae rationes eo deducuntur, ut firmissimis inde constructis demonstrationibus, aperte rei veritas sepulta fuit authoritate, philosophia victrix erumpat*, Basle, S. Henricpetri, 1573.

Thesaurus linguae Latinae, by R. Stephanus, Lyon: J. Tinghuius, 1573.

Tortellius, Johannis, *De orthographia*, Rome: S. Nicolaus Lucensis, 1471.

Trutfetter, Judocus, *Quam Judocus Eysennaienn philosophus et theologus tocius philosophie naturalis summam nuper elucubravit* . . ., Erfurt: M. Maler, 1517.

Urkunden zur Geschichte der Universität Tübingen aus den Jahren 1476–1550, ed. R. von Roth, Tübingen, 1877.

Urkundenbuch der Universität Wittenberg, Teil I (1502–1611), ed. W. Friedensburg, Magdeburg, 1926 (*Urkundenbuch* in notes).

Valla, Georgius, *Commentationes. In Ptolemei quadripartitum inque Ciceronis partitiones et Tusculanas quaestiones ac Plinii naturalis historie librum secundum*, Venice: M. Firmanus, 1502.

Velcurio, Johannes Bernhardi, *Commentarii in universam physicam Aristotelis libri quatuor*, Tübingen: U. Morhard, 1540.

Epitomae physicae libri quatuor, Erfurt: M. Saxo, 1538.

In philosophiae naturalis partem omnium praestantissimam, hoc est, Aristotelis de anima libros, epitome . . ., Basle: J. Oporinus, 1537.

Virgil, *Aeneid VII–XII, the Minor Poems*, trans. H. R. Fairclough, The Loeb Classical Library, London, 1918.

Eclogues, Georgics, Aeneid I–VI, trans. H. R. Fairclough, The Loeb Classical Library, London, rev. edn 1974.

Vives, Johannes Ludovicus (1782). *Opera Omnia*, Valencia, vol. III.

Zanchi, Hieronymus, *De naturali auscultatione*, Strasburg: W. Rihelius, 1554.

Zwingli, Huldrich, *Huldrich Zwinglis Sämtliche Werke*, ed. E. Egli *et al.*, 6–3, Corpus Reformatorum, vol. 93–3, Zurich, 1983.

SECONDARY WORKS

(Collective volumes are cited under their titles and listed alphabetically according to the first word, excluding articles and first names.)

Ahrbeck, H. (1961). 'Melanchthon als Praeceptor Germaniae', in *Philipp Melanchthon*, 133–48.

Allen, M. J. B. (1984). *The Platonism of Marsilio Ficino: A Study of His 'Phaedrus' Commentary, Its Sources and Genesis*, Berkeley, Los Angeles and London.

Althaus, P. (1970). *The Theology of Martin Luther*, trans. R. C. Schultz, Philadelphia.

Antiqui und Moderni: Traditionsbewusstsein und Fortschrittsbewusstsein im späten Mittelalter, ed. A. Zimmermann, Berlin, 1974.

Aristotelismus und Renaissance: In memoriam Charles B. Schmitt, ed. E. Keßler *et al.*, Wolfenbütteler Forschungen 40, Wiesbaden, 1988.

Arntz, J. (1965). 'Natural Law and Its History', *Concilium* 1, 5: 23–32.

Ashworth, W. (1991). 'The Habsburg Circle', in *Patronage and Institutions*, 137–67.

'Astrologi Hallucinati': Stars and the End of the World in Luther's Time, ed. P. Zambelli, Berlin, 1986.

Astrology, Science and Society: Historical Essays, ed. P. Curry, Bury St Edmunds, 1987.

Augustijn, C. (1991). *Erasmus, His Life, Works and Influence*, trans. J. C. Grayson, Toronto and London.

Backus, I. (1988). 'The Teaching of Logic in Two Protestant Academies at the End of the Sixteenth Century. The Reception of Zabarella at Strasbourg and Geneva', *Archiv für Reformationsgeschichte* 80: 240–51.

Bakker, W. de (1982). 'Bernhard Rothman: The Dialectics of Radicalization in Münster', in *Profiles of Radical Reformers: Biographical Sketches from Thomas Müntzer to Paracelsus*, ed. H. J. Goertz and W. Klaassen, Kitchener, Ont. Originally published in German, in Munich, 1978, 191–202.

Baldry, H. C. (1952). 'Who Invented the Golden Age?', *Classical Quarterly*, n.s. 2: 83–92.

Barnes, R. B. (1988). *Prophecy and Gnosis: Apocalypticism in the Wake of the Lutheran Reformation*, Stanford.

Baron, F. (1978a). 'Camerarius and the Historical Doctor Faust', in *Joachim Camerarius (1500–1574)*, 200–22.

(1978b). *Doctor Faustus: From History to Legend*, Munich.

Bauch, G. (1897). 'Wittenberg und die Scholastik', *Neues Archiv für Sächsische Geschichte und Altertumskunde* 18: 285–339.

Bauer, C. (1951). 'Melanchthons Naturrechtslehre', *Archiv für Reformationsgeschichte* 42: 64–100.

Baumeister, K. H. (1968). *Georg Joachim Rhetikus 1514–1574*, 3 vols., Wiesbaden.

Baxandall, M. (1985). *Patterns of Intention: On the Historical Explanation of Pictures*, New Haven.

Baylor, M. G. (1977). *Action and Person: Conscience in Late Scholasticism and the Young Luther*, Studies in Medieval and Reformation Thought 20, Leiden.

Beiträge zu Problemen deutscher Universitätsgründungen der frühen Neuzeit, ed. N. Hammerstein and P. Baumgart, Wolfenbütteler Forschungen 4, Nendeln, 1978.

Bellucci, D. (1988). 'Mélanchthon et la défense de l'astrologie', *Bibliothèque d'Humanisme et Renaissance* 50: 587–622.

Bender, H. S. (1980). 'The Zwickau Prophets, Thomas Müntzer, and the Anabaptists', in *The Anabaptists and Thomas Müntzer*, ed. and trans. J. M. Stayer and W. O. Packull, Dubuque and Toronto, 145–51.

Benrath, G. A. (1970). 'Die Deutsche Universität der Reformationszeit', in *Universität und Gelehrtenstand 1400–1800*, ed. H. Rüssler and G. Franz, Limburg, 63–83.

Bettoni, E. (1961). *Duns Scotus: The Basic Principles of His Philosophy*, trans. B. Bonansea, Washington.

Biagioli, M. (1990). 'Galileo the Emblem Maker', *Isis* 81: 230–58.

Bianca, C. (1980). 'Per la storia del termine atheus nel Cinquecento: fonti e traduzioni greco-latine', *Studi Filosofici* 3: 71–104.

Bizer, E. (1958). *Fides ex auditu: Eine Untersuchung über die Entdeckung der Gerechtigkeit Gottes durch Martin Luther*, Neukirchen.

(1966). *Theologie der Verheissung: Studien zur theologischen Entwicklung des jungen Melanchthon (1519–1524)*, Neukirchen.

Blume, F. (1975). *Protestant Church Music: A History*, London.

Boisset, J. (1962). *Erasme et Luther: libre ou serf arbitre*, Paris.

Borgeaud, C. (1900). *L'Académie de Calvin 1559–1798*, Geneva.

Bornkamm, H. (1961). 'Melanchthons Menschenbild', in *Philipp Melanchthon*, 76–90.

Bosshard, S. N. (1978). *Zwingli–Erasmus–Cajetan: Die Eucharistie als zeichen der Einheit*, Veröffentlichungen des Instituts für Europäische Geschichte Mainz 89, Wiesbaden.

Bouwsma, W. J. (1988). *John Calvin: A Sixteenth-Century Portrait*, New York.

Boyle, M. O'Rouke (1977). *Erasmus on Language and Method in Theology*, Toronto.

(1981). *Christening Pagan Mysteries*, Toronto.

(1983). *Rhetoric and Reform: Erasmus' Civil Dispute with Luther*, Cambridge, Mass.

Brandis, C. G. (1917). 'Luther und Melanchthon als Benutzer der Wittenberger Bibliothek', *Theologische Studien und Kritiken* 90: 206–21.

Brann, N. L. (1988). 'Humanism in Germany', in *Renaissance Humanism*, II, 123–55.

Brecht, M. (1966). *Die frühe Theologie des Johannes Brenz*, Beiträge zur historischen Theologie 36, Tübingen.

(1977). '"Iustitia Christi": Die Entdeckung Martin Luthers', *Zeitschrift für Theologie und Kirche* 74: 179–223.

(1981–7). *Martin Luther*, 3 vols., Stuttgart.

Breen, Q. (1947). 'The Terms "loci communes" and "loci" in Melanchthon', *Church History* 16: 197–209.

(1952a). 'Giovanni Pico della Mirandola on the Conflict of Philosophy and Rhetoric', *Journal of the History of Ideas* 13: 384–412.

(1952b). 'The Subordination of Philosophy to Rhetoric in Melanchthon: A Study of his Reply to G. Pico della Mirandola', *Archiv für Reformationsgeschichte* 43: 13–28.

Brooke, J. H. (1991). *Science and Religion: Some Historical Perspectives*, Cambridge.

Buchwald, G. (1884). 'Eine ungedruckte Trostrede Luthers am Krankenbett [Velcurios]', *Zeitschrift für kirchliche Wissenschaft und kirchliches Leben* 5: 428–32.

(1896). 'Archivalische Mittheilungen über Bücherbezüge der kurfürstlichen Bibliothek und Georg Spalatin's in Wittenberg', *Archiv für Geschichte des deutschen Buchhandels* 18: 7–15.

Buckley, M. J. (1987). *At the Origins of Modern Atheism*, New Haven.

Burchill, C. J. (1984). 'Girolamo Zanchi: Portrait of a Reformed Theologian and His Work', *Sixteenth Century Journal* 15–2: 185–207.

(1988). 'Aristotle and the Trinity: The Case of Johann Hasler in Strasbourg 1574–1575', *Archiv für Reformationsgeschichte* 79: 282–309.

Burgess, T. C. (1902). 'Epideictic Literature', *Studies in Classical Philology* 3: 89–261.

Büttner, M. (1975). *Regiert Gott die Welt?*, Stuttgart.

(1979). 'The Significance of the Reformation for the Reorientation of Geography in Lutheran Germany', *History of Science* 17: 151–69.

Bylebyl, J. J. (1990). 'The Medical Meaning of *Physica*', *Osiris* 2nd ser. 6: 16–41.

Callahan, J. F. (1958). 'Greek Philosophy and the Cappadocian Cosmology', *Dumbarton Oaks Papers* 12: 29–57.

The Cambridge History of Later Medieval Philosophy: From the Rediscovery of Aristotle to the Disintegration of Scholasticism: 1100–1600, ed. N. Kretzmann, A. Kenny and J. Pinborg, Cambridge, 1982.

The Cambridge History of Renaissance Philosophy, ed. C. B. Schmitt *et al.*, Cambridge, 1988.

Joachim Camerarius (1500–1574), Humanistische Bibliothek 24, ed. F. Baron, Munich, 1978.

Campana, A. (1946). 'The Origin of the Word "Humanist"', *Journal of the Warburg and Courtauld Institutes* 9: 60–73.

Caroti, S. (1982). 'Comete, portenti, causalità naturale e escatologia in Filippo Melantone', in *Scienze, credenze occulte, livelli di cultura. Convegno Internazionale di Studi (Firenze, 26–30 giugno 1980)*, ed. Istituto Nazionale di Studi sul Rinascimento, Florence, 393–426.

(1986). 'Melanchthon's Astrology', in *'Astrologi Hallucinati'*, 109–21.

Carpenter, N. C. (1958). *Music in the Medieval and Renaissance Universities*, New York.

Cavarnos, J. P. (1976). 'The Relation of Body and Soul in the Thought of Gregory of Nyssa', in *Gregor von Nyssa und die Philosophie. Zweites Internationales Kolloquium über Gregor von Nyssa*, ed. H. Dörrie *et al.*, Leiden, 61–78.

Chartier, R. (1987). *The Cultural Uses of Print in Early Modern France*, trans. L. G. Cochrane, Princeton.

Chenu, M.-D. (1964). *Toward Understanding Saint Thomas*, trans. A. M. Landry and D. Hughes, Chicago.

Chrisman, M. U. (1967). *Strasbourg and the Reform: A Study in the Process of Change*, New Haven.

Christensen, C. C. (1979). *Art and the Reformation in Germany*, Athens, Ohio.

Clark, W. (1986). 'From the Medieval Universitas Scholarium to the German Research University: A Sociogenesis of the Germanic Academic', unpublished Ph.D. dissertation, University of California, Los Angeles. University Microfilms International, Ann Arbor.

Clasen, C.-P. (1972). *Anabaptism: A Social History 1525–1618 Switzerland, Austria, Moravia, South and Central Germany*, Ithaca, NY.

Clough, C. H. (1976). 'Samuel Leigh Sotheby und seine Bibliothek', *Librarium* 19: 108–18.

Clulee, N. H. (1988). *John Dee's Natural Philosophy: Between Science and Religion*, London and New York.

Coggins, J. (1986). 'Toward a Definition of 16th Century Anabaptism: 20th Century Historiography of the Radical Reformation', *Journal of Mennonite Studies* 4: 183–207.

Cohn, N. (1970). *The Pursuit of the Millenium: Revolutionary Millenarians and Mystical Anarchists of the Middle Ages*, London.

Comito, T. (1971). 'Renaissance Gardens and the Discovery of Paradise', *Journal of the History of Ideas*, 32, 483–506.

Conermann, K. (1973). 'Doctor Faustus: Universities, the Sciences and Magic in the Age of the Reformation', in *The University World: A Synoptic View of Higher Education in the Middle Ages and Renaissance*, Medieval and Renaissance Studies Committee 2, ed. D. Radcliff-Umstead, Pittsburgh, 104–39.

Copenhaver, B. P. (1988). 'Translation, Terminology and Style in Philosophical Discourse', in *The Cambridge History of Renaissance Philosophy*, 77–110.

Cornford, F. M. (1937). *Plato's Cosmology*, London.

Courtenay, W. J. (1984). 'The Role of English Thought in the Transformation of University Education in the Late Middle Ages', in *Rebirth, Reform and Resilience: Universities in Transition 1300–1700*, ed. J. M. Kittelson and P. J. Transue, Ohio, 103–62.

(1987). 'Antiqui and Moderni in late Medieval Thought', *Journal of the History of Ideas* 43: 3–10.

Cranz, F. E. (1976). 'The Renaissance Reading of the *De Anima*', in *Platon et Aristote à la Renaissance: XVIe Colloque international de Tours*, Paris, 359–76.

Crowe, M. B. (1977). *The Changing Profile of the Natural Law*, The Hague.

The Cultural Context of Medieval Learning: Proceedings of the First International Colloquium of Philosophy, Science and Theology in the Middle Ages – September 1973, ed. J. E. Murdoch and E. D. Sylla, Boston Studies in the Philosophy of Science 26, Dordrecht and Boston, 1975.

Cunningham, A. R. (1988). 'Getting the Game Right: Some Plain Words on the Identity and Invention of Science', *Studies in History and Philosophy of Science* 19: 365–89.

(1991). 'How the *Principia* Got its Name; or Taking Natural Philosophy Seriously', *History of Science* 29: 377–92.

The Anatomical Renaissance, forthcoming.

Curley, M. J. (1980). 'Physiologus, φυσιολογία and the Rise of Christian Nature Symbolism', *Viator* 11: 1–10.

Curry, P. (1989). *Prophecy and Power: Astrology in Early Modern England*, Oxford.

Dannenfeldt, K. H. (1972). 'Wittenberg Botanists during the Sixteenth Century', in *The Social History of the Reformation*, ed. L. P. Buck and J. W. Zophy, Columbus, 223–48.

Dear, P. (1984). 'Marin Mersenne and the Probabilistic Roots of "Mitigated Scepticism"', *Journal of History of Philosophy* 22: 173–205.

(1988). *Mersenne and the Learning of the Schools*, Ithaca and London.

Deason, G. B. (1985). 'The Protestant Reformation and the Rise of Modern Science', *Scottish Journal of Theology* 38: 221–40.

Dijksterhuis, E. J. (1961). *The Mechanization of the World Picture*, trans. C. Dikshoorn, Oxford.

Dillenberger, J. (1961). *Protestant Thought and Natural Science: A Historical Interpretation*, London.

Donnelly, J. P. (1976). 'Italian Influence on the Development of Calvinist Scholasticism', *The Sixteenth Century Journal* 7.1: 81–101.

Dragona-Monachou, M. (1976). *The Stoic Arguments for the Existence and Providence of the Gods*, Athens.

Draper, J. W. (1875). *History of the Conflict between Religion and Science*, second edn, London.

Durling, R. J. (1989). 'Leonhard Fuchs and his Commentaries on Galen', *Medizinhistorisches Journal* 24: 42–7.

Eastwood, B. S. (1986). 'Plinian Astronomy in the Middle Ages and Renaissance', in *Science in the Early Roman Empire*, 197–251.

Ebeling, G. (1970). *Luther: An Introduction to his Thought*, trans. R. A. Wilson, London.

Eckermann, W. (1978). 'Die Aristoteleskritik Luthers: ihre Bedeutung für seine Theologie', *Catholica* 32: 114–30.

Edwards, M. U. Jr (1975). *Luther and the False Brethren*, Stanford.

Ehresmann, D. L. (1966/7). 'The Brazen Serpent, a Reformation Motif in the Works of Lucas Cranach the Elder and his Workshop', *Marsyas* 13: 32–47.

Ehrle, F. K. (1925). *Der Sentenzenkommentar Peters von Candia des Pisaner papstes Alexanders V: Ein Beitrag zur Scheidung der Schulen in der Scholastik des vierzehnten Jahrhunderts und zur Geschichte des Wegestreites*, Münster.

Eire, C. M. N. (1986). *War Against the Idols: The Reformation of Worship from Erasmus to Calvin*, Cambridge.

Engelland, H. (1960). 'Melanchthons Bedeutung für Schule und Universität', *Mitteilungen der Luthergesellschaft* 31: 24–41.

(1961). 'Der Ansatz der Theologie Melanchthons', in *Philipp Melanchthon*, 56–75.

(1965). Introduction to *Melanchthon on Christian Doctrine: Loci communes of 1555*, trans. C. L. Manschreck, New York, xxv–xlii.

Etherington, C. L. (1962). *Protestant Worship Music: Its History and Practice*, New York.

Evans, R. J. W. (1973). *Rudolph II and his World: A Study in Intellectual History 1576–1612*, Oxford.

Farge, J. K. (1985). *Orthodox and Reform in Early Reformation France: The Faculty of Paris 1500–1543*, Leiden.

Fatio, O. (1976). *Méthode et théologie: Lambert Daneau et les débuts de la scholastique réformée*, Travaux d'humanisme et renaissance 147, Geneva.

(1981). 'Lambert Daneau', in *Shapers of Religious Traditions*, 105–19.

Febvre, L. (1982). *The Problem of Unbelief in the Sixteenth Century: The Religion of Rabelais*, trans. B. Gottlieb, Cambridge, Mass.

Feldhay, R. (1987). 'Knowledge and Salvation in Jesuit Culture', *Science in Context* 1: 195–213.

Ficino and Renaissance Neoplatonism, University of Toronto Italian Studies 1, ed. K. Eisenbichler and O. Z. Pugliese, Ottawa, 1986.

Marsilio Ficino e il ritorno di Platone, Studi e Testi 15, ed. G. C. Garfagnini, 2 vols., Florence, 1986.

Field, J. V. (1984). 'A Lutheran Astrologer: Johannes Kepler', *Archive for the History of Exact Sciences* 31: 189–272.

Fleischer, M. P. (1979). 'The Garden of Laurentius Scholz: A Cultural Landmark of Late-Sixteenth-Century Lutheranism', *Journal of Medieval and Renaissance Studies* 9: 29–48.

Fletcher, J. M. (1984). 'The Faculty of Arts', in *The History of the University of Oxford vol. I. The Early Oxford Schools*, ed. J. I. Catto, Oxford, 369–99.

Fraenkel, P. (1961a). *Testimonia Patrum: The Function of the Patristic Argument in the Theology of Philip Melanchthon*, Geneva.

(1961b). 'Ten Questions Concerning Melanchthon, the Fathers, and the Eucharist', in *Luther und Melanchthon*, 146–64.

Freedman, J. S. (1984). *Deutsche Schulphilosophie im Reformationszeitalter (1500–1600): Ein Handbuch für den Hochschulunterricht*, Münster.

(1985). 'Philosophy Instruction within the Institutional Framework of Central European Schools and Universities during the Reformation Era', *History of Universities* 5: 117–66.

(1988). *European Academic Life in the Late Sixteenth and Early Seventeenth Centuries: The Life, Significance, and Philosophy of Clemens Timpler 1563/4–1624*, Studien und Materialen zur Geschichte der Philosophie 27, 2 vols., Hildesheim, Zurich and New York.

(1993). 'The Diffusion of the Writings of Petrus Ramus in Central Europe, c. 1570 – c. 1630', *Renaissance Quarterly* 46–1: 98–152.

French, R. K. (1986). 'Pliny and Renaissance Medicine', in *Science in the Early Roman Empire*, 252–81.

(1989). 'The Arrival of the French Disease in Leipzig', in *Maladie et société (XIIe–XVIIIe siècles). Actes du Colloque de Bielefeld*, 133–141.

French, R. K. and A. R. Cunningham, *Before Science: The Friar's Medieval Natural Philosophy*, forthcoming.

Friedensburg, W. (1917). *Geschichte der Universität Wittenberg*, Halle.

(1924). 'Die Berufung des Johannes Rhagius Aesticampianus an die Universität Wittenberg 1517', *Archiv für Reformationsgeschichte* 21: 146–7.

Friedländer, M. J. and J. Rosenberg (1978). *The Paintings of Lucas Cranach*, rev. edn, New York.

Friedman, J. B. (1974). 'The Architect's Compass in Creation Miniatures of the Later Middle Ages', *Traditio* 30: 419–29.

Friesen, A. (1990). *Thomas Müntzer, a Destroyer of the Godless: The Making of a Sixteenth Century Religious Revolutionary*, Berkeley and Los Angeles.

Funkenstein, A. (1986). *Theology and the Scientific Imagination from the Middle Ages to the Seventeenth Century*, New Haven.

Gabriel, A. L. (1963). 'Metaphysics in the Curriculum of Studies of the Mediaeval Universities', in *Die Metaphysik im Mittelalter*, Miscellanea Mediaevalia 2, ed. P. Wilpert, Berlin, 92–102.

(1974). '"Via antiqua" and "via moderna" and the Migration of Paris Students and Masters to the German Universities in the Fifteenth Century', in *Antiqui und Moderni*, 439–83.

Garin, E. (1937). 'ἐνδελέχεια e ἐντελέχεια nelle discussioni umanistiche', *Atene et Roma* 5: 177–87.

(1983). *Astrology in the Renaissance: The Zodiac of Life*, trans. C. Jackson and J. Allen, rev. C. Robertson and E. Garin, London.

The German Peasant War of 1525 – New Viewpoints, ed. B. Scribner and G. Benecke, London, 1979.

Gerrish, B.A. (1962). *Grace and Reason: A Study in the Theology of Luther*, Oxford.

(1968). 'The Reformation and the Rise of Modern Science', in *The Impact of Church upon its Culture: Reappraisals of the History of Christianity*, ed. J. C. Brauer, Chicago, 231–66.

Gestrich, C. (1967). *Zwingli als Theologe: Glaube und Geist beim Züricher Reformator*, Studien zur Dogmengeschichte und systematischen Theologie 20, Zürich.

Giard, L. (1991). 'Remapping Knowledge, Reshaping Institutions', in *Science, Culture and Popular Belief in Renaissance Europe*, ed. S. Pumfrey, P. L. Rossi and M. Slawinski, Manchester, 19–45.

Gilbert, N. W. (1960). *Renaissance Concepts of Method*, New York.

(1974). 'Ockham, Wyclif, and the "via moderna"', in *Antiqui und Moderni*, 85–125.

Gilson, E. (1954). *History of Christian Philosophy in the Middle Ages*, London.

(1957). *The Christian Philosophy of St. Thomas Aquinas*, trans. L. K. Shook, London.

Ginzburg, C. (1976). 'High and Low: The Theme of Forbidden Knowledge in the Sixteenth and Seventeenth Centuries', *Past and Present* 73: 28–41.

God and Nature: Historical Essays on the Encounter between Christianity and Science, ed. D. C. Lindberg and R. L. Numbers, Berkeley, 1986.

Goodich, M. E. (1989). *From Birth to Old Age: The Human Life Cycle in Medieval Thought, 1250–1350*, Lanham, Md.

Grafton, A. and L. Jardine (1986). *From Humanism to the Humanities: Education and the Liberal Arts in Fifteenth- and Sixteenth-Century Europe*, London.

Grane, L. (1970). 'Die Anfänge von Luthers Auseinandersetzung mit dem Thomismus', *Theologische Literaturzeitung* 95: 241–9.

Grant, E. (1982). 'The Effect of the Condemnation of 1277', in *The Cambridge History of Later Medieval Philosophy*, 537–9.

Green, L. C. (1980). *How Melanchthon Helped Luther Discover the Gospel: The Doctrine of Justification in the Reformation*, Fallbrook, Ca.

Greenblatt, S. (1992). *Marvellous Possessions: The Wonder of the New World*, Oxford.

Gregg, R. C. (1975). *Consolation Philosophy: Greek and Christian Paideia in Basil and the Two Gregories*, Cambridge, Mass.

Gregor von Rimini: Werk und Wirkung bis zur Reformation, Spätmittelalter und Reformation 20, ed. H. A. Oberman, Berlin and New York, 1981.

Grossmann, M. (1971). *Wittenberger Drucke 1502 bis 1517: Ein bibliographischer Beitrag zur Geschichte des Humanismus in Deutschland*, Vienna.

(1975). *Humanism in Wittenberg 1485–1517*, Nieuwkoop.

Gründler, O. (1964). 'The Influence of Thomas Aquinas upon the Theology of Girolamo Zanchi (1516–90)', *Studies in Medieval Culture* 1: 102–17.

Gwynn, A. (1926). *Roman Education from Cicero to Quintilian*, Oxford.

Hägglund, B. (1983). 'Luthers Anthropologie', in *Leben und Werk Martin Luthers* I: 63–76; II: 747ff.

Hall, A. R. (1983). *The Revolution in Science 1500–1750*, London.

Hallowell, R. E. (1962). 'Ronsard and the Gallic Hercules Myth', *Studies in the Renaissance* 9: 242–55.

Hammer, W. (1951). 'Melanchthon, Inspirer of the Study of Astronomy: with a Translation of his Oration in Praise of Astronomy (De orione, 1553)', *Popular Astronomy* 59: 308–19.

Hannaway, O. (1975). *The Chemist and the Word*, Baltimore.

Harrison, R. L. Jr (1978). 'Melanchthon's Role in the Reformation of the University of Tübingen', *Church History* 47: 268–78.

Hartfelder, K. *Philipp Melanchthon als Praeceptor Germaniae*, Berlin, 1889 (*Hartfelder* in notes).

(1889). 'Der Aberglaube Philipp Melanchthons', *Historisches Taschenbuch* 6–8: 231–69.

(1892). *Melanthoniana Paedagogica: Eine Ergänzung zu den Werken Melanchthons im Corpus Reformatorum*, Leipzig.

Hassel, D. J. (1962). 'Conversion Theory and "Scientia" in the *De trinitate*', *Recherches Augustiniennes* 2: 383–401.

Hayum, A. (1989). *The Isenheim Altarpiece: God's Medicine and the Painter's Vision*, Princeton.

Heckscher, W. S. (1978). 'Melancholia (1541): An Essay in the Rhetoric of Description by Joachim Camerarius', in *Joachim Camerarius (1500–1574)*, 31–120.

Hellmann, G. (1921). 'Die Meteorologie in den deutschen Flugschriften und Flugblätten des XVI. Jahrhunderts, ein Beitrag zur Geschichte der Meteorologie', in *Abhandlungen der Preussischen Academie der Wissenschaften, Physikalisch-Mathematische Klasse*, Berlin, 1–96.

Hengst, K. (1981). *Jesuiten an Universitäten und Jesuitenuniversitäten: zur Geschichte der Universitäten in der Obendeutschen und Rheinischen Provinz der Gesellschaft Jesu im Zeitalter der konfessionellen Auseinandersetzung*, Quellen und Forschungen aus dem Gebiet der Geschichte, n.s. 2, Paderborn, Munich, Vienna and Zurich.

Herrlinger, A. (1879). *Die Theologie Melanchthons in ihrer geschichtlichen Entwicklung im Zusammenhange mit der Lehrgeschichte und Kulturbewegung der Reformation dargestellt*, Gotha.

Hildebrandt, F. (1946). *Melanchthon: Alien or Ally?*, Cambridge.

Hinrichs, C. (1962). *Luther und Müntzer: ihre Auseinandersetzung über Obrigkeit und Widerstandrecht*, Arbeit zur Kirchengeschichte 29, Berlin.

Hintzenstern, H. von (1981). *Lucas Cranach d. Ä.: Altarbilder aus der Reformationszeit*, Berlin.

Hissette, R. (1977). *Enquête sur les 219 Articles condamnés à Paris le 7 mars 1277*, Louvain.

Hoffmann, N. (1982). *Die Artistenfakultät an der Universität Tübingen 1534–1601*, Contubernium 28, Tübingen.

Hooykaas, R. (1958). *Humanisme, science et réforme: Pierre de la Ramée (1515–1572)*, Leiden.

(1972). *Religion and the Rise of Modern Science*, Grand Rapids.

(1980). 'Von der "physica" zur Physik', in *Humanismus und Naturwissenschaften*, 9–38.

Höss, I. (1989). *Georg Spalatin 1484–1545: Ein Leben in der Zeit des Humanismus und der Reformation*, second edn, Weimar.

Hübner, F. (1936). *Natürliche Theologie und theokratische Schwärmerei bei Melanchthon*, Gütersloh.

Hübner, J. (1975). *Die Theologie Johannes Keplers zwischen Orthodoxie und Naturwissenschaft*, Tübingen.

Humanismus und Naturwissenschaften, ed. R. Schmitz and F. Krafft, Boppard, 1980.

Hutchinson, G. O. (1988). *Hellenistic Poetry*, Oxford.

Hutchison, K. (1987). 'Towards a Political Iconology of the Copernican Revolution', in *Astrology, Science and Society*, 95–141.

Ingegno, A. (1988). 'The New Philosophy of Nature', in *The Cambridge History of Renaissance Philosophy*, 236–63.

Jaeger, W. (1947). *The Theology of the Early Greek Philosophers*, Oxford.

Jansen, B. (1951). 'Die scholastische Psychologie vom 16. bis 18. Jahrhundert', *Scholastik 26*: 342–63.

Jardine, L. (1988). 'Humanistic Logic', in *The Cambridge History of Renaissance Philosophy*, 173–98.

Jardine, N. (1979). 'The Forging of Modern Realism: Clavius and Kepler against the Sceptics', *Studies in History and Philosophy of Science* 10: 41–73.

'Keeping Order in the School of Padua: Jacopo Zabarella and Francesco Piccolomini on the Offices of Philosophy', forthcoming.

Joachimsen, P. (1926). '*Loci communes*: Eine Untersuchung zur Geistesgeschichte des Humanismus und der Reformation', *Luther-Jahrbuch* 8: 27–97.

Jones, H. (1989). *The Epicurean Tradition*, London.

Junghans, H. (1984). *Der junge Luther und die Humanisten*, Arbeiten zur Kirchengeschichte 8, Weimar.

Jungkuntz, R. P. (1962). 'Christian Approval of Epicureanism', *Church History* 31: 279–93.

Kaiser, C. B. (1988) 'Calvin's Understanding of Aristotelian Natural Philosophy: Its Extent and Possible Origin', *Calviniana: Ideas and Influence of Jean Calvin*, ed. R. V. Schnucker, Sixteenth Century Essays and Studies 10, Ann Arbor, Michigan, 77–92.

Kaminsky, H. (1967). *A History of the Hussite Revolution*, Berkeley and Los Angeles.

Karant-Nunn, S. C. (1987). *Zwickau in Transition, 1500–1547: The Reformation as an Agent of Change*, Ohio University Press.
Kaufmann, G. (1888–96). *Die Geschichte der Deutschen Universitäten*, 3 vols., Stuttgart.
Keen, R. A. (1984). 'Notae Melanchthonianae', *Humanistica Lovaniensia*, 33: 316–17.
(1988). Introduction to *A Melanchthon Reader*, New York, 1–45.
Kelley, D. R. (1981). *The Beginning of Ideology: Consciousness and Society in the French Reformation*, Cambridge.
(1990). 'What is Happening to the History of Ideas?', *Journal of the History of Ideas* 51: 3–25.
Keßler, E. (1988). 'The Intellective Soul', in *The Cambridge History of Renaissance Philosophy*, 485–534.
Kiessling, E.C. (1971). *The Early Sermons of Luther and Their Relation to the Pre-Reformation Sermon*, repr. edn, New York.
Kisch, G. (1967). *Melanchthons Rechts- und Soziallehre*, Berlin.
Kittleson, J. M. (1977). 'Marbach vs Zanchi: The Resolution of Controversy in Late Reformation Strasbourg', *Sixteenth Century Journal* 8–3: 31–44.
Koepplin, D. and T. Frank (1974), *Lucas Cranach*, 2 vols., Basle.
Korolec, J. B. (1982). 'Free Will and Free Choice', in *The Cambridge History of Later Medieval Philosophy*, 629–41.
Koyré, A. (1961). *The Astronomical Revolution: Copernicus – Kepler – Borelli*, trans. R. E. W. Maddison, Paris.
Kraye, J. (1988). 'Moral Philosophy', in *The Cambridge History of Renaissance Philosophy*, 303–86.
Kristeller, P. O. (1961). *Renaissance Thought: The Classic, Scholastic and Humanist Strains*, New York.
(1968). 'The Myth of Renaissance Atheism and the French Tradition of Free Thought', *Journal of the History of Philosophy* 6: 233–43.
(1988a). 'Humanism', in *The Cambridge History of Renaissance Philosophy*, 113–38.
(1988b). 'Humanism and Moral Philosophy', in *Renaissance Humanism*, III, 271–309.
(1993). '"Creativity" and "Tradition"', in *Renaissance Thought and the Arts, Collected Essays*, 247–58.
Kropatscheck, F. (1901). 'Zur Biographie des Johannes Dölsch aus Feldkirch (gest.1523)', *Zeitschrift für Kirchengeschichte* 21: 454–7.
Kunst der Reformationszeit, Berlin, 1983.
Kunz, E. (1980). *Protestantische Eschatologie von der Reformation bis zur Aufklärung*, Freiburg.
Kurze, D. (1958). 'Prophecy and History', *Journal of the Warburg and Courtauld Institutes* 21: 63–85.
Kuspit, D. B. (1973). 'Melanchthon and Dürer: The Search for the Simple Style', *Journal of Medieval and Renaissance Studies* 3–2: 177–202.

Kusukawa, S. (1993). '*Aspectio divinorum operum*: Melanchthon and Astrology for Lutheran Medics', in *Medicine and the Reformation*, 33–56.

'*Vinculum concordiae*: Lutheran Method by Philip Melanchthon', forthcoming.

Wittenberg University Library Catalogue (1536), forthcoming.

Ladner, G. B. (1958). 'The Philosophical Anthropology of Saint Gregory of Nyssa', *Dumbarton Oaks Papers* 12: 59–94.

Lang, H. S. (1992). *Aristotle's Physics and its Medieval Varieties*, New York.

Lapionte, F. H. (1973). 'The Origin and Evolution of the Term "Psychology"', *Rivista Critica di Storia della Filosofia* 28: 138–60.

Leader, D. R. (1988). *A History of the University of Cambridge*, I. *The University to 1546*, Cambridge.

Leaver, R. A. (1982). *Music as Preaching: Bach, Passions and Music in Worship*, Oxford.

Leben und Werk Martin Luthers von 1526 bis 1546: Festgabe zu seinem 500. Geburtstag, ed. H. Junghans, 2 vols., Berlin, 1983.

Lechner, J. M. (1962). *Renaissance Concepts of the Commonplaces*, New York.

Leinsle, U. G. (1988). 'Methodologie und Metaphysik bei den deustchen Lutheranern um 1600', in *Aristotelismus und Renaissance*, 149–61.

Lemay, R. (1962). *Abu Ma'Shar and Latin Aristotelianism in the Twelfth Century: The Recovery of Aristotle's Natural Philosophy through Arabic Astrology*, Beirut.

(1976). 'The Teaching of Astronomy in Medieval Universities, Principally at Paris in the Fourteenth Century', *Manuscripta* 20: 197–217.

(1978). 'The Late Medieval Astrological School at Cracow and the Copernican System', in *Science and History: Studies in Honor of Edward Rosen*, ed. E. Hilfstein *et al.*, Studia Copernicana 16, Wrocław, 337–54.

(1987). 'The True Place of Astrology in Medieval Science and Philosophy: Towards a Definition', in *Astrology, Science and Society*, 57–73.

Levin, H. (1969). *The Myth of the Golden Age in the Renaissance*, London.

Lewis, C. S. (1964). *The Discarded Image: An Introduction to Medieval and Renaissance Literature*, Cambridge.

Lind, L. R. (1975). *Study in Pre-Vesalian Anatomy: Biography, Translations, Documents*, Philadelphia.

Lint, J. G. De, (1924). 'Fugitive Anatomical Sheets', *Janus* 28: 78–91.

Livingstone, D. N. (1988). 'Science, Magic and Religion: A Contextual Reassessment of Geography in the Sixteenth and Seventeeth Centuries', *History of Science* 26: 269–94.

Lloyd, A. C. (1964). 'Nosce Teipsum and conscientia', *Archiv für Geschichte der Philosophie* 46: 188–200.

Lloyd, G. E. R. (1973). *Greek Science After Aristotle*, New York.

Loescher, J. R. (1981). *The Divine Community: Trinity, Church, and Ethics in Reformation Theologies*, Kirksville, Mo.

Lohr, C. H. (1982). 'The Medieval Interpretation of Aristotle', in *The Cambridge History of Later Medieval Philosophy*, 80–98.

(1988a). 'Metaphysics', in *The Cambridge History of Renaissance Philosophy*, 537–638.
(1988b). 'The Sixteenth-Century Transformation of the Aristotelian Natural Philosophy', in *Aristotelismus und Renaissance*, 89–99.
Lohse, B. (1983). 'Philipp Melanchthon in seinen Beziehungen zur Luther', in *Leben und Werk Martin Luthers* I, 403–18; II, 860–3.
Longeon, C. (1976). 'L'usage de Latin et des langues vernaculaires dans les ouvrages de botanique de XVIème siècle', in *Acta Conventus Neo-Latini Turonensis*, ed. J.-C. Margolin, Vrin, 751–66.
Lottin, O. (1948). *Psychologie et morale aux XIIe et XIIIe siècles*, 5 vols., Louvain.
Ludolphy, I. (1986). 'Luther und die Astrologie', in *'Astrologi Hallucinati'*, 101–7.
Luther and Erasmus: Free Will and Salvation, The Library of Christian Classics 17, trans. and ed. E. G. Rupp and P. S. Watson, London.
Luther und Melanchthon: Referate und Bericht des zweiten Internationalen Kongresses für Lutherforschung, Münster, 8.–13. August 1960, ed. V. Vajta, Göttingen, 1961.
Lytle, G. F. (1981). 'Universities as Religious Authorities in the Later Middle Ages and Reformation', in *Reform and Authority in the Medieval and Reformation Church*, ed. G. F. Lytle, Washington, 69–97.
McCue, J. F. (1968). 'The Doctrine of Transubstantiation from Berengar through Trent: The Point at Issue', *Harvard Theological Review* 61: 385–430.
McDonald, W. C. (1976). 'Maximilian I of Habsburg and the Veneration of Hercules: On the Revival of Myth and the German Renaissance', *Journal of Medieval and Renaissance Studies* 6, 139–54.
McDonough, T. M. (1963). *The Law and the Gospel in Luther*, Oxford.
McInery, R. (1983). 'Beyond the Liberal Arts', in *The Seven Liberal Arts in the Middle Ages*, ed. D. L. Wagner, Bloomington, 248–72.
Mackinnon, J. (1925–30). *Luther and the Reformation*, 4 vols., London, New York and Toronto.
McLelland, J. (1976). 'Calvinist Thomism', *Viator* 7: 441–55.
McNair, P. (1967). *Peter Martyr in Italy: An Anatomy of Apostasy*, Oxford.
McNeill, J.T. (1941). 'Natural Law in the Thought of Luther', *Church History* 10: 211–27.
Mandonia, C. (1988). 'Simone Simonii', *Bibliotheca dissentium: Répertoire des non-conformistes religieux des seizième et dix-septième siècles* 9: 59–110.
Manschreck, C. L. (1958). *Melanchthon: The Quiet Reformer*, New York.
Marenbon, J. (1987). *Later Medieval Philosophy (1150–1350): An Introduction*, London.
Marrou, H. I. (1956). *A History of Education in Antiquity*, trans. G. Lamb, London.
Martin, A. L. (1988). *The Jesuit Mind: The Mentality of an Elite in Early Modern France*, Ithaca.

Mason, S. F. (1962). *A History of the Sciences*, rev. edn, New York.

Maurer, W. (1958). 'Melanchthons Anteil am Streit zwischen Luther und Erasmus', *Archiv für Reformationsgeschichte*, 49: 89–115.

(1959). 'Der Einfluß Augustins auf Melanchthons theologische Entwicklung', *Kerygma und Dogma* 5: 165–99.

(1962). 'Melanchthon und die Naturwissenschaft seiner Zeit', *Archiv für Kulturgeschichte* 44: 199–226.

(1967–9). *Der junge Melanchthon: zwischen Humanismus und Reformation*, 2 vols., Göttingen.

(1976–8). *Historischer Kommentar zur Confessio Augustana*, 2 vols., Gütersloh.

Medicine and the Reformation, ed. O. P. Grell and A. Cunningham, The Wellcome Institute Series in the History of Medicine, London, 1993.

Meijering, E. P. (1983). *Melanchthon and Patristic Thought: The Doctrine of Christ and Grace, the Trinity and Creation*, Studies in the History of Christian Thought 32, Leiden.

Meinhold, P. (1958). *Luthers Sprachphilosophie*, Berlin.

Philipp Melanchthon: Forschungbeiträge zur vierhundertsten Wiederkehr seines Todestages dargeboten in Wittenberg 1560, ed. W. Ellinger, Göttingen, 1961.

Merton, R. K. (1970). *Science, Technology, and Society in Seventeenth Century England*, New York.

Mesnard, P. (1966). 'The Pedagogy of Johann Sturm (1507–1589) and its Evangelical Inspiration', *Studies in the Renaissance* 13: 200–19.

Milton, J. R. (1981). 'The Origin and Development of the Concept of the "Laws of Nature"', *Archives Européennes de Sociologie* 22: 173–95.

Moran, B. T. (1980). 'Wilhelm IV of Hesse-Kassel: Informal Communication and the Aristocratic Context of Discovery', in *Scientific Discovery: Case Studies*, Boston Studies in the Philosophy of Science 60, ed. T. Nickles, Dordrecht and London.

(1991). 'Patronage and Institutions: Courts, Universities, and Academies in Germany; an Overview 1550–1750', in *Patronage and Institutions*, 169–83.

Mouchel, C. (1992). 'Figures et adéquation dans la doctrine oratoire de Philipp Melanchthon', *Etudes Littéraires* 24–3: 49–62.

Müller, N. (1911). *Die Wittenberger Bewegung, 1521 und 1522. Die Vorgänge in und um Wittenberg während Luthers Wartburgaufenthalt*, Leipzig.

Muller, R. A. (1979). '"Duplex Cognitio Dei" in the Theology of Early Reformed Orthodoxy', *Sixteenth Century Journal* 10–2: 51–61.

(1984). 'Vera philosophia cum sacra Theologia nusquam pugnat: Keckermann on Philosophy, Theology and the Problem of Double Truth', *Sixteenth Century Journal* 15–3: 341–65.

Murdoch, J. E. (1975). 'From Social into Intellectual Factors: An Aspect of the Unitary Character of Late Medieval Learning', in *The Cultural Context of Learning*, 271–348.

(1982). 'The Analytic Character of Late Medieval Learning: Natural

Philosophy Without Nature', in *Approaches to Nature in the Middle Ages: Papers of the Tenth Annual Conference of the Center for Medieval and Early Renaissance Studies*, ed. L. D. Roberts, New York, 171–213.

Muther, T. (1874). 'Die ersten Statuten der Wittenberger Artistenfakultät von. J. 1504', *Neue Mitteilungen aus dem Gebiet historisch-antiquarischer Forschungen* 13: 176–208.

Nauert, C. G. Jr 'Humanists, Scientists and Pliny: Changing Approaches to a Classical Author', *American Historical Review* 84: 72–85.

(1980). 'Caius Plinius Secundus', *Catologus Translationum et Commentariorum* 4: 297–422.

Neuser, W. H. (1968). *Die Abendmahlslehre Melanchthons in ihrer geschichtlichen Entwicklung 1519–1530*, Beiträge zur Geschichte und Lehre der Reformierten Kirche 26, Neukirchen.

(1987). *Bibliographie der Confessio Augustana und Apologie 1530–1580*, Bibliotheca Humanistica et Reformatorica 37, Niewkoop.

Nitschke, A. (1971). 'Luthers Beziehung zur neuzeitlichen Naturwissenschaft', in *Festschrift für Hermann Heimpel zum 70. Geburtstag am 19. September 1971*, 3 vols., Göttingen, 1, 639–66.

Nitzsch, F. (1883). *Luther und Aristoteles. Festschrift zum vierhundert-jährigen Geburtstage Luther's*, Kiel.

Nolan, E. P. (1990). *Now Through a Glass Darkely: Specular Images of Being and Knowing from Virgil to Chaucer*, Ann Arbor.

Noreña, C. G. (1970). *Juan Luis Vives*, The Hague.

North, J. D. (1980). 'Astrology and the Fortuna of Churches', *Centaurus* 24: 181–211.

(1986). 'Celestial Influence – the Major Premiss of Astrology', in *'Astrologi Hallucinati'*, 45–100.

Nutton, V. (1990). 'Anatomy of the Soul in Early Renaissance Medicine', in *The Human Embryo: Aristotle and the Arabic and European Traditions*, ed. G. R. Dunstan, Exeter, 136–57.

(1993). 'Wittenberg Anatomy', in *Medicine and the Reformation*, 11–32.

Oberman, H. A. (1981). *Masters of the Reformation: The Emergence of a New Intellectual Climate in Europe*, trans. D. Martin, Cambridge.

(1987a). 'VIA ANTIQUA and VIA MODERNA: Late Medieval Prolegomena to Early Reformation Thought', in *From Ockham to Wyclif*, ed. A. Hudson and M. Wilks, Oxford, 445–63.

(1987b). 'VIA ANTIQUA and VIA MODERNA: Late Medieval Prolegomena to Early Reformation Thought', *Journal of the History of Ideas* 48: 23–40.

(1989). *Luther: Man between God and the Devil*, trans. E. Walliser-Schwarzbart, New Haven (originally published in German as *Luther: Mensch zwischen Gott und Teufel*, Berlin, 1982).

Olson, O. K. (1981). 'Mathias Flacius Illyricus', in *Shapers of Religious Traditions in Germany, Switzerland, and Poland, 1560–1600*, ed. J. Raitt, New Haven and London, 1–17.

O'Malley, C. D. (1964). *Andreas Vesalius of Brussels 1514–1564*, Berkeley.

O'Malley, J. W. (1979). *Praise and Blame in Renaissance Rome: Rhetoric, Doctrine and Reform in the Sacred Orators of the Papal Court, c. 1450–1521*, Duke Monographs in Medieval and Renaissance Studies 3, Durham, NC.

Ong, W. J. (1958). *Ramus, Method, and the Decay of Dialogue*, Cambridge, Mass.

Overfield, J. H. (1976). 'Scholastic Opposition to Humanism in Pre-Reformation Germany', *Viator* 7: 391–420.

(1984). *Humanism and Scholasticism in Late Medieval Germany*, Princeton.

Oyer, J. S. (1964). *Lutheran Reformers against Anabaptists: Luther, Melanchthon and Menius and the Anabaptists of Central Germany*, The Hague.

Pagel, W. (1969–70). 'William Harvey Revisited', *History of Science* 8: 1–81; 9: 1–41.

Panofsky, E. (1975) *Idea: A Concept in Art Theory*, trans. J. J. S. Peake, second edn, New York.

Pantin, I. (1987). 'La Lettre de Melanchthon à S. Grynaeus: les avatars d'une apologie de l'astrologie', in *Divination et controverse religieuse en France au XVIe siècle*, ed. R. Aulotte, Paris, 85–101.

Park, K. (1988). 'The Organic Soul', in *The Cambridge History of Renaissance Philosophy*, 464–84.

Park, K. and L. Daston (1981). 'Unnatural Conceptions: The Study of Monsters in Sixteenth- and Seventeenth-Century France and England', *Past and Present* 92: 20–54.

Park, K. and E. Keßler (1988). 'The Concept of Psychology', in *The Cambridge History of Renaissance Philosophy*, 455–63.

Parker, T. H. L. (1986). *Commentaries on the Epistle to the Romans 1532–1542*, Edinburgh.

Parshall, P. W. (1978). 'Camerarius on Dürer – Humanist Biography as Art Criticism', in *Joachim Camerarius*, 11–30.

Partee, C. (1977) *Calvin and Classical Philosophy*, Studies in the History of Christian Thought 14, Leiden.

Pater, C. A. (1984). *Karlstadt as the Father of the Baptist Movements: The Emergence of Lay Protestantism*, Toronto.

Patronage and Institutions: Science, Technology, and Medicine at the European Court 1500–1750, ed. B. T. Moran, Cambridge.

Patterson, R. (1981). 'The "Hortus Palatinus" at Heidelberg and the Reformation of the World', *Journal of Garden History* 1: 67–104; 179–202.

Pauck, W. (1984). *From Luther to Tillich: The Reformers and Their Heirs*, ed. M. Pauck, San Francisco.

Pease, A. S. (1941). 'Caeli Enarrant', *Harvard Theological Review* 34: 163–200.

Pegis, A. C. (1946). 'The Middle Ages and Philosophy', *Proceedings of the American Catholic Philosophical Association* 21: 16–25.

Petersen, P. (1921). *Geschichte der Aristotelischen Philosophie im Protestantischen Deutschland*, Leipzig.
Pierre de la Ramée, in *Revue des Sciences Philosophiques et Théologiques 70 (1986): 2–100.*
Pine, M. L. (1986). *Pietro Pomponazzi: Radical Philosopher of the Renaissance*, Padua.
Popkin, R. H. (1979). *The History of Scepticism from Erasmus to Spinoza*, Berkeley.
Poppi, A. (1983). 'Scienza e filosofia nelle scuole tomista e scotista all'università di Padova nel sec. xv', in *Scienza e Filosofia all'Università di Padova nel Quattrocento*, ed. A. Poppi, Trieste, 329–43.
Posse, H. (1942). *Lucas Cranach d. Ä.*, Vienna.
Potts, T. C. (1980). *Conscience in Medieval Philosophy*, Cambridge.
Potter, G. R. (1976). *Huldrych Zwingli*, Cambridge.
Prantl, C. (1855–70). *Geschichte der Logik im Abendlande*, 4 vols., Leipzig.
Pressel, T. (1862). *J. Jonas, C. Cruciger, P. Speratus, L. Spengler, N. von Amsdorf, P. Eber, M. Chemnitz, D. Chytraeus*, Leben und ausgewählte Schriften der Väter und Begründer der lutherischen Kirche 8, Elbenfeld.
Prest, J. (1981). *The Garden of Eden: The Botanic Garden and the Re-Creation of Paradise*, New Haven.
Preus, J. S. (1974). *Carlstadt's 'Ordinaciones' and Luther's Liberty: A Study of the Wittenberg Movement*, Harvard Theological Studies 27, Cambridge, Mass.
Das protestantische Kirchenlied im 16. und 17. Jahrhundert: Text-, musik- und theologiegeschichtliche Probleme, ed. A. Dürr and W. Killy, Wolfenbütteler Forschungen 31, Wiesbaden, 1986.
Quanbeck, W. A. (1961). 'Luther and Apocalyptic', in *Luther und Melanchthon*, 119–28.
Quere, R. W. (1977). *Melanchthon's Christum Cognoscere: Christ's Efficacious Presence in the Eucharistic Theology of Melanchthon*, Nieuwkoop.
Rabin, S. J. (1987). 'Two Renaissance Views of Astrology: Pico and Kepler', unpublished Ph.D. dissertation, City University of New York, University Microfilms International, Ann Arbor.
The Radical Reformation, ed. and trans. M. G. Baylor, Cambridge Texts in the History of Political Thought, Cambridge, 1991.
Rashdall, H. (1936). *The Universities in the Middle Ages*, 3 vols., new edn, F. M. Powicke and A. B. Emden, London.
Rauscher, J. (1911). 'Der Halleysche Komet im Jahre 1531 und die Reformatoren', *Zeitschrift für Kirchengeschichte* 32: 259–76.
Reappraisals of the Scientific Revolution, ed. D. C. Lindberg and R. S. Westman, Cambridge, 1990.
Reeds, K. M. (1991). *Botany in Medieval and Renaissance Universities*, New York and London.
Reif, P. (1969). 'The Textbook Tradition in Natural Philosophy, 1600–1650', *Journal of the History of Ideas* 30: 17–32.

Renaissance Humanism: Foundation, Forms and Legacy, ed. A. Rabil Jr, 3 vols., Philadelphia, 1988.
Rice, E. F. (1958). *The Renaissance Idea of Wisdom*, Cambridge, Mass.
Risse, W. (1964). *Die Logik der Neuzeit*, 2 vols., I. *1500–1640*, Stuttgart.
Rist, J. M. (1972). *Epicurus: An Introduction*, Cambridge.
Ritter, G. (1922). *Studien zur Spätscholastik II: Via antiqua und via moderna auf den deutschen Universitäten des XV. Jahrhunderts*, Heidelberg.
Robinson, C. (1979). *Lucian and his Influence in Europe*, Chapel Hill and London.
Robinson-Hammerstein, H. (1986). 'The Battle of the Booklets: Prognostic Tradition and Proclamation of the Word in Early Sixteenth-century Germany', in *'Astrologi Hallucinati'*, 129–151.
(1989). 'The Lutheran Reformation and its Music', in *The Transmission of Ideas in the Lutheran Reformation*, ed. H. Robinson-Hammerstein, Dublin, 141–71.
Rokita, G. (1970). 'Aristoteles, Aristotelicus, Aristotelicotatos, Aristotelskunst', *Archiv für Begriffsgeschichte* 15: 51–93.
Rose, P. L. (1975). *The Italian Renaissance of Mathematics: Studies on Humanists and Mathematicians from Petrarch to Galileo*, Geneva.
Rudolf, R. (1957). *Ars Moriendi: von der Kunst des heilsamen Lebens und Sterben*, Graz.
Rump, J. (1896). *Melanchthons Psychologie, seiner Schrift de anima, in ihrer Abhängigkeit von Aristoteles und Galenos dargestellet*, Kiel.
Saxl, F. (1957). 'Holbein and the Reformation', *Lectures*, 2 vols., London, I, 277–85.
Schade, W. (1980). *Cranach, a Family of Master Painters*, trans. H. Sebba, New York.
Schaffer, S. (1987). 'Newton's Comets and the Transformation of Astrology', in *Astrology, Science and Society*, 219–43.
Scheible, H. (1984). 'Melanchthon zwischen Luther und Erasmus', in *Renaissance–Reformation: Gegensätze und Gemeinsamkeiten*, Wolfenbütteler Abhandlungen zur Renaissanceforschung 5, ed. A. Buck, Wiesbaden.
Schindling, A. (1977). *Humanistische Hochschule und freie Reichstadt: Gymnasium und Academie in Strassburg 1538–1621*, Wiesbaden.
Schmitt, Charles B. (1972). *Cicero Scepticus: A Study of the Influence of the Academica in the Renaissance*, The Hague.
(1975). 'Philosophy and Science in Sixteenth-Century Universities: Some Preliminary Comments', in *The Cultural Context of Medieval Learning*, 485–537.
(1983). *Aristotle and the Renaissance*, Cambridge, Mass.
(1984). 'Filippo Fabri's *Philosophia naturalis Io. Duns Scoti* and its Relation to Paduan Aristotelianism', in *The Aristotelian Tradition and Renaissance Universities*, London, ch. 10.
(1987). 'The Development of the Historiography of Scepticism: From the Renaissance to Brucker', in *Scepticism from the Renaissance to the*

Enlightenment, ed. R. H. Popkin and C. B. Schmitt, Wiesbaden, 185–200.

(1988a). 'The Rise of the Philosophical Textbook', in *The Cambridge History of Renaissance Philosophy*, 792–804.

(1988b). 'Towards a History of Renaissance Philosophy', in *Aristotelismus und Renaissance*, 9–16.

Schneider, J. R. (1990). *Philip Melanchthon's Rhetorical Construal of Biblical Authority: Oratio Sacra*, Text and Studies in Religion 5, Lewiston and Lampeter.

Schuchardt, C. (1851–70). *Lucas Cranach des Aeltern: Leben und Werke*, 3 vols., Leipzig.

Schupbach, W. (1982). *The Paradox of Rembrandt's 'Anatomy of Dr. Tulp'*, London.

Schwarzenau, P. (1956). *Der Wandel im theologischen Ansatz bei Melanchthon von 1525–35*, Güthersloh.

Schwiebert, E. G. (1940). 'Remnants of a Reformation Library', *The Library Quarterly* 10: 494–531.

(1950). *Luther and his Times: The Reformation from a New Perspective*, St Louis.

(1958). 'New Groups and Ideas at the University of Wittenberg', *Archiv für Reformationsgeschichte* 49: 60–79.

Science in the Early Roman Empire: Pliny the Elder, his Sources and Influence, ed. R. French and F. Greenaway, London, 1986.

Scott, T. (1979). 'The Peasants' War: A Historiographical Review', *Historical Review* 22: 693–720; 953–74.

(1989). *Thomas Müntzer: Theology and Revolution in the German Reformation*, Basingstoke and London.

Scribner, R. W. (1981). *For the Sake of the Simple Folk: Popular Propaganda for the German Reformation*, Cambridge.

(1987). *Popular Culture and Popular Movements in Reformation Germany*, London.

Serrai, A. (1990), *Conrad Gesner*, ed. M. Cochetti, Rome.

Shank, M. H. (1988). *'Unless You Believe, You Shall Not Understand': Logic, University and Society in Late Medieval Vienna*, Princeton.

Sharratt, P. (1976). 'Peter Ramus and the Reform of the University: The Divorce of Philosophy and Eloquence?', in *French Renaissance Studies 1540–1570: Humanism and the Encyclopaedia*, ed. P. Sharratt, Edinburgh, 4–20.

Sider, R. J. (1974). *Andreas Bodenstein von Karlstadt: The Development of his Thought 1517–1525*, Leiden.

Siegel, R. E. (1973). *Galen on Psychology, Psychopathology, and Function and Diseases of the Nervous System: An Analysis of his Doctrines, Observations and Experiments*, Basle.

Sigwart, C. (1889). *Kleine Schriften*, Freiburg.

Simon, G. (1979). *Kepler, astronome astrologue*, Paris.

Singer, C. J. (1952). *Vesalius on the Human Brain*, London.

Siraisi, N. G. (1990). *Medieval and Early Renaissance Medicine: An Introduction to Knowledge and Practice*, Chicago.

Skinner, Q. (1969). 'Meaning and Understanding in the History of Ideas', *History and Theory* 8: 3–53.

(1978). *The Foundations of Modern Political Thought*, 2 vols., Cambridge.

Smith, Pr. (1911). 'Luther's Homer', *Zeitschrift für Kirchengeschichte* 32: 112–13.

Sohm, W. (1912). *Die Schule Jo. Sturms und die Kirche Strassburgs in ihrem gegenseitigen Verhältnis 1530–1581*, Munich.

Solmsen, F. (1963). 'Nature as Craftsman in Greek Thought', *Journal of History of Ideas* 24: 474–96.

Sorabji, R. (1979). 'Body and Soul in Aristotle', in *Articles on Aristotle*, ed. J. Barnes *et al.*, London, IV, 42–64.

Southern, R. W. (1986). *Robert Grosseteste: The Growth of an English Mind in Medieval Europe*, Oxford.

Sparn, W. (1976). *Wiederkehr der Metaphysik: Die ontologische Frage in der lutherischen Theologie des frühen 17. Jahrhunderts*, Calwer Theologische Monographien 4, Stuttgart.

(1984). 'Hercules Christianus. Mythographie und Theologie in der frühen Neuzeit', *Mythographie der frühen Neuzeit: Ihre Anwendung in den Künsten*, ed. W. Killy, Wolfenbütteler Forschungen 27, Wiesbaden, 73–107.

Spinka, M. (1968). *John Huss: A Biography*, Princeton.

Spitz, L. W. (1963). *The Religious Renaissance of the German Humanists*, Cambridge, Mass.

Stayer, J. M. (1972). *Anabaptists and the Sword*, Lawrence, Kansas.

(1991). *The German Peasants' War and the Anabaptist Community of Goods*, Montreal and Kingston.

Stayer, J. M., W. Packull and K. Deppermann (1975). 'From Monogenesis to Polygenesis: The Historical Discussion of Anabaptist Origins', *Mennonnite Quarterly Review* 49: 83–121.

Steenberghen, F. van (1955). *Aristotle in the West: The Origins of Latin Aristotelianism*, trans. L. Johnston, Louvain.

Stegmüller, F. (1959). *Filosofia e teologia nas universidades de Coimbra e Evora no sécolo XVI*, Coimbra.

Steinmann, M. (1967). *Johannes Oporinus: Ein Basler Buchdrucker um die Mitte des 16. Jahrhunderts*, Basler Beiträge zur Geschichtswissenschaft 105, Basle.

Steinmetz, D. C. (1968). *Misericordia Dei: The Theology of Johannes von Staupitz in its Late Medieval Setting*, Leiden.

(1980). *Luther and Staupitz: An Essay in the Intellectual Origins of the Protestant Reformation*, Durham, NC.

(1991). 'Calvin and the Natural Knowledge of God', in *Via Augustini*, 142–56.

Steneck, N. H. (1976). *Science and Creation in the Middle Ages: Henry of Langenstein (d. 1397) on Genesis*, Notre Dame and London.

Stephens, W. P. (1986). *The Theology of Huldrych Zwingli*, Oxford.

Stirm, M. (1977). *Die Bilderfrage in der Reformation*, Quellen und Forschungen zur Reformationsgeschichte 45, Gütersloh.

Strahl, I. (1982). *Verzeichnis der Luther-Bildnisse*, Deutsche Staatsbibliothek Handschrifteninventare 5, Berlin.

Strauss, G. (1978). *Luther's House of Learning: Indoctrination of the Young in the German Reformation*, Baltimore, Md.

(1986). *Law, Resistance, and the State: The Opposition to Roman Law in Reformation Germany*, Princeton.

Stupperich, R. (1966). *Melanchthon*, trans. R. H. Fischer, London.

Summers, D. (1987). *The Judgement of Sense: Renaissance Naturalism and the Rise of Aesthetics*, Cambridge.

Sylla, E. D. (1975). 'Autonomous and Handmaiden Science: St Thomas Aquinas and William of Ockham on the Physics of the Eucharist', in *The Cultural Context of Medieval Learning*, 349–96.

Tachau, K. A. (1988). *Vision and Certitude in the Age of Ockham: Optics, Epistemology, and the Foundations of Semantics 1250–1345*, Studien und Texte zur Geistesgeschichte des Mittelalters 22, Leiden, 1988.

Taub, L. C. (1993). *Ptolemy's Universe: The Natural Philosophical and Ethical Foundations of Ptolemy's Astronomy*, Chicago and LaSalle.

Temkin, O. (1973). *Galenism: Rise and Decline of a Medical Philosophy*, Ithaca and London.

Thomas, J. A. C. (1976). *Textbook of Roman Law*, Amsterdam, New York and London.

Thomas-Stanford, C. (1926). *Early Editions of Euclid's Elements*, London.

Thorndike, L. (1923–58). *A History of Magic and Experimental Science*, 8 vols., London.

(1949). *The Sphere of Sacrobosco and its Commentators*, Chicago.

(1975). *University Records and Life in the Middle Ages*, New York.

Thulin, O. (1930). *Johannes der Täufer im Geistlichen Schauspiel des Mittelalters und der Reformationszeit*, Leipzig.

(1955). *Cranach-Altäre der Reformation*, Berlin.

(1961). 'Melanchthons Bildnis und Werk im zeitgenössischer Kunst', in *Philipp Melanchthon*, 180–93.

Tigerstedt, E. N. (1969). 'Plato's Idea of Poetical Inspiration', *Commentationes Humanarum Litterarum Societas Scientiarum Fennica* XLIV–II.

(1974). *The Decline and Fall of the Neoplatonic Interpretation of Plato: An Outline and Some Observations*, Commentationes Humanarum Litterarum 52, Helsinki.

Trinkaus, C. (1970). *In Our Image and Likeness: Humanity and Divinity in Italian Humanist Thought*, 2 vols., London.

(1985). 'The Astrological Cosmos and Rhetorical Culture of Giovanni Gioviano Pontano', *Renaissance Quarterly* 38: 446–72.

Tuck, R. (1993). *Philosophy and Government, 1572–1651*, Cambridge.

Ueberweg, F. (1926–8). *Grundriss der Geschichte der Philosophie*, ed. B. Geyer *et al.*, 5 vols., Berlin.

Vasoli, C. (1986). 'De Pierre de la Ramée à François Patrizi: thèmes et raison de la polémique autour d'Aristote', *Revue des Sciences Philosophiques et Théologiques* 70: 87–98.

Via Augustini: Augustine in the Later Middle Ages, Renaissance and the Reformation, Studies in Medieval and Reformation Thought 48, ed. H. A. Oberman and F. A. James III., Leiden, 1991.

Vignaux, P. (1959). *Philosophy in the Middle Ages*, trans. E. C. Hall, New York.

Viner, J. (1972). *The Role of Providence in Social History: An Essay in Intellectual History*, Philadelphia.

Vlastos, G. (1947). 'Equality and Justice in Early Greek Cosmologies', *Classical Philology* 42: 156–78.

Vogel, J. (1907). 'Zur Cranachforschung', *Zeitschrift für bildende Kunst* 18: 219–26.

Volz, H. (1954). 'Excurs I', *Archiv für Reformationsgeschichte* 45: 228.

Vona, P. di (1968). *Studi sulla scolastica della Controriforma*, Florence.

Walker, D. P. (1955). 'Ways of Dealing with Atheists: A Background to Pamela's Refutation of Cecropia', *Bibliothèque d'Humanisme et Renaissance* 17: 252–77.

(1984). 'Medical Spirits and God and the Soul', in *Spiritus. IVo Colloquio Internazionale Roma, 7–9 gennaio 1983*, ed. M. Fattori and M. Bianchi, Rome, 223–44.

Warburg, A. (1919). *Heidnisch-antike Weissagung in Wort und Bild zu Luthers Zeiten*, Sitzungsberichte der Heidelberger Academie der Wissenschaften, Stiftung Heinrich Lanz, Philosophische-historische Klasse 26.

Weber, B. (1989). 'Martin Luther als Hercules Germanicus 1522', in *Zentralbibliothek Zürich: Schatzkammer der Überlierferung*, ed. A. Cattami and B. Weber, Zurich, 39–41, 156–7.

Weber, H. W. (1969). *Der Einfluß der protestantischen Schulphilosophie auf die orthodoxlutherische Dogmatik*, Darmstadt.

Webster, C. (1993). 'Paracelsus: Medicine as Popular Protest', in *Medicine and the Reformation*, 57–77.

Weinberg, B. (1961). *A History of Literary Criticism in the Italian Renaissance*, 2 vols., Chicago.

Weisheipl, J. A. (1964). 'Curriculum of the Faculty of Arts at Oxford in the Early Fourteenth Century', *Mediaeval Studies* 26: 141–85.

Wellisch, Hans H. (1984). *Conrad Gessner: A Bio-Bibliography*, Zug.

Wells, L. H. (1964). 'A Remarkable Pair of Anatomical Fugitive Sheets in the Medical Library, University of Michigan', *Bulletin of the History of Medicine* 38: 470–6.

Westman, R. S. (1975). 'The Melanchthon Circle, Rheticus, and the Wittenberg Interpretation of the Copernican Theory', *Isis* 56: 165–93.

(1980a). 'Humanism and Scientific Roles in the Sixteenth Century', in *Humanismus und Naturwissenschaft*, 83–99.

(1980b). 'The Astronomer's Role in the Sixteenth Century: A Preliminary Study', *History of Science* 18: 105–47.

(1990). 'Proof, Poetics and Patronage: Copernicus' Preface to De Revolutionibus', in *Reappraisals of the Scientific Revolution*, 167–205.
Wetzel, R. (1991). '*Staupitz Augustinianus*: An Account of the Reception of Augustine in Tübingen Sermons', in *Via Augustini*, 72–115.
White, A. D. (1955). *A History of the Warfare of Science with Theology in Christendom*, London.
White, L. Jr (1975). 'Medical Astrologers and Late Medieval Technology', *Viator* 6: 295–308.
Wicher, H. B. (1986). 'Nemesius Emesenus', *Catalogus Translationum et Commentariorum* 6: 31–72.
Wieland, G. (1982a). 'The Reception and Interpretation of Aristotle's Ethics', in *The Cambridge History of Later Medieval Philosophy*, 657–72.
(1982b). 'Happiness: The Perfection of Man', in *The Cambridge History of Later Medieval Philosophy*, 673–86.
Wilkins, W. G. (1929). *The Delphic Maxims in Literature*, Chicago.
Williams, A. (1948). *The Common Expositor: An Account of the Commentaries on Genesis 1527–1633*, Chapel Hill.
Williams, G. H. (1962a). *The Radical Reformation*, London.
(1962b). *Wilderness and Paradise in Christian Thought: The Biblical Experience of the Desert in the History of Christianity and the Paradise Theme in the Theological Idea of the University*, New York.
Wingren, G. (1958). *The Christian's Calling: Luther on Vocation*, trans. C. C. Rasmussen, Edinburgh.
Wippel, J. F. (1977). 'The Condemnations of 1270 and 1277 at Paris', *Journal of Medieval and Renaissance Studies* 7: 169–201.
(1982). 'Essence and Existence', in *The Cambridge History of Later Medieval Philosophy*, 385–410.
Wrightsman, B. (1970). 'Andreas Osiander and Lutheran Contributions to the Copernican Revolution', unpublished Ph.D. thesis, University of Wisconsin.
(1975). 'Andreas Osiander's Contribution to the Copernican Achievement', in *The Copernican Achievement*, ed. R. S. Westman, Berkeley, 213–43.
Yates, F. A. (1975). *Astraea: The Imperial Theme in the Sixteenth Century*, London and Boston.
Zambelli, P. (1986). 'Many Ends for the World: Luca Gaurico, Instigator of the Debate in Italy and in Germany', in *'Astrologi Hallucinati'*, 239–63.
Zeeden, E. W. (1985). 'Grundlage und Wege der Konfessionsbildung in Deutschland im Zeitalter der Glaubenskämpfe', in *Konfessionsbildung: Studien zur Reformation, Gegenreformation und katholischen Reform*, ed. V. Press and E. W. Zeeden, Stuttgart, 67–112.

Index

IDEAS IN CONTEXT

1 RICHARD RORTY, J. B. SCHNEEWIND and QUENTIN SKINNER (eds.)
Philosophy in History
*Essays in the Historiography of Philosophy**

2 J. G. A. POCOCK
Virtue, Commerce and History
*Essays on Political Thought and History, chiefly in the Eighteenth Century**

3 M. M. GOLDSMITH
Private Vices, Public Benefits
Bernard Mandeville's Social and Political Thought

4 ANTHONY PAGDEN (ed.)
The Languages of Political Theory in Early Modern Europe*

5 DAVID SUMMERS
The Judgment of Sense
*Renaissance Nationalism and the Rise of Aesthetics**

6 LAURENCE DICKEY
Hegel: Religion, Economics and the Politics of Spirit, 1770–1807*

7 MARGO TODD
Christian Humanism and the Puritan Social Order

8 LYNN SUMIDA JOY
Gassendi the Atomist
Advocate of History in an Age of Science

9 EDMUND LEITES (ed.)
Conscience and Casuistry in Early Modern Europe

10 WOLF LEPENIES
Between Literature and Science: The Rise of Sociology*

11 TERENCE BALL, JAMES FARR and RUSSELL L. HANSON (eds.)
Political Innovation and Conceptual Change*

12 GERD GIGERENZER *et al.*
The Empire of Chance
*How Probability Changed Science and Everyday Life**

13 PETER NOVICK
That Noble Dream
*The 'Objectivity Question' and the American Historical Profession**

14 DAVID LIEBERMAN
The Province of Legislation Determined
Legal Theory in Eighteenth-Century Britain

15 DANIEL PICK
Faces of Degeneration
A European Disorder, c. 1848–c. 1918

16 KEITH BAKER
Approaching the French Revolution
*Essays on French Political Culture in the Eighteenth Century**

17 IAN HACKING
The Taming of Chance*

18 GISELA BOCK, QUENTIN SKINNER and MAURIZIO VIROLI (eds.)
Machiavelli and Republicanism*

19 DOROTHY ROSS
The Origins of American Social Science*

20 KLAUS CHRISTIAN KÖHNKE
The Rise of Neo-Kantianism
German Academic Philosophy between Idealism and Positivism

21 IAN MACLEAN
Interpretation and Meaning in the Renaissance
The Case of Law

22 MAURIZIO VIROLI
From Politics to Reason of State
The Acquisition and Transformation of the Language of Politics 1250–1600

23 MARTIN VAN GELDEREN
The Political Thought of the Dutch Revolt 1555–1590

24 NICHOLAS PHILLIPSON and QUENTIN SKINNER (eds.)
Political Discourse in Early Modern Britain

25 JAMES TULLY
An Approach to Political Philosophy: Locke in Contexts*

26 RICHARD TUCK
Philosophy and Government 1572–1651*

27 RICHARD R. YEO
Defining Science
William Whewell, Natural Knowledge and Public Debate in Early Victorian Britain

28 MARTIN WARNKE
The Court Artist
The Ancestry of the Modern Artist

29 PETER N. MILLER
Defining the Common Good
Empire, Religion and Philosophy in Eighteenth-Century Britain

30 CHRISTOPHER J. BERRY
The Idea of Luxury
*A Comceptual and Historical Investigation**

31 E. J. HUNDERT
The Enlightenment's 'Fable'
Bernard Mandeville and the Discovery of Society

32 JULIA STAPLETON
Englishness and the Study of Politics
The Social and Political Thought of Ernest Barker

33 KEITH TRIBE
German Economic Thought from the Enlightenment to the Social Market

34 SACHIKO KUSUKAWA
The Transformation of Natural Philosophy: The Case of Philip Melancthon

Titles marked with an asterisk are also available in paperback